GOD'S DESIGN®

Life

| The World of Plants | The Human Body | The World of Animals |

MASTERBOOKS CURRICULUM

Debbie & Richard Lawrence

Fourth Edition: January 2016
Master Books Edition Second printing: August 2019

ISBN: 978-1-68344-127-4
ISBN: 978-1-61458-651-7 (digital)

Cover by Diana Bogardus
Book design: Diane King
Editor: Gary Vaterlaus

Unless otherwise noted, Scripture quotations are from the New King James Version of the Bible. Copyright 1982 by Thomas Nelson, Inc. Used by permission. All rights reserved.

God's Design® for Life is a complete life science curriculum for grades 3–8. The books in this series are designed for use in the Christian school and homeschool, and provide easy-to-use lessons that will encourage children to see God's hand in everything around them.

The publisher and authors have made every reasonable effort to ensure that the activities recommended in this book are safe when performed as instructed but assume no responsibility for any damage caused or sustained while conducting the experiments and activities. It is the parents', guardians', and/or teachers' responsibility to supervise all recommended activities.

Please consider requesting that a copy of this volume be purchased by your local library system.

Printed in the United States of America

Please visit our website for other great titles:
www.masterbooks.com

For information regarding author interviews,
please contact the publicity department at (870) 438-5288

Master
Books®
A Division of New Leaf Publishing Group
www.masterbooks.com

The World of Plants

Unit 1: Introduction to Life Science   13

Lesson 1   Is It Alive? 14
Lesson 2   What Is a Kingdom? 18
Lesson 3   Classification System 21
Special Feature   Carl Linnaeus 24
Lesson 4   Plant & Animal Cells 26
Special Feature   Cells 30

Unit 2: Flowering Plants & Seeds   31

Lesson 5   Flowering Plants 32
Lesson 6   Grasses 35
Lesson 7   Trees 38
Special Feature   Redwoods 41
Lesson 8   Seeds 42
Lesson 9   Monocots & Dicots 45
Lesson 10   Seeds—Where Are They? 48
Special Feature   George Washington Carver 52

Unit 3: Roots & Stems   54

Lesson 11   Roots 55
Lesson 12   Special Roots 58
Lesson 13   Stems 61
Lesson 14   Stem Structure 64
Lesson 15   Stem Growth 66

Unit 4: Leaves — 69

Lesson 16   Photosynthesis 70
Lesson 17   Arrangement of Leaves 74
Lesson 18   Leaves—Shape & Design 77
Lesson 19   Changing Colors. 81
Lesson 20   Tree Identification: Final Project 84

Unit 5: Flowers & Fruits — 87

Lesson 21   Flowers. 88
Lesson 22   Pollination 91
Special Feature   Pierre-Joseph Redoute 94
Lesson 23   Flower Dissection 95
Special Feature   A Rose by Any Other Name 98
Lesson 24   Fruits 99
Lesson 25   Annuals, Biennials, & Perennials 102

Unit 6: Unusual Plants — 105

Lesson 26   Meat-eating Plants 106
Lesson 27   Parasites & Passengers 109
Lesson 28   Tropisms. 112
Lesson 29   Survival Techniques. 115
Lesson 30   Reproduction without Seeds. 117
Lesson 31   Ferns 120
Lesson 32   Mosses. 123
Lesson 33   Algae. 126
Lesson 34   Fungi 129
Lesson 35   Conclusion 132
Glossary 133
Challenge Glossary 135

The Human Body

Unit 1: Body Overview		139
Lesson 1	The Creation of Life	140
Lesson 2	Overview of the Human Body	142
Special Feature	Leonardo da Vinci	144
Lesson 3	Cells, Tissues, & Organs	146

Unit 2: Bones & Muscles		149
Lesson 4	The Skeletal System	150
Lesson 5	Names of Bones	153
Lesson 6	Types of Bones	156
Lesson 7	Joints	159
Lesson 8	The Muscular System	162
Lesson 9	Different Types of Muscles	165
Lesson 10	Hands & Feet	167

Unit 3: Nerves & Senses		170
Lesson 11	The Nervous System	171
Lesson 12	The Brain	174
Lesson 13	Learning & Thinking	177
Special Feature	Brain Surgery	180
Lesson 14	Reflexes & Nerves	182
Lesson 15	The Five Senses	185

Lesson 16   The Eye 188

Lesson 17   The Ear. 191

Lesson 18   Taste & Smell 194

Unit 4: Digestion   197

Lesson 19   The Digestive System. 198

Lesson 20   Teeth 201

Lesson 21   Dental Health 204

Lesson 22   Nutrition. 206

Special Feature   Florence Nightingale 209

Lesson 23   Vitamins & Minerals. 211

Unit 5: Heart & Lungs   214

Lesson 24   The Circulatory System. 215

Lesson 25   The Heart 219

Lesson 26   Blood. 222

Special Feature   Blood—Who Needs It? 225

Lesson 27   The Respiratory System 226

Lesson 28   The Lungs 229

Unit 6: Skin & Immunity   232

Lesson 29   The Skin 233

Lesson 30   Cross-section of Skin 236

Lesson 31   Fingerprints. 239

Lesson 32   The Immune System 243

Lesson 33   Genetics. 246

Special Feature   Gregor Mendel 249

Lesson 34   Body Poster: Final Project 251

Lesson 35   Conclusion 253

Glossary 254

Challenge Glossary 256

The World of Animals

Unit 1: Mammals   261

Lesson 1   The World of Animals 262

Lesson 2   Vertebrates 264

Lesson 3   Mammals 266

Lesson 4   Mammals: Large & Small 269

Lesson 5   Monkeys & Apes 273

Special Feature   Man & Monkeys 276

Lesson 6   Aquatic Mammals 278

Lesson 7   Marsupials 282

Unit 2: Birds & Fish   285

Lesson 8   Birds 286

Special Feature   Charles Darwin 290

Lesson 9   Flight 291

Lesson 10   The Bird's Digestive System 295

Lesson 11   Fish 298

Lesson 12   Fins & Other Fish Anatomy 301

Lesson 13   Cartilaginous fish 304

Unit 3: Amphibians & Reptiles — 307

Lesson 14   Amphibians. 308
Lesson 15   Amphibian Metamorphosis 311
Lesson 16   Reptiles 314
Special Feature   When Did the Dinosaurs Live? 317
Lesson 17   Snakes 319
Special Feature   Rattlesnakes. 322
Lesson 18   Lizards 323
Lesson 19   Turtles & Crocodiles. 326

Unit 4: Arthropods — 329

Lesson 20   Invertebrates. 330
Lesson 21   Arthropods 333
Lesson 22   Insects 336
Lesson 23   Insect Metamorphosis 339
Lesson 24   Arachnids 342
Lesson 25   Crustaceans. 345
Lesson 26   Myriapods. 347

Unit 5: Other Invertebrates — 350

Lesson 27   Mollusks. 351
Lesson 28   Cnidarians. 354
Lesson 29   Echinoderms 358
Lesson 30   Sponges. 361
Lesson 31   Worms 363

Unit 6: Simple Organisms — 366

Lesson 32   Kingdom Protista 367
Lesson 33   Kingdom Monera & Viruses. 370
Special Feature   Louis Pasteur—Got Milk?. 373
Lesson 34   Animal Notebook: Final Project 375
Lesson 35   Conclusion 377
Glossary 378
Challenge Glossary 380
Index 381
Photo Credits. 385

Welcome to
GOD'S DESIGN®

LIFE

You are about to start an exciting series of lessons on life science. *God's Design® for Life* consists of: *The World of Plants*, *The World of Animals*, and *The Human Body*. It will give you insight into how God designed and created our world and the things that live in it.

No matter what grade you are in, third through eighth grade, you can use this book.

3rd–5th grade

Read the lesson.

 Do the activity in the light blue box (worksheets will be provided by your teacher).

 Test your knowledge by answering the **What did we learn?** questions.

 Assess your understanding by answering the **Taking it further** questions.

Be sure to read the special features and do the final project.

There are also unit quizzes and a final test to take.

6th–8th grade

Read the lesson.

 Do the activity in the light blue box (worksheets will be provided by your teacher).

 Test your knowledge by answering the **What did we learn?** questions.

 Assess your understanding by answering the **Taking it further** questions.

 Do the challenge section in the light green box. This part of the lesson will challenge you to do more advanced activities and learn additional interesting information.

Be sure to read the special features and do the final project.

There are also unit quizzes and a final test to take.

When you truly understand how God has designed everything in our universe to work together, then you will enjoy the world around you even more. So let's get started!

The World of Plants

UNIT 1

Introduction to Life Science

1 Is It Alive?

2 What Is a Kingdom?

3 Classification System

4 Plant & Animal Cells

◊ **Identify** the six characteristics of living things.

◊ **Identify** the five kingdoms of living things.

◊ **Identify** the method of classification of living things.

◊ **Describe** the need for scientific names.

◊ **Describe** basic parts of a cell using models.

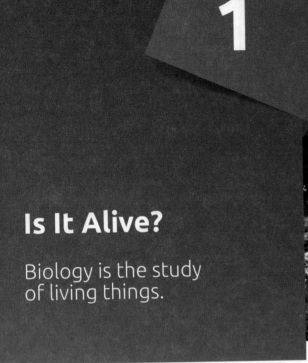

1

Is It Alive?

Biology is the study of living things.

How do we know if something is alive?

Words to know:

respiration

Challenge words:

spontaneous generation   abiogenesis

law of biogenesis   chemical evolution

How can we tell if something is alive?
Look at the things around you. Is an animal alive? Is a plant alive? Is the table alive? How about your computer? Some things are obviously alive while other things are obviously not alive. Still other things might be a little more confusing. We are getting ready to study plants, and the study of plants is part of the study of life science. Before we can study life science, we need to know what is considered alive scientifically and what is not. It will help you to identify living things if you realize that all living things have six common characteristics:

1. Living things eat or absorb nutrients. All living things need food and water. Most animals take in food and water through their mouths. Plants absorb nutrients from the soil through their roots.

2. Living things perform **respiration**—they "breathe" or exchange oxygen and carbon dioxide as they turn food into energy. Both plants and animals need oxygen to survive. Animals get oxygen from their surroundings in many different ways. We are most familiar with animals that breathe with lungs. But some animals, such as fish, breathe with gills, and others, such as Earthworms, can

absorb oxygen through their skin. Plants also "breathe" by exchanging carbon dioxide and oxygen through their leaves. During the day, when sunlight is abundant, plants use carbon dioxide to produce food through photosynthesis; however, at night, plants use oxygen to break down some of that food for energy to grow. The type of respiration performed by all living things is called cellular respiration. It involves using oxygen to break down sugars to release energy needed for the processes of life. Different processes are used to exchange the gases required for and produced by cellular respiration—how it "breathes"—but all organisms use energy.

3. Living things grow. All plants and animals have a life cycle in which they are born, develop and grow, and then die.

4. Living things reproduce. Animals and plants reproduce in many different ways, but God designed each living thing to be able to produce more of its own kind. Most animals have babies and most plants produce seeds, but there are other ways of reproducing such as dividing or producing spores.

5. Living things move and respond to their environment. Animals can move in many different ways: some run, some fly, some slither, some swim. Plants can't move around like animals but they do respond to their environment. Plants turn their leaves to face the sun. Their roots grow down and their stems grow up. Many flowers close at night and open in the morning. This is their way of moving and responding.

6. Living things have cells. Even though we can't see plant and animal cells without the aid of a microscope, we know that all living things are made up of living cells.

Are Plants Alive Biblically?

When we talk about the study of living things from a scientific perspective, we use a definition of living things that is based on what we can observe about the organism God has created. But, according to the Bible, there is a difference between plant life and animal and human life. Throughout the Bible, the Hebrew words *nephesh chayyâh* are used to describe human and animal life. When referring to mankind, *nephesh chayyâh* means "living soul" or "soulish creature," and when it refers to animals, it means "living creature." However, this word is never applied to plant life. There is a plain distinction. It is easy to see that plants do not experience pain, suffering, or death in the same way that humans and animals do. Plant death is not the death of a "living soul" or "living creature."

As you consider the six characteristics above, keep in mind that we are using the scientific definition of a living thing. To see a biblical example of the distinction, read the following passages and compare how they talk about humans or animals and plants: Genesis 2:7, 6:17, 7:15, 7:22; Leviticus 17:10–12; Psalm 104:24–30; Matthew 6:25–34.

🧠 What did we learn?

- What are the six questions you should ask to determine if something is biologically alive?
- Does the Bible refer to plants as living things?

🚀 Taking it further

- Do scientists consider a piece of wood that has been cut off of a tree living? (Hint: Is it growing? Can it respond?)
- Is paper alive?
- Is a seed alive?

Is it alive? scavenger hunt

Use a copy of the "Is it Alive? Scavenger Hunt" worksheet to determine whether items inside and outside of your house are alive or not.

 # Law of biogenesis

Now that you know how to determine if something is alive, you understand that living things come from living things. An apple tree produces seeds that grow into new apple trees; a dog gives birth to puppies that grow up to be dogs. This observation is completely consistent with the Bible when it says in Genesis that plants and animals were created to reproduce after their own kind. Also, in Matthew chapter 7, Jesus said that people could tell a plant by its fruit—a thorn bush does not produce grapes and a thistle plant does not produce figs. Today, scientists better understand plant and animal reproduction and realize that DNA in the cells determines what kind of plant or animal will be produced.

However, people did not always understand that living things must come from living things. At one time, people thought that rats were produced by garbage because they observed that rats were more abundant when there was more garbage. People also thought that rotting meat produced maggots, which grow into flies, because they observed that when meat was left to rot, maggots often appeared within a few days. This idea is called spontaneous generation. People believed that these animals were somehow suddenly produced by their surroundings. It took the work of a some very persistent scientists to dispel this idea.

In about 1665 an Italian scientist named Francesco Redi did several experiments to show that spontaneous generation did not occur. He believed that maggots came from flies, not from rotting meat. To prove this he put some meat into three different jars. The first jar was left open to the air. The second jar was covered with a layer of gauze which allowed air to pass through. The third jar was covered with a thick parchment that prevented anything from passing into or out of the jar. What do you think happened in each of the three jars?

In the first jar maggots appeared in a few days, just as people had seen before. In the second jar, eggs and later maggots were found on top of the gauze, but no maggots were found inside the jar. There were no eggs, maggots, or flies in or around the third jar. This experiment showed that the maggots came from eggs that were laid by flies which were attracted by the smell of the decomposing meat. When the jar was sealed the flies did not smell the meat and did not lay their eggs, so there were no maggots. This experiment did much to dispel the idea of spontaneous generation; however, many people still believed that simple organisms such as bacteria might still be produced without parents.

In the 1800s Louis Pasteur worked to show that even simple organisms such as bacteria only come from other bacteria. Pasteur experimented with different samples of broth. He showed that bacteria freely reproduced in an open container of broth. He then boiled the broth to kill all of the bacteria. Some of this broth was exposed to the air and other broth was kept in a sealed container. The broth exposed to the air developed new bacteria but the sealed jar did not. Pasteur believed that bacteria were entering the jar on dust particles in the air. To show that this was true, he created a bottle with a zigzag neck that allowed air to enter but prevented dust and other particles from entering the jar. The broth in this jar did not develop any bacteria even after four years. In fact, even after 100 years, no bacteria were found in this jar, which is now on display in the Pasteur Institute in Paris. Pasteur's experiments laid to rest the idea of spontaneous generation.

These experiments proved that life only comes from other life. This is such an important idea that it is called the law of biogenesis. Every experiment has shown that in order to get something that is alive, you must start with one or more living things and that you always get what you started with. Bacteria produce bacteria, flies produce flies, and people produce people. This is exactly how God designed the world to work.

Despite the fact that biogenesis is what we always observe, many scientists today believe that at one time life came from nonlife. They refer to this occurrence as abiogenesis or chemical evolution. These scientists believe that many millions of years ago under just the right circumstances, chemicals accidentally combined to form proteins, which are

Louis Pasteur

the building blocks of living cells, and that these proteins combined to form simple living creatures. Scientists have even tried to reproduce this event in the laboratory; however, even with a very controlled environment, no one has ever built living cells from just chemicals. Even if they could produce life in a lab, all it would prove is that intelligence can produce life. It would not prove that life can evolve from chemicals on its own.

God's Word is true, and as you learn more about living things, you will be amazed at how beautifully God designed each living thing to reproduce to continue the cycle of life.

2

What Is a Kingdom?

It's alive, but what is it?

How are plants different from animals?

Words to know:

taxonomy	anatomy
zoology	kingdom
botany	

Challenge words:

dichotomous key

Once we determine that something is alive, how do we tell what it is? Scientists have grappled with this question for centuries. Carl Linnaeus is credited with developing the method of classification, or **taxonomy**, that we use today. But that classification system has been modified over the centuries to reflect new understanding of the living world.

The study of living things can be divided into three broad categories. The study of animals is called **zoology** while the study of plants is called **botany**. We use the word **anatomy** to talk about the different parts of plants, animals, or humans. But as scientists have learned more about the world of living things that God created, they have discovered that not everything fits neatly into plants or animals.

One system divides all living things into five kingdoms. A **kingdom** is a group of living things that has broad common characteristics.

The first two kingdoms are *plants*, which include all green plants that perform photosynthesis, and *fungi*, which cannot make their own food. The final three kingdoms are *animals*, which are multi-celled creatures, *protists*, which are single- and multi-celled creatures, and *monerans*, which are bacteria. Some scientists divide the kingdom Monera into two groups (Eubacteria and Archaea) based on their differing characteristics. For simplicity, we are going to treat them as one kingdom.

Because most protists and monerans are microscopic, plants and animals are the living things that most people recognize. To separate living things into different kingdoms, we must look at what is the same and what is different, and then sort them based on their differences. By answering the following questions, we can begin to determine whether a living thing is a plant or an animal.

For both plants and animals:

- Is it alive? All plants and animals are alive.

- Does it have cells? All plants and animals have cells.

- Does it reproduce after its own kind? God created

all plants and animals with the ability to make more plants and animals just like themselves.

- Does it need oxygen? All plants and animals need oxygen. We will see that the way they obtain that oxygen can be very different from one living thing to another, but they all use it.

- Do they demonstrate God's design? All plants and animals are special and created just the way God wanted them to be. You will see this great master plan as you study the plants and animals in more detail.

For plants only:

- Do the cells have chlorophyll? Chlorophyll is what makes leaves green. Plants have it; animals don't.

Fun Fact

Did you know that plants were created before there was even a sun? According to Genesis chapter 1 plants were created on Day Three of creation, and the sun, moon, and stars were created on Day Four. The plants could not have survived very long if the sun had not been created the next day.

- Does it make its own food? Plants use chlorophyll to change the sun's energy into food for the plant. Animals cannot do this and must eat either plants or other animals that eat plants.

- Does it need the sun to survive? Many animals live in places that receive little or no sunshine. But all green plants must have sunshine to make food.

- Do they need carbon dioxide? Plants use carbon dioxide in photosynthesis when they make food. Animals do not need carbon dioxide. It is a waste product that they must get rid of.

For animals only:

- Can it move about freely? Although plants and animals both move in some sense, animals move about freely in their environment. Plants are rooted to the ground and therefore cannot move from one place to another.

Plants are different from animals because plants can produce their own food using carbon dioxide, chlorophyll, and the sun. Also, plants are limited in their movement. Animals, on the other hand, move freely, but must eat plants or other animals for food.

Animal or plant game

Purpose: To play a game as you identify the characteristics of plants and animals

Materials: "Clue Cards" handout, poster board, pen, scissors

Procedure:

1. Divide a piece of poster board into three sections as shown here. Label the left column *Animals*, the right column *Plants*, and the center section a few inches up from the bottom *Both*.

Animals   Plants

Both

2. Cut out the clue cards, mix them up, and place them face down on the table.

3. Have a person draw the first card and place it in the correct column. If the card describes a characteristic of plants only put it in the *Plants* column, if it describes only animals put it in the *Animals* column. If it describes both plants and animals put it in the *Both* column.

4. Have the next person draw the next card and so on. If someone has difficulty choosing the correct column, review the questions in this lesson or let the others help.

What did we learn?

- What do plants and animals have in common?
- What makes plants unique?
- What makes animals unique?

 # Taking it further

- Are mushrooms plants?
- Why do you think they are or are not?

 # Dichotomous key

When scientists try to identify a living organism, they often use charts that have been developed by careful observation. These charts begin with two questions or options that describe a particular characteristic that helps divide the organisms into two groups. Based on the answer to the first question, the chart then presents two new questions/options to further help identify characteristics of the organism. Because there are always two possible answers, the chart is called a dichotomous key. To see how this works, use the dichotomous keys below to help you identify the animals and plants that are shown. Choose one of the plants or animals listed at the bottom of the chart. We will use the cat for our example. Go to the top of the chart and ask yourself the question, "Does this animal have a backbone or no backbone?" It has a backbone, so you follow that branch of the chart. The next question is, "Is this animal warm-blooded or cold-blooded?" The cat is warm-blooded so you move down that branch. Finally ask, "Does this animal have hair or feathers?" The cat has hair so you follow that branch and identify the animal as a cat. Follow the branch for each plant and animal on each chart. It is okay if you do not know the answers for every question for every example. This will still give you an idea of how these charts work. These charts are very simple compared to the detailed charts used by scientists.

Animal Identification Key

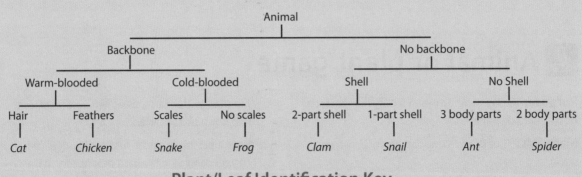

Plant/Leaf Identification Key

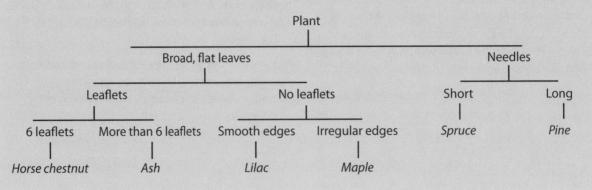

Introduction to Life Science

3

Classification System

Taxonomy—classification of living things

How are living things classified?

Words to know:

phylum	family
vascular tissue	genus
class	species
order	binomial classification

Determining if something is a plant or an animal is just the beginning of classification. One modern classification system uses a seven-level method for describing what something is. The top level is the kingdom. As we learned in the last lesson, there are five kingdoms recognized today: plants, animals, fungi, protists, and monerans. Once a specimen is determined to fit into one of these kingdoms, it is then placed into a phylum (FI-lum). A phylum (plural: phyla) separates the specimens in a kingdom by common characteristics. For example, animals are separated into a phylum based on whether they have a backbone or not—vertebrates and invertebrates. One of the characteristics used to divide plants into phyla is whether or not they have vascular tissue, a series of tubes to carry nutrients throughout the plant.

Each phylum is then divided into classes—again according to common characteristics. Each class is divided into orders. Each order is divided into families. A family is divided into genera (plural of genus). And each genus is divided into species. This may seem complicated, but a couple of examples should help you understand how this works.

The strawberry plant is classified below:

Kingdom	Plant	
Phylum	Tracheophyta	Has vascular tissue
Class	Angiosperm	Reproduces with flowers, fruits, and seeds
Order	Rosales	Flower grows from beneath ovary
Family	Rosaceae	Flowers grow up to four inches wide
Genus	*Fragaria*	Leaves grow in groups of three
Species	*vesca*	Strawberry

Now let's look at an example of an animal classification. Your pet dog is classified below:

Kingdom	Animal	
Phylum	Vertebrate	Has a backbone
Class	Mammal	Has hair, nurses young, warm-blooded
Order	Carnivore	Flesh-eating
Family	Canidae	Dog-like
Genus	*Canis*	Dog
Species	*familiaris*	Domestic

Fun Fact

Mountain lion, cougar, catamount, wildcat, and puma all refer to the same animal, depending on where you live. So it's a good thing that scientists use Latin names, like *Puma concolor*, to describe living things to avoid confusion.

Generally, a living thing is identified by its Latin genus and species names. For example, the family dog would be identified as a *canis familiaris*. This **binomial**, or two-name, **classification** system was adopted by Carl Linnaeus in the 18th century and is still used today to help scientists easily identify what they are talking about. Common names are not used for scientific purposes because the common name can be different from one area to another or even from one person to another. For example, one group of people might call a plant a chickpea plant and another group might call it a garbanzo bean plant. So using the Latin names helps avoid confusion.

Dividing plants and animals into this classification system can be subjective. And scientists do not always agree on where a creature or plant should be placed. Also, some modern scientists are attempting to change the classifications to reflect supposed evolutionary chains. There is no evidence for these evolutionary classifications, and good scientists use what can be observed and tested to make good conclusions.

Finally, when evolutionists talk about one animal evolving into another, they are referring to one kind of creature or plant changing into another. For example, they say that dogs, bears, seals, and raccoons all came from a common weasel-like ancestor millions of years ago. But what we actually observe is that dogs reproduce dogs, bears make bears, etc. Some wild dogs such as wolves and domestic dogs can interbreed. They came from a common dog kind that was on the Ark and survived the Flood. But a dog is still a dog, and a cat is still a cat.

What did we learn?

- What are the five kingdoms recognized today?
- How do scientists determine how to classify a living thing?
- What are the seven levels of the classification system?

Taking it further

- Why can pet dogs breed with wild wolves?
- How many of each animal kind did Noah take on the Ark?

Remembering the system

You can memorize one of the following sayings to help remember the classification system:

Keep	Penguins	Cool	Or	Find	Good	Shelter
Kings	Play	Chess	On	Fine	Green	Squares
(Kingdom	Phylum	Class	Order	Family	Genus	Species)

Look up the classification for some of your favorite plants or animals in a reference guide or on the Internet.

Plant classification

You will be able to understand plants better if you understand how scientists classify plants. First, plants are divided into two groups: plants with vascular tissue and plants without vascular tissue. Plants are further divided based primarily on how they reproduce.

Plants with vascular tissue have a series of tubes throughout the plant. These tubes function very much like the blood vessels in a human. They carry nutrients throughout the plants. Whether a plant has vascular tissue or not determines which phylum the plant belongs to.

Nonvascular plants are divided into three groups: mosses, liverworts, and hornworts. Together these are called bryophytes. These nonvascular plants have leaves and stems, but do not have true roots. They reproduce by spores, not with flowers. The bryophytes tend to grow in clumps in moist areas. You may find them growing on tree trunks or along streams, but don't confuse them with the algae growing in the water. Even though algae contain chlorophyll, they are not plants since they do not have leaves, stems, and roots.

Vascular plants are divided into two subphyla: plants that produce seeds and plants that do not produce seeds. Seedless plants reproduce using spores. These plants include horsetails, ferns, and club mosses.

Vascular plants with seeds are further divided into two classes: gymnosperms and angiosperms. Gymnosperms are plants that produce seeds that are not enclosed in fruit. These plants

Ginkgo tree

primarily reproduce with seeds that form in cones. Angiosperms are plants that produce seeds that are enclosed in fruit.

There are three main groups of gymnosperms. The largest group is the conifers. These plants have needle-like or scaly leaves and have the cones that we are familiar with such as pine cones or spruce cones. The second group of gymnosperms is the cycads (SI-kadz). These plants produce very large cones that grow out of the center of a large circle of palm tree style leaves. There are only a few species of cycads flourishing today, although many species are common in the fossil record. The sago palm is the most commonly cultivated cycad. The third group of gymnosperms is the ginkgoes. Ginkgoes have fleshy cones and unique fan-shaped leaves. Ginkgoes are native to China and are the only gymnosperms that shed their leaves. Ginkgoes are sometimes called living fossils because they were thought to be extinct, only found in the fossil record, until they were rediscovered in China.

Finally, angiosperms are divided into two main sub-classes based on the types of seed that the plant produces. Plants that produce two-part seeds are called dicots. Plants that produce seeds with only one part are called monocots. Angiosperms are the most common types of plants. You will learn much more about these plants in the following lessons.

Now that you have learned about how the plant kingdom is divided up, take the information above and draw a key or chart similar to the dichotomous keys you used in the previous lesson.

Thallose liverwort

Carl Linnaeus

1707–1778
Father of Taxonomy

Carl Linnaeus (also known as Carolus Linnaeus) came into the world on May 23, 1707, in southern Sweden. His father Nils Linnaeus was a Lutheran pastor, as well as an avid gardener and amateur botanist, which tells you where Carl got his love of plants. His father and mother hoped he would follow in his father's footsteps and become a pastor. Carl did follow him—right out to the garden, every chance he got. By the time he was five, his father gave him his own garden to take care of. In school, Carl got the nickname of "Little Botanicus" because of his love of plants.

Carl was originally studying to become a priest, but on the advice of his teachers, Carl got permission to study medicine. At this time, every doctor had to prepare and prescribe drugs derived from plants. This move suited Carl, and in his autobiography he wrote that studying had become as much fun as it was unpleasant before.

Even though he enjoyed his studies, Carl did not go into medicine but instead spent his time giving lectures on botany. Later, he applied to the Royal Science Society in Uppsala, Sweden, and received a grant for a scientific journey to Lapland in northern Sweden. From a natural history point of view, Lapland was still unknown. In May of 1732, Carl went north and studied the plants in Lapland. Carl Linnaeus's journals were so complete that his trip to the north attracted attention from both inside and outside of Sweden.

By this time Linnaeus had started his work on grouping plants together, but not everyone agreed with him. A botanist named Johann Siegesbeck criticized his work. However, Carl did not let this bother him. He continued his work and he even named a useless European weed *Siegesbeckia* in honor of his critic. It is not certain who got the last laugh as this weed was later found to have medicinal uses.

Through his work, Linnaeus was able to influence several students to travel as far as America in search of new plants. He also worked to find plants or crops that would grow in Sweden that could be exported in order to reduce Sweden's dependency on imports. He also tried to find native plants that could be used for tea, coffee, flour, and fodder (food for livestock), but was unsuccessful in this venture.

Carl's real claim to fame, though, is that he was the first to consistently use the two-Latin-name system (binomial) for classifying plants and animals. The first name defines the genus, or grouping of similar organisms, and the second part defines the species. For example, a human is classified as *Homo sapiens*; *Homo* meaning primate and *sapiens* meaning humanity (though we know that humans are not related to primates, such as apes).

You may wonder if Carl Linnaeus was a Christian. If you read his writings, you will see that he was. He wrote in the preface to a late edition of *Systema Naturae*, "The earth's creation is the glory of God, as seen from the works of nature by man alone."

Linnaeus did not believe in evolution. In his early years, he believed that species were unchangeable as he wrote, "The invariability of species is the condition for order in nature." He was saying that the descendants of a deer or woodpecker would be the same as the original animal.

In later years, he abandoned the concept that species were fixed and invariable and suggested that species might alter through the process of acclimatization (or adaptation). In other words, species can change to fit their environment.

We see evidence of these kinds of changes. For example, moths that blend in with their environment are not eaten so they survive to reproduce whereas those that did not blend in get eaten. After a few generations, the overall color of the population has changed to fit the environment. This is not a change from one kind of animal to another kind; it is merely a change in the dominant color of the overall population.

Linnaeus did not believe that the process of change was open-ended or unlimited. One kind does not change into another kind. The moths are still moths. They did not change into a frog or some other animal. Whatever changes have occurred within a kind have arisen from the original kind that God created.

Although the system we use today to group plants and animals is somewhat different from what Carl Linnaeus used, his early work laid the foundation for what we use today. Carl Linnaeus helped us develop a way to organize what we see around us and helped direct us to the Creator of that order.

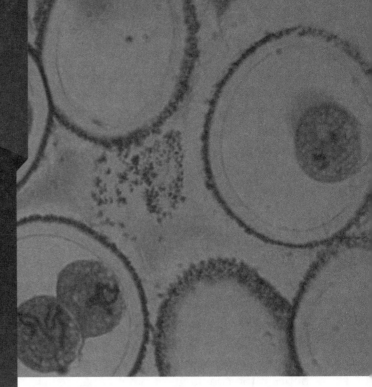

4

Plant & Animal Cells

The smallest unit of life

What are the basic parts of a cell?

Words to know:

cell	cytoplasm
organelle	cell wall
cell membrane	chloroplast
nucleus	tissue
vacuole	organ
mitochondria	

Challenge words:

mitosis	telophase
prophase	cytokinesis
metaphase	meiosis
anaphase	

You have learned that all living things are made of cells, so plants and animals have cells— but what is a cell? A **cell** is the smallest structural unit of an organism that is capable of functioning independently. Some living organisms exist only as a single cell, while an average-sized man contains from 60 to 100 trillion cells. Understanding cells helps us to understand the detail and intricacies of what God created so we can appreciate how everything works together.

Animal cells contain many specialized parts, called **organelles**. Five of these main structures are:

- **Cell membrane**—acts like the "skin" of the cell. It surrounds and protects the rest of the cell. It also recognizes other cells.

- **Nucleus**—the "brain" of the cell. It is the control center of the cell. It also contains the genetic code used to produce new cells.

- **Vacuoles**—storage "warehouses" that store food for the cell, as well as storage of waste.

- **Mitochondria**—the "power stations" of the cell. They break down the food and with the addition of oxygen produce energy for the cell.

- **Cytoplasm**—the "transportation network" of the cell. It is the liquid that fills the cell and allows all the other parts of the cell to move around inside the cell.

Animal cells can have many different shapes depending on the function of the cell, but the majority of them are round.

Plant cells have the same basic organelles as animal cells, as well as these two additional structures:

Animal cell

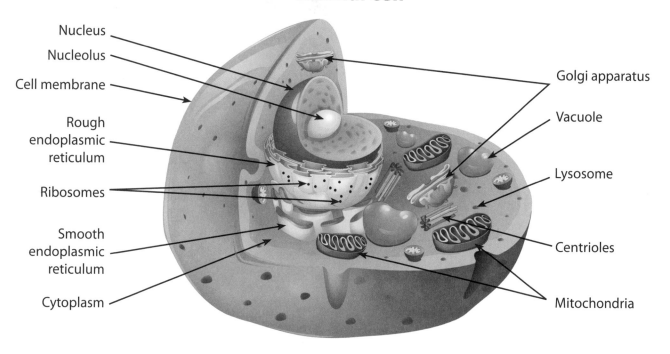

Nucleus
Nucleolus
Cell membrane
Rough endoplasmic reticulum
Ribosomes
Smooth endoplasmic reticulum
Cytoplasm

Golgi apparatus
Vacuole
Lysosome
Centrioles
Mitochondria

• **Cell wall**—provides support for the cell. It surrounds the cell membrane and gives it strength and form. This allows plants to be rigid even though they do not have a skeleton like most animals do.

• **Chloroplasts**—the "food factories" of the cell. They make sugars using water and carbon dioxide in the presence of chlorophyll and sunlight. The presence of chloroplasts is a major factor in determining if a living thing is a plant rather than an animal.

Plant cell

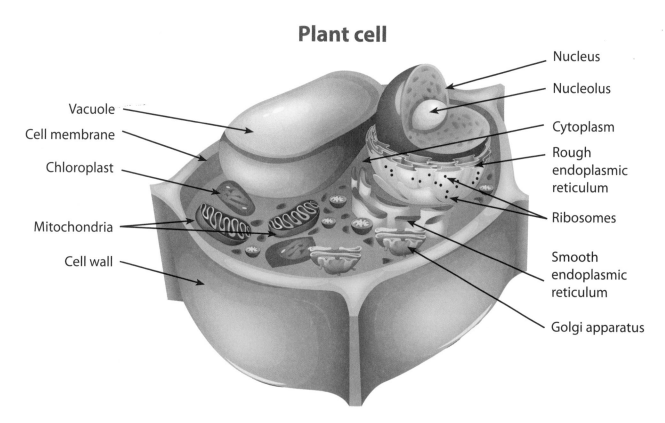

Vacuole
Cell membrane
Chloroplast
Mitochondria
Cell wall

Nucleus
Nucleolus
Cytoplasm
Rough endoplasmic reticulum
Ribosomes
Smooth endoplasmic reticulum
Golgi apparatus

Plant cells generally have a square or rectangular shape. The cell wall helps the plant cell hold its shape, which in turn helps the entire plant hold its shape.

Even though each cell can function on its own, plants and animals were designed for cells to work together with other cells. A group of cells working together to perform a function is called a tissue. A group of tissues working together is called an organ. To appreciate how small a cell is, realize that one average tree leaf has approximately 50 million cells.

 # What did we learn?

- What parts or structures do all plant and animal cells have?

- What structures are unique to plants?

- What distinguishes animal cells from plant cells?

 # Taking it further

- A euglena is a single-celled living organism that can move around by itself. It eats other creatures, but it also has chlorophyll in its cell. Is it a plant, an animal, or something else?

 # Other organelles

Research and write the function of these other organelles in animal and plant cells by looking them up in an encyclopedia or the Internet:

- centrioles
- lysosome
- nucleolus
- smooth endoplasmic reticulum
- rough endoplasmic reticulum
- ribosome
- golgi apparatus

Making a model of a cell

Purpose: To make a model of a cell

Option A—Construction paper model

Materials: construction paper, glue, scissors

Procedure:

1. Cut pieces of construction paper to resemble the parts of a cell (see previous pictures). Use different colors of construction paper for each part of the cell.

2. Glue them together to make a model of each kind of cell. Be sure to make a rectangular cell with a cell wall and green chloroplasts for a plant cell, and a round cell without those structures for an animal cell.

Option B—Gelatin model

Materials: gelatin, zipper bag, red grape, raisins, green grapes, shoe box

Procedure:

1. Mix the gelatin according to the box directions and place in the refrigerator for about 1 hour.

2. Fill a zipper bag about ¾ full of the thickened gelatin. The bag represents the cell membrane and the gelatin represents the cytoplasm.

3. Insert a red grape for the nucleus and several raisins for the mitochondria.

4. Squish the ingredients around to see how the parts of the cell move. If you move most of the cytoplasm away from an area, that would represent an empty space for a vacuole where food could be stored. This is your basic animal cell model.

5. To make a plant cell model, add several green grapes to represent chloroplasts.

6. Now place the bag inside a small shoe box. The sides of the box support the bag and give it strength just as the cell wall does in a plant cell.

7. To represent a tissue, stack several boxes together to make a tower.

8. You can stack more boxes together to make a bridge, pyramid, or other structure to represent an organ.

Introduction to Life Science

Mitosis

All living things are composed of cells. Some very tiny creatures consist of only one cell, and some don't even have a nucleus. But most plants and animals consist of millions of cells. Even though a plant or animal may have millions of cells, it still begins with only one cell. So how does one cell become a whole plant or animal? This happens through an amazing process called mitosis. Mitosis is cell division that results in two identical cells.

As you just learned, the nucleus of a cell controls everything that goes on in that cell. The nucleus can do this because is contains a vast amount of information. This information is stored in special molecules called DNA. All of the information needed to "build" the particular organism is found in the DNA. Inside the nucleus, the DNA is divided into several long strands called chromosomes.

When a cell is ready to divide, the cell makes a complete copy of each chromosome. When this is done, complete mitosis begins. Mitosis takes place in four major phases. During prophase the wall around the nucleus breaks down and the chromosomes are duplicated. In the second phase, called metaphase, the chromosomes line up in the center of the cell. In the next phase, the duplicates of each chromosome

are pulled apart and one set of chromosomes ends up at each side of the cell. This is called anaphase. The final phase is telophase. During telophase a new envelope develops around each set of chromosomes forming two nuclei. Also, in a process called cytokinesis, the cell membrane pinches together to form two new cells. In plant cells, a new cell wall also forms down the center of the cell to divide the cytoplasm. This results in two new cells, often called daughter cells, which are both identical to the original cell.

Through mitosis, plants and animals develop and grow and replace old worn out cells. The most amazing thing of all is that these identical cells somehow know to develop into different kinds of cells after division occurs.

Nearly every cell in a plant or animal experiences mitosis. The only exception is reproductive cells. Egg and sperm cells in animals, and ovules and pollen cells in plants experience a different kind of cell division call meiosis, which produces cells with only one set of chromosomes instead of two.

If you have access to a microscope you may be able to see cells that are experiencing mitosis.

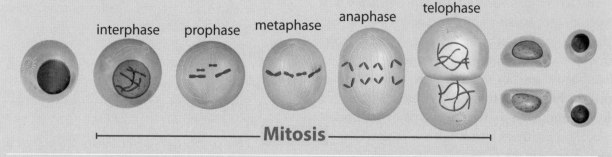

interphase   prophase   metaphase   anaphase   telophase

— Mitosis —

Purpose: To examine cell division

Materials: microscope, slide, onion, sharp knife, blue food coloring or iodine solution

Procedure:

1. Cut a very thin slice of onion and place it on a slide. Add a drop of blue food coloring or iodine solution to make the parts easier to see.

2. Observe it under a microscope. You should be able to see individual cells that look somewhat like rectangles.

Inside each cell you should be able to see a dark spot which is the nucleus. You may be able to see some cells that have chromosomes lined up in the center or that are being pulled apart. These are cells that are undergoing mitosis.

3. Whether you have a microscope or not, search the Internet and you will find many web sites that show actual cell division or animations of cell division to give you a better understanding of the process.

Cells

Who discovered cells and when? Since most cells cannot be seen with the naked eye, it took the invention of the microscope for them to be seen. The inventor of the microscope was Anton Van Leeuwenhoek from Holland; he was the first person to see microorganisms. However, the first person to record seeing cells was Robert Hooke of Britain, who improved on Anton's microscope by making a compound microscope, one with two lenses, and adding an illumination system. This happened around 1665.

Hooke used this new microscope, one of the best of its day, to study organisms. When he studied the box-like cells of cork, it reminded him of the cells of a monastery. Therefore, he called them cells and the name stuck. So, if you discover something new, choose its name wisely. It just might stick.

Robert Hooke was perhaps one of the greatest experimental scientists of his day. He was largely educated by his father. He was a homeschooler. Among his inventions are the universal joint, iris diaphragm, anchor escapement, and balance spring, which made more accurate clocks possible. He also improved or invented some of the meteorological (weather) instruments of that time. He was a man of many talents.

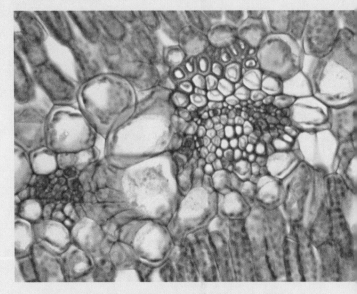

Some facts about cells:

- Cells are the smallest living things known.
- It would take around 10,000 human cells to cover the head of a pin.
- Egg yolks are cells.
- One of the largest cells is the ostrich egg yolk.
- Nerve cells can be up to 3 feet (1 m) long.
- All living organisms are made up of one or more cells.
- All cells come from other cells. They do not just appear.

UNIT 2

Flowering Plants & Seeds

5 Flowering Plants

6 Grasses

7 Trees

8 Seeds

9 Monocots & Dicots

10 Seeds—Where Are They?

◊ **Describe** the function of each of the organs of flowering plants.

◊ **Describe** why grasses are important to mankind.

◊ **Distinguish** between deciduous and evergreen trees.

◊ **Distinguish** between monocots and dicots.

Flowering Plants

God's gift of life to the world

What are the parts of a flowering plant?

Words to know:

roots	leaves
stems	flowers

God created plants on the third day of creation. Genesis 1:12 says, "And the earth brought forth grass, the herb that yields seed according to its kind, and the tree that yields fruit, whose seed is in itself according to its kind. And God saw that it was good." Most plants that we are familiar with are flowering plants. These plants reproduce by seeds that are formed in their flowers. Plants have four distinct organs that do specialized tasks. Can you name them?

The four plant organs are:

- **Roots**—anchor the plant to the soil, absorb water and minerals, and store food.
- **Stems**—hold up the plant's leaves and flowers, transport water and nutrients throughout the plant, and store food. Trees, shrubs, and some vines have stiff woody stems. Flowers, grasses, and other vines have soft flexible stems.

- **Leaves**—manufacture food. Photosynthesis takes place mostly in the leaves.
- **Flowers**—perform reproduction by producing fruits and seeds. Flowers may not always look like you expect them to!

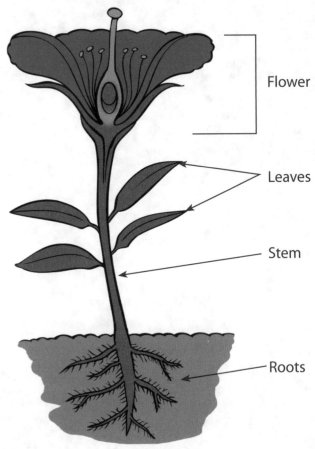

Flower

Leaves

Stem

Roots

Even though almost all plants have these structures, each type of plant is unique. God designed plants with a vast array of sizes, shapes, colors, and purposes. Many plants are easily distinguishable. Even the smallest child knows the difference between a tree and grass, or a rose and a corn stalk. One of the easiest ways to identify plants is by examining their flowers. Each type of plant has a unique flower. Examining these flowers can reveal the wonder and the variety of creation.

What did we learn?

- What are the four major parts of a plant?
- What is the purpose for each part?

Taking it further

- What characteristics other than the flowers can be used to help identify a plant?
- What similarities did you notice between the flowers you examined?
- What differences did you see?
- Can you use size to determine what a plant is? Why or why not? (Hint: Is a tiny seedling just as much an oak tree as the giant oak that is 100 years old?)
- Why might you need to identify a plant?

Examining flowers

We are familiar with many flowers, but there are some unusual ones. Grass, when allowed to grow tall enough, will bloom with very tiny flowers. Most weeds will bloom if allowed to grow. Many wild flowers are considered weeds when growing in our yards but are considered beautiful when growing in the mountains or prairies. Dandelions are a great example of this.

Purpose: To describe and identify flowers

Materials: field guide, notebook, flowers

Procedure:

1. Describe some flowers you are familiar with, such as rose, daisy, carnation, or tulip. Discuss what makes each one unique and how you might try to identify a flower you are not familiar with.

2. Examine a field guide for flowers. Look for identification techniques. These should include but not be limited to:
    - General shape of the flower (bell, ray, etc.)
    - Number and arrangement of petals
    - Color
    - Size

3. Go outside and use the field guide to identify as many flowers as possible in your garden, yard, or nearby field. Dried or pressed flowers may also be used, but are harder to match to the pictures and description in a field guide.

Tiger lily

Daisy

Rose

Carnation

Tulip

🎖 Plants in industry

Flowering plants are vitally important. Not only are they the source of food for nearly every food chain on Earth, but they are also used in many other ways as well. Plants are used in many industries. For example, cotton is used in clothing, trees are used in building, and reeds are used to make baskets. Plants are also very important in making medicines. Choose one of these areas, or another where plants are used in industry, and research the use of plants. Make a short presentation to your class or family so they will understand the importance of plants.

Reeds are used to make baskets.

Cotton plants

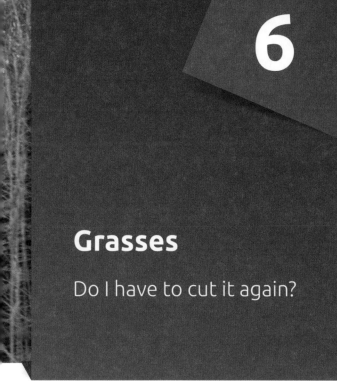

6

Grasses

Do I have to cut it again?

What kinds of grasses are there?

Words to know:

turf grass

cereal grass

forage grass

ornamental grass

A very common flowering plant is grass. One third of all land is covered with some type of grass. Grass is a very important food source for many animals as well as for humans. "But humans can't eat grass," you may argue. Well, that is true for the grass you grow in your yard and for many other grasses as well. But several types of grass, including wheat and oats, are very important foods for humans. Grasses are grouped in the following ways:

- **Turf grass:** This is usually short—only a few inches tall. This is the type of grass used in lawns, on golf courses, at parks, etc.

- **Cereal grass:** This type of grass includes the grains such as wheat, barley, rye, oats, corn, and rice. Breads and cereals are a major source of food for all humans, making this the most important group of grasses on Earth.

- **Forage grass:** This is taller than turf grass. These grasses grow wild in prairies and savannahs. They are also grown by farmers. This is a major source of food for grazing animals including

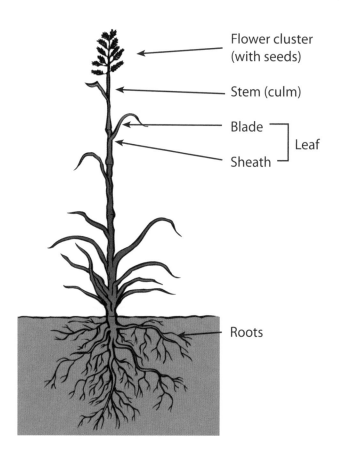

Flower cluster (with seeds)

Stem (culm)

Blade ⎤
        ⎥ Leaf
Sheath ⎦

Roots

Fun Fact

The first lawn mower was invented by Edwin Budding in the early nineteenth century. In 1870 Elwood McGuire designed a mower that appealed to the homeowner. By 1885 the U.S. was building 50,000 push mowers a year and shipping them everywhere.

wild animals such as deer and antelope, and domestic animals such as cattle and horses.

- **Ornamental grass**: This type of grass is very tall and usually used in landscaping. Pampas grass is a popular ornamental grass.
- Miscellaneous grass: This type includes sugar cane and bamboo.

🧠 What did we learn?

- Name four types of grass.
- Describe the roots of a grass plant.
- Why are grasses so important?

🚀 Taking it further

- Why can grass be cut over and over and still grow, while a tree that is cut down will die?
- Why is grass so hard to get rid of in a flower garden?
- What part of grass plants do humans eat?
- What part of grass plants do most animals eat?
- Why can a cow eat certain grasses that you can't?

Fun Fact

One of the most widely grown grasses is wheat. Over the years different varieties of wheat have been developed. Durum wheat is grown and processed to make pasta. Bread wheat is grown and processed to make flour for baking bread and many other foods. Bread wheat has a high amount of a substance called gluten. Gluten helps bread dough be stretchy and hold its shape as it rises. Durum wheat has only a small amount of gluten, so it is better suited for making pasta.

The kernel of the wheat is what is harvested and then ground to make flour.

Examining grass

Purpose: To examine the structure of grass

Materials: grass plant, magnifying glass

Procedure:

1. Carefully uproot a grass plant. Be sure to include as much of the root system as possible, as well as all the foliage growing above ground.

2. Using a magnifying glass, observe the following:

   • Grass has a fibrous root system. It has lots of small roots growing in many directions. Up to 90% of a grass plant's weight is in the roots.

   • The stem is hollow. It grows up through the center of the plant.

   • Leaves grow from the base of the plant. They have a sheath around them. This helps protect the leaves as they grow.

   • If the plant is tall enough, you may observe flower clusters at the top of the stem. These flowers are usually very small and not very noticeable.

   • If the plant has matured enough, seeds could be observed at the top of the stem.

 # Grass comparison

There are many different kinds of grass used for many different purposes. It is fun to observe and compare different grasses as they grow.

Purpose: To compare grass seeds

Materials: different grass seeds (such as Kentucky blue grass, corn, rye, fescue, wheat, oats), potting soil, baking dish, craft stick, "Grass Comparison" worksheet

Procedure:

1. Obtain as many different kinds of grass seed as you can. You should be able to obtain Kentucky bluegrass seed and corn seeds at any store that sells lawn and garden supplies. Other types of grass seed include rye, fescue, wheat, and oats.

2. Once you have obtained at least two different kinds of grass seeds, observe what each type of seed looks like and record your observations on the "Grass Comparison" worksheet.

3. Next, place two inches of potting soil in a baking dish.

4. Plant several of the first type of seed at one end of the dish. Do not plant the seeds more than ¼ inch deep.

5. Write the type of seed on a craft stick and push the stick into the soil near where you planted the seeds.

6. Plant some of the second kind of seed in another area of the dish and write the type of seed on another craft stick and place it in the soil near where you planted the seeds.

7. Repeat this process for each kind of grass seed that you have.

8. Water the soil each day and record your observations on the worksheet.

9. Continue watering your plants for two weeks. At the end of two weeks, answer the questions on the worksheet.

7

Trees

Did George Washington
really chop down
a cherry tree?

How are trees classified?

Words to know:

woody plants
herbaceous plants
deciduous
angiosperm

evergreen
conifer
gymnosperm
bark

Challenge words:

crown
growth habit

Plants that grow with a single, tall, woody stem are called trees. These plants need no support and can grow to great heights. Shrubs differ from trees in that they have many stems and low branches. Shrubs generally do not get as tall as trees. Shrubs and trees are both woody plants, which means they have stiff stems unlike grasses and many flowering plants that have bendable stems. Those plants are called herbaceous plants.

Trees can be grouped into two categories: deciduous and evergreen. Deciduous trees lose their leaves in the winter or dry season; evergreen trees do not. Trees such as oak, maple, apple, cherry, and dogwood are broad-leaved deciduous trees, but some deciduous trees, like larch and cyprus, have needles. Evergreen trees include pine, spruce, fir, and cedar, but some broad-leaf trees are evergreen, magnolias for example, especially in tropical areas.

Another way to group trees is based on where the seed is found. Angiosperms reproduce with flowers, fruits, and seeds. The seeds are in the fruit. The word angiosperm means "covered seed." Most deciduous trees are angiosperms and have broad leaves.

Gymnosperms ("naked seed") have cones instead of flowers. The seeds are not in a fruit. Conifers, or coniferous trees, are gymnosperms because instead of flowers, they have cones in which their seeds form. Most coniferous trees are evergreen. Many people may not think that conifer trees have leaves. However, their leaves are often called needles. Ginkgos and cycads are examples of gymnosperms that have broad leaves.

Fun Fact

The tallest known tree in the world is called Hyperion. It is a redwood tree located in a remote part of Redwood National Park, in California. This giant was measured at 379 feet, 4 inches (115.6 meters). That is more than twice as tall as the Statue of Liberty including the base.

A cross-section of a tree trunk showing the growth rings

Trees are different from herbaceous plants because they have a layer of bark as do some vines and most shrubs. Bark cells help protect the tree throughout its long life. Trees also have growth rings. As new cells are formed in the region between the bark and the wood, the trunk gets thicker. In cold regions, these cells are produced only during the growing season and not during the winter. Some years the conditions are better for growing than others so the growth rings can vary in size from year to year, and sometimes multiple rings can grow in one year. If a tree is cut down, the rings can be clearly seen inside the trunk (or stem) showing approximately how many years the tree has been growing.

🧠 What did we learn?

- What makes a plant a tree?
- How are deciduous and evergreen trees different?
- How are angisperms and gymnosperms different?

🚀 Taking it further

- Do evergreen trees have growth rings?
- How long do you think a tree lives?

🧪 What kind of tree is this?

Purpose: To learn the difference between deciduous and evergreen trees

Materials: index cards, marker or crayon

Procedure:

1. Label index cards with the following vocabulary words: angiosperm, gymnosperm, broadleaf, needles, flowers, cones, seeds, bark, growth rings, oak, maple, cherry, fir, pine, spruce, and conifer.

2. For each index card, decide if that word applies to deciduous or evergreen trees. Then use a marker or crayon to draw a simple tree (like those shown here) on the back of the card. Some words apply to both kinds of trees, so draw both pictures if appropriate.

Deciduous   Evergreen

3. After completing all cards, sort the cards by the pictures on the back. This will help give an idea of the differences between the two kinds of trees.

🎖 Tree shapes

Although trees are most often identified by their fruit and their leaves, many trees also have a distinctive shape. Most deciduous trees have trunks that do not go all the way to the top of the tree. Instead branches grow up and out from the trunk. These branches form the crown of the tree. Oak trees often have a rounded crown; elm trees usually have a narrow tall crown.

Many evergreen trees on the other hand have trunks that go most of the way up especially conifers. The lower branches tend to grow longer than the upper branches giving most evergreen trees a more triangular shape. The way a tree grows, or the shape its branches form, is called its growth habit. You will learn more about growth habits when you study stem structures in lesson 14.

Purpose: To study the growth habit of trees

Materials: paper, pen or pencil

Procedure:

1. Carefully observe the shape and growth habits of several trees. Try to observe both deciduous and ever-green trees.

2. For each tree, make a detailed drawing of the tree showing its shape and branch structure.

3. Label the drawing with the tree name if you know what kind of tree it is. Use a field guide to help iden-tify the tree.

4. Write a description of its growth habit below your drawing.

5. Make sketches of any flowers, cones, fruit, or seeds you find on the tree.

6. Make a bark rubbing of the tree's bark by placing a blank piece of paper against the trunk and rubbing the paper with a crayon or pencil.

7. Make a leaf rubbing or collect a few needles to glue onto your drawing.

8. Compile all of your drawings and rubbings into a notebook. Save these drawings to include in your final project, which you will do in lesson 20.

Redwoods

The Biggest Living Things on Earth

What do you think of when someone asks you, "What is the biggest living thing on Earth?" Do you think of an elephant or a blue whale? While these are very large mammals, they are not the largest living things on Earth. For that answer we need to look into the woods at the trees themselves. The largest living thing on Earth, the organism with the most mass, is a redwood tree, or sequoia. There are three types of sequoia trees: the Coastal Redwood, the Sierra Redwood, and the Dawn Redwood. The name *sequoia* comes from the Cherokee word for patriarch.

Let's look at a few interesting facts about these truly amazing trees:

1. A redwood's trunk can be from 8 to 20 feet (2.4–6 m) across.

2. Many redwoods grow to be over 300 feet (90 m) tall.

3. One redwood tree was large enough to build 22 five-room houses from its wood.

4. Some redwoods are believed to be over 2,200 years old. That means they were already 200 years old when Jesus came to Earth as a man.

5. The redwood forest has the highest amount of biomass per square foot of any place on Earth. There is as much as 8 times more living material in a redwood forest than in a tropical rainforest.

6. These trees are so tall that they can't pump water to their topmost branches. At the top, the tree absorbs water through its leaves. That is why the tallest redwoods only grow in areas that have a lot of fog.

7. The bark of the redwood can be up to one foot (30 cm) thick.

8. When fire hurts the bark of a redwood it chars

into a heat shield, thus reflecting the heat away from the tree.

9. The tree itself is either distasteful or poisonous to most pests, and the wood resists rot caused by water.

10. The wood was used to make car batteries until the 1960s because it can withstand strong acid.

11. A live redwood that gets knocked over can continue to grow. The limbs pointing upward can turn into new trees.

12. One tree was so large that a road has been put through it.

You can see these amazing trees in northern California's Sequoia National Park.

8

Seeds

Germination—the beginning of life

How do seeds grow into plants?

Words to know:

germinate   dormant

Challenge words:

seed dormancy   embryo dormancy

external dormancy   scarification

seed coat dormancy   stratification

internal dormancy   double dormancy

Seeds have the potential to produce new plants. God designed each plant to "yield seed according to its kind, and the tree that yields fruit, whose seed is in itself according to its kind." (Genesis 1:12) This means that a bean seed grows into a bean plant, a watermelon seed grows into a watermelon plant and so on. You won't get a tomato if you plant an apple seed. When you want to grow a new plant, you usually buy a package of seeds and plant them in your garden. You water the ground, and after a few days you see a plant coming up through the dirt. But, have you ever wondered why those seeds don't begin to grow into new plants while they are in the package?

Seeds must have just the right conditions before they will germinate, or begin to grow. What do you think those conditions might be? If you plant a seed in the winter, will it grow right away or does is wait to start growing until the spring time? It waits until spring. Why do you think that is?

Most seeds need three things before they will start to grow: water, oxygen, and warmth. Seeds don't sprout in the package because they are too dry. The seeds remain dormant, kind of like being asleep, until they have just the right conditions to germinate. What would happen if a seed germinated without these conditions? The plant that sprouts from the seed would not be likely to survive. Without water and oxygen the plant cannot

Fun Fact

The U.S. Department of Agriculture has a special center called the National Center for Genetic Resources Preservation, whose goal is to conserve genetic resources of crops and animals important to U.S. agriculture and landscapes. Most of the information is stored as seeds. At the main storage facility in Fort Collins, Colorado, there are over 1.5 billion seeds being stored in coolers and freezers. Stored at 0°F (-18°C), many believe the seeds may stay good nearly indefinitely.

perform respiration and break down the food it needs to grow so it would soon die. Without warmth the plant would freeze. A seed that germinates in poor conditions is basically wasted if the plant does not survive. If seeds continued to sprout in poor conditions, it is possible that some plants could become extinct. So God designed seeds to only germinate when the plant is likely to become strong and healthy.

Fun Fact

The oldest mature seed that was germinated into a viable plant was a 2,000-year-old Judean Date Palm seed, recovered from excavations at Herod the Great's palace on Masada in Israel; this seed was germinated in 2005.

What did we learn?

- What conditions must be present for most seeds to sprout or germinate?

- Why do seeds require these three conditions to begin growing?

- Is soil necessary for seeds to germinate?

Taking it further

- If plants don't need soil to germinate, why do plants need soil to grow?

- Our seeds germinated in the dark. Can the plants continue to grow in the dark?

- How long can seeds remain dormant?

Germination

Purpose: To test the hypothesis that a seed needs water, oxygen, and warmth to germinate

Materials: five glass jars (one with airtight lid), paper towels, bean seeds, steel wool, black construction paper, "Germination Data Sheet"

Procedure:

Label the jars 1–5. Jar number 4 needs to have an airtight lid.

Jar 1: This is the control that has all three conditions: water, oxygen, and warmth.

1. Place a couple of moist (not dripping) paper towels loosely in the jar.

2. Place 3 or 4 bean seeds between the side of the jar and the paper towel.

3. Place the jar in a windowsill or other warm place.

4. Keep the paper towels moist for several days.

Jar 2: This jar will have no warmth.

1. Prepare the jar as above but place it in the refrigerator.

2. Keep the paper towels moist.

Jar 3: This jar will have no water.

1. Prepare this jar as above but use dry paper towels.

2. Place it in the window sill with Jar 1.

3. Do not add water to the towels at any time.

Jar 4: This jar will have no oxygen.

1. Prepare this jar the same as jar 1, but place a piece of steel wool inside the top of the jar and seal it with an airtight lid. The steel wool will react with the oxygen in the jar to use it up, leaving no oxygen in the jar.

2. Place this jar with jars 1 and 3.

3. Do not open this jar or add more water.

Jar 5: This jar will have no light but will have water, oxygen, and warmth. This jar is necessary because we introduced an unexpected variable when we placed jar 2 in the refrigerator. Most refrigerators are dark when the door is closed, so we need to make sure that the lack of light is not what is keeping the seeds from germinating in the refrigerator.

1. Prepare jar 5 like jar 1.

2. Make a tube around the jar with black construction paper and tape it so it can slide on and off to check the progress of the seeds. Make a paper lid to set over the top of the tube to block out the light.

Conclusion: Check each jar every day for several days and record what you see on your "Germination Data Sheet." After a few days you should see some of the seeds in jars 1 and 5 begin to sprout, while the beans in the other jars do not. Discuss these observations with your parent or teacher. Save the plants growing in jar 1 for use in later lessons.

🏅 Seed dormancy

Although you have just set up an experiment to demonstrate the conditions under which most seeds will germinate, you should know that not all seeds will germinate under these conditions. Some seeds will remain dormant even when the needed conditions for germination are present until one or more other conditions are met. This is called seed dormancy.

There are two types of seed dormancy. External or seed coat dormancy occurs when the seed coat prevents the oxygen and water from reaching the seed, thus preventing germination. The second type is internal or embryo dormancy. Internal dormancy occurs when the inner tissues of the seed do not respond until certain additional conditions have been met. Both types of dormancy exist to prevent the seed from sprouting before conditions are favorable for the plant to grow. If a seed fell from a plant in the fall and germinated right away because it was still warm and there was oxygen and water available, the new plant might not survive the winter. Therefore, God designed seeds to wait for the right conditions.

Seeds with external dormancy have tough or thick seed coats. Something must happen to the seed coat to break it down or crack it open before the seed will germinate. Breaking the seed coat is called scarification. Scarification generally happens during the winter. Freezing temperatures or bacteria in the soil can break down or crack the seed coat. In other cases, the scarification occurs in the digestive system of an animal that has eaten the seed. Scarification allows the seeds to germinate in the spring when temperatures warm up and water is available.

In agriculture it is sometimes desirable to scarify the seeds so they can be planted without waiting for natural processes to do the job. Commercial growers often soak seeds in sulfuric acid to break down the seed coat. In other instances, seeds are soaked in hot water to soften and break down the seed coat. Seeds that have been scarified are planted right away because they will not store well.

Internal dormancy also prevents seeds from germinating at the wrong time; however, this dormancy is not dependent on the seed coat. Many types of seeds require that the internal moisture drop below a certain level before the seeds can germinate. This allows the seed to dry out during the winter and then be ready to germinate in the spring. Often commercial growers dry seeds quickly and then package them to sell in the spring.

Other seeds with internal dormancy must experience an extended period of cold temperatures or a period of warm moist temperatures followed by a period of cold temperatures before they will germinate. This process is called stratification. Stratification occurs during the winter months, thus the seeds are ready to germinate in the spring. Again, commercial growers often perform stratification of seeds by chilling seeds in refrigerators so they are ready to plant at the appropriate time.

Finally, some seeds have double dormancy. They must be scarified and stratified before they will germinate. The scarification must occur first, followed by the stratification. Through all these processes it is apparent that God designed seeds to be able to survive harsh conditions and to germinate when conditions are favorable to the growth of new plants.

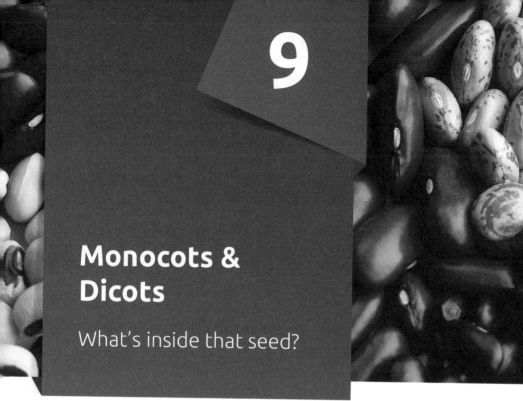

Monocots & Dicots

What's inside that seed?

How many parts does a seed have?

Words to know:

embryo	plumule
seed coat	radicle
cotyledon	endosperm
monocot	hilum
dicot	

Challenge words:

hypogeal	epigeal

Seeds were designed by God to produce new plants. Each seed has an embryo or "baby" plant inside of it. It also has a seed coat on the outside to protect the seed until conditions are right for germination. The largest part of the seed is the cotyledon (cot-el-LEE-dun), which supplies nourishment for the sprouting plant. Upon germination, the cotyledon sometimes becomes the first embryonic leaves of the seedling. Some seeds have just one cotyledon and are called monocots, and some have two cotyledons and are called dicots.

Dicot seeds can easily be split in half, but monocots cannot. Plants can grow for several days (and sometimes weeks) using the nourishment from the cotyledons. But eventually, the plant must be put into soil to receive nutrients through its roots.

On the inside of the seed are the plumule and the radicle. The plumule is the part that grows

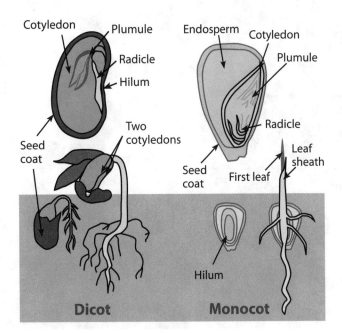

Dicot

Monocot

into the stem and leaves of the plant. The radicle develops into the roots. In some seeds, you can also see the endosperm. This is an area in the seed made up of mostly starch, which provides nutrients for the newly developing plant. Seeds with an endosperm still have a cotyledon. The cotyledon absorbs energy from the endosperm and transfers it to the developing plant.

On the outside of a seed is a scar called the hilum that shows where the seed was attached to the ovary in the flower. This is a little bit like your belly button.

It is amazing that a hard little seed has the potential to become a large plant, able to make more seeds and continue the cycle.

🧪 Seed dissection

Purpose: To dissect seeds and identify their parts

Materials: bean seeds, corn seeds, scalpel or sharp knife, magnifying glass, jar, paper towels

Preparation: Soak several bean and corn seeds in a cup of water overnight.

Dicot—Procedure:

1. Remove several of the bean seeds, which are dicots, from the water in which they have been soaking.

2. Carefully examine the outside of the seeds. You should be able to identify the seed coat and the hilum (see diagram above).

3. Remove the seed coat from one of the beans. What can you observe about the seed coat? Compare this to the seed coat of a bean that has not been soaked in water. How has the water affected the seed coat?

4. Now, use your fingernail to split the seed open. The two halves of the seed are the cotyledons.

5. Now find and identify the plumule and radicle. Can you see the plant's very first leaves?

Monocot—Procedure:

1. Remove several of the corn seeds, which are monocots, from the water and carefully examine the outside of these seeds. How does the seed coat of the corn differ from the seed coat of the beans?

2. Find the hilum of this seed (see diagram above left).

3. Using a knife, an adult should carefully cut the seed open. Monocot seeds have only one cotyledon. Also, monocots store the food for the embryo in the endosperm surrounding the cotyledon. The cotyledon absorbs nutrients from the endosperm during germination.

4. Identify the plumule and radicle using the diagram.

5. Take several of the corn seeds and "plant" them in a jar or plastic cup using moist paper towels to hold the seeds against the inside of the jar, just as you did with the beans in lesson 8, jar 1.

6. Place this jar with jar 1 so these seeds can germinate. We will continue to use these jars in future lessons. Remember to keep the towels moist but not drippy. If possible, you will want to keep these seeds growing for several weeks to observe the complete life cycle of a plant from seed to flower.

🧠 What did we learn?

- What differences did you observe between the monocot and dicot seeds?

- What parts of each seed were you able to identify?

- What is the plumule?

- What is the radicle?

- What is the purpose of the cotyledon?

🚀 Taking it further

- Why did you need to soak the seeds before dissecting them?

- What differences do you think you might find in plants that grow from monocot and dicot seeds?

🏅 Where do seeds germinate?

As you learned in the last lesson, seeds must have special conditions before they will germinate. They must have water; geminating seeds absorb up to 200% more water than the dormant seed contained. If you have any dry seeds left, compare the size and shape of the dry seeds with the seeds that have soaked in water overnight. You will probably see that the soaked seeds are bigger and less wrinkled.

Seeds also need oxygen. The germinating seeds need oxygen to begin cellular respiration. Recall from lesson 1 that even though plants make their own food, they must also be able to break down that food and turn it into energy. This is cellular respiration and it requires oxygen to react with the sugar in the plant. The food stored in the cotyledon is usually stored in the form of starch, so an enzyme called *diastase* converts the starch into sugar and then the oxygen reacts with the sugar to give the new plant energy to grow.

Once favorable conditions exist, germination generally occurs in one of two ways. Hypogeal germination is where the cotyledons stay underground as the plant emerges. Peas experience hypogeal germination. Other plants experience epigeal germination. The cotyledons of these seeds come up out of the ground and may appear to be leaves. However, they will have the same shape as the seed and not the normal shape of the leaves of the plant. The first true leaves will grow on the stem above the cotyledons. Observe your bean and corn plants as they grow and determine which plants experience hypogeal germination and which experience epigeal germination.

If you have access to other kinds of seeds, you can dissect them to determine which are monocots and which are dicots. Do you still have some grass seed left from lesson 6? Do they appear to be monocots or dicots? You can also plant other types of seeds and see which ones you are able to get to germinate.

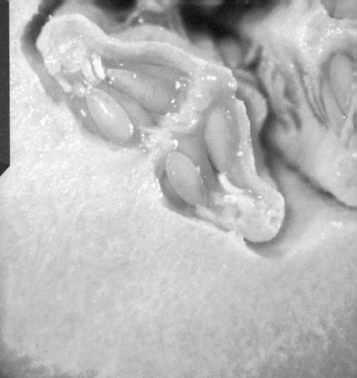

10

Seeds—Where Are They?

They get around.

How are seeds dispersed?

Words to know:

disperse

Challenge words:

seed dispersal   dispersing agent

All flowering plants produce seeds in their flowers, but we don't always see them. Where is grass seed? We often cut our grass before it has a chance to flower. Where are the ornamental flower seeds? We often throw the flower away or cut it back before the seeds are produced. Where are seeds for trees? Some places to look for seeds are in pinecones and in fruits. Seeds can also be found just about anywhere that plants grow naturally. Many times when we consider a plant to be dead, it is actually in its final stages of producing and dispersing its seeds so it can produce new plants in the future. So, look for flowers that have lost their bloom and you will probably find seeds. You often have to look very closely because many seeds are very small, especially seeds for garden or ornamental flowers.

God not only had a plan for plants to produce seeds, but He also had a plan for getting those seeds to new places. What would happen if all of a plant's seeds fell right next to the plant? The plants would quickly get too crowded and not grow well. So God designed plants with special ways to disperse or scatter their seeds. What ways can you think of? Many plants have delicious fruit around the seeds so animals will eat the fruit. In many cases, the animals

An apple's seeds are in the core.

A pile of maple seed "helicopters"

eat the seeds along with the fruit. The fruit is digested but the seeds pass through the animal and are deposited in a different location along with its waste. Animals also help disperse seeds when the seeds get caught in their fur, like the burrs that get caught in your socks when you hike in the woods. Later those seeds fall off and are then in a new location.

Seeds can also be dispersed by wind. Many seeds are designed to float on the wind. Have you ever tried to catch dandelion fluff? Those floating white umbrellas are seeds moving to a new location. Maple trees produce seeds that twirl like helicopters and float on the wind as well.

A third method of seed dispersal is the exploding seed pod. Some plants literally shoot their seeds out when they are ready. These seeds may go a few feet from the plant or many miles, depending on the weather conditions. The touch-me-not, vetch, and meadow cranesbill send their seeds out in this manner. Whatever the method for getting seeds spread out, God designed plants so that they continue to make more plants.

What did we learn?

• What are three ways seeds can be moved or dispersed?

• Where are good places to look for seeds?

Taking it further

• How do people aid in the dispersal of seeds?

• What has man done to change or improve seeds or plants?

• If a seed is small, will the mature plant also be small?

• Do the largest plants always have the largest seeds?

• Why do you think God created many large plants to have small seeds?

• Can you name a plant that disperses its seeds by the whole plant blowing around?

Fun Fact

The huge fire that occurred in Yellowstone National Park in 1989 seemed to many to be a disaster. But scientists discovered that many of the pinecones in the forests only open up and disperse their seeds in extreme heat such as during a fire. These seeds grow in the fertile soil left behind by the fire. So we see that God planned a way to grow a new forest to replace the one destroyed by the fire.

Fun Fact

Certain orchids of the tropical rain forest produce the world's smallest seeds. One seed weighs about one 35-millionth of an ounce and some seeds are only about 1/300 of an inch (.085 mm) long. The coco de mer is a spectacular giant palm that grows in the Seychelles in the Indian Ocean. The nut of the coco de mer is the largest seed produced by any plant. It can weigh up to 44 pounds (20 kg).

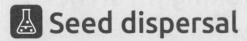

Seed location

Purpose: To see where seeds are found

Materials: several types of fruit, pinecones

Procedure:

1. Gather several types of fruits and open them up and find their seeds.

2. Compare the seeds. Which seeds have softer seed coats? Which are harder? Which seeds appear to be dicots? Which are monocots? Compare their sizes, shapes, colors, etc.

3. Observe several pinecones. Are there any seeds easily seen?

4. Remove several of the scales from one of the cones. Two seeds should be seen at the base of each scale if the pinecone has not already dropped its seeds. As pinecones mature, they become larger, and as the air becomes hotter and dryer, the scales open up, allowing the seeds to drop out.

5. To observe the effects of heat on pinecones, place several pinecones whose scales are tightly shut in a foil-lined baking dish and bake them at 200 degrees Fahrenheit for 30 minutes.

6. Remove the pan from the oven and observe the scales. While the pinecones are baking you can do the next activity: seed dispersal.

Seed dispersal

This activity can probably be done in your yard but if you do not have many plants with seeds around, plan a trip to the park or a nature area to do this activity, or use a book with pictures.

Using the "Seeds Get Around" worksheet, go outside and try to find at least one seed from each category on the worksheet. Draw a picture or glue the seed to the worksheet.

🏅 Water dispersal

The movement of seeds away from the parent plant is called seed dispersal. Seed dispersal is very important to prevent the new plants from competing with the parent plants and with each other. What resources would plants be competing for if they are growing near each other? How does seed dispersal show God's plan for plant survival?

We already discussed several ways that seeds are dispersed. When something other than the plant itself helps to disperse the seeds that force is called a dispersing agent. Animals and people can be dispersing agents. So can the wind. One important agent not mentioned yet is water. Many plants that grow in or near water have seeds that are dispersed by the movement of the water.

Seeds that fall into a stream or a river can be taken many miles away from the parent plant before they wash up on shore where they can begin growing. Other seeds fall into the ocean and are taken away by the tide. One of the largest seeds in the world, the coconut, is dispersed by water. How can a seed as large as a coconut float in the water to be carried to a new location?

Purpose: To see which seeds are likely to be dispersed by water

Materials: several types of seeds (include a coconut if possible), "Water Dispersal Test" worksheet

Procedure:

1. On the "Water Dispersal Test" worksheet, write the name of each type of seed you are going to test.

2. Write "yes" in the "Will it Float?" column if you think the seed will float. Write "no" if you do not think it will float. This is called making a hypothesis. This should be a good guess based on what you know about things that float and things that sink.

3. Fill a sink with water and gently drop one of each kind of seed into the water.

4. Fill in the chart with the results of your test. Write "yes" if it floated and "no" if it sank.

5. Check your results against your predictions. Were you surprised at your results? Checking your hypothesis is very important. If some of your predictions were wrong, examine the seeds more closely to try to understand why you got an unexpected result.

6. If you have a coconut available, have an adult help you open it up. How is the coconut shaped on the outside? How is it shaped on the inside? The inside of a coconut is hollow. This makes it able to float even though it is much larger and heavier than some other seeds.

George Washington Carver

1864–1943

"It is not the style of clothes one wears, neither the kind of automobile one drives, nor the amount of money one has in the bank, that counts. These mean nothing. It is simply service that measures success."

—*George Washington Carver*

George Washington Carver was a very rare man. He started off in life with nothing, as a slave. He was born around 1864 on the Moses Carver plantation in Diamond Grove, Missouri. Shortly before he was born, his father died in an accident. While he was still a baby, he and his mother were kidnapped by Confederate night riders (slave raiders); his brother James was left behind. Moses Carver, his owner, found him and paid his ransom after the war, but his mother was never heard of again. Susan and Moses Carver gave George their last name and reared him and his brother as their own children. They must have done a very good job instilling the right values in him when you consider his later life.

When George was young, he was too ill or weak to work in the fields so he spent his time doing household chores and gardening. He also spent long hours exploring the woods, developing a keen interest in plants at an early age. He spent his childhood collecting rocks and plants and earned the nickname, "The Plant Doctor."

At age twelve George left home in order to continue his education in a more formal setting. Since there were no schools in his area that allowed black students to attend, he moved to Newton County in southwest Missouri. Here he worked as a farmhand and studied in a one-room schoolhouse. He later went to Minneapolis, Kansas, for high school.

In 1890 George enrolled at Simpson College to study painting and piano, in which he excelled. His teacher was Etta Budd, whose father was a professor at Iowa State College. She helped him find work with different families around Indianola. As his art teacher and friend, she wanted to help him.

Miss Budd saw that George had a real talent with plants. She told him he would never be able to support a family working as a painter. And she offered to go with him to Iowa State to study science. After he thought about it, he decided to go.

Etta discovered that at Iowa State, George was not allowed to eat with the other students, but instead had to eat his meals in the kitchen because he was black. Etta found this situation to be unacceptable. She brought him into the dining hall where the white students ate. There she ate with him until the students in the school accepted him.

Carver was a brilliant student and excelled in biology. Upon graduation he was offered a teaching position. Carver was not only the first black student at Iowa State College of Agriculture and Mechanic Arts (today, Iowa State University), but he was also the first black person hired as a teacher there.

A few years later, Booker T. Washington convinced Carver to move south to work at Tuskegee Normal and Industrial Institute for Negroes as the Director of Agriculture. Carver worked there until his death in 1943.

Carver had a strong desire to help the people of the South. Growing cotton depletes the soil, so Carver sought ways to help the southern farmers become profitable after the Civil War. He devised a crop-rotation plan with soil-enriching plants such as peanuts, peas, soybeans, sweet potatoes, and pecans. Carver convinced the farmers to use his rotation method to rebuild the soil. The problem was that there was little demand for peanuts and soybeans.

So Carver invented 300 uses for peanuts and hundreds more for soybeans, pecans, and sweet potatoes. Some of his inventions utilizing these crops included adhesives, axle grease, bleach, buttermilk, chili sauce, fuel briquettes, ink, instant coffee, linoleum, mayonnaise, meat tenderizer, metal polish, paper, plastic, pavement, shaving cream, shoe polish, synthetic rubber, talcum powder, and wood stain.

Of the hundreds of inventions he came up with, Carver only patented three. The rest he gave away to benefit mankind. It is easy to see why he was considered a great man. When asked about charging for his inventions, he would respond with, "God gave them to me. How can I sell them to someone else?" In 1940 he donated his life savings to establish the Carver Research Foundation at Tuskegee, for continuing research in agriculture.

Carver was a very remarkable man. He was once offered a position with a salary of over $100,000 per year. (That is about the same as a million dollars per year today.) He turned the offer down so he could continue his research on behalf of his countrymen and the South.

"He could have added fortune to fame, but caring for neither, he found happiness and honor in being helpful to the world."

– Epitaph on the grave of George Washington Carver.

UNIT 3

Roots & Stems

11 Roots

12 Special Roots

13 Stems

14 Stem Structure

15 Stem Growth

◊ **Explain** the types and functions of roots.

◊ **Explain** the types and functions of stems.

◊ **Describe** the growth of plant stems.

11

Roots

A great foundation

How do roots help a plant?

Words to know:

vascular tissue	fibrous root
root cap	taproot

Challenge words:

primary root growth	Zone of elongation
secondary root growth	Zone of differentiation
zone of cell division	Root hair

You may recall from our lesson on cells that many cells working together form a tissue, and that many tissues working together form an organ. Plants have four main organs: roots, stems, leaves, and flowers. Each organ plays an important role.

Do you recall what roots do for the plant? Roots provide the foundation for plants. They help anchor the plant to the ground and keep it from blowing away or falling over. Roots also provide necessary nourishment and water for the rest of the plant. Fine root hairs absorb water and minerals from the soil. Then **vascular tissues**, similar to blood vessels in an animal, carry the water and minerals up to the stem. The vascular tissue also brings food back down from the leaves. The storage tissues in the roots store extra food for the plant.

Root growth occurs at the tip of the root. The **root cap**, at the very end of the root, helps protect the root tip as it pushes its way through the soil.

Plants generally have one of two basic types of root systems. Some plants, such as grasses, have a **fibrous root** system in which the roots spread out in many different directions. They appear to have a lot of little roots and no central root. Plants with fibrous roots generally grow from monocot seeds. Dicots usually produce plants that have a taproot system. **Taproots** have one large central root growing down with many smaller side roots growing outward. Taproots can go deep into the ground. They help plants get water in very dry areas.

Fun Fact

When you look at a plant, think about what is going on below the surface of the soil. There is generally as much of the plant underground as there is above the ground. Think about that the next time you see a tree that is 60 feet (18 m) tall!

Fibrous roots   Taproot

 # What did we learn?

- What are the four organs of a plant?
- What are the jobs that the roots perform?
- How can you tell what kind of root system a plant has?

Fun Fact

The deepest observed living root, at least 195 feet (59.4 m) below the ground surface, was observed during the excavation of an open-pit mine in Arizona.

🚀 Taking it further

- What kind of plants might you want to plant on a hillside? Why?
- Why are the roots of plants like carrots and beets good to eat?
- Why would a plant with a tap root be more likely to survive in an area with little rainfall than a plant with fibrous roots?

 # Root observation

Can you name some common edible roots? Possible ideas would be carrots, turnips, beets, sugar beets, and radishes.

Purpose: To examine root structures

Materials: carrot, magnifying glass, paper towels

Procedure:

1. Examine an unpeeled carrot with a magnifying glass.

2. Carefully slice one carrot lengthwise. Identify the vascular tissue, storage tissue, root hairs, root tip, and if possible the root cap.

3. Use the magnifying glass to examine the root structures that are visible in the jars of beans and corn that you have been growing since lessons 8 and 9.

Questions:

- Do carrots have a fibrous root or taproot system?

- Are carrot seeds more likely to be monocots or dicots? With the exception of grasses, the majority of the plants we are familiar with are dicots.

- How are the roots of the beans and corn similar and how are they different?

- Were any corn or bean seeds planted "upside down." Are the roots growing upside down?

① Root growth

Root growth is very important to any plant. There are two ways that a root grows. First it grows longer. This is called primary root growth. Second, it gets fatter. This is called secondary root growth.

Primary root growth happens in two ways. First, the cells at the tip of the root perform cell division. This creates new cells which push the root deeper into the soil. The region where cells are actively dividing is called zone of cell division, located under the root cap. The part of the root just above the zone of cell division is the zone of elongation. Here the cells themselves become longer, also adding to the length of the root.

Secondary root growth occurs as new cells are produced around the central core. These new cells add to the diameter of the root, causing it to become fatter. Secondary root growth occurs in the area above the zone of elongation, which is called the zone of differentiation (or *zone of maturation*). In this region cells arrange themselves to form the tubes needed to make vascular tissue for transporting the water and nutrients that are absorbed from the ground.

Root hairs form on the outside of the zone of differentiation. Root hairs are tube-like projections responsible for absorbing nearly all of the water and nutrients needed by the plant. Root hairs are very small, usually less than a centimeter long, and very narrow, yet they greatly increase the root's surface area. A plant may have as many as 250,000 root hairs per square inch of root surface. This provides a huge surface area for absorbing water.

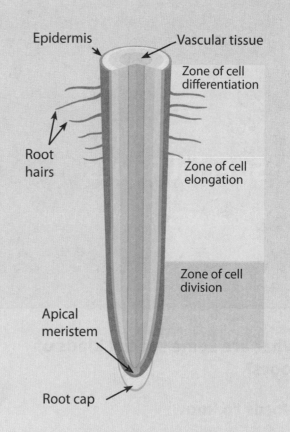

Roots are specially designed for moving through the soil. Not only do the cells add to the length of the root, but the root cap secretes a slimy substance that makes it easier for the root to move between the particles of soil. In addition, because the cells in the root tip are very active, they produce a relatively large amount of carbon dioxide. This combines with water in the soil to produce carbonic acid, which helps to loosen up the particles of soil around the root tip, making it even easier for the root to grow.

Purpose: To observe root hairs on the tip of a root

Materials: radish seeds, magnifying glass

Procedure:

1. Fold a paper towel into quarters.

2. Place several radish seeds between the folds and moisten the paper towel.

3. Place the towel in a warm area and keep the towel moist for several days.

4. When the seeds have sprouted, carefully remove one and use a magnifying glass to observe the root hairs.

12

Special Roots

Not always underground

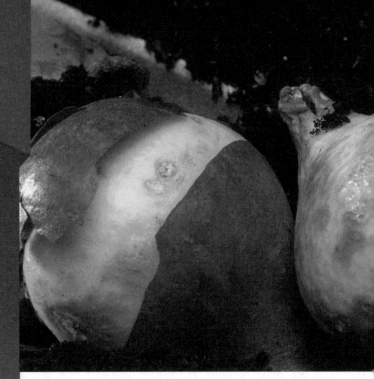

What are some special kinds of roots?

Words to know:

adventitious roots

aerial roots

pneumatophores

prop roots

parasitic roots

haustoria

Challenge words:

epiphyte

In the previous lesson you learned that plant roots grow in one of two different configurations –fibrous roots or tap roots. This is true for the vast majority of plants. However, some plants have roots growing in unusual places or in unusual ways. These unusual roots are called **adventitious** (ad-ven-TIH-shuhs) **roots**. Adventitious roots can take on many different forms.

Have you ever planted a tulip bulb or looked closely at an onion? You might think that the bulb itself is a root with root hairs growing out of the bottom. However, the bulb is actually a special type of stem and the roots grow individually out of the disc at the bottom of the stem. This is an unusual way for roots to grow so they are classified as adventitious.

Aerial roots, roots that grow in the air instead of in the ground, are another type of adventitious root. There are actually several different kinds of aerial roots and they each serve a different function. In places like the tropical rain forest where there are many large trees, it is difficult for most plants to survive on the ground because the trees block the light from reaching the forest floor. So some plants actually grow on the sides of the trees, up higher where they can receive sunlight. However, this means their roots cannot reach the ground. These plants have special roots that can absorb moisture directly from the air.

Other plants have roots that provide support as they grow up the sides of trees, buildings, and other structures. Ivy plants and many other plants have roots that curl around trellises, fences, and other structures. In addition, some orchids have

Cypress knees are pneumatophores.

Mangrove trees have prop roots.

Mistletoe is a common parasitic plant.

roots that have chlorophyll, allowing them to perform photosynthesis.

Another type of aerial root is call a **pneumatophore** (new-MAT-o-for). Pneumatophores are roots that do not grow down, but actually grow straight out or even grow up from the sides of a plant. Most plants that have pneumatophores grow in locations where the plants cannot get enough oxygen from the soil, often because the soil is frequently flooded. So these special roots absorb oxygen from the air. One plant that produces pneumatophores is the mangrove tree. Mangroves grow in very wet soil that is often covered with water.

Prop roots are another type of aerial root. Prop roots grow from the sides of the stem or even from the branches down into the ground. They provide extra support for the plant when the soil is loose or marshy and regular roots are not sufficient to hold the plant in place. Mangroves also grow prop roots to help anchor them to the soil.

Finally some plants have **parasitic roots**. Parasitic roots are ones that grow near the roots of another plant then send out special shoots called **haustoria** (haw-STOHR-ee-uh), which tap into the adjacent plant's roots and "steal" nutrients from the other plant. This is often harmful to the other plant. Mistletoe has parasitic roots.

What did we learn?

- What are adventitious roots?
- What are aerial roots?
- What are prop roots?

Taking it further

- Why do you think that some plants have specialized roots?
- Why do some plants need prop roots?

Root poster

Make a poster explaining all of the different roots you have learned about. Collect pictures of different kinds of roots or draw your own, then use the pictures to make a poster.

Be sure to explain the purpose or function of each kind of root. You should include taproots and fibrous roots on your poster, as well as the roots covered in this lesson.

 # Banyan trees

The banyan tree is a type of fig tree. It starts life as an epiphyte, which is a plant that grows on another plant just for support. Often a banyan tree seed is deposited on a branch or trunk of a tree by a bird that has eaten the figs of a banyan tree. Once this seed germinates, it sends out roots that begin growing downward toward the ground. As the banyan tree gets larger, it sends out more aerial roots that fuse together and often cover the host tree. If the roots grow closely enough they can eventually kill the host. Thus the banyan tree is often called the strangler fig.

The banyan continues to send out prop roots from its branches and can spread out using these roots. So over time, a banyan tree can become very large. Older trees have been known to grow up to 650 feet (200 m) in diameter and 100 feet (30 m) tall.

Fun Fact

Legend has it that Alexander the Great once camped under a banyan tree that was so large it provided shelter for his entire army of 7,000 men.

Banyan trees are native to India but can be found in most of southern Asia and on many tropical islands. They have large leathery leaves and produce a type of rubber as well as a sticky, milky sap. The banyan tree has many uses. First, it is often used as a meeting place because it provides a large shady area. Its sap is used in gardening, to make a polish for copper and bronze, as well as for a medical treatment for skin inflammation and bruising. The roots are often used to make rope, and the bark can be used to make paper. Banyan trees are also very interesting to look at. So if you get a chance, enjoy a rest under the shade of one of these amazing trees.

13

Stems

Connecting it all together

How does the stem help the plant?

Words to know:

xylem	tendril
phloem	thorn
tuber	stolon
bulb	runner

Challenge words:

diffusion	capillarity
osmosis	transpiration

The second organ of the plant that we will study is the stem. Do you recall the functions of the stem? The stem provides support for the plant, serves as a transportation network, and sometimes acts as a storage facility. The stem connects the roots with the leaves and flowers of the plant. It includes the main stem as well as any branches that the plant may have. Woody plants such as trees often have bark on the outside of their stems. Woody plants have stems that get thicker each year and are usually stiff. Woody plants generally come back year after year without dying down to the ground in the wintertime. Herbaceous plants have flexible stems. Some herbaceous plants grow year after year. But many herbaceous plants complete their life cycles in one growing season and then die.

In addition to supporting the plant, the stem's main function is to transport water and nutrients from the roots to the leaves and to transport food from the leaves to the roots. The stem accomplishes this by a series of tubes. The tubes that take water and minerals up the plant are called xylem (ZI-lum). Tubes that take the food from the leaves to the rest of the plant are called phloem (FLO-em).

Some stems also store food for the plant. People often think that potatoes are roots. But they are actually special stems called tubers that store extra food for the plant. Bulbs such as onions are also special stems that store food. Because this part of the stem is underground, we may think of it as a root, but it is really a stem.

Many plants have other special stems as well. Grape vines, and many other vines, in addition to regular stems, have special stems called tendrils that grab onto trellises, fences, buildings, and nearly anything else around, including other plants. Rose bushes have special stems called thorns that help protect the plant from animals. Strawberries have special stems called stolons, or runners, which allow them to spread easily over an area and produce new plants.

What did we learn?

- What are the main functions of a stem?
- What do we call the stem of a tree?

Taking it further

- If a tree branch is 3 feet above the ground on a certain day, how far up will the branch be 10 years later?
- What are some stems that are good to eat?

What goes up?

Purpose: To examine the transport system of plants

Materials: food coloring, stalk of celery, bean and corn plants

Procedure:

1. Add a few drops of food coloring to a glass of water until the water is a dark color.

2. Cut off the bottom ½ inch of a stalk of celery to open the xylem and phloem.

3. Place the cut end of the celery in the glass of colored water.

4. After an hour or two you should be able to observe the colored water moving up the stalk of celery. After several hours the color will become visible in the leaves of the celery. You are observing the xylem tubes in action, which are transporting the water up the plant to the leaves.

5. Next, observe the bean and corn plants that have been growing since lessons 8 and 9. What do their stems look like? How are they similar? How are they different?

6. Carefully take two or three of the bean plants and transplant them into a cup of potting soil.

7. Do the same for two or three corn plants. These plants are getting too big to survive much longer on the food stored in the cotyledons of the seed and will need to get nourishment from the soil. Remember to keep the soil moist.

8. If you wish, you can continue growing the rest of the bean and corn plants in the cups without soil and compare their progress with those that you transplanted into the soil.

Water movement in plants

Gravity is constantly pulling down on everything on Earth. It pulls down on you and me and it pulls down on plants. So, if gravity is constantly pulling down on everything, how does water move up the stem of a plant? There are at least three different processes involved in moving the water and nutrients up the plant.

The first process is a special type of diffusion called osmosis. Diffusion occurs when molecules move from an area of higher concentration to an area of lower concentration. Osmosis is the diffusion of water across a membrane. In plants, osmosis occurs as water molecules pass through the cell membrane of the cells in the root hairs. Because the concentration of water inside the cell is less than the concentration of water outside, water passes through the cell membrane into the cell. Then because the cells inside the root have a lower concentration of water than the root hair cells, the water moves into the inner cells. This lowers the concentration of water in the outer cells allowing more water to move into them.

Inside the xylem, another force called capillarity helps to move the water upward. Capillarity is the attraction that the water molecules have for each other and the walls of the xylem tubes. Water molecules have a slight attraction to each other due to their molecular structure. This attraction helps to draw the water up the stem. You can observe capillarity by placing the edge of a paper towel in a dish of water. Even though only the edge of the paper towel is in the dish, water will quickly move up the towel.

Capillarity can raise water only a few feet, so another force must exist to draw the water farther up the plant. Transpiration is the evaporation of water from the plant into the atmosphere. When water evaporates from the leaves, it lowers the water pressure; this allows water from below to flow upward into the leaf. All three processes—osmosis, capillarity, and transpiration—work together to move liquids up the stem of a plant.

Roots & Stems

Stem Structure

How they are put together

How is a branch structured?

Words to know:

shoot	lateral bud
terminal bud	node
axillary bud	internode

Challenge words:

excurrent branching	deliquescent branching

A stem is the major part of a plant that you see above ground. It provides the main shape and structure of the plant. Trees have a single large stem (trunk) with many smaller stems branching off of the main stem. Bushes have lots of smaller stems growing directly out of the ground. These stems also branch out, but are generally much smaller than tree branches. Flowers and garden plants also have stems and many of them branch out as well. Stems may look very different from one plant to another, but they serve the same purposes. The stem's main purpose is to transport nutrients and food throughout the plant.

A **shoot** is a new stem that grows from the seed or off of the main stem. As the shoot grows, it forms buds. The **terminal bud** is the bud at the end of the stem. This is where most of the stem's growth occurs.

Other buds form along the stem. These buds are called **axillary buds**, or **lateral buds**. Lateral buds grow into flowers or new shoots that form new branches. If a plant grows aerial roots they will start from a lateral bud. Leaves also grow from lateral buds.

The point where a leaf grows on a stem is called a **node**. Most leaves grow from the sides of the stem or from the end of the stem. However, in many grasses the leaves grow from the bottom of the stem. The area of the stem between two nodes is called the **internode**. The diagram shows the major structures of a stem. 🌿

Terminal bud
Lateral buds
Node
Internode

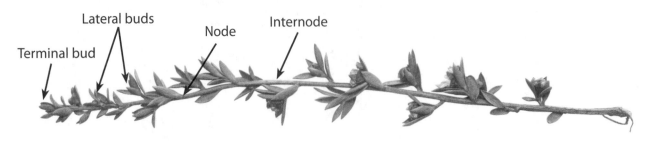

What did we learn?

- What are the major structures of a stem?
- Where does new growth occur on a stem?
- What gives the plant its size and shape?

Taking it further

- What will happen to a plant if its terminal buds are removed?
- How are stems different between trees and bushes?

- In your experience, do flower stems have the same structures, including terminal buds, nodes, etc., as bush and tree stems?

Examining stems

If possible, examine a bush or tree that has new growth. Try to identify each part of the stem. Look for terminal and lateral buds, new shoots, nodes, and internodes.

After examining the plant, draw a picture of the stem. Be sure to identify all the parts that you observed.

Branching

Just like roots, stems also have primary growth (growing in length) and secondary growth (growing in diameter). Primary growth occurs at the tips of the branches at the terminal buds and the lateral buds. In the spring, meristematic cells in the buds begin to divide causing the buds to lengthen. As the terminal bud grows it also produces hormones which control the growth in the lateral buds. Most plants produce more lateral buds than they need. Some of the lateral buds receive the hormone to make them grow and others remain dormant. However, if some of the growing buds are damaged the remaining buds can be stimulated to grow in their place. This is God's back up plan to ensure that the plant grows well even if a hailstorm damages the plant or an animal eats some of the buds. If the extra lateral buds are not needed they eventually fall off.

As you learned in lesson 7, different plants have different growth habits. This is because some plants have strong growth in the terminal buds and other plants have strong growth in the lateral buds. Plants that have strong growth in the terminal buds have a more vertical growth habit. These plants are said to have excurrent branching. Trees such as pines, firs, and redwoods have this type of growth.

Plants that have strong growth in the lateral buds have a more horizontal growth habit. This type of growth is called deliquescent branching. Oaks and willows, and most other deciduous trees, have this type of growth.

Secondary growth occurs in stems as the cells inside the stem divide and grow. This causes the

Oak trees exhibit deliquescent branching.

Fir trees exhibit excurrent branching.

stem to become larger in diameter. Secondary growth occurs primarily in trees and shrubs. You will learn more about secondary growth in the following lessons.

Look at the growth habit for the plants that you just examined. Is the growth primarily vertical or horizontal? Can you easily see a trunk or primary stem most of the way up the plant? Then the plant has excurrent branching. If you see lots of branches dividing over and over, the plant has deliquescent branching. Which plants in your yard have excurrent branching and which have deliquescent branching?

Roots & Stems

15

Stem Growth

Further up and further out

Why do trees have rings?

Words to know:

epidermis

cuticle

cambium cells

heartwood

sapwood

Challenge words:

vascular bundles

The stems of all plants grow longer and branch out to some extent. In young plants, the outer layer of the stem is called the epidermis. This is the same name given to your skin. And just as your skin helps protect your body, the epidermis of the stem protects the plant. The very top layer of the epidermis is called the cuticle and contains a waxy substance that prevents the plant from losing or absorbing too much water. In herbaceous plants, those that only live one year, or those that die down to the ground each winter, young flexible stems are the only type of stem that we see. However, in woody plants that continue to grow larger each year, like trees and shrubs, the stems grow outward as well as lengthwise.

Inside the epidermis are special cells called cambium cells. These are thin-walled cells located around the xylem and phloem cells. As the stems become more mature, they develop more xylem and phloem cells. The cambium cells also expand and push outward on the epidermis. The epidermis cells begin to harden and die. These dead cells eventually become bark. After several years of growth, the bark can become very thick on some trees. The bark on other trees remains relatively thin, depending on the type of tree. Because bark cells are dead, they cannot grow and stretch as the tree trunk enlarges. Therefore, the bark often cracks or peels as the trees become more mature. Still, the bark serves the purpose of protecting the tree from drying out and from disease.

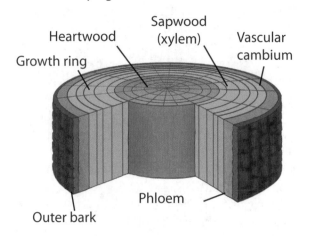

The growth in the cambium, xylem, and phloem cells only occurs during the spring and summer. The cells produced during the spring are a lighter color and bigger than those produced during the summer in temperate regions. As you learned in lesson 7, this produces different colored bands inside the tree, with one band of light- and dark-colored cells for each growing season. In very wet years, there may be multiple rings in a single year.

If a tree lives long enough, eventually the xylem cells near the center of the tree are no longer able to transport fluids. These cells continue to provide support for the tree, but water and other materials no longer flow through the center of the tree. The wood in the center of the tree becomes very hard and is called heartwood. The xylem and phloem that are farther from the center of the tree still transport the needed nutrients. The wood in this part of the stem is called sapwood, which contains the xylem. The living phloem cells are part of the inner bark.

What did we learn?

- What are epidermis cells?
- What is bark?
- Name three types of cells inside a stem.

Taking it further

- Can we tell a tree's age from the rings inside the trunk? Why or why not?
- If you wanted to make a very strong wooden spoon, which part of the tree would you use?
- Why don't herbaceous plants have bark?

Looking at tree rings

Below is a cross section of a tree trunk. Notice the different colored bands. Each set of light and dark bands represents one year of growth. During years where there is plenty of water and favorable conditions, the tree produces a larger number of new cells than in years that do not have as much water or that are too hot or too cold. See how many rings you can count and try to figure out how old the tree is. Some rings, particularly the outer rings, are difficult to distinguish so everyone will probably get a different number. Do you notice any rings that are significantly wider or narrower than the rest? What can you guess about the growing conditions during those years?

Scientists have developed a way to take a very thin sample of wood from the inside of a living tree to see the number of rings. This does not harm the tree, but allows the scientist to calculate the tree's age.

Vascular tissue

Woody plants and herbaceous plants all have xylem, phloem, and cambium cells; however, this vascular tissue is arranged differently inside the different types of stems. As you just learned, the vascular tissues are arranged in rings inside a woody stem. Just inside the bark is a ring of phloem tissue. This tissue carries the food down from the leaves of the tree or shrub. Because the phloem is close to the outside of the tree, we are able to drill into a maple tree in the spring and get sap to make maple syrup.

Inside the ring of phloem tubes is a ring of vascular cambium cells. These cells are the ones that divide to form new phloem and xylem cells. Inside the cambium ring is a ring of xylem tissue. The xylem transports water and other materials up from the roots to the rest of the plant. As more xylem and phloem cells are produced, the trunk gets bigger around. As you just learned, if you look at a cross-section of a tree, you see the rings of xylem that have been formed each year. The ring of phloem near the outside of the tree is not as obvious, but is vital to the health of the tree.

Herbaceous stems do not have the same ring structure that woody stems have. The xylem and phloem are found in groups called **vascular bundles**. In dicot stems there is a ring of cambium cells and the bundles are arranged around this ring. Each bundle contains both xylem and phloem tissue with the xylem tissue toward the center of the stem and the phloem tissue toward the outside of the stem within each bundle. This structure is similar to the structure for a young tree or shrub, but the vascular

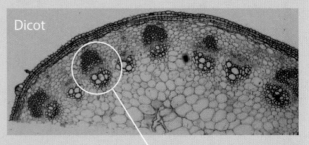

Dicot

Vascular bundle

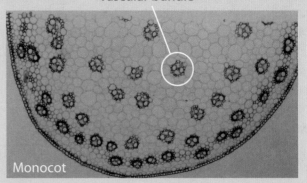

Monocot

tissue does not develop into full rings because the stems only grow for one growing season. In herbaceous monocots, the vascular bundles are more evenly distributed throughout the stem rather than in a circular pattern. Also, some monocots do not contain cambium cells.

In lesson 13, you watched fluids moving up the stem of a stalk of celery. Do you remember how the xylem were arranged in the celery? They were arranged in a circular pattern. Would that indicate that celery is a monocot or a dicot?

UNIT 4

Leaves

16 Photosynthesis

17 Arrangement of Leaves

18 Leaves—Shape & Design

19 Changing Colors

20 Tree Identification—Final World
    of Plants Project

◊ **Describe** how plants perform photosynthesis.

◊ **Describe** the different shapes and arrangements of leaves.

◊ **Explain** why leaves change colors in the fall.

◊ **Use** a field guide to identify plants.

Photosynthesis

Making food for the world

How do plants make their own food?

Words to know:

photosynthesis   chlorophyll

stomata   catalyst

guard cells

Challenge words:

glucose   starch

sucrose

Leaves are the power plants of the world. They provide food for every living thing on land and thus demonstrate God's love and provision for everything on Earth. You may argue that many animals do not eat plants but only eat other animals and that humans get energy from meat as well as from plants. But keep in mind that the animals that are being eaten got their energy from the plants that they ate and are passing that energy on to the people or animals that are eating them. Thus, all energy ultimately comes from the plants that are eaten. The plants produce this food through an amazing process called **photosynthesis**. Photosynthesis comes from two Greek words that mean "light" and "putting together." Plants use light's energy to combine simple compounds to make sugar for food energy.

Fun Fact

It is estimated that the plants and algae of the world produce 300 billion tons of sugar and starch each year. About 75% of that food is produced in the sea by algae.

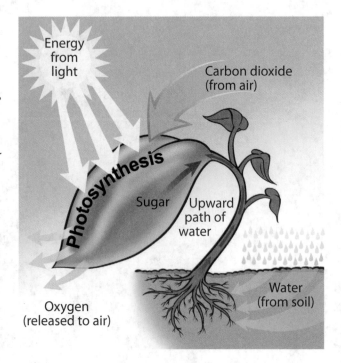

Energy from light

Carbon dioxide (from air)

Photosynthesis

Sugar

Upward path of water

Oxygen (released to air)

Water (from soil)

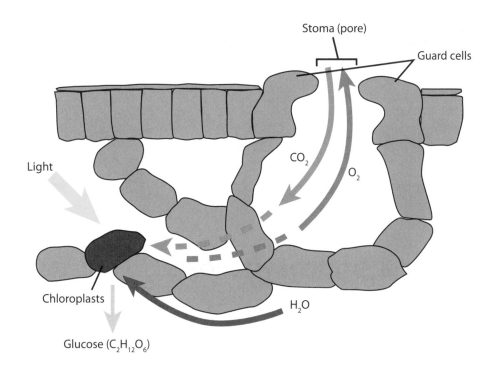

Light

Stoma (pore)

Guard cells

CO_2

O_2

Chloroplasts

H_2O

Glucose $(C_2H_{12}O_6)$

Photosynthesis is a truly amazing process. The roots send water up to the leaves through the stem. The leaves absorb carbon dioxide from the air through stomata (singular *stoma*), which are tiny holes in the underside of the leaf. Guard cells on each side of the stomata open and close them to allow carbon dioxide to enter or oxygen to exit the leaf. Then, the chloroplasts in the leaves use the energy from sunlight to break apart the water molecules. These molecules combine with the carbon dioxide to make sugar (glucose) and oxygen. The sugar is then changed to starch or fat and stored in the vacuoles of the cells, while the oxygen is released into the air. The food in the vacuoles is then stored in fruit, seeds, stems, roots, and leaves, where it is used by the plant for growth or eaten by animals and humans.

The chloroplasts in the plant cells contain a green pigment called chlorophyll. This is what makes leaves and stems green and what makes photosynthesis possible. Chlorophyll is a catalyst, which is a substance that causes a chemical reaction to take place very quickly but is not used up in the process. The rate that plants make food through photosynthesis is affected by many factors.

If water and carbon dioxide are not readily available, the plant cannot make food quickly. Also, if the temperature is below 65°F (18°C) or above 85°F (30°C), the process slows down. Finally, if sunlight is not available photosynthesis cannot occur.

Perhaps the most amazing thing about photosynthesis is that its waste product—oxygen—is one of the most essential elements for sustaining life on Earth. Plants use carbon dioxide to produce oxygen for people and animals to breath, and the people and animals use that oxygen to break down the food they eat which produces more carbon dioxide for the plants to use in photosynthesis. When we talked about respiration in lesson 1, we mentioned that all organisms use energy to perform the functions of life. Even plants need to use oxygen to change the sugars they make into energy through cellular respiration. But they use less oxygen than they produce, making all of the extra oxygen available for animals to breathe. In a sense, photosynthesis and cellular respiration are opposite processes that complement one another in amazing ways to allow life to prosper. God created a perfect recycling system to keep our air clean and provide food for all His creatures, including us.

What did we learn?

- What are the "ingredients" needed for photosynthesis?

- What are the "products" of photosynthesis?

- How did God specifically design plants to be a source of food?

- How does carbon dioxide enter a leaf?

 # Taking it further

- On which day of creation did God create plants?

- On which day did He create the sun?

- In our experiment, we found that the plant that got less sunlight grew more slowly than the one that had full sunlight. Is this true for all plants?

 # Sunlight & photosynthesis

Purpose: To test the effects of sunlight on photosynthesis

Materials: three fast-growing potted plants, two cardboard boxes, scissors or knife, "Photosynthesis Data Sheet"

Procedure:

1. Label 3 fast-growing plants (mint plants are a good choice) with the letters A, B, and C.

2. Place all three plants in the windowsill or other sunny area.

3. Measure the height of each plant and record it on the "Photosynthesis Data Sheet."

4. Cut several holes about the size of a half dollar into a cardboard box. About half of the total area of the box should be cut away.

5. Place this box over plant B.

6. Do not cut any holes in the other box and place it over plant C. Plant A should not have a box over it.

7. Each day, for the next several days, remove the boxes and pour the same amount, approximately ¼ cup of water, on the soil of each plant.

8. Measure the height of each plant and record that on your data sheet.

9. Make observations about the plants and the soil and record these on your data sheet as well. As soon as you are done making observations, replace the boxes.

Conclusion: After several days, you should begin to see significant differences in the growth of the three plants. By limiting the amount of sunlight available to two of the plants, you are reducing their ability to perform photosynthesis and therefore their ability to grow. At the end of the experiment, write your conclusions on the bottom of the data sheet summarizing what you learned from this experiment.

Leaves

The photosynthesis reaction

Photosynthesis occurs when chloroplasts break apart water and carbon dioxide molecules in the presence of sunlight, and then recombine those atoms to form sugar and oxygen. This is a very simplistic explanation of photosynthesis. Let's take a closer look at what is really happening. The molecules that are coming into the leaves are carbon dioxide and water. A molecule of carbon dioxide contains one carbon atom and two oxygen atoms, CO_2. You probably already know that water, H_2O, contains two hydrogen atoms and one oxygen atom. These molecules are broken apart and the atoms are used to build sugar and oxygen molecules.

The type of sugar that is formed as a result of photosynthesis is called glucose. Glucose production takes place in two phases, called the light-dependent reactions and the light-independent reactions. One molecule of glucose contains six carbon atoms, twelve hydrogen atoms, and six oxygen atoms, $C_6H_{12}O_6$. Oxygen atoms are more stable in pairs, so the oxygen atoms that are not used to build the glucose molecule combine together in pairs to form O_2. Obviously you can't build a glucose molecule from just one carbon dioxide and one water molecule. You must actually have six of each of these molecules to build just one glucose molecule. When you use six carbon dioxide molecules and six water molecules to build one glucose molecule, you have twelve oxygen atoms left over which combine to form six O_2 molecules. We have taken a lot of words to explain this process, but scientists prefer to use symbols to explain how this works. The scientific explanation looks very much like a mathematical equation (see below).

Once photosynthesis is complete, the plant now has glucose that can be used for energy. However, it is more efficient to transport and store larger molecules than the relatively small glucose molecules so glucose molecules are linked together to form sucrose, which is a larger sugar molecule, or starch, which is a long chain of glucose molecules linked together. These larger molecules are stored in fruit, leaves, stems, and roots for later use by the plants that made them and for use by the animals and people that eat them.

Leaves

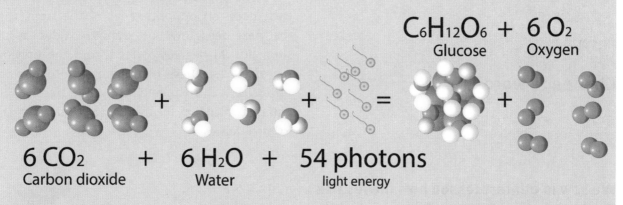

$6\ CO_2$ + $6\ H_2O$ + 54 photons = $C_6H_{12}O_6$ + $6\ O_2$

Carbon dioxide Water light energy Glucose Oxygen

Purpose: To better understand the photosynthesis process

Materials: "Photosynthesis Building Blocks," scissors, tape

Procedure:

1. Make copies of the "Photosynthesis Building Blocks." You will be starting with six carbon dioxide molecules and six water molecules.

2. Cut the molecules into separate atoms.

3. Tape the atoms together to form one glucose molecule and six oxygen molecules. If you have more than one copy of the worksheet, you can make more than one glucose molecule.

4. Tape two glucose molecules together to form sucrose. If you really like to cut and tape, you can make several glucose molecules and tape them together in a chain to form starch.

17

Arrangement of Leaves

Maximizing sunlight

How are leaves arranged on a plant?

Words to know:

opposite leaf
   arrangement

whorled

rosette

alternate leaves

Challenge words:

bract

succulent leaves

spine

We saw in our last lesson how leaves use water, carbon dioxide, and sunlight, with the help of chlorophyll, to make food through a process called photosynthesis. We also found that if a plant does not get enough sunlight it will not be able to make enough food and it grows more slowly. Therefore, it is reasonable to think that plants should have their leaves exposed to as much sunlight as possible. And that is exactly what we see when we examine how leaves grow on different plants. God designed plants so their leaves can have maximum exposure to the sunlight.

Leaves grow in one of four specially designed arrangements on stems. Where the leaf grows from the stem is called a node. How the nodes are arranged and how many leaves grow from each node determines the arrangement of the leaves.

Some plants have two leaves that grow from each node on opposite sides of the stem, then the next set grows on opposite sides of the stem but 90 degrees rotated from the previous set of leaves. These plants are said to have an **opposite leaf arrangement**. Maple trees, coleus, and mint plants all have an opposite arrangement for their leaves.

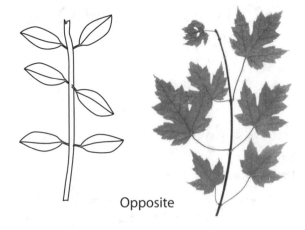

Opposite

Many trees' leaves are arranged in an alternate pattern. Only one leaf grows from each node. A leaf grows on one side of the stem, and then the next leaf grows farther up and on the other side of the stem. Plants with **alternate leaves** include apple, oak, and birch trees.

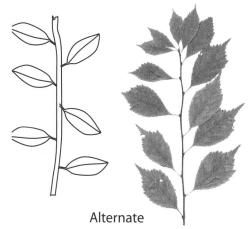

Alternate

Some plants have three or more leaves that grow from the same node on a stem. This arrangement is called **whorled**. A lily is an example of a plant with a whorled leaf arrangement.

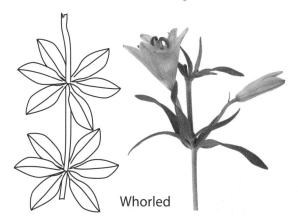

Whorled

The final arrangement of leaves is the **rosette**. All the leaves on these plants grow from the bottom of the stem like petals of a flower. A dandelion is an example of a plant with leaves in a rosette arrangement.

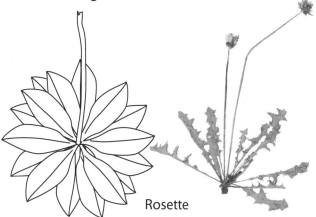

Rosette

In addition to the arrangement of the leaves, God also designed the leaves with the ability to turn toward the sun and follow the movement of the sun, thus further maximizing their exposure to sunlight. This works in a fairly simple manner. When one side of a plant is exposed to a large amount of light, the plant attempts to maximize the amount of photosynthesis it can perform by exposing a larger surface area to the light. The tip of the plants can measure the amount of light coming from each direction. It then sends large concentrations of the plant hormone auxin to the cells of the shady side of the plant. This chemical causes those cells to lengthen, and the whole plant bends towards the light source. Plant leaves usually maintain approximately a 90-degree angle toward the sunlight.

🧪 Observing leaf arrangement

Purpose: To illustrate leaf arrangements

Materials: sketch pad or paper, pen or pencil

Procedure:

1. Take your drawing supplies into the yard and observe a tree, bush, or plant of your choice.

2. Determine what leaf arrangement it has, then draw and label a picture of the plant. Be sure to emphasize the leaf arrangement in the drawing.

3. Repeat this exercise for as many plants as you care to examine.

4. Combine your drawings into a book. Make a cover for your book. Then share what you have learned with other people.

🧠 What did we learn?

- What are four common ways leaves can be arranged on a plant?

- Why do you think God created each of these different leaf arrangements?

- Why is it important for sunlight to reach each leaf?

🚀 Taking it further

- How does efficient leaf arrangement show God's provision or care for us?

- What other feature, besides leaf arrangement, aids leaves in obtaining maximum exposure to sunlight?

🏅 Special leaves

Just as there are specialized roots and stems that perform certain functions, there are also specialized leaves that perform special functions. You have already learned that tendrils are special stems that curl around solid objects, but some tendrils are actually specialized leaves that curl around solid objects. Tendrils are very sensitive to touch and respond when they encounter a solid object.

Bracts are another special kind of leaf. Often, bracts are leaves that are brightly colored to attract pollinators to a plant with small flowers. They serve the same role as the petals in most plants. Probably the most popular plant with bracts is the poinsettia. What many people think of as bright red petals, are actually bright red leaves that surround very small flowers.

Plants that grow in very dry areas often have special leaves that help conserve water. A cactus has leaves called spines. These are needle-like leaves that have very little surface area so they do not lose much moisture through evaporation. Other desert plants have succulent leaves. Succulent leaves store water. They often have fewer stomata so water stays inside the leaves. These leaves have a swollen or fleshy appearance. An aloe plant is a popular succulent. If you have access to a plant with succulent leaves, you can cut a leaf open and see the water that is stored in it.

Finally, some leaves are used by plants to trap insects. You will learn more about these special leaves in lesson 26. God has designed leaves to provide food for the world and has designed some leaves for other special purposes as well.

A poinsettia has special red leaves surrounding small flowers.

An aloe plant has succulent leaves.

Cactus spines are special leaves.

18

Leaves—Shape & Design

What's your shape?

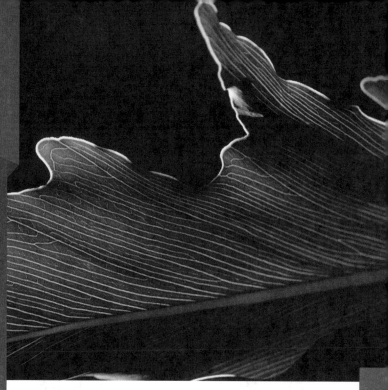

What patterns do veins make in leaves?

Words to know:

venation

pinnate

palmate

petiole

Challenge words:

leaf margin

entire margin

toothed margin

lobed margin

simple leaves

compound leaves

Most plants around us are broad-leaved plants. Their leaves are wide and relatively flat. There is great variety in the shape of these leaves, so much variety that the shape of a leaf can be used to help identify the plant itself. But there are also many plants that have narrow leaves, needles, or scales.

Grasses have narrow leaves. These leaves are long, thin, and flat. Evergreen or conifer trees have needles. These leaves are hard and thin. They can be as short as ½ inch (1.3 cm) or as long as five inches (12.7 cm). Needles can be flat or square. Their length, shape, and arrangement help us identify the

type of tree they come from. Some evergreen trees such as junipers have flat scale-like leaves.

No matter what the leaves look like, they serve the same purpose—to produce food for the plant. The xylem and phloem from the stems continue into the leaves to bring them water and minerals from

Grasses have narrow leaves, and evergreen tree needles are hard and thin.

Pinnate leaves

Palmate leaves

the roots and to carry the food produced by the leaves back to the rest of the plant. The xylem and phloem appear as veins in the leaves. The arrangement of these veins is referred to as venation.

Monocots, primarily grasses, have narrow leaves with parallel veins. Dicots, most of the broad-leaved plants, have veins in one of two arrangements. The veins can be pinnate (feather-like) or palmate (hand-like). Leaves with pinnate veins have one vein down the center of the leaf with smaller veins branching off to each side. A pinnate arrangement works well for leaves that are longer than they are wide. Nutrients can be taken down the center and out to the edges of the leaf efficiently.

Leaves with palmate veins have two or more major veins with smaller veins branching off of these major veins. Wider leaves need more than one major vein in order to efficiently move nutrients throughout the leaf.

God designed these various arrangements of veins to allow for the most efficient transportation of needed materials into the leaf and of food out of the leaf.

What did we learn?

- What general shape of leaves do monocots and dicots have?
- How can we use leaves to help us identify plants?
- How do nutrients and food get into and out of the leaves?

Taking it further

- Describe how the arrangement of the veins is most efficient for each leaf shape.

Observing leaves & veins

Purpose: To observe various leaf shapes and vein arrangements

Materials: sketch pad or paper, pen or pencil, cup, red food coloring, crayons

Procedure:

1. Go into the yard and observe several blades of grass. Be sure to notice the long, thin, flat shape of the leaves. Also note the parallel lines or veins in the leaves.

2. Observe the broad leaves of several trees or bushes.

3. Select a tree or bush with large leaves and carefully remove one or more leaves and take them into the house.

4. Draw a picture of the leaf. Pay close attention to the color and arrangement of the veins. Does the leaf have pinnate or palmate arrangement?

5. Fill a cup with water and add a few drops of red food coloring.

6. Stir the water. Make a diagonal cut across the petiole (the "stem" that attaches the leaf to the tree) with a knife or scissors.

7. Put the leaf in the water so the cut end of the leaf can pull up the colored water.

8. Observe the leaf each day for three days and draw a picture of the leaf each day. You should be able to observe the color spreading up the leaf throughout the veins.

9. Another fun idea is to make a leaf rubbing. Place another leaf on a hard surface, lay a piece of paper over it and color back and forth over the leaf with a crayon. This will help bring out the details of the shape of the leaf as well as the arrangement of the veins.

10. Also, observe the leaf shapes and vein arrangements of the bean and corn plants from lessons 8 and 9.

Questions:

- How are the shapes and vein arrangements different?
- Which plant has broad leaves?
- Which has long narrow leaves?
- Which plant is a monocot?
- Which plant is a dicot?

Leaf shapes & margins

One of the most important skills for a good scientist to develop is the skill of careful observation. There is much more to observing leaf shape than just looking at whether the leaves are broad or thin and looking at the venation. First you need to look at the general shape of the leaf. Although every plant has leaves with a shape that is unique to that plant, many plants have leaves with similar shapes. Some leaves are elliptical—they are wide in the center and narrow at the ends. Other leaves are oval with very rounded edges. Some leaves are heart shaped or arrow shaped. Others are ovate or triangular with rounded corners.

Arrow-shaped leaves

Heart-shaped leaves

Entire margin

Toothed margin

Lobed margin

Once you have identified the general shape of the leaf you need to examine the edges of the leaf. The edge of a leaf is called the leaf margin. There are three basic types of leaf margins. Leaves with smooth edges are said to have an entire margin. Other leaves have jagged edges called a toothed margin. Finally, some leaves have very large indentations around the edge and are said to be lobed or to have a lobed margin. You learned in the last lesson that leaves are arranged on the stem to allow maximum exposure to the sun. The shape of the leaves also contributes to the amount of sunlight that reaches the other leaves. Lobed leaves allow light to pass through to leaves lower down on the plant.

Finally, you need to determine whether the leaf you are looking at is simple or compound. Most leaves are simple leaves, there is one leaf growing from the main leaf stalk or petiole. However, compound leaves have several leaflets growing from the petiole. A compound leaf is often confused with a branch with several leaves on it. You can determine if you are looking at several simple leaves or one compound leaf by examining how the leaves are attached. If they all lie flat in the same plane, instead of alternating around the center, then you are looking at a compound leaf instead of several simple leaves. Examine the pictures and become familiar with the different shapes, margins, and complexities of the leaves so you will be better able to identify the plants they come from.

Simple leaf

Compound leaves

19

Changing Colors

The beauty of autumn

Why do leaves change color in the fall?

Challenge words:

xanthophyll

anthocyanin

carotene

Fall can be the most beautiful time of year. Leaves change from green to bright red, orange, purple, and yellow. Then they fade to brown before falling to the ground. But why do the leaves change color and how do the trees know when to change?

Leaves are green in the spring and summer because of chlorophyll. The other colors are still there but they are drowned out or covered up by the much more abundant chlorophyll. When the length of sunlight each day becomes shorter as winter approaches, the trees seal off the connection between the leaf and the branch. Without new nutrients, no new chlorophyll is formed. As the old chlorophyll deteriorates, the other colors become visible. Eventually, all of the nutrients are used up, the leaf withers, and it falls off.

God designed leaves to fall off so that trees can survive the harsh environment of winter. Trees cannot continue to move liquids around in thin leaves with the temperatures below freezing. Also, the amount of water needed for photosynthesis is often not available in the winter. So many deciduous trees lose their leaves and rest in their growth during the winter. Similarly, evergreen trees rest during the winter. But, because their leaves are not as fragile, they do not lose them each fall.

What did we learn?

- How do trees know when to change color?
- Why do trees drop their leaves?
- Why don't evergreen trees drop their leaves in the winter?

 # Taking it further

- Do trees and bushes with leaves that are purple in the summer still have chlorophyll?
- What factors, other than daylight, might affect when a tree's leaves start changing color?

 # An autumn picture

Purpose: To make a picture of autumn colors

Materials: colored leaves, construction paper, newspaper, heavy book, tag board

Procedure:

1. If it is autumn, collect several different colored leaves. If no leaves are available, cut paper leaves of various shapes and colors from colored construction paper.

2. If the leaves are still pliable, place them between sheets of newspaper and place a heavy book on top of them for several days until they dry out. This will keep them looking good for a longer period of time.

3. Cut out a picture frame from tag board or poster board.

4. Glue the leaves along the edges of the picture frame.

5. Use the frame to demonstrate the beauty that God created all around us, as well as His provision by designing trees to survive the winter.

 # Leaf pigments

Although most leaves are green, there are four basic pigments that can be found in leaves. Chlorophyll is the most abundant and is what gives leaves their green color. However, other pigments are found in leaves as well. Xanthophyll (ZAN-tho-fill) is a yellow pigment. Many leaves contain xanthophyll as well as chlorophyll. Some leaves look more yellow than green, others look very green, but still contain xanthophyll.

Another pigment that seldom shows through on leaves before fall is carotene. Carotene produces a yellowish-orange pigment. A third pigment found in leaves is anthocyanin (an-tho-SI-a-nin). This pigment produces bright red, blue, and purple colors.

These pigments are not only found in leaves. They are responsible for many of the beautiful colors found in flowers and fruits. Carotene is what makes carrots orange and anthocyanin is responsible for the color of beets and plums.

Purpose: To determine what pigments are present in a plant using paper chromatography

Materials: leaves, coffee filter, coin, fingernail polish remover, dish, tape

Procedure:

1. Gather two or three different leaves. Try to find ones with different colors or different shades of green.

2. Cut a 1-inch wide strip from a coffee filter for each leaf that you collected.

3. Place a leaf over the paper near the bottom of the strip.

4. About 1 inch from the bottom of the paper, roll a quarter or other coin across the leaf, using it to press some of the leaf pigment into the filter paper.

Leaves

5. Repeat this process for each leaf on its own strip of paper.

6. Before continuing, predict what color of pigments you expect to find in each leaf. Write your predictions on a piece of paper.

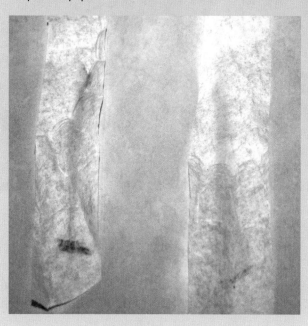

7. Pour fingernail polish remover into a small dish to a depth of ½ inch.

8. Place the dish on a counter near the wall and tape each strip of paper to the wall so that it is hanging down with the bottom edge of the strip just touching the polish remover. The polish remover will slowly move up the paper. As it does, it will dissolve the pigments and move them up the paper, too. Different pigments have different weights and will move up a different amount. This will allow you to see the different pigments that are in each leaf.

9. When the polish remover has moved up several inches, remove the strips and place them on a flat surface to dry.

10. Once the strips are dry, compare the pigments found in the various leaves.

Questions:

- Did each leaf have the color of pigments you expected?

- Are you surprised to find so many different colors in them?

Tree Identification: Final World of Plants Project

How do I know what tree it is?

Leaves

How many trees can you identify?

Why should you want to learn how to identify trees? You can enjoy trees by looking at them and sitting in their shade. Maybe you'd like to climb into a tree and build a tree house. But to truly enjoy and appreciate the diversity of God's creation, it helps to be able to identify the different plants around us. It is a lot like being a detective as you look for clues.

There are many ways to identify a plant. We use flowers, fruit, and leaves. For mature trees, we can also use the shape of the tree, its bark, and the pattern left on the branches where the leaves were attached. Shape and bark are especially useful for making identification in the winter when leaves and flowers are not available. Leaves are generally available for a longer period of time than flowers and fruit, so they are one of the most useful ways to identify trees or other plants.

To begin with, you need to determine several things about the leaves of the tree. Are they broad leaves, needles, or scales? Are they simple leaves or compound leaves? Compound leaves have several leaflets on each leaf. Look at the arrangement of the leaves. Examine their shape and the arrangement of the veins in the leaves. All of these things give you clues to the tree's identity. Once you have determined these things, you can use a field guide to help identify the tree. Field guides will give you additional things to look for such as the size of the leaves or the length and arrangement of needles. A good field guide will have pictures of the leaves and often will have pictures of mature trees to aid in identification. If you have access to the Internet, you can get practice identifying trees by their leaves by using an online Dichotomous Tree Key. There are a variety available from universities and state agricultural or conservation extension services.

Flowers, fruits, and seeds, including cones and pods, can also be very helpful in identifying a plant. The shape of the plant can be deceiving if the plant has been pruned excessively. Trees and plants growing in the wild are more likely to have the expected shape than those growing in gardens and parks.

So be a detective, get your field guide, and start practicing. Practice is the best way to learn to tell one plant from another. Eventually, you will be able to identify many plants without the use of a book.

What did we learn?

- What are some ways you can try to identify a plant?

- What are the biggest differences between deciduous and coniferous trees?

🚀 Taking it further

- Why do we need to be able to identify trees and other plants?

⚗️ Final project: leaf notebook

This project will take several days to complete. It will be done in three parts. Part one is to go to an area with a wide variety of trees such as a park or arboretum. There you will collect samples, make observations, and make identifications. Part two is to bring your samples home and prepare them for display. Part three is to prepare a notebook using the information and samples you gathered.

Purpose: To make a tree identification notebook

Part One

Materials: tree field guide, index cards, pencil, zipper bags

Procedure:

1. For each tree, examine the leaves, bark, etc., as described in the lesson. Write all of your observations on an index card. This could include leaf type (needle, broad, scale), size, shape, bark color and texture, leaf arrangement, leaf colors, fruit, flowers, etc.

2. Sketch the general shape of the tree and sketch or describe any other unusual or interesting features you observe.

3. Using the field guide, identify the tree and write the identification on the index card.

4. Carefully remove a leaf from the tree and place the leaf and the index card together in a zipper bag. You can also collect samples of flowers, seeds, pods, cones, etc., and place them in the bag with the leaf.

5. Repeat this procedure for each tree you wish to identify, being sure to place each leaf in a separate bag with its own identification card.

Part Two

After you return from collecting leaves, immediately set up a leaf press. This can be as simple as using several heavy books and some newspaper, or you can look on the Internet or in a field guide or other book for examples of building a more elaborate press. The important thing is to press the leaves flat and remove the moisture so they will be able to be displayed without rotting or curling up.

Materials: newspaper, heavy books

Procedure:

1. Spread a layer of newspaper on the counter.

2. Carefully lay several leaves on the paper.

3. Place a number next to each leaf and number the matching index card with the same number.

4. Be sure all the leaves are flat, and then cover them with another layer of newspaper.

5. Place heavy books on top of the newspaper and allow the leaves to sit in the press for several days until they are dry.

Part Three

After the leaves are all pressed and dried, put together a notebook displaying what was learned. Be creative in how you display your leaves and information. Below are just a few suggestions:

- Organize leaves alphabetically, or by type of trees (e.g., pines, oaks, elms, etc.)

- Cut colored paper into rectangles or other shapes to put behind each leaf.

- Type up the information on the index card, or if neatly written, include the card in the display.

- Place the leaves and information on pages of a photo album, or glue to cardstock and place inside plastic protector sheets in a binder.

- Make an index or table of contents as well as a title page.

Keep your eyes open for different varieties of trees. You can always add new samples to your notebook.

Finishing your notebook

You should include the information you gathered on growth habits from lesson 7 in your notebook. Also include any information you can find on each tree that you find interesting. Try to make your notebook something others will enjoy reading.

UNIT 5

Flowers & Fruits

21 Flowers

22 Pollination

23 Flower Dissection

24 Fruits

25 Annuals, Biennials, & Perennials

◊ **Identify** and **describe** the parts of a flower using models.

◊ **Describe** the purpose of a fruit.

◊ **Explain** different plant life cycles

Flowers

The beauty of sight and scent

What are the parts of a flower?

Words to know:

sepal	ovule
petal	ovary
stamen	fruit
pollen	staminate
pistil	pistillate

Challenge words:

composite flower	disk flower
head	ray flower

The fourth organ of a plant is the flower. (Remember that only angiosperm plants have flowers while gymnosperms produce seeds in structures like cones.) Its purpose is reproduction—it produces the seeds that grow into new plants. There is great variety in flowers: variety in shape, size, fragrance, and color. But nearly all flowers have the same basic parts. Most flowers have sepals, petals, stamens, and pistils.

Sepals are usually green. They protect the flower as it develops by covering the petals until it is ready to bloom. Once the flower blooms, the sepals are usually found at the base of the flower and could be mistaken for small leaves.

Fun Fact

The corpse flower (*Amorphophallus titanum*) is the stinkiest plant on the planet. It grows to an average height of 6½ feet (2 m) and when it blooms it releases an extremely foul odor similar to rotten flesh, which can be smelled half a mile away. It is also known as the *devil's tongue*. This foul-smelling flower was discovered in 1878 in the rainforest of central Sumatra in Western Indonesia.

The **petals** are the most familiar part of a flower. They are the colorful and fragrant part of the flower. Their purpose, besides giving pleasure to those who look at them, is to attract pollinating animals through sight and smell.

The **stamens** are the parts of the flower that produce pollen. **Pollen** is a fine powder necessary for fertilization of the ovules. Stamens are considered the male parts of the flower.

The **pistil** is considered the female part of the flower. It consists of three parts: the lowermost enlarged part called the **ovary**, the style which serves as a conduit between the ovary and the stigma, the uppermost part which recieves the pollen. The ovary produces **ovules**, which are unfertilized seeds or eggs. When combined with pollen, the ovules become seeds.

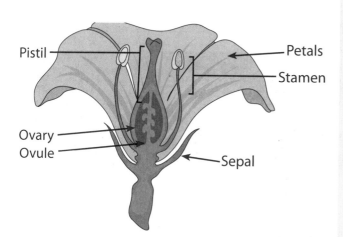

Fun Fact

The orange, brown, and white parasitic plant, *Rafflesia arnoldi*, has the largest flowers. These attach themselves to the cissus vines of the jungles of Southeast Asia. The flower measures up to 3 feet (1 m) across, and weighs up to 24 pounds (11 kg). The rafflesia also smells like rotting meat when it blooms. Although the corpse flower grows taller than the rafflesia, it is technically a collection of smaller flowers so the rafflesia is the largest single bloom.

🧪 Flower model

Purpose: To make a model of a flower

Materials: "Flower Pattern" sheet, scissors, construction paper, hole punch, modeling clay, cornmeal, soda straw, pipe cleaners

Procedure:

1. Cut out each pattern on the "Flower Pattern" sheet.

2. Using the pattern, trace the flower petals on a piece of colorful construction paper.

3. Trace the sepal on a piece of green construction paper.

4. Cut each part out and carefully punch a hole in the center of each piece using a hole punch.

5. Place a 1-inch ball of modeling clay on a piece of construction paper to use as a base for the flower.

6. Place a soda straw, representing the stem, in the clay and press the clay down onto the paper.

7. Put one end of a pipe cleaner through the petal then through the sepal and into the straw, leaving about 1–2 inches sticking out.

8. Cut four 1-inch pieces from a second pipe cleaner.

9. Stick each of these through the petal and sepal into the straw, keeping about ½ inch sticking out. The longer piece represents the pistil and the shorter pieces represent the stamens.

10. Sprinkle a small amount of corn meal on the stamens to represent pollen.

11. You can also cut leaf shapes from the green construction paper using the leaf patterns and tape or glue them to the sides of the straw.

12. Review the purpose of each part of the flower with your parent or teacher.

Fruit is the ripened and often swollen ovary containing the seeds. Using this definition, apples and oranges are fruit, but so are cucumbers, pumpkins, wheat grains, and acorns.

God has designed each of these parts to work together to produce the seed that will grow into another plant.

Most flowers have both stamens and pistils, but some flowers have only one or the other. Flowers with only stamens are called staminates, and those with only pistils are called pistillates.

 # What did we learn?

- What are the four parts of the flower and what is the purpose or job of each part?

 # Taking it further

- Why do you think God made so many different shapes and colors of flowers?

- If you were to design a flower, what would it look like? Draw a picture of it.

 # Composite flowers

One of the largest families of flowers is the composite family. You are probably already familiar with many of the flowers in this family. They include the sunflower, daisy, dandelion, marigold, and thistle. So what makes these flowers special? They are called composite flowers because what you might consider to be one flower is actually hundreds of tiny flowers on one stalk that together resemble a single flower.

Daisies, sunflowers, and many other composites actually have two different kinds of flowers. The center of the flower is called the head and it contains disk flowers. These flowers are packed tightly together to form the center of the structure. Around the edge of the head are what appear to be the petals of the flower, but these are actually individual flowers called ray flowers. In some composite flowers, only the disk flowers produce seeds, in others both the

Thistle

disk flowers and ray flowers produce seeds.

Some composite flowers only have ray flowers. Dandelions do not have a head with disk flowers. The ray flowers of the dandelion each produce a seed so a single stalk may produce hundreds of dandelion seeds. A few composite flowers only have disk flowers and do not have rays. Thistles are an example of a composite flower with only disk flowers.

Other common composite flowers include asters, dahlias, zinnias, black-eyed Susans, and chrysanthemums. When you see these flowers, closely examine them to see the individual flowers.

Sunflower

Flowers & Fruits

22

Pollination

The buzzing bee's job

How does a plant produce seeds?

Words to know:

pollination   pollinator

self-pollination   nectar

cross-pollination

Challenge words:

nectar guide   pollen guide

Pollination is the uniting of pollen and ovule to form a seed. Some plants are **self-pollinating**, which means the pollen produced by the flower is used by that same plant to produce a seed. However, most plants need to have pollen from another plant of the same type brought to its flowers in order to produce seeds. This is called **cross-pollination**. But how does pollen get from one plant to another?

Sometimes pollen is transferred by the wind or even the rain, but most of the time an animal such as a bee, wasp, moth, or even a hummingbird transfers pollen. These animals are called **pollinators** and they are attracted to the flowers by color and scent. The petals attract pollinators. Flowers also produce a sweet liquid called **nectar** to attract pollinators. The animal drinks the nectar of the flower. While moving around, pollen particles stick to the animal's body. Then it flies to another flower for more nectar, where the pollen may fall off. If the pollen lands on the pistil, pollination begins.

The pollen sends a tube down into the pistil until it makes contact with the ovule. This begins the creation of a seed. As the seed matures, the petals fall off, the ovary swells, producing fruit, and finally, when the seeds are mature, they are dispersed.

The yellow pollen grains can be seen on this bee.

What did we learn?

- What animals can pollinate a flower?
- How can a flower be pollinated without an animal?
- Does pollen have to come from another flower?

Taking it further

- Why do you suppose God designed most plants to need cross-pollination?

 # Pollination flip book

Purpose: To create a book illustrating pollination

Materials: scissors, crayons or colored pencils, stapler, "Flip Book" worksheet

Procedure:

1. Color each page on the "Flip Book" worksheet. Color the flowers identically.

2. Cut the pages apart, put them in order, and then staple the top edges together to form a book.

3. Flip quickly through the pages, and you will see a flower being pollinated to form a seed.

4. After making the flip book, examine your corn and bean plants from lessons 8 and 9. Look for flowers and/or the beginnings of fruit indicating that pollination has taken place. This is the last time we will be examining these plants.

Conclusion:

In your flip book, page 1 shows a bee drinking nectar. You can draw pollen on the bee's body.

Page 2 shows the flower after the bee is gone and shows pollen on the pistil.

Page 3 shows the pollen tube beginning to grow.

Page 4 shows the tube going down into the ovary.

Page 5 shows the tube going down farther.

Page 6 shows the tube going all the way down to the ovule, completing fertilization.

Pollen

Pollination is vital to the survival of plants. Without pollination, new seeds are not formed. But how does the right pollen get from plant to plant? A bee may visit several types of flowers and get more than one kind of pollen on its body. How does the plant know which pollen is right for it? Even though pollen looks like tiny dust to us, the pollen produced by each plant is unique to that plant. The shape and texture of the pollen grains are different for every type of plant. Thus when a bee enters a flower, only the pollen with the right shape and texture will stick to the pistil in that flower. So pollen from a tomato plant cannot pollinate a snap dragon.

Pollen grains from a variety of common plants magnified 500 times

Flowers & Fruits

Getting the bee or other pollinator to visit a flower is very important to that plant's survival. God has designed flowers with many ways to attract pollinators. Some flowers have a sweet scent that attracts bees or moths. We usually like to have these flowers in our homes. Roses and lilacs are two examples of flowers that attract pollinators by scent. Some flowers, such as the corpse flower, produce a smell like rotting flesh. This may not attract very many people, but it is just the right scent to attract flies, which are its main pollinator.

Other flowers attract pollinators by their bright colors. Hummingbirds are especially attracted to the color red which is why hummingbird feeders have red on them. The red petals of many flowers attract hummingbirds for pollination.

Some flowers have patterns on their petals that direct the pollinator to the nectar. They may have stripes or dashes that seem to point to the center of the flower. These patterns are called nectar guides or pollen guides. Pansies have dark centers and lines that guide the pollinator to the nectar. Some of these guides are not visible to the human eye, but are visible under ultraviolet light. Bees and other insects can see a higher spectrum of light than humans so some flowers have been designed to point the way to the nectar with a pattern that can only be seen by the pollinators.

Flowers & Fruits

The shapes of many flowers also contribute to their likelihood of being pollinated. Some flowers are bell shaped which requires the pollinator to crawl inside to reach the nectar and thus increases the possibility of pollination.

Flowers that do not need pollinators, ones that are pollinated by the wind for example, often have small unimpressive petals and no scent; they are not needed. These are often the plants that cause the most problems with allergies because their pollen is easily spread by the wind and thus easily spread to people who are allergic to the pollen. Ragweed is an example of this type of flower. The ragweed flower is very small and has no scent.

You can see the differences in pollen if you examine pollen grains with a magnifying glass or microscope. Obtain one or more samples of pollen and look at them closely with a magnifying glass or microscope. A microscope will best demonstrate the different shapes of the various pollen samples.

Pierre-Joseph Redoute

1759–1840

Pierre-Joseph Redoute is well known for his beautiful drawings and paintings of roses. However, he did more in his life than just draw roses. Redoute was born in 1759 into a family of painters. His father was a painter, as was his grandfather. Pierre-Joseph had little education, but he had a lot of talent. He left home at age 13. Leaving the small country of Luxembourg where he was born, he traveled to Belgium where he hoped to make a living as an interior decorator, doing portraits and commissioned religious works. He loved flowers but was told he could never make a living painting them.

During his travels, Pierre-Joseph become acquainted with other painters and learned from them. Later he joined his older brother in Paris where they painted scenery for the opera. While there, he was brought to the attention of a botanist who asked Pierre-Joseph to paint pictures of plants for his new book. This was something he enjoyed immensely.

After some time in Paris, Redoute was appointed to be the court artist for Queen Marie-Antoinette, and painted the gardens at Petite Trianon. During the French Revolution and the "Reign of Terror" that followed, he was appointed to document the gardens that had become national property.

Later, during the time of Emperor Napoleon, Redoute's career went very well. He produced his most lavish books with plants from around the world. He did his most famous work for the Empress Josephine, Napoleon's first wife. He painted the roses in Josephine's beautiful gardens. This book became his most famous work.

Rosa centifolia foliacea.   Rosier à cent feuilles, foliacé.

After the death of Empress Josephine, Redoute was appointed Master of Design for a museum in 1822.

Redoute died in 1840, around the age of 80. The paintings he did of roses, most of which he did in the Empress Josephine's gardens, are still considered some of the best paintings of roses ever done. Although he was told he could never succeed by painting flowers, Redoute continued to follow his dream and became known as the "Rembrandt of Roses" and the "Raphael of Flowers." He gave us some of the most inspiring paintings of flowers that exist.

23

Flower Dissection

Seeing what's inside

What is the role of each part of a flower?

Words to know:

filament   stigma

anther   style

Challenge words:

receptacle

The best way to appreciate the parts of a flower is to actually observe these parts. By dissecting a flower, you will be able to really visualize the pollination process. As you dissect a flower, you should be able to see not only the major parts that you have already learned about which include the sepal, petals, stamen, and pistil, but you should be able to see the individual parts that make up the stamen and pistil.

The stamen, which is the male part of the flower, consists of a long stem-like part called a **filament** and a bulge at the top called the **anther**. The anther produces the pollen. The filament supports the anther making it easy for pollinators to bump up against it and collect the pollen to take it to other flowers.

The pistil, which is the female part of the flower,

Fun Fact

Did you know that when you eat broccoli you are actually eating the flowers of the plant? Broccoli is harvested after the plant produces flower buds but before the buds have a chance to open up.

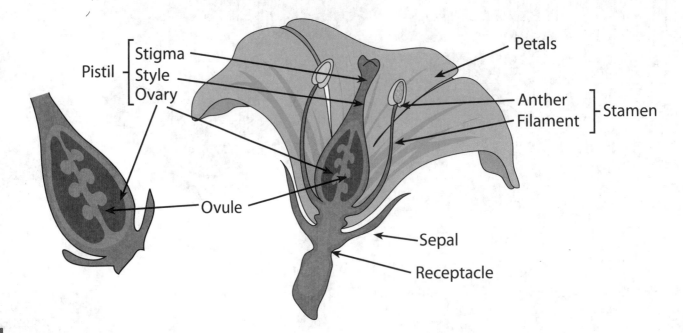

has three main parts. The top of the pistil is called the stigma. The stigma is sticky and is the part that receives the pollen when a bee or other pollinator brings pollen into the flower. The stigma is supported by a stem called the style. The style is often the tallest part in the center of the flower because it is important for the pollinator to easily bump up against the stigma. At the bottom of the style is the ovary. The ovary contains the ovules, which when pollinated develop into seeds.

 Flower dissection

Purpose: To dissect a flower and examine its parts

Materials: flower (such as lily or alstroemeria), knife or razor blade, tweezers

Procedure:

Examine a flower. Be sure to look carefully for each of the following items.

1. Identify the sepals (usually green and found near the base of the flower). Note, some flowers do not have sepals or lose their sepals after the flower has opened, so your flower may not have sepals

2. Identify the petals. Note their color, scent, and texture. Gently remove the petals and set them aside.

3. Identify the filament and anther of the stamens. The anthers will often have pollen (a sticky yellow substance) on the ends. Gently remove the stamens.

4. Identify the pistil. It should be all that is left of the flower. Most pistils are thin with a bulging area at the bottom. This bulging area is the ovary where the ovules (beginnings of seeds) are. Going up from the ovary you will see the style and at the top you will see the stigma.

5. A parent or teacher should gently cut open the pistil with a sharp knife or razor blade.

6. Locate any ovules. These are generally the size and shape of the flower seed, but are often white or green.

 Optional activity

If you have other flowers available, such as ones growing in your yard, dissect them as well. Some flowers have small parts that may be difficult to identify. Compare how easy or hard it was to identify the parts of the flowers in your yard with the flower chosen for dissection. Compare and contrast the different flowers' reproductive parts.

Review all of the flower parts shown in the diagram, then dissect a real flower and see if you can locate all of these parts.

 # What did we learn?

- How many ovules did you find?

- What did they look like?

- If possible, compare them to the mature seeds that are ready to be planted.

 # Taking it further

- Why are the ovules in the flower green or white when most seeds are brown or black?

- If you planted the ovules, would they grow into a plant?

Composite flower dissection

Purpose: To dissect a composite flower and examine its parts

Materials: composite flower such as a daisy or sunflower, magnifying glass

Procedure:

1. Carefully examine the head and the rays. Look at each type of flower and see how they are similar and how they are different. Examine how the flowers connect to the stem.

2. Carefully remove one of the ray flowers. Use your fingernail to gently open the bottom of the flower. Examine it closely with a magnifying glass. See if you can identify the pistil and stamen.

3. Remove one of the disk flowers. Again gently open the base of the flower and use a magnifying glass to identify the pistil and stamen. These parts are very small and may be difficult to find.

4. Look at how the flowers are connected to the receptacle. The receptacle is the area where the flower connects to the stem. Underneath the receptacle you may find bracts. These special leaves will probably be green and may resemble the sepals on other flowers. The arrangement of bracts is one way that different species of composite flowers are identified.

Questions:

- How do the flowers in the composite flower compare to the flower you previously dissected?

- How are they the same? How are they different?

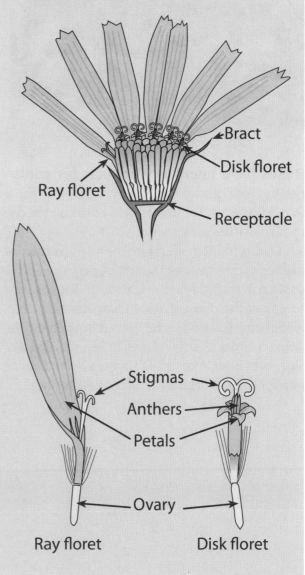

Ray floret   Disk floret

A Rose by Any Other Name Would Smell as Sweet

Roses have been very popular for centuries. In China, the rose has been cultivated for more than 3,000 years. The Chinese had books on the cultivation of roses as far back as 500 BC.

During the Roman Empire, the rose was used for medicinal purposes, as a source of perfume and as confetti in many of their celebrations. The rose was so popular at that time that many Roman nobles made large rose gardens for the public to enjoy. The Romans had a "Festival of Rosalia" on the island of Sicily every year. After the fall of the Roman Empire, interest in roses declined until the Renaissance.

In England during the 1400s, two different colors of roses were used to symbolize two different families who wanted to control England. The Lancasters used the red rose and the Yorks used the white rose. The power struggle between the two families, and most of England, was called "The War of the Roses." King Henry VII ended the struggle by uniting the families in marriage. The new family became known as the Tudors and they were symbolized by the Tudor rose, a white rose edged in red. This is still the symbol of royalty in England today.

During the 1700s the rose was so popular that the royalty of France would use roses and rose water (made by distilling rose petals in water) as a form of money. Napoleon's wife, Josephine, installed a rose garden west of Paris in the 1800s. This is where Pierre-Joseph Redoute did most of his work. Her interest in all exotic plants, and roses in particular, encouraged many people to begin developing different varieties of roses.

In the 1800s the Chinese way of cultivating roses was introduced into Europe. Since that time more than 150 species of roses have been developed. Most of the roses that are sold today can trace their "roots" back to China, thus making roses some of the oldest cultivated flowers on Earth.

24

Fruits

Is it ripe yet?

What kinds of fruit are there?

Words to know:

simple fruit

multiple fruit

aggregate fruit

Challenge words:

succulent fruit

pome

dry fruit

nut

drupe

legume

berry

grain

Once pollination has occurred in a flower and the ovule has been fertilized, the job of the petals is complete so they begin to wither and fall off. But the job of the ovary is just beginning. As the seeds mature, the ovary of the flower swells and ripens. This process is called producing fruit. When you hear the word fruit, what do you think of? Do you think of bananas, peaches, apples, and oranges? These are all fruits. However, any ripened ovary is a fruit from a biological perspective. So a cucumber, walnut, and bean pod are also fruits.

Most fruits are simple fruits. **Simple fruits** form from one flower that has one pistil and one ovary. Some examples of simple fruits include oranges, grapes, tomatoes, peaches, cherries, and olives. Some simple fruits have only one seed inside and others have multiple seeds from multiple ovules.

But not all plants produce simple fruit. **Aggregate fruit** forms from a flower that has multiple pistils. Some common aggregate fruits are strawberries, blackberries, and raspberries. Each little seed on the outside of a strawberry came from a separate ovary inside a single flower. These separate ovaries combine to produce the single strawberry.

Pineapple flowers each form a fruit that fuse together into a single core.

The third type of fruit we commonly see is called **multiple fruit**. Multiple fruit forms one "piece" of fruit from several flowers. The most common examples of multiple fruit are the pineapple and the fig. In the pineapple, each flower forms a fruit. These fruits fuse together into a single core.

The main purpose of ripened fruit is to disperse the mature seeds so the life cycle of the plant can be complete. Many fruits are attractive to animals. When the animal eats the fruit, the seeds pass through the digestive system and are deposited in another location. Some fruits form into dried seed-pods that explode open. Still others form in such a way as to be carried off by the wind. Recall what we learned about seed dispersal. The fruit has completed its job when the mature seeds are dispersed.

Now that you have learned about the four organs of a plant, you should better understand the life cycle of a flowering plant. It begins as a seed. When conditions are right, the seed germinates and the plant begins growing. The leaves perform photosynthesis to make food for the growing plant. As the plant matures it produces flowers that attract pollinators. After pollination, new seeds are formed and dispersed to begin the cycle again.

What did we learn?

- What is the main purpose of fruit?
- What are the three main groups of fruit?
- Describe how each type of fruit forms.

Taking it further

- What is the fruit of a wheat plant?
- Which category of fruit is most common?
- Why do biologists consider a green pepper to be a fruit?

Fruit identification

Purpose: To examine the three types of fruit

Materials: apple, strawberry, pineapple, sharp knife

Apple—Procedure:

1. Carefully examine an apple. Look at the outside of the apple, and then carefully slice the apple in half.

2. Observe the outer fleshy layer—the part we like to eat. Then observe the inner papery layer around the seeds. The apple is a simple fruit that develops from a flower with a single pistil. Simple fruits with a fleshy outer layer and a papery inner layer are called pomes.

3. If you slice an apple across the center, you should be able to see the five chambers of the ovary, each with several ovules that form seeds. The fleshy part outside the core is the receptacle, and the dried sepals can be seen at the bottom where the flower used to be.

Strawberry—Procedure:

1. Carefully examine a strawberry. Each "seed" developed from a separate pistil inside the same flower. This is called an aggregate fruit.

2. Carefully slice the strawberry in half from the top to the bottom. Notice the central core of the fruit. This is formed from the receptacle of the flower.

Pineapple—Procedure:

1. Carefully examine a pineapple. Each diamond-shaped area is a separate fruit. Each fruit formed from a separate flower.

2. Now carefully slice the pineapple in half. Notice the core in the center of the pineapple. This is where each fruit has fused together.

Now cut up your fruit and make a yummy fruit salad.

🏅 Fruit divisions

As you just learned, most fruits are simple fruits. Simple fruits can be divided into two groups. If the fruit has a thick fleshy outer layer it is called a succulent fruit. Most of what are commonly called fruits, as well as many "vegetables," are succulents. Other fruits do not have a fleshy outer layer; instead they have a dry cover. These are called dry fruits. Each of these groups is further divided into smaller groups.

The succulent fruits are divided into three main groups. If a fruit has a fleshy outer layer with only one hard covered seed in the center it is called a drupe. Can you think of any fruits with single hard seeds in the center? Peaches, plums, apricots, cherries, and olives are all drupes. You may not think of an olive as a fruit, but it has the same structures as cherries and other fruits in this category so scientifically it is a drupe.

Succulent fruits with many seeds are called berries. When you think of berries you probably think of strawberries and raspberries. These are not berries according to this definition because they are aggregate fruit and not simple fruit. What fruit can you think of that have many seeds inside?

Oranges and grapes are berries by this definition. Some vegetables are berries as well. Tomatoes and cucumbers are considered berries.

The third group of succulent fruit is called pomes. A pome (pōm) is a fruit that has a papery inner core around the seeds. What fruits can you think of that have a papery core? Apples and pears are pomes.

There are three main groups of dry fruits as well. Nuts are dry fruits with hard shells. You are probably familiar with many different nuts. This group includes walnuts, hazelnuts, pecans, and chestnuts. Peanuts do not fit into this group, however, because they do not have a hard outer shell. Instead, peanuts have a pod and so are part of the legume group. Legumes are dry fruits that form a pod around the seeds. The third group of dry fruit is the grains. The fruit of the grass family are grains. This includes many of the cereal grains and bread grains such as wheat, corn, rye, and oats.

Test how well you understand these definitions by completing the "Fruit Classification" worksheet.

Cherry
Drupe

Tomato
Berry

Apple
Pome

Pecan
Nut

Peanut
Legume

Wheat
Grain

Annuals, Biennials, & Perennials

How long do they grow?

What is the life cycle of plants?

Words to know:

annual   perennial
biennial

Challenge words:

ephemeral

Every spring, plant nurseries, home improvement stores, and even supermarkets are filled with racks of flowering plants. And every spring, homeowners buy these plants to take home and put in their gardens and flowerpots. Why do we go through this yearly ritual? Why do we have to buy new plants each year? We do this because different plants have different lengths of life cycles.

Annuals are plants that live for only one growing season. These are mostly what you see for sale each spring. Annuals grow from seed, to mature plant, to flowers with ripe seeds in only a few months. At the end of the summer or fall, the plants produce seeds, wither, and die. These plants do not grow again. Therefore, to have the same beautiful flowers next year, many people buy new plants in the spring. Some popular annuals include petunias, marigolds, and zinnias.

In addition to many decorative flowers, most crops are annuals as well. Peas, beans, and grains complete their life cycles in one growing season. Most food crops are planted as seeds in the spring and harvested in the fall. These plants were designed by God to provide food for people living in climates that are not suitable for plant growth year round.

Annual

Biennial

Perennial

Some plants, however, do not complete their life cycles in only one season. Some plants require two growing seasons to produce seeds. These plants are called biennials. During the first season, biennials grow relatively small plants and store most of the food that is produced in its roots, stems, or leaves. The next year, the plant uses the stored food to help produce flowers and eventually seeds. Some common biennials include carrots, beets, and cabbages. We usually harvest these biennials after the first season so we can eat the plants and benefit from the stored food. Therefore, we often do not see the flowers of these plants. However, if we allow the plants to grow a second year we will see the flowers and seeds that are necessary for reproduction.

Finally, some plants continue to grow year after year. These plants are called perennials. Perennials grow and produce flowers and seeds each year. During the winter, many of these plants either rest or appear to die, but new growth occurs in the spring from the roots and stems of the plant. Trees and shrubs are the most common perennials. Other perennials include most wildflowers, peonies, and asparagus.

What did we learn?

- What is an annual plant?
- What is a biennial plant?
- What is a perennial plant?

Taking it further

- Why don't we often see the flowers of biennial plants?
- Why don't people grow new plants from the seeds produced by the annuals each year?

Plant word search

Complete the "Plant Word Search."

Ephemerals

Some plants have a very short life cycle. They may complete their full life cycles in as little as six weeks. These plants are called ephemerals, which means transitory or quickly fading. Ephemerals grow very quickly, produce flowers and seeds, and then die all within just a few short weeks. Why do you suppose God created some plants with the ability to go through their life cycles so quickly?

Many ephemerals are found in the desert where growing conditions are very harsh. These plants remain in seed dormancy for very long periods of time. However, when rain comes, these seeds suddenly spring to life and the plants grow very quickly. The water will not last long so plants cannot survive if they require months to mature.

Another place where a short growing season is required is on the woodland floor. During the summer, the leaves of the trees prevent most of the sunlight from reaching the forest floor, so most plants cannot grow there during the summer. But in the spring, before the trees leaf out, there is abundant sunshine on the forest floor. This is when many ephemeral plants grow. They only have a few weeks of sunshine, and God has designed them to complete their life cycle very quickly.

Some plants have a short life cycle and can complete several life cycles in one growing season. Most of these plants are considered weeds and can be very annoying, especially to farmers. The Bible says that weeds are a result of the curse placed on the earth at the Fall of man (see Genesis 3:17–19). So you see there are several reasons why some plants have very short life cycles.

These trilliums are spring ephemerals.

UNIT 6

Unusual Plants

26 Meat-eating Plants

27 Parasites & Passengers

28 Tropisms

29 Survival Techniques

30 Reproduction Without Seeds

31 Ferns

32 Mosses

33 Algae

34 Fungi

35 Conclusion

◊ **Describe** the unique features of carnivorous plants.

◊ **Explain** the different tropisms and how they benefit plants.

◊ **Describe** how various plants are adapted to harsh environments.

◊ **Describe** how plants reproduce without seeds.

◊ **Explain** why algae and fungi are not plants.

26

Meat-eating Plants

Will it eat me?

How do plants eat insects?

Words to know:

carnivorous

Have you ever seen a Venus flytrap? This is a plant that traps an insect between special leaves and slowly digests it. But the Venus flytrap is not the only **carnivorous**, or meat-eating, plant. There are several types of plants that trap and digest small animals, usually insects.

Meat-eating plants are green plants that have chlorophyll and perform photosynthesis. So why do they also eat insects? Most meat-eating plants live in wet boggy soil that does not have enough nutrients. They trap insects to supplement their diet. This is a little bit like taking a vitamin pill.

Carnivorous plants have various ways to trap their meals. The sundew has leaves that are covered

with short sticky hairs. When an insect lands on the leaf, it becomes stuck and the leaf slowly curls around it. Pitcher plants have long tube-shaped leaves, similar in shape to a trumpet. The rim of the pitcher produces nectar to attract insects. When the insect stops to sample the nectar it slips inside the pitcher and is then trapped by slippery walls and downward pointing hairs at the bottom.

The Venus flytrap (above) is designed with special leaves that work a little like a mousetrap. When

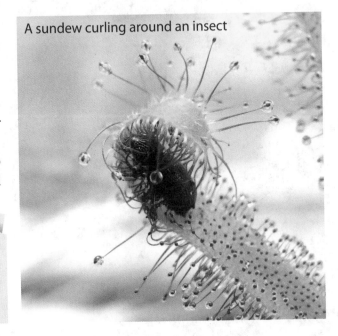

A sundew curling around an insect

Fun Fact

There are five carnivorous plants that are native to the United States: pitcher plant, bladderwort, butterwort, sundew, and Venus flytrap.

A pitcher plant with a trapped fly

- What is a carnivorous plant?
- Why do some plants need to be carnivorous?
- How does a carnivorous plant eat an insect?

 Taking it further

- Where are you likely to find carnivorous plants?
- How might a Venus flytrap tell the difference between an insect on its leaf and a raindrop?

an insect lands on the special leaf, it moves the trigger bristles, which signal the leaf to begin closing. The leaves are edged with teeth-like spikes that quickly close around the insect preventing it from escaping.

Once the insect is trapped in one of these plants, the plant secretes an acid that begins to digest the insect's body. It may take several days to digest the insect. The plant cannot digest the exoskeleton—the hard outer shell of the insect. When it is done digesting the rest of the insect, it may open its leaves to let the wind blow the exoskeleton away. Most of the time, however, the exoskeleton remains in the trap and attracts unwary spiders. Check your teacher's guide for this course for additional information on learning more about carniverous plants.

Fun Fact

The largest carnivorous plants are in the genus *Nepenthes*. These large vines can grow over 30 feet (9 m) long. These tropical pitcher plants have traps designed to capture some of the largest prey, including creatures as large as frogs. Very rarely, captures of birds or rodents have been reported.

Making a trap

In this activity, you will design a trap. The simplest trap is one where one end of a box is propped up by a stick. The prey knocks over the stick and is trapped in the box. You can make a simple trap like this or may design a more elaborate trap. You can use a small toy as the insect and pretend to catch the insect inside your trap.

Discuss how the trap works and how it is similar and different from the plant traps described in the lesson.

🏅 Cobra lily

One of the most interesting looking carnivorous plants is the cobra lily. The cobra lily is not a true lily but a pitcher plant. Special leaves grow up and bend over to form a pitcher that resembles the head of a cobra. It even grows leaves that resemble a tongue.

When an insect lands on the "tongue" it is attracted by the scent of nectar and crawls up the tongue inside the pitcher. The top of the pitcher has several windows that allow light to pass through. When the insect is ready to leave it usually flies toward the light thinking it is an exit, but instead of escaping, it hits the top of the pitcher. This knocks the insect into the neck of the pitcher, which is lined with downward facing

Cobra lily

hairs and a slippery fluid. It quickly becomes trapped and is digested by the plant.

Most carnivorous plants produce enzymes that digest the bodies of the insects that become trapped. But the cobra lily does not produce these enzymes. Instead, it relies on bacteria to break down the bodies of its prey and then absorbs the nutrients.

Cobra lilies grow in swampy mountain bogs in southwestern Oregon and northern California.

If you were to design a carnivorous plant what would it look like? How would it trap insects or other animals? Use your imagination and draw a picture of your meat-eating plant. Be sure to give it a name.

Unusual Plants

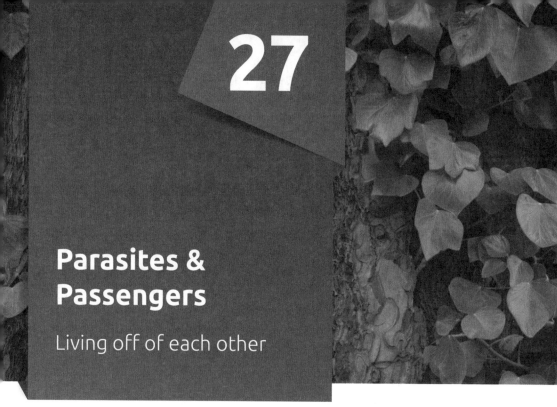

27

Parasites & Passengers

Living off of each other

How do parasitic plants survive?

Words to know:

parasite

host

passenger plant

vine

Although most plants around us live and grow the way we have discussed in the previous lessons, a few do not. Some plants are parasites. This means that they obtain the water, minerals, and food they need by stealing them from other plants. Parasitic plants often have roots when they are young, but once they tap into another plant those roots wither and the plant gets all of its nourishment from the host plant.

Parasites attach themselves to the host using special organs called *haustoria*, which are suckers that penetrate into the stem or roots of the host so it can suck the liquids from the host plant. Some common parasitic plants include mistletoe, dodder, and eyebright.

Some plants live and grow on other plants without tapping into them or harming them in any way. These plants are called passengers. Passenger plants are found most commonly on trees. These plants usually grow on trees in order to have better access to sunlight. Many passenger plants grow in the trees of the rain forest.

One passenger plant is the moth orchid. These orchids are often found in the branches of trees in the

Spanish moss is a passenger plant.

Moth orchid on a tree

rain forests. They have three kinds of roots. One kind of root anchors the plant to the host. The second kind of root is an aerial root that absorbs water directly from the air. And the third kind of root absorbs minerals from its surroundings. These orchids produce flowers that produce seeds. The seeds are scattered by the wind and blown into the bark of other trees where they germinate and grow new plants.

Unlike the moth orchid, which is fairly large, most passenger plants are small. The most common passenger plants in North America are mosses and lichens.

Similarly, **vines** are plants that use other plants for support, but they have their own root systems. One common vine is the wild grape. As birds eat the fruit, they deposit the seeds near trees as they rest in the branches. The seed sprouts and the vine begins to grow up the side of a tree, spreading its leaves out as it grows. Vines can also grow up the sides of buildings or cliffs or on trellises in gardens. Poison ivy vines also have small aerial roots that make them look fuzzy. Other vines include true ivy vines, honeysuckle, pole beans, and Virginia creeper.

Parasite model

Purpose: To demonstrate how a parasite steals nutrients from a host

Materials: soda straw, knife, coffee stirrer or small straw

Procedure:

1. Cut a small hole in the side near the center of a soda straw. The hole should be the same size as a coffee stirrer or smaller straw.

2. Insert a coffee stirrer into the hole so that the edge is in the center of the straw. Angle the coffee stirrer so that it is pointing slightly down—not straight out to the side. This stirrer represents the haustoria, or suckers, that the parasitic plant sends into the host plant.

3. Place the straw under running water in a sink.

Conclusion: Observe how most of the water flows out of the bottom of the straw but some of the water flows out of the coffee stirrer. This smaller amount of water represents the nutrients that would flow into the parasitic plant.

Search for parasites & passengers

If possible, go outside and search for parasitic plants and passenger plants. Large trees are the most likely place to locate these types of plants. Look for mistletoe, lichen, and moss. Mistletoe is a common parasite. Lichen and moss are passengers. Poison ivy, honesyuckle, and Virginia creeper are vines. If you find something growing on a tree, closely observe how it is growing. Is it attached to the outside only, or does part of the plant penetrate into the stem?

A field guide is useful in helping you identify the plants you find. *Reader's Digest North American Wildlife* is a good resource to have available anytime you explore nature. Many other field guides are available at your library as well.

Unusual Plants

Fun Fact

Mistletoe, considered sacred by the British Druids, was believed to have many miraculous powers. Among the Romans, it was a symbol of peace, and it was said that when enemies met under it, they discarded their arms and declared a truce. From this comes our Christmas custom of kissing under the mistletoe. England was the first country to use it during the Christmas season.

What did we learn?

- What is a parasitic plant?
- What is a passenger plant?
- How do passenger plants obtain water and minerals?

Taking it further

- Where is the most likely place to find passenger plants?
- Do passenger plants perform photosynthesis?
- Do parasitic plants perform photosynthesis?

Plant research

There are many interesting parasitic and passenger plants. Choose one of the plants from the following lists, or another parasitic or passenger that you are interested in, and find out all you can. You may want to search the Internet for epiphytic plants, which is the scientific name for passenger plants.

Draw a picture of your plant and its host or find photos of the actual plant. Make a presentation to your class or family, telling them what you learned.

Parasites
- Mistletoe
- Rafflesia
- Dodder
- Love Vine

Passengers
- Moth orchid
- Spanish moss
- Lichen
- Old man's beard

Unusual Plants

28

Tropisms

How plants respond

How does a plant know which way to grow?

Words to know:

tropism

geotropism

hydrotropism

heliotropism/
     phototropism

Challenge words:

positive tropism

negative tropism

chemotropism

thermotropism

thigmotropism

Do seeds grow if they are planted upside down? Will a plant grow if it is far from the river or other water source? How can a plant survive if something blocks the light? God has designed plants so they know how to grow. The earth gives clues to the plants to help them survive. These "survival techniques" are called tropisms (from a Greek word meaning "turning"). A **tropism** is a response by the plant to a certain stimulus or condition. Plants experience several tropisms.

Geotropism—Roots always grow down and out and stems always grow up from a seed regardless of which direction it is planted in the ground. The plant knows how to do this because it responds to the pull of gravity. If a plant in a pot gets knocked

These trees were knocked over when young and then began to grow straight up again. This is an example of geotropism.

Plants turn toward light sources to maximize photosynthesis.

a leaf, some cells contract and others expand to turn the leaf toward the sun. As the sun moves through the sky, the leaves follow it. If something blocks the sun, the plant will grow toward any available light, allowing it to bypass whatever may be in its way. These are responses to light.

God designed plants with these abilities to increase their chances of survival. Tropisms demonstrate God's brilliant design.

over so that the roots and stem are now sideways, after a few days the roots will begin growing downward and the stem will begin growing upward again in response to gravity.

Hydrotropism—Roots can sense water and will grow towards it. Some plants, willows for example, can send roots more than 30 feet (9 m) sideways to reach a source of water. Dicots with taproots often go down 20–30 feet (6–9 m) to find water.

Heliotropism (also called **phototropism**)—Leaves turn to face the sun to obtain the maximum energy for photosynthesis. As the sun hits

What did we learn?

- What is geotropism?
- What is hydrotropism?
- What is phototropism or heliotropism?

Taking it further

- Why are tropisms sometimes called "survival techniques"?
- Will a seed germinate if it is planted 5 feet (1.5 m) from the water?
- Where are some places you would not want to plant water-seeking plants such as willows?

Observing heliotropism

Purpose: To observe phototropism/heliotropism

Materials: house plant

Procedure:

1. Place a houseplant near a window. Observe which direction the leaves are facing.

2. After a day or two, observe the plant again. You should be able to see that the leaves are all facing toward the window.

3. Turn the plant 180 degrees and leave it for another two days.

4. Observe the leaves again. They will have turned around to face the window again.

⬤ More tropisms

Tropism is the response of a plant to a certain stimulus. Positive tropism means that the plant moves toward the stimulus; negative tropism means the plant moves away from the stimulus. Hydrotropism is a positive tropism because the roots of the plant move toward the water. Phototropism or heliotropism is also a positive tropism because leaves move toward the light and stems grow toward the light. Geotropism is positive for the roots and negative for the stems because the roots move toward the pull of gravity and the stems move away from the pull of gravity.

In addition to these responses, other tropisms have been observed in certain plants. Chemotropism is a response to chemicals. In many flowering plants, the pollination process is a positive chemotropism. The ovary releases a chemical. This causes the pollen tube to move toward it. This completes the pollination process.

Thermotropism is a response to heat or cold. Some leaves will curl up when the air around them becomes cold. This is a negative tropism. Some plants have roots that respond to heat. When the soil above the plant becomes warm the roots move toward the heat, but when it becomes too hot, the roots move away from the heat.

Some plants also experience thigmotropism, which is a response to touch. Can you think of any plants that we have studied that respond to touch? Tendrils have a positive response to touch. They curl around solid objects that they come in contact with. Plant roots on the other hand have negative thigmotropism. As roots grow they move away from something solid. This allows the roots to find spaces between the bits of dirt and more easily penetrate the soil.

Complete the "Tropisms" worksheet by drawing a picture demonstrating each tropism listed.

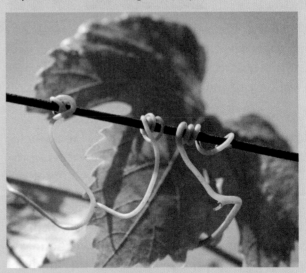

Grape vine tendrils coil and latch on for support. This is an example of thigmotropism.

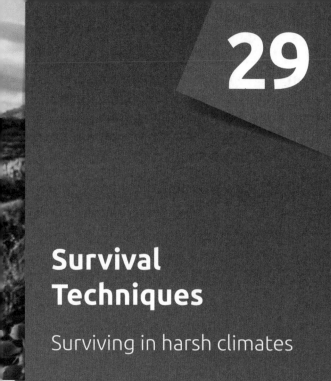

29

Survival Techniques

Surviving in harsh climates

How can plants survive in harsh conditions?

Words to know:

succulent

Plants can be found growing in nearly every part of the world. But all climates are not necessarily conducive to plant growth. Some climates have too much or too little water. Some climates are very hot or very cold. But God designed plants that can grow in even these very harsh climates. In addition to tropisms, God has given these plants special survival techniques to help them deal with the harsh conditions.

We have learned how some plants that grow where there are few nitrates due to too much water can supplement their "diet" by digesting insects. Conversely, plants that live where there is very little water have been designed to make the most of what water is available. These plants are called succulents and can often go for weeks or even months without water. When water is available, the cactus and other succulents absorb as much water as they can, storing it in their fleshy stems. They are designed with ridges in their stems that can expand to hold more water when it is

available. Also, to keep the water from evaporating, cacti have needle-like leaves with very little surface area so water does not evaporate quickly. The cactus's needles also help keep animals from eating its stem and taking its water.

Other plants have been designed to survive in alpine areas where there is often high wind, cold temperatures, and little available water. These alpine plants are small and grow low to the ground to survive the wind. They often grow in dense groups to provide protection and insulation to the whole group of plants. When summer comes to the high mountain areas, these plants

Alpine plants are small and grow low to the ground.

Fun Fact

The cardón cactus is the world's largest cactus. It is found in the American southwest, mostly in Baja California. Some of the largest cardónes have been measured at nearly 70 feet (21 m) high and weigh up to 25 tons.

bloom and reproduce very quickly to take advantage of the short growing season. Also, many alpine plants have tiny hairs on their leaves to protect them from the intense sun at high altitudes. These hairs can also act as insulation to protect the leaves from extreme cold.

Each of these plants shows the wonder of God's design and His provision for all parts of His creation.

What did we learn?

- How do some plants survive in hot dry climates?
- How do some plants survive in cold windy climates?

Taking it further

- Why do alpine plants need protection from the sun?

Examining a cactus

Carefully examine a small cactus. Using a magnifying glass, examine the needles and the fleshy stem. Look for folds in the stem that might expand to hold more water or shrink when water is not available. Discuss how this plant was designed to survive in the harsh climate of a desert.

Designed for survival

In order to survive, plants require many different things. You will appreciate all of the ways God has designed plants for survival when you complete the "Designed for Survival" worksheet.

We have talked about many different ways that plants have been designed to survive in various conditions. Review the lessons in this book for ideas to put on the worksheet. You can start with the designs listed in this lesson, but there are many more listed throughout the previous lessons.

30

Reproduction without Seeds

There are other ways.

How can a plant reproduce without seeds?

Words to know:

vegetative reproduction   rhizome

vegetative propagation

Challenge words:

cloning   cutting

grafting   genetic modification

rootstock   GMO

scion

Some plants that reproduce by producing seeds can also reproduce in other ways as well. A small piece of the plant can be used to start a new

plant. This is called vegetative reproduction or vegetative propagation. There are several ways that vegetative reproduction can take place. One way is when a plant sends out special creeping stems called stolons. This is the main way that gardeners get new strawberry plants. After the plant is done producing fruit, it sends out runners, or stolons, that grow new plants at the end of the runners.

Many plants that bloom in the early spring, such as tulips or crocuses, grow from bulbs. Bulbs often produce new bulbs underground that can be used to grow new plants. Some plants, such as the iris, grow rhizomes, special stems that grow

Some plants reproduce by sending out creeping stems called stolons.

Fun Fact

The creosote plant that grows in the American southwest reproduces vegetatively. It is believed that some of the creosote plants growing today have the exact same genetic make-up as plants that were growing thousands of years ago.

Unearthed bamboo rhizomes

way to get new plants, vegetative reproduction is often used because it can have faster results. 🧬

🧠 What did we learn?

- What are some ways that plants can reproduce without growing from seeds?

🚀 Taking it further

- Why can a potato grow from a piece of potato instead of from a seed?

- Will the new plant be just like the original plant?

underground, and produce new plants. Other special underground stems are tubers. Potatoes are tubers and new potato plants can be started from a small part of a potato.

Finally, some plants reproduce by growing new roots from a cut stem or leaf. Ivy and many other houseplants can be cut and placed in water to encourage new roots to grow. Then the new plant can be placed in soil. Although seeds are the primary

Unusual Plants

🧪 Growing a new potato plant

Purpose: To grow a new potato plant without using seeds

Materials: a potato with "eyes"—small white growths on the side of the potato, jar, potting soil

Procedure:

1. Cut out a square of the potato around the eye.

2. Plant this part of the potato in a jar filled with potting soil. It should be planted about two inches below the surface.

3. Keep the soil moist but not too wet.

4. In 10 to 14 days, you will see a potato plant begin to grow from the piece of the original potato.

🏅 Cloning plants

Most plants reproduce sexually by the uniting of pollen and ovule to produce a seed. When this happens, DNA from the plant producing the pollen unites with DNA from the plant producing the ovule and the resulting seed has unique DNA that is a combination of the parent plants' DNA. God designed plants to reproduce this way so that problems that occur in the DNA are not as likely to be passed on to the next generation.

When plants experience vegetative reproduction, the new plant has the exact DNA as the plant that it came from. When a strawberry plant sends out runners, the new plants will have the same DNA as the parent plants. When the potato eye that you planted grows a new potato plant it will have the same DNA as the potato plant that the potato came from. This is a form of cloning. Cloning is producing offspring with identical DNA to the parent. This form of reproduction occurs naturally in some plants. Cloning is also used in many areas of agriculture.

One of the most widespread uses of vegetative reproduction in agriculture is in fruit tree reproduction. Although sexual reproduction keeps plants healthy, the fruit is different from one plant to the next. This is okay in the wild, but people expect a golden delicious apple to taste like a golden delicious apple. They do not want it to taste like a Granny Smith apple or a sour wild apple. Growing fruit trees from seed can have unexpected results. Therefore, commercial tree growers use vegetative reproduction to produce clone trees that produce fruit with the desired qualities.

The most common form of vegetative reproduction used to grow new fruit trees is grafting. The first part of grafting is growing the rootstock. Usually, roots and a stem are taken from an existing root structure to form a new rootstock. Sometimes trees are grown from seeds to produce new rootstock. The rootstock is chosen for its hardiness and ability to support the tree that will be grafted to it, not for its fruit.

Once the rootstock is ready, a stem or a bud, referred as a scion (SI-un), is cut from the desired tree and a cut is made in the rootstock. The cut side of the bud is placed next to the cut in the rootstock and the two pieces are taped together and the cut is sealed with grafting wax. With the cambium cells of both plants next to each other, the two plants begin to grow together. This completes the grafting process. What results is a tree that produces fruit that is identical to the tree that the bud came from.

Other plants are propagated by a process called cutting. This is a very simple process. A stem or branch from one plant is cut off and placed in soil. The cutting grows roots and becomes a new plant genetically identical to the original. Forsythia bushes are often propagated in this way.

Cloning ensures that each new plant is genetically identical to its parent; however, sometimes it is desirable to make a plant that is very different from its parent plant. Scientists have developed ways to modify the genes in the DNA in particular plants to obtain new plants with different characteristics. This practice is called genetic modification. Although people have been breeding plants to get desired results for centuries, the idea of actually modifying the DNA is a relatively new one. Plants that have been developed by genetic modification are called genetically modified organisms or GMOs.

Do some research to find out how genetic modification works, how it is being used, what foods you might be eating that are GMOs, and what controversies surround this interesting field of science. Be sure to share what you learn with someone else.

The grafts can be clearly seen on these almond trees.

31

Ferns

Seedless plants

How do ferns reproduce?

Words to know:

frond   spore

Challenge words:

fiddlehead

Not all plants have flowers and produce seeds. Plants without seeds include ferns and mosses. Ferns are similar to other plants because they have roots, stems, vascular tissue, and leaves with chlorophyll. These leaves are called **fronds**. But ferns do not have flowers or seeds.

So how do ferns reproduce? Ferns produce microscopic **spores** on the backs of their leaves. These spores do not contain a baby plant like a seed does. They contain just enough informa-tion to grow a tiny leaf-like structure, which then

Fun Fact

A typical fern plant may produce up to one billion spores per year.

produces an egg and sperm which, when united, form the beginnings of a new fern plant. This method of reproduction is very different from the way most plants reproduce; therefore, ferns are classified separately from most other plants.

Young ferns

Fun Fact

One of the first plants to begin growing after a volcanic eruption is the fern. The big island of Hawaii has many beautiful fern forests growing where lava once covered the ground.

Ferns generally need a lot of water so they usually grow in areas with lots of rain. Ferns are generally small plants but a few grow up to 60 feet (18 m) tall in the rain forests.

Fun Fact

There are over 12,000 species of ferns in the world, most of these found in the tropics.

- How are ferns like other plants?
- What are fern leaves called?
- How are ferns different from other plants?
- How do they reproduce?

Taking it further

- Why can't ferns reproduce with seeds?

Fern fronds

Closely examine this picture, showing fern fronds with spores on the back. Then paint a picture of a fern frond. After the paint is dry, glue small amounts of corn meal or sand on the frond to represent the spores.

If you have a fern plant available, place a frond on the table, cover it with a piece of paper, and color back and forth over it with a crayon to make a tracing, or rubbing, of the leaf. Then glue the corn meal onto your rubbing to show the spores.

Unusual Plants

Fern structure

Although ferns have many of the same structures that are found in other plants, they do not grow the way that most plants grow. Instead of having a vertical stem, most ferns have a horizontal stem called a rhizome. The rhizomes grow just below the surface. As in most plants, the roots grow down from the stems.

Since the stems of the fern plant are underground, the fronds, or leaves, grow up from the ground. They start out as a small rolled up structure called a fiddlehead, which is actually the developing petiole of the frond. As it grows, the fiddlehead unrolls and develops into a frond.

Ferns are abundant in the fossil record showing that in the past ferns covered much of the earth. Fern fossils are often found in coal beds. These fossils are nearly identical to ferns found today, showing that ferns have not changed or evolved. Also, many of the fossilized ferns clearly show the beautiful lacy

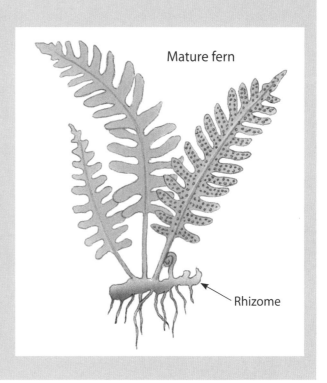

Mature fern

Rhizome

Fossil ferns are identical to modern ferns.

A fiddlehead

texture of a living frond, indicating that the leaves were covered quickly while the plant was still alive, not slowly as evolutionary theories indicate. This is consistent with the idea of plants becoming buried quickly during the worldwide Flood in Genesis.

Add ground, rhizomes, and roots to your painting to show the whole structure of a fern plant.

32

Mosses

Do you really find moss on the north side of trees?

How do mosses grow and reproduce?

Challenge words:

peat

Another group of non seed-bearing plants is mosses. These are tiny plants with thin, green leaves, stems, and root-like structures. Most mosses absorb more water through their leaves than through their roots. Mosses do not have flowers or seeds. They reproduce with spores in a similar way to that of ferns.

Fun Fact

Most animals don't eat lichens—they are hard to digest and have little nutritional value. But reindeer eat lots of them. Why? A certain lichen, called *reindeer moss*, contains a chemical that helps a reindeer's cells keep working at low temperatures. When the reindeer make their yearly journey across the icy Arctic region, this chemical keeps them from freezing, just like antifreeze keeps a car from freezing up in the cold winter.

Mosses have two stages in their life cycles. One stage is the green moss plant stage with which you are probably familiar. The second stage is the capsule and stalk stage. In this stage, the plant produces a stalk like a thin stem with a capsule on the end. This capsule produces the spores that later produce new moss plants.

Most mosses are very small, but they can grow in large clumps or groups. Mosses are found wherever there is a consistently wet environment. The

Unusual Plants

idea that moss always grows on the north side of a tree comes from the fact that in winter sun shines on the south side, making it warmer and dryer and therefore less likely to grow moss. But the truth is that moss will grow anywhere that is wet enough. Mosses love bogs and swamps, but will also grow in forests and even in the tundra.

🧠 What did we learn?

- How do mosses differ from seed-bearing plants?
- How do mosses differ from ferns?
- How do mosses produce food?

🚀 Taking it further

- Are you likely to find moss in a desert? Why/why not?

🧪 Find the moss

Using art supplies, draw pictures of a forest or swamp. Then glue dried moss in the places you are most likely to find it. Be sure to include the bases of trees, under rocks, or on fallen logs.

After making the pictures, go out in your yard and search for moss. Look under rocks, on old logs, or in damp shady areas. Use a magnifying glass to observe the small leaves.

Peat moss

One of the most important mosses is called sphagnum moss. Sphagnum moss, also called peat moss, has leaf-like structures that can absorb and hold water. This gives peat moss a spongy texture. This is important for many reasons. First, this moss helps prevent soil erosion by quickly absorbing rain water that would otherwise wash away soil. When peat moss dies, it is used as a soil additive to increase the ability of the soil to hold water. Many people add peat moss to the soil when planting trees and other plants to help keep moisture near the roots of the new plants.

Peat moss grows primarily in swampy bogs. As it begins to decay it becomes compressed by the weight of the water and other plants. These layers are called peat. The acid in the moss prevents it from completely decaying, so in certain bogs the peat is several feet thick. In Ireland and other areas, people cut squares of peat from the bogs, dry them and use them as fuel.

Peat moss and many other mosses are also important in the formation of soil. The plants secrete an acid that helps to break down the minerals in rocks. This helps create new soil and to add minerals to the soil. This is just one way that God designed the world to be able to sustain life.

Blocks of peat drying in Scotland

Purpose: To demonstrate the water absorbing qualities of peat moss

Materials: peat moss, three paper cups, dirt, water

Procedure:

1. Place ½ cup of peat moss in a paper cup.
2. Place a ½ cup of dirt from your yard in a second cup.
3. Place ¼ cup of peat moss and ¼ cup of dirt together in a third cup and stir the dirt and peat moss together.
4. Pour ¼ cup of water into each sample.
5. Let the water sink in then feel the texture/moisture of each sample.
6. Wait 1 hour then feel the texture and moisture of each sample again. Which samples are still moist?
7. Test the samples again after 1 more hour. Which samples are moist now?
8. See if any of the samples are still moist after 24 hours.

Conclusion: What difference did adding peat moss make to the ability of the soil to hold water? You should find that the peat moss and the soil with the peat moss mixed in both held the moisture longer than the dirt by itself. This is why many people add peat moss to their soil.

Unusual Plants

Algae

Are all green things plants?

Why are algae important organisms?

Words to know:

algae

primary consumer

secondary consumer

diatom

Challenge words:

filament

algin

carrageenin

Have you ever walked along a lake or pond and noticed green scum on the top of the water? Or maybe you have seen an area in the ocean that is a different color from the rest of the water. Have you ever pulled long, green, stringy material from a pond or stream or seaweed from the ocean? If so, then you have seen algae.

Algae are plantlike organisms that generally live in the water. They do not have roots, leaves, stems, flowers, or seeds so they are not truly plants. They contain chlorophyll and produce their own food, like plants, but are classified in the kingdom Protista.

Algae are very important organisms. They provide food for many fish and other sea creatures.

They are the beginning of most aquatic food chains. Nearly everything in the ocean eats algae or eats something that has eaten algae. Animals that eat algae or plants are called primary consumers. Animals that eat other animals that have eaten algae or plants are called secondary consumers.

In addition to food, algae are used in a variety of manufactured products. Diatoms are yellow algae that have silica in their cell walls. Large deposits of dead diatoms have been found and are used in toothpastes, scouring powders, tiles, and bricks. Diatom deposits are also used in explosives to help

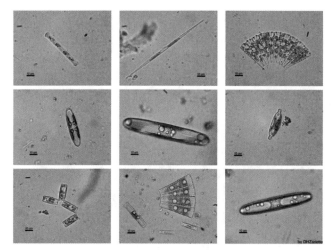

Microscopic images of common freshwater diatoms

Algae are used as wrappers for sushi.

stabilize the explosive material. Algae are used in many food products including wrappers for sushi and other oriental foods and as thickeners in ice cream, pudding, and salad dressings.

Most important of all, algae produce more than half of the oxygen in the world. Algae are the most abundant life form on Earth, with the exception of bacteria, thriving in the surface layer of the oceans. Scientists believe they perform as much as 70% of all photosynthesis in the world. This makes algae one of the most beneficial organisms on Earth.

🧠 What did we learn?

- Why are algae such important organisms?
- What gives algae its green color?

🚀 Taking it further

- Why are some algae yellow, brown, blue, or red?

⚗️ Food chain picture

Scientists often talk about food chains. There were not any food chains in God's original creation since all animals (and man) ate only plants (Genesis 1:29–30). However, after the Fall of man, animals began to eat each other. Today, food chains begin with plants or algae. Animals eat the plants. Then other animals eat those animals and so on. Most aquatic food chains begin with algae. In one food chain, algae are eaten by microscopic animals such as rotifers. The rotifers are eaten by tiny fish such as minnows. The minnows are eaten by perch, and the perch are eaten by birds.

Purpose: To illustrate a food chain

Materials: colored pencils, construction paper, scissors

Procedure:

1. Draw a picture of a lake using colored pencils.

2. Cut out different animals in the food chain from construction paper.

3. Glue the animals on the picture in the order that they occur in the food chain. Be sure to make an area of the lake greenish where the algae are and start your food chain in that location.

4. Identify the primary and secondary consumers of the algae.

Amazing algae

Algae are generally classified by their color. There are green, yellow, brown, and red algae. All algae contain chlorophyll, which is green. But many algae contain other pigments as well, giving them different colors. The green algae comprise the largest group of algae. Many green algae live as single cells, but others connect together. If several cells connect end to end they are called a filament. Other green algae survive in large groups called colonies. Spirogyra is one of the most common filament algae. These algae form long green threads. Inside each cell is a spiral shaped chloroplast which performs photosynthesis. Spirogyra can be found in nearly any pond.

You have already learned about yellow algae called diatoms which contain silica. Brown algae are often called seaweed. We generally think of algae as being very small, and most are microscopic; however, the brown algae are multi-cellular and can be up to 200 feet long. Kelp is the largest algae. The longest kelp ever recorded was 10.5 miles (17 km) long. Kelp is also one of the most useful brown algae. It contains a substance called algin which is used in making many products including chocolate milk, ice cream, mayonnaise, and lotions. Algin is a sticky substance in kelp that helps to keep these products smooth and creamy.

A few seaweeds are red algae. Red algae is also useful in manufacturing different products. Carrageenin is a gelatin-like substance found in many red algae that is used to thicken different foods including some ice cream. Red algae is also used to make agar, which is the medium that scientists use

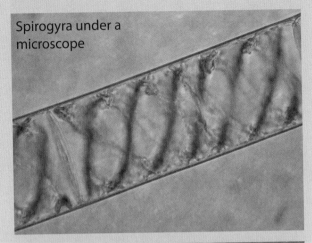

Spirogyra under a microscope

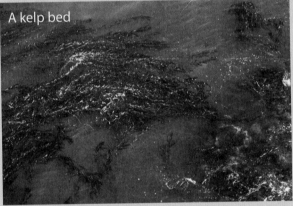

A kelp bed

to grow bacteria in the laboratory.

As you can see, in addition to producing the majority of the oxygen in the world, algae are very useful in many commercial applications. You can view algae yourself if you have a microscope.

Purpose: To examine pond water for algae

Materials: pond water, microscope

Procedure:

1. Obtain a sample of pond water and examine it with a microscope. You will likely find several types of algae,

but you are almost certain to see spirogyra, which are easily recognizable by their long green chains.

2. Draw pictures of any algae that you see and try to identify them.

34

Fungi

Are these really plants?

Are fungi plants?

Words to know:

fungi

What makes an organism a plant? The accepted definition of a plant is something that can create its own food through photosynthesis and has the tissues to make roots, stems, and leaves. By this definition, fungi are not plants. **Fungi** are classified in their own kingdom and include mushrooms, toadstools, molds, yeasts, and mildews.

Because fungi do not have chlorophyll, they must take nutrients from other plants or animals and convert them into food. Most fungi reproduce by spores or by budding.

Many fungi can be harmful. Many are poisonous. You must be especially careful when eating

mushrooms. Never eat wild mushrooms or mushrooms that come from someplace other than a food store as they may cause serious illness or even death. Some fungi spoil our food. Have you ever grabbed a loaf of bread or a bag of bagels from your cupboard only to find that mold was growing on the food? Some fungi cause diseases such as athlete's foot. And others, such as corn smut, damage crops.

Fun Fact

The ancient Egyptians are believed to be the first civilization to use yeast to make their bread rise. Aren't you glad they did? Otherwise, we might not have all those great sandwiches and bread rolls.

As bad as some of these fungi are, there are many more fungi that are useful to people. Some mushrooms are good for food. Yeast is used to make our bread fluffy. Some molds are used to make medicine and save people's lives. Other molds are used to give cheeses their unique flavors. Finally, fungi aid in the decay of dead plants and animals. Without fungi and bacteria to aid in the decaying process, the world would soon be filled with dead plants and animals.

 # What did we learn?

- Why are fungi not considered plants and given their own kingdom?

- What are some good uses for fungi?

 # Taking it further

- What other conditions might affect mold growth other than those tested here?

- How can you keep your bread from becoming moldy?

 ## Grow that mold

Purpose: To better understand the conditions that foster mold growth

Materials: six pieces of bread (homemade bread or bread without preservatives works best), three plastic sandwich bags, "Mold Data Sheet."

Procedure:

1. Place one slice of bread in each of the 3 sandwich bags and seal the bags.

2. Place one slice of bread without a bag and one slice in a bag in a warm dry area such as a cupboard in the kitchen.

3. Place one slice of bread without a bag and one slice in a bag in a cold area such as the refrigerator.

4. Place the remaining slices in a moist area such as a bathroom.

5. Now, make a hypothesis (an educated guess) about which slices you expect to see mold grow on. What

are the reasons for your hypothesis? Write your hypothesis at the top of the "Mold Data Sheet."

6. Observe each slice of bread once a day for several days until you see significant mold growth. Write your observations on the "Mold Data Sheet" each day.

7. After several days, review the hypothesis and see if you got the results you expected. Why was your hypothesis correct or incorrect?

Spore print

Mushrooms reproduce by spores. The spores are produced in the cap of the mushroom. You can view these spores if you make a spore print. It is fun and interesting to make spore prints.

Purpose: To observe the spores produced by a mushroom.

Materials: fresh mushroom, knife, index card, hair spray

Procedure:

1. Cut the stem of the mushroom off and place the cap on an index card in a location that it will not be disturbed.

2. Leave the mushroom on the card overnight.

3. The next day, carefully remove the cap from the card. You will see the pattern of the ribs inside the cap. This pattern is made by the spores from inside the mushroom cap.

4. Carefully spray a light coat of aerosol hair spray over the print to preserve it. After the hair spray dries, you can pick up the card and examine the print in more detail.

Unusual Plants

Conclusion

Appreciating the world of plants

Thank God for plants.

God has created a wonderful world of plants. We look around us, and everywhere we see flowers, trees, bushes, and grass. When we eat, we are aware of God's provision as we see all of the fruits, vegetables, and grains that are available to eat everyday. Plants provides food, shelter, and clothing for us. Plants clean the air by recycling our exhaled carbon dioxide, and through photosynthesis they make food and produce oxygen. Thank God today for the wonderful world of plants!

Write a poem to express your wonder at God's design for the world of plants.

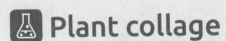

Plant collage

Purpose: To make a plant collage

Materials: dried leaves, flowers, grass, twigs, seeds, seed pods, cones, bark, etc.

Procedure:

1. Glue the plant materials to a piece of tag board and make a beautiful picture to remind you of God's wonderful world of plants.

World of Plants — Glossary

Adventitious roots   Roots that grow in unexpected places or in unexpected ways

Aerial roots   Roots that take water from the air

Aggregate fruit   Formed from one flower with multiple pistils and ovaries

Algae   Plantlike organisms that often live in the water; Kingdom Protista

Alternate leaf arrangement   One leaf grows from each node on alternating sides of the stem

Anatomy   The study of the human body

Angiosperm   Plant that reproduces with flowers, fruit, and seeds

Annual   Plant that completes life cycle in one growing season

Anther   Part of the stamen that produces pollen

Axillary bud/Lateral bud   Bud growing from side of stem

Bark   Dead, hardened epidermis cells in woody stems

Biennial   Plant that completes life cycle in two growing seasons

Binomial classification   Two-name system of classification developed by Carl Linnaeus

Botany   The study of plants

Cambium cells   Cells that divide to produce more xylem and phloem

Carnivorous   Meat eating

Catalyst   Substance that speeds up a chemical reaction

Cell   Smallest unit of an organism that can survive on its own

Cell membrane   Outer coating or "skin" of a cell

Cell wall   Rigid outermost layer of a plant cell

Cereal grass   Grains such as wheat and oats

Chlorophyll   Green substance in chloroplasts that makes photosynthesis possible

Chloroplast   Part of a cell that transforms sunlight into food (glucose)

Conifer   Plant that reproduces with seeds in cones

Cotyledon   Food stored in seed to supply nourishment to new plant

Cross-pollination   Flower is pollinated with pollen from another plant

Cuticle   Top layer of epidermis

Cytoplasm   Liquid that fills a cell

Deciduous   Trees that lose their leaves in the winter

Diatoms   Yellow algae with silica in their cell walls

Dicot   Seed with two cotyledons

Disperse/Dispersal   Movement of seed away from parent plant

Dormant   A condition in which the seed in inactive or "asleep"

Embryo   "Baby" plant inside a seed

Endosperm   Additional nutrients absorbed by cotyledon during germination of monocots

Epidermis   Outer layer of cells in a young stem

Evergreen   Trees that do not lose their leaves in the winter

Fibrous roots   Roots spread out in many directions

Filament   Stalk of the stamen that supports the anther

Flowers   Organs that produce fruits and seeds for reproduction

Forage grass   Taller grass eaten by grazing animals

Fronds   "Leaves" of a fern

Fruit   Ripened ovary

Fungi   Organisms that cannot make their own food including mushrooms and yeast; Kingdom Fungi

Geotropism   The ability to sense up and down, response to gravity

Germinate   When seeds begin to grow

Guard cells   Cells which open and close the stomata

Gymnosperm   Plant that reproduces with cones and seeds

Haustoria   Shoots sent from parasitic roots to tap into another plant's roots

Heartwood   Dead xylem cells in center of tree that no longer transport materials

Heliotropism/Phototropism   The ability to sense light; response to light

Herbaceous plants   Plants with bendable stems

Hilum   Location on seed where it was attached to the ovary of the plant

Host   Plant from which a parasite takes nutrients

Hydrotropism   The ability to sense water, response to water

Internode   Stem between two nodes

Kingdom   Group of living things that have broad common characteristics

Leaves   Organs that manufacture food for the plant

Mitochondria   Part of a cell that breaks down food into energy

Monocot   Seed with one cotyledon

Multiple fruit   Formed when several flowers form fruit that fuse together

Nectar   Sweet liquid that attracts pollinators

Node   Point where leaf attaches to stem

Nucleus   Control center or "brain" of a cell

Opposite leaf arrangement   Two leaves grow on opposite sides of the stem from one node

Organ   A group of tissues working together to perform a function

Ornamental grass   Very tall grass used for landscaping

Ovary   Part of the pistil that produces the ovules

Ovule   Unfertilized seed, egg

Palmate   Palm-like venation

Parasite   Plant that gains nutrients by tapping into and taking them from other plants

Parasitic roots   Roots that tap into another plant's roots to steal nutrients and water

Passenger plant   Attached to other plants but does not harm them

Perennial   Plant that grows year after year

Petal   Part of the flower that attracts pollinators—often brightly colored and scented

Petiole   The part of the leaf that attaches to the stem

Phloem   Tubes that transport food from leaves back down to the roots

Photosynthesis   Process that changes light, water, and carbon dioxide into sugar and oxygen

Phylum, class, order, family, genus, species   Different levels of how living things in a kingdom are divided into groups by common characteristics

Pinnate   Feather-like venation

Pistil   Female part of the flower—contains ovules

Pistillate   Flower that produces only pistils

Plumule   Part of embryo which develops into the stem and leaves

Pneumatophore   Roots that grow above ground to absorb oxygen from the air

Pollen   Fine powder needed for reproduction

Pollination   Uniting of pollen with an ovule

Pollinator   Animal that distributes pollen

Primary consumers   Animals that eat plants

Prop roots   Roots growing out from the side of a stem then into the ground to provide stability

Radicle   Part of the embryo which develops into the roots

Respiration   Exchange of oxygen and carbon dioxide in living cells

Rhizomes   Special underground stems that grow horizontally

Root cap   Covering that protects tip of root

Roots   Organs that anchor plants and absorb water and nutrients

Rosette leaf arrangement   Leaves grow from the bottom of the stem

Sapwood   Area of stem with active xylem and phloem cells

Secondary consumers   Animals that eat the primary consumers

Seed coat   Protective covering on outside of seed

Self-pollination   Flower is pollinated with pollen from the same plant

Sepal   Part of the flower that protects the developing flower

Shoot   New stem growth

Simple fruit   Formed from one flower with one pistil and one ovary

Spores   Reproductive organs of non-flowering plants

Stamen   Male part of the flower—produces pollen

Staminate   Flower that produces only stamens

Stems   Organs that hold up plants and provide their basic shape

Stigma   Part of the pistil that receives the pollen

Stolons/Runners   Special stems that produce new plants

Stomata   Holes on the underside of a leaf

Style   Stalk of the pistil that supports the stigma

Succulents   Plants that have the ability to store large amounts of water

Taproot   One large central root with many smaller roots branching out

Taxonomy   Method of classifying living things

Tendrils   Special stems that grab onto things

Terminal bud   Bud at the end of a stem

Thorns   Special stems for protection

Tissue   Group of cells working together to perform a function

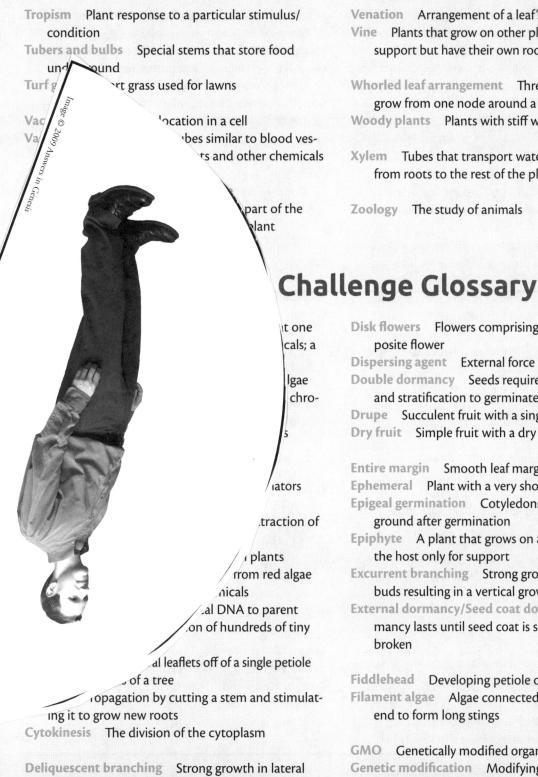

Tropism   Plant response to a particular stimulus/
   condition
Tubers and bulbs   Special stems that store food
   und... round
Turf g...   ...rt grass used for lawns

Vac...   ...ocation in a cell
Va...   ...bes similar to blood ves-
   ...ts and other chemicals

...part of the
...lant

...t one
...cals; a

...lgae
...chro-

...iators

...traction of

...plants
...rom red algae
...nicals
...al DNA to parent
...on of hundreds of tiny

...al leaflets off of a single petiole
...s of a tree
...opagation by cutting a stem and stimulating it to grow new roots
Cytokinesis   The division of the cytoplasm

Deliquescent branching   Strong growth in lateral
   buds resulting in horizontal growth habit
Dichotomous key   Chart presenting two options at
   each level for classification
Diffusion   Movement of molecules from an area
   of higher concentration to an area of lower
   concentration

Venation   Arrangement of a leaf's veins
Vine   Plants that grow on other plants or structures for
   support but have their own root systems

Whorled leaf arrangement   Three or more leaves
   grow from one node around a stem
Woody plants   Plants with stiff woody stems

Xylem   Tubes that transport water and nutrients
   from roots to the rest of the plant

Zoology   The study of animals

Challenge Glossary

Disk flowers   Flowers comprising the head of a com-
   posite flower
Dispersing agent   External force aiding in dispersal
Double dormancy   Seeds require both scarification
   and stratification to germinate
Drupe   Succulent fruit with a single hard seed
Dry fruit   Simple fruit with a dry outer layer

Entire margin   Smooth leaf margin
Ephemeral   Plant with a very short life cycle
Epigeal germination   Cotyledons move above
   ground after germination
Epiphyte   A plant that grows on another plant using
   the host only for support
Excurrent branching   Strong growth in terminal
   buds resulting in a vertical growth habit
External dormancy/Seed coat dormancy   Dormancy lasts until seed coat is softened and/or
   broken

Fiddlehead   Developing petiole of a fern frond
Filament algae   Algae connected together end to
   end to form long stings

GMO   Genetically modified organism
Genetic modification   Modifying a plant's genes to
   obtain desired results
Glucose   Sugar produced in photosynthesis
Grafting   Propagation by combining a bud onto a
   rootstock.
Grain   Dry fruit of the grass family
Growth habit   Way the branches of a tree grow; a
   tree's shape

Head Center of a composite flower

Hypogeal germination Cotyledons remain below ground after germination

Internal dormancy/Embryo dormancy Dormancy lasts until certain temperature or moisture requirements are met

Law of biogenesis Life can only come from life

Leaf margin The edge of a leaf

Legume Dry fruit with a pod around the seeds

Lobed margin Deeply indented leaf margin

Meiosis Cell division that results in reproductive cells

Metaphase Second phase of mitosis in which the chromosomes line up in the middle of the cell

Mitosis/Fission Cell division resulting in two daughter cells identical to the original cell

Nectar/Pollen guide Markings on flowers to direct pollinators to the nectar

Negative tropism Movement away from the stimulus

Nut Dry fruit with hard outer shell

Osmosis Diffusion through a membrane

Peat Layers of decaying peat moss

Pome Succulent fruit with a papery core around the seeds

Positive tropism Movement toward the stimulus

Primary growth Growth that results in longer roots, stems, etc.

Prophase First phase of mitosis in which the nuclear envelope dissolves

Ray flowers Flowers that look like petals on a composite flower

Receptacle Where the flower attaches to the stem

Root hairs Tube-like projections on roots that are responsible for absorbing most of the water

Rootstock Root and stem grown specifically for grafting

Scarification Actions that result in breaking of seed coat

Scion Stem or bud that is grafted onto a rootstock

Secondary growth Growth that results in thicker roots, stems, etc.

Seed dormancy Seeds will not germinate because certain conditions have not been met

Simple leaf Only one leaf per petiole

Spines Needle-like leaves designed to conserve water

Spontaneous generation Belief that animals were suddenly produced by their surroundings

Starch A string of glucose molecules linked together

Stratification Seeds experience an extended period of cold temperature

Succulent fruit Simple fruit with a thick fleshy outer layer

Succulent leaves Fleshy leaves that store water

Sucrose More complex sugar formed by combining two glucose molecules

Telophase Final phase of mitosis in which nuclear envelopes develop around the chromosomes and cell divides into two separate cells

Thermotropism Response to changes in temperature

Thigmotropism Response to touch

Toothed margin Jagged leaf margin

Transpiration Evaporation of water from plants

Vascular bundles Groups or bundles of xylem and phloem

Xanthophyll Yellow pigment in plants

Zone of cell division Region where cells are actively dividing

Zone of differentiation/Zone of maturation Region where cells line up to form vascular tissue

Zone of elongation Region of root that lengthens due to lengthening of cells

The Human Body

UNIT 1

Body Overview

1 The Creation of Life

2 Overview of the Human Body

3 Cells, Tissues, & Organs

◊ **Describe** the function of the major organ systems in the human body.

◊ **Explain** how cells, tissues, organs, and systems are related.

The Creation of Life

God created them male and female.

How is man different from the rest of the creatures God created?

After God created the Earth, plants, sun, moon, stars, and animals, He created man. God spoke the entire universe into existence, but He made man out of the dust of the ground with His own hands and breathed life into his body. God created man to be His companion and friend. The special relationship that man has with God is unique in all of creation.

God also made a woman for man so he would not be alone on the Earth. God made woman from a rib taken from the side of man, and together He charged them with caring for the world He had created.

God gave man and woman wonderful bodies. It has taken scientists thousands of years to even begin to understand the complexity of the human body. Even today, with all of the technology available to us, we have only a small understanding of how everything in the human body really works.

As you study the lessons in this book and learn more about how your body was designed and how it works, remember that God made you special. God wants you to have a relationship with Him.

🧠 What did we learn?

- On which day of creation did God make man?
- In whose image did God create man?
- According to Genesis 1:26, over what were man and woman to rule?

🚀 Taking it further

- Since we are created in God's image, how should we treat our bodies?

Fun Fact

There are over 7 billion people alive on the Earth and each one of them is unique and created in God's image.

Self-portrait

Read Genesis 1–2. Discuss how God created humans and why He created them. Then read Psalm 139:13–18. Discuss how God knew each of us even before we were born. Remember that He loves us and has a plan for each of our lives.

Write the words "God Made Me Special" at the top of a sheet of drawing paper. Then using a mirror, try and draw a self portrait.

Body systems

There are eleven recognized systems in the human body. We will be studying eight of those systems in some detail in this book and will briefly look at the other three. On a piece of paper, list as many of the body's systems as you can. Then write a short description of what each system does. Which system do you know the most about? Which system do you know the least about? Which system is the most interesting to you?

Body Overview

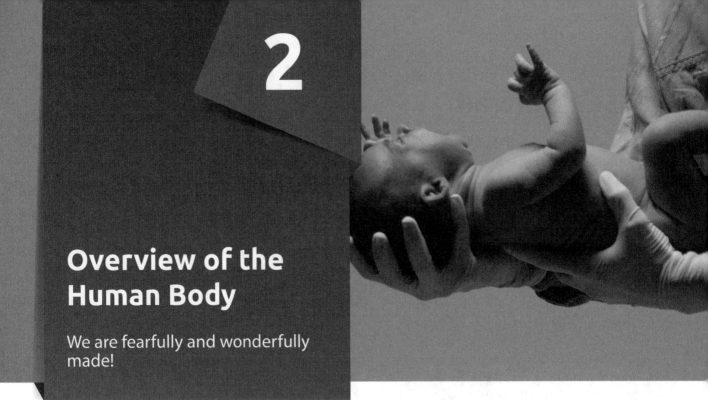

2

Overview of the Human Body

We are fearfully and wonderfully made!

What systems did God give the body to help it accomplish all of the tasks it must perform?

Challenge words:

endocrine system	kidneys
hormone	reproductive system
excretory system	uterus

Perhaps the most amazing of all of God's creations is the human body. It is a complex set of systems all working together. The human body includes systems to move, breathe, eat, think, and feel. These are all wonders of creation. But most animals also have these systems working in their bodies. So what makes people different from animals?

The Bible says that we are created in God's image. We have souls that can relate to God. As we study the wonder of God's creation, remember that we are His handiwork. God designed humans to be very creative like Him. We have been given the ability to think and reason far beyond anything an animal can do. We resemble our Creator and we are separate from the animals.

Some of the remarkable systems that God created for the human body include:

- Skeletal and muscular systems for strength and movement
- Respiratory system for breathing
- Circulatory system for transporting nutrients
- Digestive system for eating
- Nervous system for thinking and feeling
- Skin for protection
- Immune system to fight against disease and other "intruders"

As you learn more about each of these systems, you will marvel at God's creative genius in putting our bodies together.

What did we learn?

- Name as many of the body's systems as you can and describe what each system does.

Taking it further

- Which body systems are used when you walk across a room?

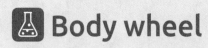

Body wheel

Color each section of the "Body Wheel." Then cut out both circles and connect them with a paper fastener in the center. Turn the top wheel and read the description of each system of the body.

Other systems

Look at the list you made from lesson 1. Did you include all eight of the body systems mentioned in this lesson? If not, add any you missed to your list. You are probably somewhat familiar with these body systems, and we will study each system in more detail throughout the remaining lessons in this book. However, there are three other systems that are also important to your body that you might not be as familiar with. We will look at these three systems briefly here. If you want to learn more about these systems, you can study an anatomy book or look in a high school biology book

First is the endocrine system. The endocrine system produces chemical messengers called hormones. These chemicals are produced in special glands and are then secreted into the blood. Hormones control many functions in your body including growth, heart rate, the rate of digestion, waking, and sleeping. You don't have to think about these things. God designed your body to automatically regulate these functions by producing the necessary chemicals.

The second system is the excretory system. This system was designed to remove wastes from the body. Without this system, poisonous substances would build up in your body and eventually kill you. But God designed our bodies to efficiently remove and eliminate unneeded and harmful substances. The main organs of the excretory system are the kidneys, which remove waste substances from the blood, producing urine, which is then eliminated from the body.

Finally, every person has a reproductive system. One of the first commands God gave to Adam and Eve was to be fruitful and multiply. God loves children and designed the human body to be able to create new life. A man's body is designed so that he can become a father. A woman's body is designed to carry the developing child in her womb, called the uterus, until it is ready to be born and then to nourish the new baby with milk from her body. The creation of a new life is a miraculous process designed by God.

Did you include these systems on your list? These are systems that you might not have thought about. Add these systems to your list and include a brief description of each. Every system of your body is necessary and amazing. Enjoy your study of each system and thank God for His wonderful creation.

Body Overview

Leonardo da Vinci

1452–1519

Artist, inventor, engineer, genius—which was Leonardo? He was all of these. He was born on April 15, 1452, to Ser Piero da Vinci, a young lawyer, and Caterina, a peasant girl. His name meant "Leonardo, from Vinci." It is believed he was a vegetarian throughout his life. In fact, there are stories that he loved animals so much that he would buy caged animals only to let them go. He studied at home, learning reading, writing, and arithmetic.

When Leonardo was young, his father asked him to paint a round shield. The story goes that Leonardo thought it would be neat to paint a really creepy scene on the shield. He examined all sorts of vermin such as lizards, maggots, and bats to use in the painting. When he showed the shield to his father, his father was so impressed with the realism of the animals, that he knew his son could only be an artist.

Leonardo was successful at nearly everything he did. He was reported to be strikingly handsome with great strength. He also had a fine singing voice. He quickly learned to play the lyre, and he would sing and beautifully improvise with it. But good looks, strength, and musical talent were just the beginning. He was most gifted in art and science.

In 1469, at the age of 17, Leonardo and his father moved to Florence, Italy where he worked under the master artist, Verrocchio. It soon became apparent that his skills surpassed that of his teacher's. In 1472 Leonardo joined the painter's guild of Florence where he had contact with many other great Florentine artists. At this time, Leonardo started working for himself. Not only was he doing paintings, he was also sketching water pumps, military weapons, and other machines. One of the more unusual characteristics about Leonardo was that he was not only left-handed, which is not too uncommon, but he wrote many of his papers and works from right to left and backwards. Many of his notes can only be read in a mirror.

In 1482 the Duke of Milan hired Leonardo as a painter and engineer. During his 17 years under the duke, he completed six paintings and worked as an adviser on architecture, fortifications, military matters, hydraulics, and mechanical engineering. In 1489 Leonardo did some of his earliest drawings of human anatomy, and even though most of his drawings were completely wrong, he produced extremely accurate cross-sectional representations of the skull. By 1495 Leonardo felt he had achieved his goal in understanding the human anatomy and he abandoned his work in this area for eight years.

During his time with the duke, Leonardo spent many hours studying geometry. This took time away from his painting. But he wrote a book on the elementary theory of mechanics. It was also during his time under the duke that he started exploring the possibility of constructing a telescope, looked into flying machines, designed advanced weapons, including tanks and other vehicles for war, and designed submarines. During this period, Leonardo achieved new heights of scientific thought.

When the Duke of Milan died, his son wanted Leonardo to make a bronze sculpture of his father on horseback. The sculpture was to be four times bigger than life size and weigh about 80 tons. But this task proved too challenging even for Leonardo. Leonardo studied for years, developing new casting methods, but when the French invaded, he had only been successful in building a 22-foot clay model. He left Florence in 1499 when the French soldiers used the model for target practice.

Leonardo spent the next few years traveling through southern Europe. From 1502 to 1503 he worked as a military engineer for Cesare Borgia. After this, he returned to Florence for three years. It was during this time he painted what is perhaps his most famous work, the "Mona Lisa." In 1504, Leonardo received word of his father's death. His father's estate went to his half brothers and sisters, so he left Florence for Milan only to return the following year to fight for his uncle's estate, which he eventually inherited.

In the winter of 1507–1508 his interest in the human anatomy was revived when he witnessed an old man die. The man claimed to be one hundred years old. The old man told Leonardo before dying that he felt fine, only weaker. Leonardo wanted to know how this man could have such a peaceful death, so he studied this man's anatomy and found an absence of fat. This study allowed Leonardo to complete the most detailed records of a single subject. During his lifetime, Leonardo made hundreds of sketches of the human body.

In 1509 Leonardo returned to Milan and spent time on other scientific studies including a project to change the course of the Abba River. From 1510 to 1513 he concentrated on the study of human

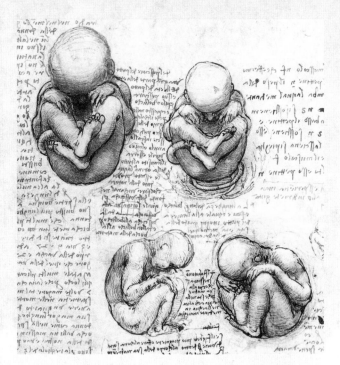

anatomy and developed a new way to do science. The old way was to interpret everything with what you already knew; the new method was to first observe and then see if it fit with what you understood. During this time, Leonardo did some of his most famous anatomical drawings—one of them being the "Embryo in the Womb," which is still found in some medical textbooks today.

In 1513 Leonardo went to Rome under the protection of Giuliano de Medici, the brother of Pope Leo X. He had a workshop and undertook a variety of projects for the Pope. He was also able to continue his studies in human anatomy. However, the Pope would not allow him to dissect any cadavers.

Following the death of Giuliano de Medici, Francis I of France offered Leonardo the position of Premier Painter, Engineer, and Architect of the King. Leonardo accepted the position and went to work for the king of France where he lived in a house near the royal chateau at Amboise. He worked for King Francis until his death, and legend has it that when he died in 1519, King Francis was at his side, cradling Leonardo's head in his arms. Leonardo da Vinci was buried in the cloister of San Fiorentino in Amboise, France. The world will remember him as a painter, architect, engineer, and scientist with one of the brightest minds of the Middle Ages.

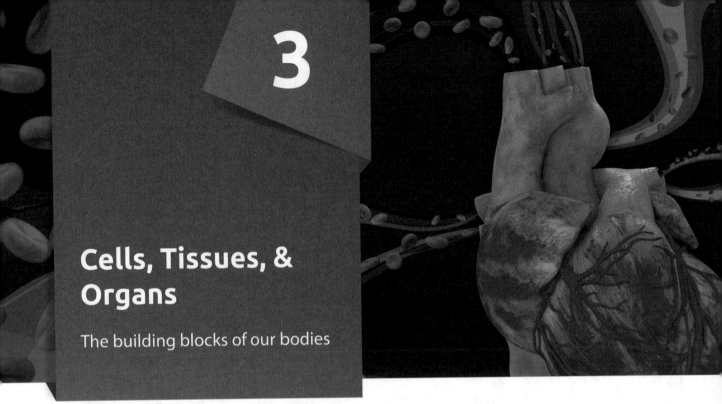

3

Cells, Tissues, & Organs

The building blocks of our bodies

Body Overview

How are organs related to cells?

Words to know:

cell	nucleus
tissue	cytoplasm
organ	mitochondria
cell membrane	vacuole

Challenge words:

muscle tissue	epithelial tissue
nerve tissue	connective tissue

The systems of the human body begin with cells. Cells are the smallest part of the human body that can function on their own. Cells are essentially the building blocks of your body. Many cells working together form a tissue, and many tissues working together form an organ. Each system is comprised of cells, tissues, and organs all working together to perform a certain function.

Although various kinds of cells may look different, they all have some similar features. All cells have a cell membrane, which surrounds and protects the rest of the cell, somewhat like your skin. Also, every cell has a nucleus, which functions as the brain of the cell. Cells are filled with a liquid called cytoplasm, which allows the other parts of the cell to move around inside the cell. All cells have mitochondria, which break down food into energy for the cell. And finally, cells have vacuoles, which store food or any variety of nutrients a cell might need to survive. They even store waste products until the waste can be eliminated from the cell so the rest of the cell is protected from contamination.

Even though all cells have these common characteristics, the cells in each system are specially designed for their jobs. Red blood cells, which move throughout the body inside the blood vessels, are round and smooth. They are shaped like disks, or little lifesavers, so they easily flow over each other and move easily through the blood vessels. Also, their cell membrane is designed to easily allow gases to pass through so oxygen can be released to other parts of the body and carbon dioxide can be absorbed and transported to the lungs where it is removed from the body. White blood cells look like white balls but can change their shape to surround germs that get inside the body. Skin cells are rectangular and fit tightly together to keep germs on the outside and moisture on the inside of the body.

Muscle cells are long and stretchy, allowing them to expand and contract so our bodies can move. Bone cells crisscross to make strong structures. Nerve cells have an irregular shape that includes a cell body and a long part with finger-like tendrils that allows signals to move efficiently throughout the body. This lets the brain "talk" to all parts of the body very quickly. A nerve cell can be over one yard (1 m) long. God designed each cell to look and act differently based on its function in the body.

The cells, or building blocks, work together to make tissues and the tissues work together to make organs such as muscles, lungs, the brain, and your skin. We group these organs together into systems by what they do for us. For example, the heart and blood work together to take oxygen and nutrients to every part of the body, so we group them together and call them the circulatory system. The brain, spinal cord, and all of our nerves work together to communicate messages to the body, so we group them together and call them the nervous system. We will study each system of the human body separately to better understand its function.

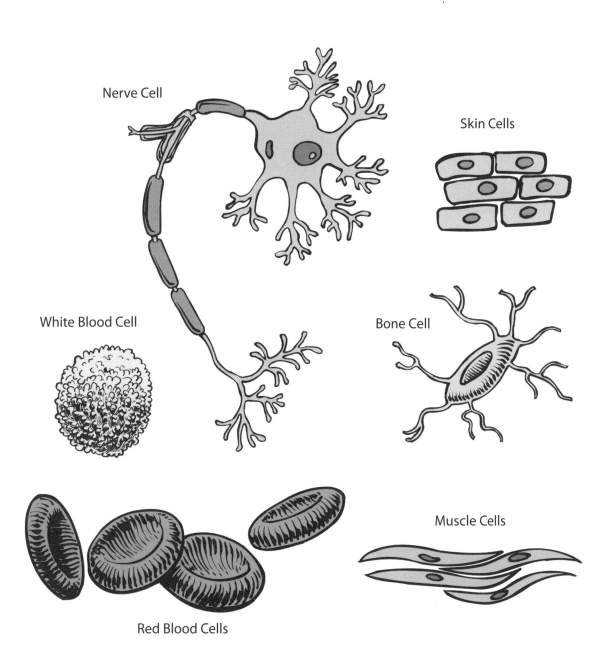

Nerve Cell

Skin Cells

White Blood Cell

Bone Cell

Red Blood Cells

Muscle Cells

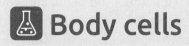 # Body cells

Complete the "Body Cells" worksheet. Use the pictures on the previous page as a guide.

 # What did we learn?

- What is the function of each of the following kinds of cells: skin cells, red blood cells, white blood cells, bone cells, nerve cells, and muscle cells?

 # Taking it further

- How has God uniquely designed red blood cells to transport oxygen?

- How are nerve cells specially designed to carry signals?

- How did God design skin cells to perform their special functions?

- With all these cells working together, what do you think is the largest organ in the body?

Tissue types

The human body contains many organs and tissues. These tissues are classified into four different categories.

- **Muscle tissue** is designed to contract. Its main function is movement. Muscle tissue moves your bones when you decide to move an arm, leg, or other body part. It also moves parts inside your body without you even thinking about it such as making your heart beat or your stomach move to digest your food.

- **Nerve tissue** controls body activities and coordinates functions. Nerves are directly connected to most muscles and send them the necessary signals to make the muscle tissue contract. Your brain is made of nerve tissue, which coordinates all of the input from your body and also allows you to think.

- **Epithelial tissue** lines all of your body parts, both inside and out. Epithelial tissue secretes liquid that lubricates all the parts of your body to reduce friction as your body parts move. It also covers and protects each part of your body.

- **Connective tissue** holds your body together. Many connective tissues are solid; however, blood and lymph are considered connective tissues even though they are liquids because they connect all of the parts of the body together as they circulate throughout the body.

Based on what you just learned about the different kinds of tissues, identify which type of tissue each of the following body parts belongs to. Some of these are tricky so don't be surprised if you get some wrong.

- Skin
- Muscles
- Tendons
- Lining of the mouth
- Brain
- Inside of lungs
- Fat
- Bones

UNIT 2

Bones & Muscles

4 The Skeletal System

5 Names of Bones

6 Types of Bones

7 Joints

8 The Muscular System

9 Different Types of Muscles

10 Hands & Feet

◊ **Identify** the major bones of the body.

◊ **Describe** the relationship between muscles and bones.

◊ **Distinguish** between voluntary and involuntary muscles.

The Skeletal System

Structure and strength

What allows bones to move?

Words to know:

skeletal system   tendon

muscular system   cartilage

Challenge words:

axial skeleton   appendicular skeleton

What gives the human body its strength, shape, and form? Two systems work together to do this: the skeletal and muscular systems. The skeletal system gives the body strength and determines its general size and shape. The muscular system helps the bones to move and gives us our general appearance.

Fun Fact

Babies actually have more bones than adults. The bones in a baby's head are not fused like they are in an adult. This allows for easier birth. As the child grows, the bones grow and fuse together, so an adult actually has fewer separate bones than a newborn baby.

The adult human body has 206 bones. Eighty bones are in the head, ribs, and spine; sixty bones are in the hands and feet; sixty bones are in the legs and arms; four bones make up the shoulder girdle; and two bones make up the pelvic girdle. Bones are made mostly from calcium and make up approximately 20% of your body weight. Bones are very strong—as strong as reinforced concrete!

Bones provide structure and strength to your body. They also provide protection. Your ribs surround your

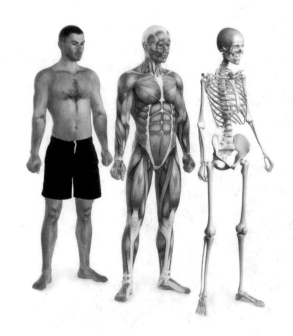

heart, lungs, and other internal organs and protect them from injury. But bones do much more than this. They also produce blood cells. About 2 million red blood cells are made inside your bones every second! White blood cells, stem cells, and lymph cells are also produced in the center of your long bones by a substance called bone marrow. Also, bones are an important storage facility for calcium and phosphorus, two chemicals which your body uses to make new tissues.

Bones are connected to muscles by cord-like structures called tendons. This allows the muscles to move the bones when the muscles contract. Cartilage is a smooth material, which forms a cushion between bones where they meet so they do not rub against each other. Cartilage also connects the ribs to the sternum, which is the vertical bone in the center of your chest. Without your skeletal system, you would be a squishy lump or just a bag of flesh that is unable to move.

What did we learn?

- What are three jobs that bones perform?
- How are muscles connected to bones?
- What keeps bones from rubbing against each other at the joints?
- How many bones does an adult human have?
- What is the main mineral in bones?

Taking it further

- What do you think is the largest bone in the body?
- Why does this bone need to be so large?
- What do you think are the smallest bones in the body?

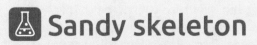 Sandy skeleton

Cut out and assemble "Sandy Skeleton." It is not necessary for younger children to cut exactly on the lines in order to put the skeleton together.

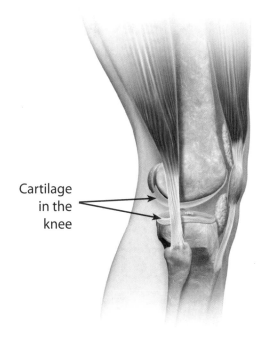

Cartilage in the knee

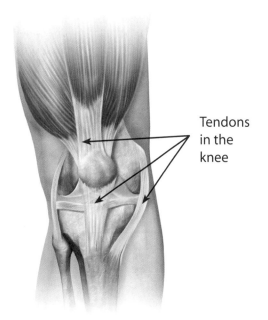

Tendons in the knee

① Your skeleton

The skeletal system is divided into two broad categories called the axial skeleton and the appendicular skeleton.

The appendicular skeleton consists of all the bones in your arms, legs, hips, shoulders, hands, and feet. These are the bones that provide strength, form, and mobility. There are 126 bones in the appendicular skeleton.

The axial skeleton consists of all the bones in the skull, face, neck, spine, sternum, and ribs. These are the bones that are generally in the center part of your body. The axial skeleton provides protection to all your vital organs such as your brain, heart, and lungs. There are 80 bones in the axial skeleton.

The bones in your spine are called vertebrae and between each vertebra there is a cushioning pad made of cartilage. As you sleep at night, these cartilage pads absorb a small amount of water. This causes your spine to expand slightly. But as you walk around all day, gravity pulls down on your body and some of the water is squeezed out of the cartilage pads and they compress. This means that you are probably slightly shorter at night than you are first thing in the morning. Test this to find out how much your height changes. Carefully measure your height first thing in the morning. Then, measure your height again just before you go to bed and see if you notice a difference.

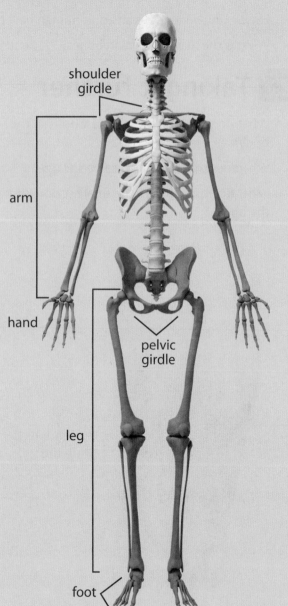

shoulder girdle

arm

hand

pelvic girdle

leg

foot

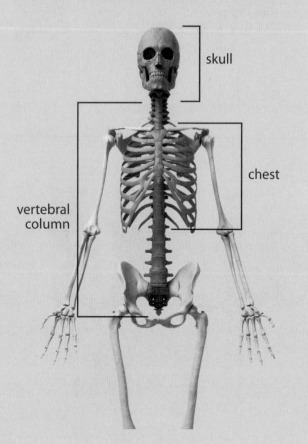

skull

chest

vertebral column

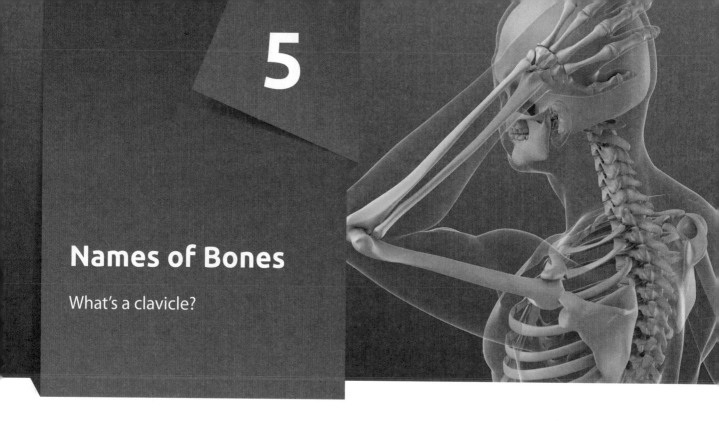

5

Names of Bones

What's a clavicle?

Bones & Muscles

How many bones in your body can you name?

Words to know:

cranium	incus
vertebrae	stapes
mandible	ulna
clavicle	radius
phalanges	humerus
patella	femur
sternum	fibula
carpals	tibia
metacarpals	scapula
malleus	

Many of the bones in our bodies have familiar names and others seem peculiar. It is fun to learn the names of the bones in the body, and it is important. Knowing the names of bones will help you better understand and appreciate what your bones do. Look at the diagram on the next page, and locate the bones mentioned below as you read about them.

Your skull is called your cranium. The bones in your spine are called vertebrae. Your mandible is your jawbone. Your clavicle is also called your collarbone. Phalanges are the bones in your fingers and toes. Your patella is your kneecap. The sternum is the vertical bone in the middle of your chest that is connected to some of your ribs. Carpals and metacarpals can be found in your hands and wrists, while the malleus, incus, and stapes (also called the hammer, anvil, and stirrup) are found in your ear. The ulna, radius, and humerus are your arm bones and the femur, fibula, and tibia are your leg bones. Finally, your shoulder blades are called scapulas. Did you find all of these bones in the diagram?

If you can remember the names of these bones, you will know most of the major bones in your body. Use the diagram to review the names of these bones every day until you have them memorized.

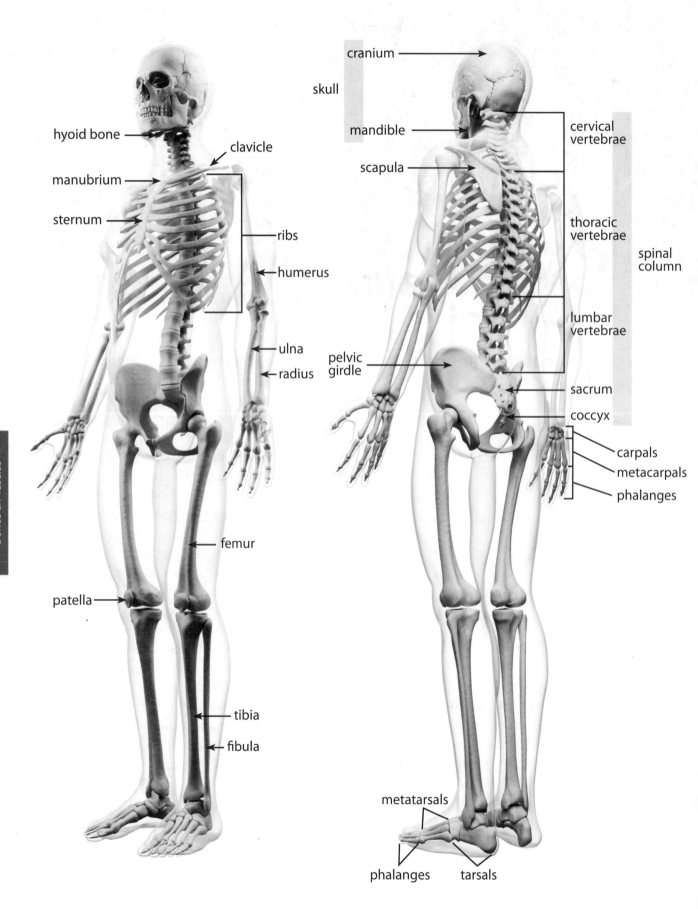

hyoid bone

clavicle

manubrium

sternum

ribs

humerus

ulna

radius

femur

patella

tibia

fibula

cranium

skull

mandible

scapula

cervical vertebrae

thoracic vertebrae

spinal column

lumbar vertebrae

pelvic girdle

sacrum

coccyx

carpals

metacarpals

phalanges

metatarsals

phalanges

tarsals

Bones & Muscles

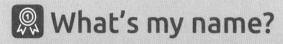

Label those bones

Put on a swimming suit and write the names of bones where they are located on your body with a washable gel pen. You can write many of the names on yourself or you can write on a friend or sibling and let them write on you.

If a washable gel pen is not available, you can write the names on sticky notes and stick them on your body.

After you are done labeling your bones, make up a bone rap or song.

You can also use some of these sayings to help you remember the names of some of your bones:

- If you bump your head you can crack your cranium.

- Your humerus is just above your funny bone.

- The patella caps off your knee.

- Put your hand on your jaw to "handible" your mandible.

- I keep my lungs in a cage: my rib cage.

Now make up your own sayings to help you remember the names of other bones.

What's my name?

Complete the "What's My Name?" worksheet.

What did we learn?

- Review the names of the bones by pointing to each bone as you name it.

- Is your cranium above or below your mandible?

- What is moving if you wiggle your phalanges?

Taking it further

- What happens if you cross your legs and gently hit just below your patella?

- Why do we have Latin names for body parts?

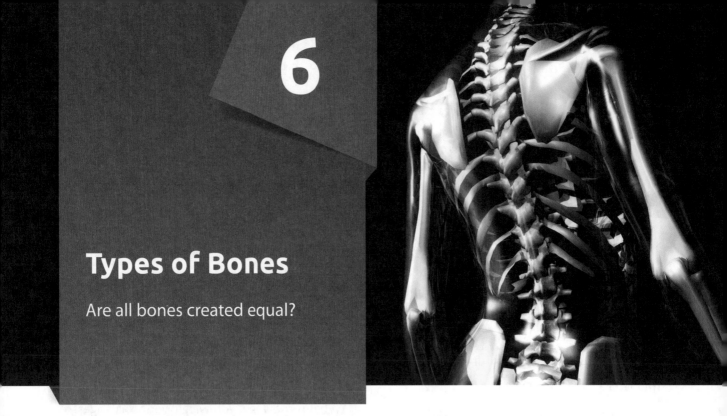

Types of Bones

Are all bones created equal?

Bones & Muscles

How is a rib different from a femur?

Words to know:

short bones   flat bones

long bones   irregular bones

Challenge words:

fracture   compound fracture

simple fracture   collagen

Bones are classified into four basic types according to their shapes. There are long bones, short bones, flat bones, and irregular bones. Leg and arm bones are examples of long bones. These are the bones that give you your height and bear most of your weight. Also, long bones are factories for new red blood cells that are produced in the marrow in the center of the bones. Approximately 2 million red blood cells are produced each second inside the long bones. Long bones also produce many of the white blood cells and platelets in your blood (we'll learn about these in lesson 26).

Short bones are roughly cube-shaped and are located in the wrists/hands and ankes/feet. They give us dexterity and flexibility in walking and allow us to do most of the functions we do each day. Short bones include carpals and metacarpals, as well as tarsals and metatarsals. The phalanges (our finger and toe bones) are actually classified as long bones even though they are fairly short.

Flat bones include the shoulder blades (scapula), skull (cranium), ribs, and pelvis. Their primary function is the protection of vital organs. These bones protect the brain, heart, lungs, and other internal organs.

All other bones are irregular bones because they all have different shapes. Some of the irregular bones include the vertebrae and facial bones. The vertebrae are round bones that are hollow in the center. Their primary function is to protect the spinal cord. There are 26 individual bones stacked on top of each other in a curved column. This design allows us to easily bend and move in many different ways.

Fun Fact

Humans and giraffes have the same number of bones in their necks. A giraffe's neck vertebrae are just much, much longer.

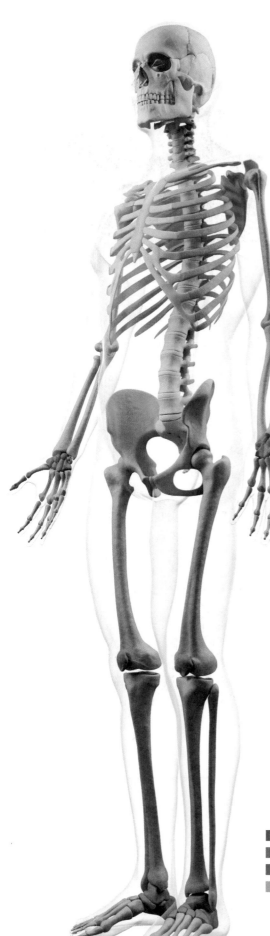

Facial bones give our faces form and structure. Along with the facial muscles and fat, these bones help people identify you as the unique person you are.

Each type of bone has a special function and performs in a way to make the human body one of God's greatest creations.

What did we learn?

- Which bones are designed mainly for protection of internal organs?
- Which type of bones helps determine what your face will look like?
- Which type of bones works closely with your circulatory system to replace old blood cells?

Taking it further

- Why are the long bones filled with marrow and not solid?
- What is the advantage of having so many small bones in your hands?

Simon says

Review the names of the bones you have learned by labeling the bones on Sandy Skeleton. Then take turns playing "Simon Says" with someone, asking each other to point to specific bones using their scientific names.

■ Long bones
■ Short bones
■ Flat bones
■ Irregular bones

🏅 Broken bones

Bones are very strong—stronger than reinforced concrete. But sometimes an unusual force can cause a bone to break. A break in a bone is called a fracture. Most broken bones are classified as simple fractures. This means that the bones remain inside the body after they are broken. However, occasionally the broken bone will pierce the skin. This is classified as a compound fracture.

When a bone breaks, the parts must be realigned and held in place while the fracture heals. God designed bones so that they are very efficient at repairing themselves. Some cells clot the broken blood vessels right away to control bleeding. Then new blood vessels form quickly to supply the area with nutrients and raw materials for constructing new bone.

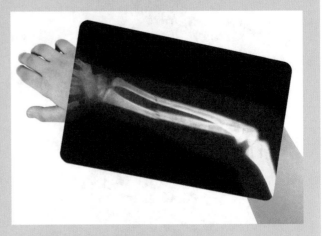

Next, special bone cells fill in the break with cartilage. This cartilage is slowly replaced with new bone cells. This process can take several weeks, but once it is complete, the bone may actually be stronger than it was before the break.

Purpose: To understand what gives bones their strength

Materials: two cleaned chicken leg bones, cup, vinegar

Procedure:

1. Place one chicken leg bone in a cup and cover it with vinegar. What do you see happening?

2. Cover the cup so the vinegar does not evaporate.

3. Set the second bone next to the cup in the open air.

4. After three or four days, compare the bones. The bone that was not in the vinegar should be very dry.

5. Try to break the bone that was in the air. It should break easily. Examine the break. Try to place the bone back together. What would have to happen to repair the break? God has designed chicken bodies to be able to repair broken bones too.

6. Now examine the bone from the vinegar. How does it feel?

7. Try to break this bone. What happened?

Conclusion: The bone that was in the vinegar should be very flexible and should bend but not break. The vinegar has chemically reacted with the calcium in the bone leaving behind only the collagen. Collagen is a flexible protein that builds the structure of the bone. Without the calcium, however, the bone is not strong. Your bones need calcium, too, so it is important to eat foods with calcium so your bones will be strong. A few foods that contain a lot of calcium are milk, cheese, soy products, beans, almonds, and orange juice.

Bones & Muscles

Joints

Connections are important

How is your knee similar to a door?

Words to know:

hinge joint

ball and socket joint

pivot joint

ellipsoid joint

saddle joint

gliding joint

Challenge words:

ligament

synovial fluid

All the bones in your body are connected together at joints. Different types of joints provide different movement. A few joints in the cranium are immovable and some joints, such as the vertebrae, are only slightly moveable. But most joints are freely moveable. This is what makes the body so flexible and allows humans to do so much.

There are six types of joints found in the body.

- **Hinge joint**: Knees and the middle and end joints of your fingers are hinge joints. They can move in one plane, or back and forth, only.

- **Ball and socket joint**: Hips and shoulders are ball and socket joints. They can move in two planes which means they can rotate in place.

- **Pivot joint**: Your neck is a pivot joint. This means it rotates around a fixed point.

- **Ellipsoid joint**: You find ellipsoid joints where fingers connect to the hand. These joints move in two directions without rotating. Your fingers

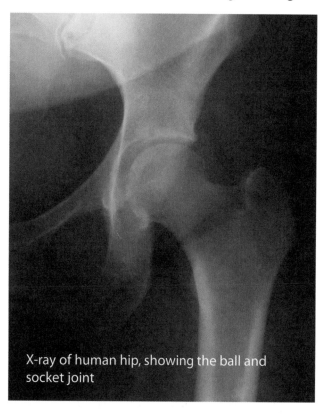

X-ray of human hip, showing the ball and socket joint

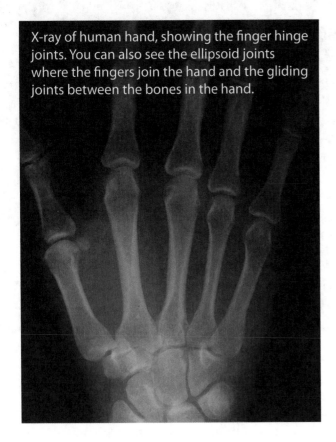

X-ray of human hand, showing the finger hinge joints. You can also see the ellipsoid joints where the fingers join the hand and the gliding joints between the bones in the hand.

in two directions but the joint is shaped like a horse's saddle, giving it more flexibility than your fingers.

- **Gliding joint**: Hand bones form gliding joints. One bone slips or glides over another.

God designed each joint for its specific function. He did not create fingers that can turn in any direction because fingers would not work as well that way. It would be harder to pick things up if fingers bent backwards. But God designed your shoulders to move in nearly every direction so you could reach all the things you need to reach, including that itch in the middle of your back.

can move up and down and side to side but cannot rotate.

- **Saddle joint**: Where your thumb connects to your hand is a saddle joint. Your thumb moves

🧠 What did we learn?

- What was the most common joint found around your house?

🚀 Taking it further

- Which came first, the joints in the body or the joints in your house?
- Why do you need so many different kinds of joints in your body?

Scavenger hunt

Search your house for examples of different types of joints. Try and identify the different types of joints you find.

Examples could be:

- door hinges
- sliding doors
- joints in pets
- LEGO® pieces
- nut crackers
- pliers, or other tools

This list is just to get you started. You will be amazed at how many different joints there are around your house.

🏅 Amazing joints

A joint is much more than just the point where two bones come together. In order for a joint to work properly, the bones must be held in place, yet be able to move freely. This sounds like an impossible task, yet God designed strong flexible cords called ligaments to hold the bones in place while allowing them to move within the joint.

Also, the bones cannot rub against each other when they move, or they would quickly wear out. To prevent this, the ends of bones are covered with a slippery substance called cartilage. Cartilage is tough but allows the bones to slide easily. The cartilage is also coated with a slippery fluid that keeps things moving smoothly. This substance is called synovial fluid. The ligaments completely encase the joint, which not only holds the bones in place, but also holds the synovial fluid inside the joint. All of these things work together to hold the bones together.

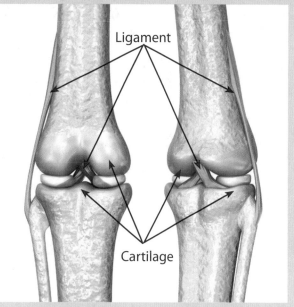

Illustration of a human knee showing the cartilage and ligaments.

Purpose: To build a model joint

Materials: two wooden pencils, rubber bands, tacks

Procedure:

1. Place two wooden pencils end to end. These represent two bones.

2. Place a rubber band lengthwise across the "joint" where your two "bones" come together. Stretch it slightly and use tacks to attach each end to one of the pencils. Rotate the pencils and add another rubber band parallel to the first one. Repeat until you have rubber bands surrounding the joint. The rubber bands are like the ligaments that hold your joints together.

3. See if you can move your pencil joint around and still keep the pencils close together.

Bones & Muscles

8

The Muscular System

Making it move

What pairs of muscles allow you to swing a hammer?

Words to know:

muscular system	trapezius
bicep	gluteus maximus
tricep	diaphragm
pectoral	

Do you like to run and jump? Do you like to play soccer or the piano? Then be glad for your muscular and skeletal systems. The muscular system works together with the skeleton to allow us to move our bodies. The muscles are attached to the bones by cords called tendons. When a muscle contracts, it gets shorter and pulls the bone. For example, to bend your arm, the muscle on the front of your arm above the elbow (called a bicep) contracts, causing your arm to bend.

Fun Fact

It takes more muscles to frown than it does to smile. So smile—it's easier.

But muscles cannot stretch or "uncontract" by themselves. After moving a bone, the muscle relaxes but does not stretch out again. Another muscle on the other side of the bone must contract to move the bone and stretch the first muscle out again. Muscles work together in pairs. There are pairs of muscles in many different locations all over your body allowing you to move in many different directions.

It is important to learn the names of some of the muscles. Some of the more important muscles include biceps and triceps in your upper arm, pectoral muscles in your upper chest, trapezius muscles in your upper back and shoulders, and the gluteus maximus muscles in your rear. One very specialized muscle is the diaphragm below your lungs. This muscle contracts to expand your chest cavity and allow air to enter your lungs.

Look at the diagrams here or in an anatomy book to see where all of these muscles are found in the body. There are also many other muscles in your body that you can learn about as well.

Your muscles make up about 40 percent of your body weight. They are also the part of your body that gives it most of its shape. The muscles in your face, along with a layer of fat, determine what your face looks like. The muscles in your face also help you express feelings by changing the expression on your face.

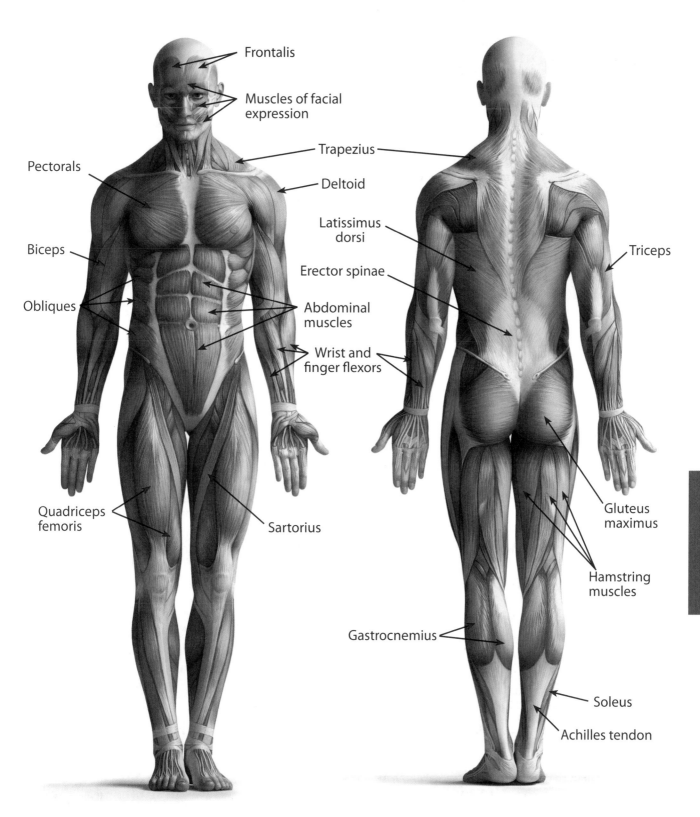

Frontalis

Muscles of facial expression

Trapezius

Deltoid

Latissimus dorsi

Erector spinae

Abdominal muscles

Wrist and finger flexors

Triceps

Pectorals

Biceps

Obliques

Quadriceps femoris

Sartorius

Gluteus maximus

Hamstring muscles

Gastrocnemius

Soleus

Achilles tendon

Bones & Muscles

 What did we learn?

- How does a contracted muscle feel?
- How does a muscle get stretched?

🚀 Taking it further

- How does a muscle know when to contract?
- How does your face express emotion?

Find the pairs

Purpose: To discover muscle pairs on your body

Materials: none

Procedure:

1. Stretch out your left arm and feel the bicep. It should feel long and stretched.

2. Now feel the back side of your arm. Your tricep will feel hard.

3. Next, bend your arm and feel the muscles again. Now the bicep should feel shorter and harder and the tricep should feel long and stretched.

Try to discover as many other pairs of muscles as possible. Try bending your legs, swinging a straight leg, making a fist, and smiling and frowning. Not all muscle pairs are easily identifiable. Smiling and frowning require many muscles, not just a single pair of muscles.

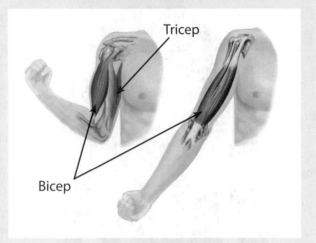

Muscle jobs

You learned in lesson 3 that muscle cells expand and contract. These special cells are what give muscles their strength and flexibility. Each cell contracts when it receives an impulse from the nerve that is attached to it. The cells in most muscle tissue are lined up in parallel rows so they can all contract together in the same direction. This gives muscles a striped appearance.

Many muscles are designed to move bones, but muscles have other jobs too. You probably already know that your heart is a muscle but it was not designed to moves bones; it was designed to move blood. Your heart pumps blood throughout your whole body. However, you may not know that muscles that move bones, such as your leg muscles, also help move the blood in your legs. When your leg muscles contract they squeeze the veins in you legs, helping to push the blood back toward your heart.

You may have heard that exercise is good for your circulation. This is true because the movement of your muscles helps move the blood through the blood vessels.

Other muscles help move your food through your digestive system. Beginning in your throat, down your esophagus, in your stomach, and throughout your intestines, muscles contract and expand to move your latest meal through the digestive process. Finally, muscles in your arms and legs help move lymph fluid throughout your body, in the same way they help move blood. You will learn more about the lymph system in lesson 32.

Use a magnifying glass to closely examine a piece of raw steak. Look for parallel lines of meat. These are the muscle tissues that are lined up parallel to allow the muscles to contract in a strong way.

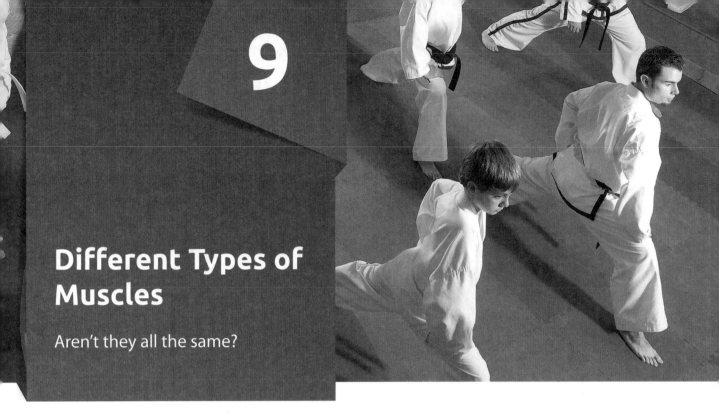

Different Types of Muscles

Aren't they all the same?

9

How are the muscles in your heart different from the muscles in your digestive tract?

Words to know:

voluntary muscles

smooth muscles

involuntary muscles

Challenge words:

striated muscle tissue

smooth muscle tissue

cardiac muscle tissue

The muscles we learned about in the last lesson are ones that move when your brain tells them to. You can decide to make them move and they do. They are called voluntary muscles. But the body has other muscles that move without you having to think about it. These are called involuntary muscles. One of these muscles, your heart, keeps your blood moving around your body. It automatically contracts and relaxes continuously whether you are awake or asleep. Your diaphragm muscle, which expands your chest cavity so you can breathe, is an involuntary muscle that you can also control to a small extent.

Other involuntary muscles are called smooth muscles. These muscles line your digestive tract and automatically move the food through your intestines. Involuntary muscles are vital to keeping you healthy and keeping your body functioning. You have enough to think about without having to think about digesting your food or making your heart beat.

Muscles play such an important part in your body that you need to take good care of them. To have healthy muscles you must eat right and exercise. Muscles are built with nutrients called proteins, so when you eat meat and dried beans, or drink milk, you are giving your body foods that help to build muscle.

It is important to stretch your muscles before you exercise.

Muscles were designed to be used. As we use them, they become larger and stronger. Using muscles every day will keep them healthy. This will give you more energy and endurance for everything you do. Muscles can be torn by too much force or by a sudden force. So it is important to stretch out your muscles and start your exercise slowly so you don't tear your muscles. Take good care of your muscles so they will help you remain strong and healthy.

What did we learn?

- What are the two types of muscles?
- How can we keep our muscles healthy?
- How do your muscles learn?
- What are some advantages of exercising?

Taking it further

- Do you need to exercise your facial muscles?

Muscle memory exercises

Your muscles and your brain work together to help you move and do activities. If you do something over and over again, your brain and your muscles learn to do it very efficiently. Practice the following activities every day for three days. You will notice that your muscles "gain a memory" and improve from the first time to the last time.

Activity 1: Have someone use a stopwatch and time how long you can stand on one foot. You should be able to stand longer each day.

Activity 2: Write your name with the hand you do not normally write with. Do this three times each day. You should see an improvement in your writing after three days.

Activity 3: Hold your arm in front of you with your thumb and pointer finger about ½ inch apart. Have someone hold a yardstick between your fingers with the 0 end lined up with your finger and thumb. When they drop the stick, grab it with your finger and thumb as quickly as possible. Read the number where you grabbed the yardstick. As you practice, you should be able to grab it faster (at a lower number).

Muscle tissue

You learned that there are two different kinds of muscles: voluntary and involuntary. These different types of muscles are made of different types of muscle tissue. Remember how we learned that voluntary muscles have a striped appearance? The tissue that forms voluntary or skeletal muscles is called striated muscle tissue because of this striped appearance. Most muscle tissue is striated tissue.

The heart, however, is made up of special muscle tissue. The heart is composed of cardiac muscle tissue. Cardiac tissue is similar to striated tissue, except that the cardiac muscle cells are specially designed to be able to contract and relax over and over again without becoming tired. The muscles in your legs get tired fairly quickly if you are running or exercising, but cardiac muscle tissue does not get tired, even after years of constant use.

The third type of muscle tissue is smooth muscle tissue. Smooth muscle cells are very different from striated and cardiac muscle cells because they are designed for a different purpose. Smooth muscles were designed to make long, strong contractions rather than relatively short contractions. These long contractions efficiently move food through the digestive system, move blood through blood vessels, and hold your eyelids open. Each type of muscle tissue is very effective for the purposes for which it was designed.

Think about the purpose of each of the muscles listed below. Then decide if they are likely to be made of striated, cardiac, or smooth muscle tissue.

- Diaphragm
- Tongue
- Esophagus
- Mother's womb
- Hand muscle
- Heart

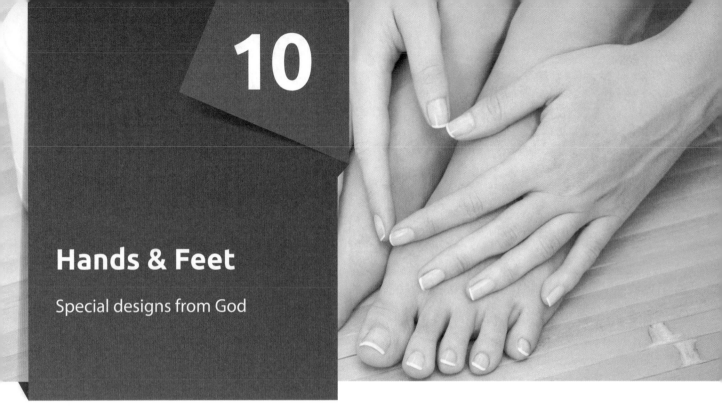

Hands & Feet

Special designs from God

How did God design hands and feet for their unique jobs?

Words to know:

friction skin

God designed each part of the human body for a special purpose. Two of the most amazing parts of the body are our hands and feet. Hands were designed for grasping, holding, and picking things up. In order to move a bite of food to your mouth, you use over 30 joints and 50 muscles. Thumbs make nearly all functions of the hand possible. The use of his hands has allowed man to accomplish the many technological, mechanical, and design marvels that we have today. In addition to having a soul, man's intellect and his ability to build and manipulate things sets him apart from all of God's other creatures.

Hands have the ability to pick up something as small as a pin and as large as we can get our hands around. Your hand can hold something as delicate as a kitten and as hard as a brick. Our hands allow us to play musical instruments, type on a computer keyboard, and scratch an itch. We would be very limited in what we could do if God did not design our hands with so much complexity. Hands have

a much higher concentration of nerves and more joints than any other part of the body, which allows you to do all those fun things.

Feet were designed to support the weight of the body, and to withstand the pounding of walking, running, and jumping. Your feet can distinguish between very small changes in the surface you are walking on. Feet help us to keep our balance and to go wherever

Our hands are designed to hold many different things.

We can have fun using the hands that God gave us.

gripping and walking. Also, fingers and toes all have nails on the ends that help protect them from injury when you bump them.

we want to go. We use our feet for hiking, swimming, and even for tickling. God made our feet tough and sensitive so we could safely navigate our world.

Both hands and feet were designed with special ridged skin called **friction skin** to help with

What did we learn?

- Which is the most important finger?
- Why is the thumb so important?
- What are some special features God gave to hands and feet?

Taking it further

- What activities or jobs require special use of the hands?
- What jobs require special use of the feet?

Design appreciation

Purpose: To appreciate design of your hands and feet

Materials: a helper, pencil, cup

Procedure:

1. Try walking on your hands (get someone to help hold up your legs). How do your hands feel? Could you walk on your hands all day long?

2. Try writing your name by holding the pencil between your toes. How does this work? Why is it easier to write with your fingers than your toes?

3. Try picking up a cup without using your thumb. Now try picking it up again using your thumb and only one of your other fingers. God designed your hand with an opposing thumb—moving in the opposite direction from the fingers—to allow you to grasp objects. You can still do most things without one of your fingers

but without your thumb it is almost impossible to do most activities that require grasping.

4. Try snapping your fingers without using your thumb. You can't do it. Hands and feet are perfectly designed for their functions.

🏅 Right- or left-handed?

People are often asked if they are right-handed or left-handed; however, there is not a clear definition of handedness. When asking this question most people think about which hand they use to write with. However, scientists often use a broader definition such as which hand can perform certain tasks more quickly. Some people define handedness simply as which hand you prefer to use. Regardless of the definition, most people use one hand more frequently than the other.

The vast majority of people are right-handed, between 70 and 90%. Another 10% of people are left-handed. The remaining population is either mix-handed—alternating which hand they use for certain tasks—or they are ambidextrous—using both hands equally well. Men are slightly more likely to be left-handed than women.

Scientists have determined that the left side of the brain controls movement on the right side of the body, and the right side of the brain controls movement on the left side of the body. So, many tests have been done to determine if there are differences in how the brain works based on handedness. These studies have not produced any conclusive results. Some people think that the side of the brain that controls the majority of speech processes may be related to handedness since speech is controlled primarily by the left side of the brain in those who are right-handed and is often controlled equally by both sides of the brain or even by the right side of the brain in people who are left-handed. However, this is not conclusive.

Because most people are right-handed, tools and other items have been designed in ways that make many tasks more difficult for non-right-handed people. Using scissors, writing from left to right on a piece of paper or white board, using many hand tools, and playing certain instruments can be challenging for left-handed people. But most people learn to adapt or find new ways to do necessary tasks.

The cause of handedness is not well understood. Some people think that conditions inside the womb may contribute to a child's handedness but there is no hard evidence for this. Other people believe there is a genetic influence. Families where both parents are left-handed seem to have a higher rate of left-handed children. But a gene or set of genes that control handedness has not been determined. Other people believe that parents, teachers, and other external pressures influence children to choose to use their right hand even if they would otherwise choose to use their left hand. What scientists do know is that most children exhibit a preferred hand by the time they are two years old even if they often switch back and forth, and by the age of three most children are decidedly right- or left-handed.

Whether you are left-handed, right-handed, or mixed-handed, you can be thankful that you have such an amazing thing as hands. Hands allow us to do so many wonderful things.

UNIT 3

Nerves & Senses

11 The Nervous System

12 The Brain

13 Learning & Thinking

14 Reflexes & Nerves

15 The Five Senses

16 The Eye

17 The Ear

18 Taste & Smell

◊ **Describe** how the nervous system is related to the rest of the body.

◊ **Describe** how different parts of the brain control different functions.

◊ **Explain** how each of the five senses gathers information.

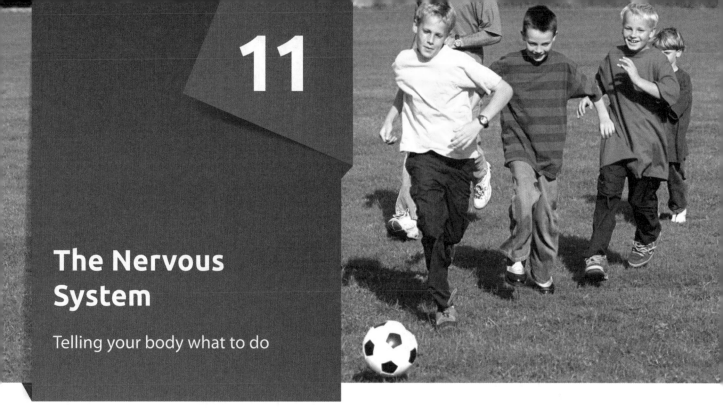

11

The Nervous System

Telling your body what to do

How does your finger know what your brain wants it to do?

Words to know:

nervous system

central nervous system

peripheral nervous system

Our muscular system would be useless to us without the nervous system, because our muscles would not move. The nervous system begins with the brain—the control center of the entire body. Connected to the brain is the spinal cord, which goes down your back. Branching off of the spinal cord is a series of nerves, which branch out to every part of the body. Together, the brain and the spinal cord are called the central nervous system; and the nerves, along with other organs such as the eyes and ears, are called the peripheral nervous system.

The nervous system has two functions. First, it sends information from the brain to the body; and second, it sends information from various parts of the body to the brain. It is a two-way information highway. When the brain is controlling the body, signals travel down the spinal cord to nerves in the muscle or other body part to be controlled. Most signals are sent automatically, like ones causing your

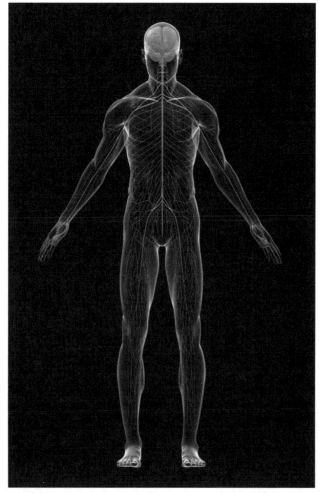

The human nervous system includes our brain, spinal cord, and many nerves throughout our body.

Response time test

Purpose: To show how long it takes for a message to complete a trip from the eyes, to the brain, to the hand

Materials: small object, ruler, stop watch

Procedure:

1. Place your hand flat on a table.

2. Have someone hold a small object such as an eraser 3 inches above your hand. Watch the object closely. Have them drop the object. As soon as you see the object begin to fall, move your hand out of the way.

3. If the object hits your hand before you got it out of the way repeat the process but have the object released from 4 inches above your hand. Repeat, increasing the height by one inch, until you find the lowest height at which you can move your hand out of the way of the falling object.

4. Once you have determined this height, use a stopwatch to time how long it takes for the object to fall that distance.

Conclusion: In order for you to move your hand out of the way of a falling object, your eyes have to send a message to your brain that the object is falling, your brain has to process this information and then send a message to the nerves attached to your arm muscles signaling the muscles to pull back your hand. The time you measured is the time it took for these messages to complete the trip from eyes to brain to arm.

Fun Fact

Your funny bone is not a bone at all. It is a nerve between the bones in your elbow. When struck, it sends a message to your brain, which results in a tingly feeling in your arm and fingers.

heart to beat, your lungs to breathe, and your eyes to blink. Other signals are the result of conscious thought such as signals that tell your hand to pick up a pencil or your body to lie down on the bed.

When receiving information from the body, sensory organs such as eyes, ears, or nerves in the skin send signals from the nerves up the spinal cord to the brain, where the brain processes the information and then decides what to do. Here again, many signals sent to the brain are automatic. For example, when you are running, a message saying you need more oxygen is sent to your brain from your lungs and muscles. Then your brain tells your body to increase your rate of breathing and your heart rate. Other signals occur when you purposely look at, smell, taste, listen to, or touch something. These processes will be explored more fully in later lessons.

 # What did we learn?

- What are the three main parts of the nervous system?

- In the response time test, what messages were sent to and from the brain?

 # Taking it further

- Name ways that information is collected by your body to be sent to the brain.

Nervous system coloring page

Get a copy of the "Nervous System Coloring Page" and identify and color the different parts of the nervous system. Remember that the brain and the spinal cord are the central nervous system and the collection of nerves is the peripheral nervous system.

 # Unique humans

In addition to sending and receiving signals, the human nervous system is designed to do something that no other creature can do. Humans have the ability to think, reason, and communicate with language. Humans can make decisions and show complex creativity. The human nervous system is believed by many biologists to be the most highly organized system in any living creature.

Many people will argue that animals communicate, think, and reason. And on a limited basis this is true. But animal communication and thinking is very limited and basic. Man's communication and thinking is on a whole different level. People talk and freely share ideas just for the enjoyment of socializing. This does not happen between animals. People imagine and pretend. They invent and create. All of these are characteristics we get from God, the Creator.

People also act differently than animals. People serve each other. They recognize and meet the needs of other people. Animals generally are only interested in their own survival. They may help others in their herd or band, but do not show compassion and servanthood the way humans do.

Most importantly, people are valuable to God in a way that animals never will be. God loved us so much that he sent his own son to die in our place. This is what really makes humans different from the animals.

Make your own list of things that humans can do that animals cannot do. What accounts for each of these abilities?

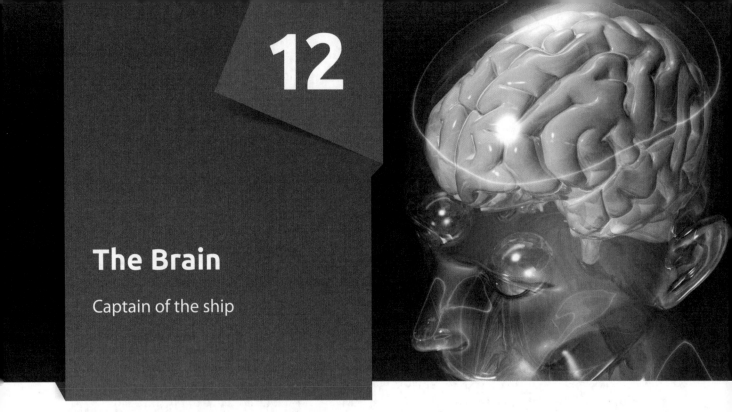

The Brain

Captain of the ship

How does the brain control all of the different activities you do?

Words to know:

cerebrum	medulla oblongata
corpus callosum	thalamus
cerebellum	pituitary gland
brain stem	hippocampus

The major organ of the nervous system is the brain. The brain receives, processes, and sends out billions of messages each second. It has three major parts: the cerebrum, the cerebellum, and the brain stem. The cerebrum (suh-REE-bruhm) is the upper part of the brain and the largest part. It controls thought, memory, and learned behavior. This is the part of the brain you use for decision making. Different areas in the cerebrum control different things. One area controls thinking, another controls speech, another memory, and so on.

The cerebrum is divided into two halves called the right hemisphere and the left hemisphere. The right side of the cerebrum, or right hemisphere, controls movement on the left side of the body, and the left hemisphere controls movement on the right side of the body. Until recently it was believed that the right hemisphere was the "big picture" part of the brain and was where artistry, music, and intuition originated and that the left hemisphere is where logic, mathematics, and critical thinking took place. But many recent studies have shown that this is mostly false. Most people use both sides of their brain together for most types of thinking. Certain specific tasks may always be done on one side of the brain, but you use both sides together to learn music or solve a math problem.

The two hemispheres of the cerebrum are connected by a large mass of nerves in the center of the brain called the corpus callosum (KOR-puhs kuh-LOH-suhm). This part of the brain coordinates the communication between the two sides of the cerebrum. Magnetic Resonance Imaging (MRI) has been used in recent years to evaluate all parts of the brain and has shown that part of the corpus callosum is often larger in musicians than in non-musicians, and that it is larger in left-handed people than in right-handed people. Also, people with dyslexia, a condition that can cause learning problems, often have a smaller corpus callosum than non-dyslexic people. This has nothing to do with intelligence, only with how efficiently the two sides of the cerebrum might communicate.

The second major part of your brain is the cerebellum (ser-uh-BEL-uhm). This is the lower

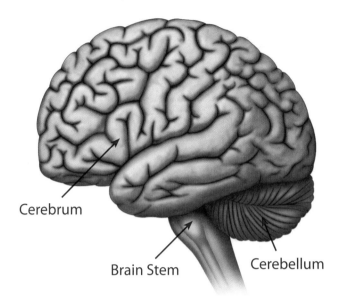

Cerebrum

Brain Stem

Cerebellum

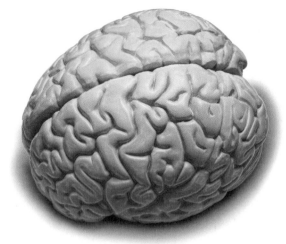

This model of a human brain shows the left and right hemispheres.

part of the brain. It controls balance and voluntary muscles. This part controls most of your movement. When learning a new activity, the cerebrum works with the cerebellum to think about how to do it. With practice, this function becomes more automatic and the cerebellum moves the muscles automatically. Remember when you tried to write your name with the wrong hand in lesson 9? Your cerebrum had to think very hard about how to move the muscles in that hand and arm to make your name look right. But if you practiced writing with that hand over and over, eventually your cerebellum would take over and you would not have to think about it so much, just like when you write your name with your normal writing hand.

The third major part of the brain is the brain stem. This is the part of the brain that connects to the spinal cord. All the messages to and from the brain pass through this part of the brain. The medulla oblongata (muh-DUHL-uh ob-lawng-GAH-tuh) in the brain stem is responsible for controlling involuntary muscles and regulating automatic activities, which are the necessary life functions. The brain stem regulates breathing, eye movement, heartbeat, blood pressure, waking and sleeping, and many reflexes.

Finally, several smaller parts of the brain, located near the brain stem, control other important functions. The thalamus (THAL-uh-muhs) routes messages to the correct part of the brain, the pituitary gland controls growth, and the hippocampus (hip-uh-KAM-puhs) helps with storage and retrieval of short-term memory. All of the parts of the brain function together to make everything else in the body work the way God designed it. This is why you need to wear your bike helmet so you don't hurt your brain if you have an accident. The brain is so complex that we can only marvel at its design, and try to copy its functions, without truly understanding it.

🧠 What did we learn?

- What are the three major parts of the brain?
- Which part of the brain controls growth?

🚀 Taking it further

- Which part of the brain would be used for each of the following: running, dilating your eyes, learning your math facts?
- Is your brain the same thing as your mind?

⚗️ Brain model

Using an anatomy book, make a model of the brain using different colors of clay for each of the major parts of the brain.

🏅 Brain anatomy

Use an anatomy book to locate the following parts of the brain, then add them to your brain model:

- Corpus callosum
- Olfactory lobe
- Medulla oblongata
- Optic nerve
- Pituitary gland

Label the various parts of your model. You can make little flags of paper with the words and glue the papers to toothpicks. Stick these flags into your model.

For even more fun, see if you can find out in which part of the brain each of the following functions takes place:

- Thought
- Smell
- Heartbeat regulation
- Memory
- Eyesight
- Speech
- Muscle control
- Pupil dilation

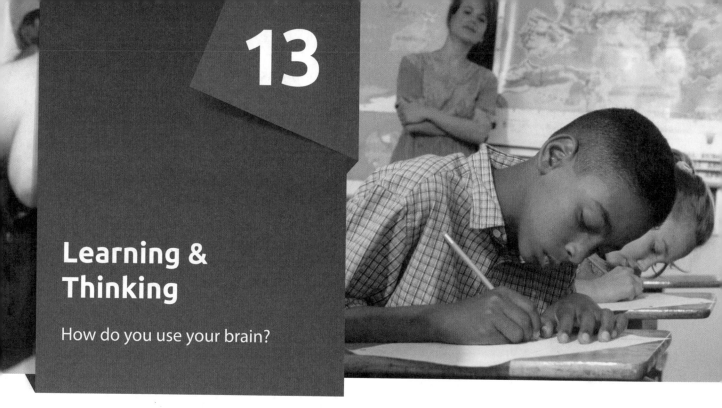

Learning & Thinking

How do you use your brain?

How do you exercise your brain?

Words to know:

cerebral cortex

The human brain is so complex we can never hope to fully understand it. God has designed our brains to not only control our bodies and to react to the world around us, but to learn and think so we can understand and enjoy the world God has created. Thinking and learning take place in the frontal lobe of the cerebrum. Also, personality, judgment, and self-control are coordinated from this part of the brain. And just as exercising your muscles makes them stronger, so exercising your brain makes it stronger.

Fun Fact

In 2003, a man who was barely conscious for nearly 20 years regained speech and movement because his brain spontaneously rewired itself. Doctors discovered that his brain had grown tiny new nerve connections to replace the ones sheared apart in a car crash.

The brain quickly learns to do things in the most efficient way so we need to constantly be challenging our brains with new ideas and tasks. We learn in many different ways. We learn by putting in new information using our five primary senses of sight, sound, touch, taste, and smell. These senses each connect to different parts of the cerebrum.

The hippocampus, located near the brain stem, stores and retrieves items for short-term memory. Long-term memories are stored and retrieved from the cerebral cortex, the outermost layer of the cerebrum. Most people will remember something better if it has a meaning than if it is just a picture or a sound. You can remember words or math facts better than the face of a stranger you saw only once. Also, learning something more than once greatly increases your ability to remember it. This is why you may study the human body in elementary school and then learn human anatomy again in high school.

Some people are better at math or logic and other people are better at music or art. This does not mean that we should just learn and practice the things that we are good at. We can all improve in every area by practice. So it is important that you continue to learn new things—even if they

Nerves & Senses

Practicing your math facts will make it easier to remember them.

are hard for you—so your brain will continue to be strong. You also need to get enough sleep each night. Lack of sleep makes it difficult to perform tasks that require higher level thinking and causes your brain to work harder than necessary. And eating healthy food and avoiding junk food gives your brain what it needs to grow. So exercise your body and your brain every day.

What did we learn?

- Which part of the brain does each of the following: stores short-term memories, stores long-term memories, controls learning and thinking, controls the senses?

- Which side of the brain controls the left side of the body?

- What is necessary for a healthy brain?

Taking it further

- List ways you can learn something.

- What is something you have trouble learning?

Brain exercises

Purpose: To exercise your brain

Materials: six index cards, colored markers

Activity 1—Procedure:

1. Take six index cards. On each index card, use a colored marker to write the name of a color. But do not write the color of the ink. For example, use the blue marker to write the word ORANGE, the orange marker to write the word GREEN, the green marker to write the word RED.

2. Now lay the index cards on the table and read the words out loud. This should be relatively easy.

3. Next, look at the word but say the color of the ink not the word that is written on the card. This will probably be much more difficult.

Conclusion: Our brains have been trained to read words regardless of the color of ink. It is more difficult to say the color when we automatically read the word first. This exercise is a good way to force your brain to think in ways it does not ordinarily think.

Activity 2—Procedure:

Look at the pictures below. What do you see? Our brains are trained to interpret what we see based on what we are familiar with. In the left picture, do you see a duck or a rabbit? In the right picture, do you see a vase or two people facing each other?

With practice, most people can see both images, but without concentration, a person usually sees only one image at first glance. So stretch your brain and look for both images.

⓵ Logic puzzles

Try these logic puzzles to exercise your cerebrum:

1. Four people must cross a river in a boat. Two people weigh 50 pounds each and the other two weigh 100 pounds each. They have a boat that can only hold a maximum of 100 pounds without sinking. Describe how all four people can cross the river in the boat.

2. You are in a strange land and you need to find the nearest town. You know that one group of people living in the area always tells the truth and that the second group of people always tells a lie. You come to a fork in the road and do not know which way to go. Standing at the fork are two people, one from each group, but you cannot tell which one is from which group. You can only ask one person one question. What question will you ask to be sure you take the correct road to reach the nearest town?

Now that you have done a few logic puzzles, see if you can make up a logic puzzle of your own. There are many games available today that require logical thinking skills. Try to find one and play it. It will improve your brain power.

Brain Surgery

The brain is very complex and still far more powerful than the most advanced computers. Very little was known about the human brain until the last 100 years or so. However, this did not stop man from conducting brain surgery. "Trepanning," the process of putting a small hole 1 to 2 inches (2.5–5 cm) in diameter into the skull of a living patient, goes back to ancient times. Records and bones show that this procedure was practiced in Ancient Egypt, as well as in Greece and Rome. Records show that the operation has also been done in the Middle East, in China, among the Celtic tribes, in India, among the Mayans, Aztecs, and the Brazilian Indians, in the South Seas, and in Africa.

If so little was known about the brain, why was there such widespread trepanning? No one really knows. The surprising part of all this is that the survival rate among patients that had this procedure may have been as high as 65 to 70% in ancient times. This is a much higher survival rate than what brain surgery patients experienced in the 14th through the 18th centuries. Did the ancient people have knowledge about the brain from before the Flood that was later lost? We may never know.

During the Middle Ages, no real advancement was made in understanding the brain. Then in the 1800s, Eduard Hitzig, a German doctor working at a military hospital, conducted some experiments. His patients had suffered head injuries on the battlefield, leaving part of the skull missing. Using a battery, he stimulated the back area of their brains. He found that by doing so he was able to make their eyes move.

Later, he teamed up with Gustav Fritsch and ran experiments on dogs. They found, through stimulating the dogs' brains, that specific areas of the brain controlled specific movements.

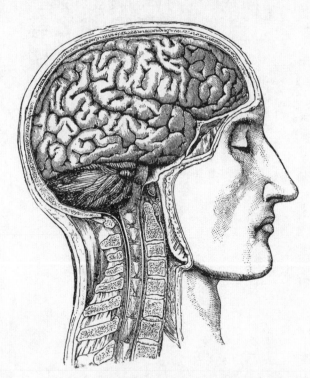

Later, John Jackson learned more by observing epileptic seizures in his wife. He found that the seizures always followed the same pattern. He believed that electrical pulses starting in one part of the brain and radiating out to other parts caused the seizures. From these observations he determined that the brain was divided into different sections, each controlling a different motor function.

Scientists discovered that the brain also affects personality when a man named Phineas Gage was injured in 1848. While working as a railroad construction supervisor, an explosion accidentally sent a rod through the left side of his skull. The rod, about an inch in diameter, entered though his left cheek and exited through the top of his head. He recovered from the injury, but months later started showing startling changes in his personality. He became anti-social, foul-mouthed and a liar, which was very unlike his original personality. This was believed to be a result of his injury.

These 19th-century discoveries were the beginning of understanding the brain. Today, scientists have a better understanding of the brain. They know how electrical signals travel throughout the nervous system. They know which regions in the brain control thought and movement. Doctors can "look" at a person's brain without opening the skull using CAT scans (computerized axial tomography) and MRI (magnetic resonance imaging).

Using modern technology, surgeons today can do many types of operations that greatly benefit the patient without causing damage to the brain. Brain surgery today has a 98% success rate. Technology allows surgeons to make smaller incisions compared to surgery in the past. Also, microscopic cameras allow the surgeons to see exactly what they are doing so they only touch the necessary parts of the brain. Brain surgery has come a long way from the trepanning of ancient times.

But even with all of their knowledge, people still don't really understand how the brain helps us think, feel, and make decisions. God, in His infinite wisdom, has created our brains with a complexity that we will never fully understand.

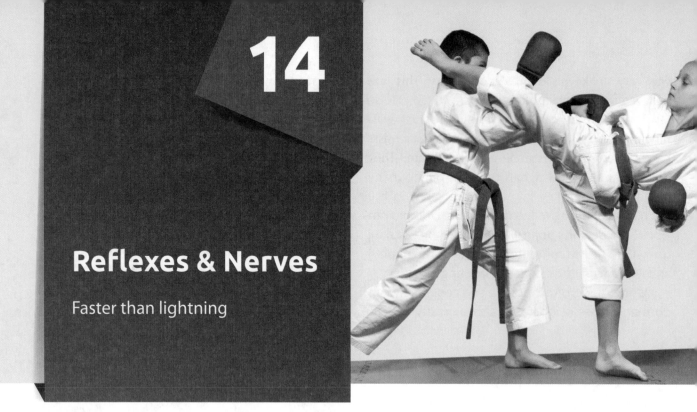

14

Reflexes & Nerves

Faster than lightning

How do electrical signals travel through your body?

Words to know:

reflex   neuron

Challenge words:

sensory neurons   dendrite

motor neurons   axon

interneurons   Schwann cells

association neurons   myelin

Some functions of your nervous system are automatic—you don't have to think about them. One automatic function is called a reflex. A reflex is when your body moves quickly in response to something. For example, if something flies toward your face, you automatically close your eyes. If you set your hand on something hot, you quickly jerk it back. God designed us to have reflexes so we would be less likely to get hurt.

Reflexes occur when a danger signal, such as "it's hot," is sent to the spinal cord and another message is sent directly to the hand to make it move, without the message having to go all the way to the brain. This path is shorter so it is quicker, allowing us to react more quickly to a dangerous situation. If we are not in danger, messages generally go all the way to the brain to be processed.

Whether the message goes all the way to the brain or just to the spinal cord, nerves receive the information from outside the body. All of our senses contain nerves. There are special nerves in the eyes, ears, nose, and tongue, but most nerves that receive

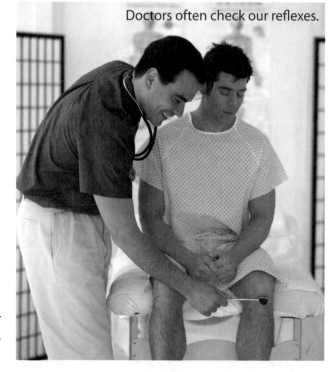

Doctors often check our reflexes.

information are on the surface of our skin. Nerve cells called **neurons** send pulses of electricity to the brain.

We have nerves all over our bodies, but they are more concentrated in our hands, feet, and face than in other parts of our bodies. More nerves are needed in our fingers to enable us to detect subtle differences in the things we touch. There are several different types of nerves in the skin. These different nerves detect different sensations. Some nerves detect touch/texture, pain, or temperature. Others detect vibration and rapid pressure changes. Still others detect slight pressure changes. All of these nerves work together to help us interpret the world around us.

 # What did we learn?

- How do reflex reactions differ from other nervous system messages?
- Why do we have reflexes?
- What are some different types of sensations detected by your nerves?

 # Taking it further

- What reflexes might you experience?
- How does the sense of touch differ from your fingertips to the back of your arm?
- Why do you need a larger number of nerves on the bottoms of your feet?

 # Test your reflexes & nerves

To test your reflexes, a doctor may have hit your knee lightly with a rubber hammer. Were you surprised to see your leg jump? You can do the same thing at home.

Purpose: To test your own reflexes

Materials: toothpicks or pencils, blindfold

Activity 1—Procedure:

Sit with one leg crossed over the other and have someone gently strike your leg just below the kneecap with the side of his hand. If you are relaxed, you should see your leg kick out even though you didn't mean for it to.

Activity 2—Procedure:

1. Have someone blindfold you or sit in such a way that you cannot see what they are doing.

2. Have them gently press the two points of the pencils against your finger tip with the tips touching each other. How many points do you feel? You should only feel one point.

3. Lift and repeat with the tips slightly apart.

4. Repeat, spreading the points farther apart until you can feel two distinct points. Measure how far apart the tips were when you felt two points.

5. Now repeat this exercise on the back of your arm. The points should be much farther apart before you can distinguish two separate points.

Conclusion: You can repeat this exercise on various parts of your body such as the bottoms of your feet or your back. You should discover that nerves are much closer together on the fingers and feet than other places.

🏅 Nerve cells

God designed your body with millions of nerves, also called neurons, to help you do all the things you need to do. These nerve cells are divided into three different categories. First, you have sensory neurons. Sensory neurons receive information from outside the body and send messages to the brain. The nerves in your skin are sensory nerves. You also have sensory nerves in your mouth for taste and in your nose for smell. The optic nerves in your eyes and the auditory nerves in your ears are sensory nerves as well.

The second type of nerves is motor neurons. Motor neurons transfer electrical impulses from the brain to your muscles. These are the nerves that make your arms and legs move. They also carry messages to your heart to make it keep beating and to your diaphragm to make you keep breathing.

Finally, you have interneurons, also called association neurons. Interneurons are the nerves in your brain and spinal cord that receive and interpret the information from the sensory nerves and then pass instructions to the motor nerves. These nerves work somewhat like the logic circuits in a computer.

Nerve cells have a nucleus that controls the metabolism of the cell. The nucleus is located in the cell body. Connected to the cell body are hundreds or even thousands of tiny fingers called dendrites. Dendrites receive input. This input can come from outside your body or from another nerve cell. The electrical impulse received by the dendrite is then passed on to the cell body which in turn passes it on to the axon. The axon is a long projection that carries the impulse away from the cell body to another neuron. The axon is covered by special cells called Schwann cells which produce a material called myelin. Myelin acts as insulation, preventing electrical signals from jumping between nerve cells. The electrical signals in your nervous system always travel from the dendrites toward the axons. Dendrites are usually relatively short, but axons can be very long, sometimes as long as one yard (one meter).

Draw a diagram of a nerve cell and label all of the parts. Do some research on multiple sclerosis, a disease of the nervous system. Find out what causes it and how it affects the nerves.

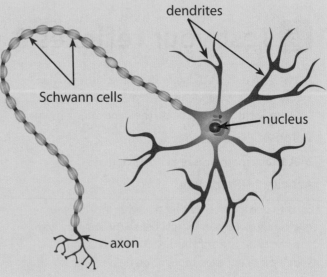

dendrites

Schwann cells

nucleus

axon

Nerves & Senses

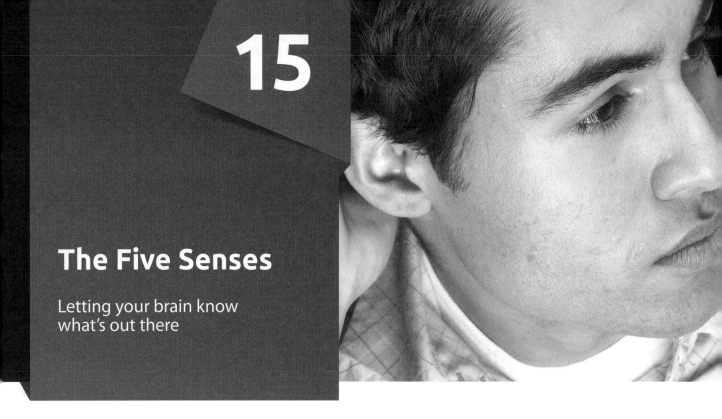

15

The Five Senses

Letting your brain know
what's out there

How many different ways can you sense an orange?

Challenge words:

Braille

We input information to our nervous system through our five primary senses: touch, taste, smell, sight, and hearing. Most people use all five senses together in various degrees throughout the day. We get the most information through our sense of sight. But if one sense is not working properly, the other senses can help compensate.

A blind person has heightened hearing and touch to help make up for not seeing. The use of touch can help a blind person read using the Braille alphabet of raised dots. Similarly, a deaf person has a heightened

sense of sight and touch. A deaf person can often feel something that a hearing person could not.

In addition to our five primary senses, scientists have identified many more senses, maybe more than 20. Some of these secondary senses include proprioception—the ability to tell where your body parts are relative to other body parts; equilibrioception—the sense that allows you to keep your balance and sense body movement in terms of acceleration and direction; and tension sensors—these are found in such places as your muscles and allow the brain the ability to monitor muscle tension. Together, these senses tell us where the parts of our body are in relation to

Nerves & Senses

Fun Fact

The nerves throughout your body can send pain messages to the brain. Medicines can help relieve pain, but the brain can also produce its own pain relievers called endorphins. Soothing music can also help your brain block pain messages so you don't feel so uncomfortable.

Blind people read using the Braille alphabet of raised dots.

things around us. They send messages to the brain so it knows where our body parts are. Our senses also help us keep our balance. Receptors in the inner ear help tell us when we are off balance.

We often associate the sense of touch with our fingers or hands. But actually, this sense occurs throughout your entire body. As we discussed in the previous lesson, more nerves are located in the hands and feet, but there are nerves that touch the world around you everywhere you have skin. These nerves can sometimes cause curious results. Have you ever wondered what causes goose bumps?

Nerves attached to the hairs on your skin detect breezes or cold temperatures and your brain causes small muscles attached to the hair follicles to contract. This movement causes goose bumps and helps to warm you up. It also alerts your brain to have you take more action if necessary to warm you up.

A few parts of your body do not have nerves. Your hair, fingernails, and toenails do not have nerves. This is why you can cut your hair and your nails without feeling pain. We will explore the sense of touch in today's activity, and we will learn more about the other senses in following lessons.

Feeling hot, feeling cold

Nerves in your skin can distinguish many different sensations including temperature, pressure, pain, and vibration.

Purpose: To understand how our body reacts to temperature differences

Materials: 3 bowls, jacket with zipper, straight pins, bag of ice

Activity 1—Procedure:

1. Set up three bowls of water: one hot (not hot enough to burn the skin), one warm (about room temperature), and one cold.

2. Place one hand in the bowl of hot water and the other hand in the bowl of cold water for 1–2 minutes.

3. At the end of that time, immediately place both your hands in the bowl of warm water. How does the warm water feel to each hand?

4. Keep your hands in the warm water for 1–2 minutes. How does the water feel to each hand at the end of that time?

Conclusion: Over time, if the same message is sent to the brain over and over, and it is not an emergency type of signal, the brain will often start ignoring it. So your hands do not notice how hot or cold the water is. Also, the brain makes assumptions about temperature in a relative way. If something is much colder or hotter than what you have been experiencing, the brain notices it more strongly. That is why the warm water feels cold to the hand that was in the hot water and it feels hot to the hand that was in the cold water.

Activity 2—Procedure:

1. Put on a jacket with a zipper but leave it unzipped.

2. Place 2–3 straight pins on a table.

3. Hold a bag of ice in your hands for 2–3 minutes, then try to zip up the jacket.

4. Next, try to pick up the pins one at a time. This may seem difficult to do with very cold hands.

Conclusion: Extended cold signals are eventually ignored by the brain, making it slower to respond to other inputs from that hand. This makes the hand feel numb and unable to do many of the normal tasks. If an area of skin is exposed to extreme cold for long periods of time, the skin can be damaged. But if it is cold for only a short period of time, like in this experiment, the signals quickly begin flowing again and normal activity resumes once your hands warm back up.

What did we learn?

- What are your five senses?
- Which of these senses usually gives us the most information?
- How does your brain compensate for the loss of one of your senses?

 # Taking it further

- You have nerves all over your skin, so why don't you feel your clothes all day long?
- Your eyes see your nose all day long. Why don't you notice it all the time?
- If you are in the hot sun for a while then you go inside, the room feels cold. Why?

 # Braille system

Because people without the sense of sight still need a form of written communication, Louis Braille developed a special alphabet for blind people. His alphabet is a system of raised dots that represent letters and numbers. The Braille system starts with a matrix of six dots in two columns with three dots in each. The location of the raised dots in this matrix determines the letter. For example if there is a dot in the upper left hand position only, this represents the letter *a*. If there is a dot in the two upper positions only, this represents the letter *c*. Below is a chart showing all of the letters of the Braille alphabet.

The patterns that are used for A through I are the same as the patterns used for 0 through 9. So a special pattern precedes numbers to notify the reader that what follows is a number and not a word.

There are machines that are designed to print books and other papers using the Braille alphabet. Blind people can use these machines to write letters and to have written communication with other people.

Write a message on a piece of paper in Braille using small dots of glue for the raised dots. Allow the glue to dry, then try to read the message with your fingers. Allow a schoolmate or family member to try to read your Braille message as well. Why do you think that Braille was designed to be read with fingertips instead of your palm or the side of your hand?

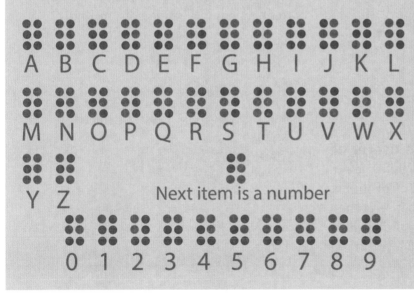

Louis Braille

16

The Eye

Window to the world

How does your eye see in brightly lit and dark rooms?

Words to know:

cornea	rods
pupil	cones
lens	optic nerve
retina	iris

Challenge words:

aqueous humor   vitreous humor

One of the most complex and useful of our five senses is sight. The organ for sight is the eye. The eye receives light rays that bounce off of objects around us. The light passes through the **cornea**, the front of the eye, and enters the **pupil**, which is the dark circle in the middle of your eye. It then passes through the **lens**, which focuses and projects an upside down image on the **retina**, which is the back of the eye. Receptors in the retina called **rods** and **cones** detect light and color and change the image into electrical signals that are sent to the **optic nerve**, which sends the message on to the brain. The brain interprets the signal, turns the image right side up, and lets you see the object. All of this happens in a fraction of a second.

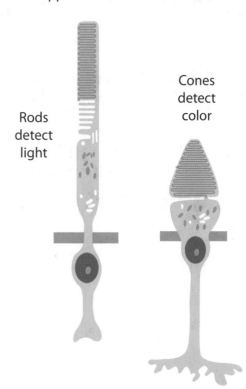

Rods detect light

Cones detect color

Fun Fact

It's estimated that up to 8% of boys have some degree of color blindness, whereas less than 1% of girls have the same condition.

Nerves & Senses

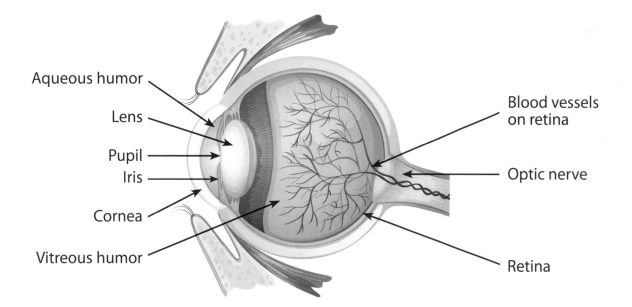

Aqueous humor

Lens

Pupil

Iris

Cornea

Vitreous humor

Blood vessels on retina

Optic nerve

Retina

Your brain controls the parts of your eye to help you see most efficiently. The brain causes muscles in the iris, the colored part surrounding your pupil, to widen or narrow the pupil to allow in the best amount of light. In a dark room your pupils get very wide to enable you to use all available light. In very bright light the pupils get very small to protect the eye and optic nerve from overload. The brain also changes the shape of the lens to keep objects in focus. This allows you to look at objects that are very near as well as at things that are far away. The brain also controls the muscles that move the eyes to keep them working together.

Your brain and eyes work together to help you recognize things you are familiar with. You use four kinds of "clues" to help you determine what something is: shape, size, brightness, and color. A favorite toy can be recognized hiding under a bed by its size and shape even if you can't see it very well. If you don't have enough light, or you can't see all of something, your brain automatically fills in the gaps and tries to match it to something you know. This can result in your eyes being fooled into seeing something they don't really see. Illusionists use this knowledge to trick their audiences all the time.

allows you to see more sides of an object

What did we learn?

- Name four important parts of the eye.
- How does your brain compensate for different amounts of light in your surroundings?
- How does your brain help you to focus on items that are near and items that are far away?
- Why did God design our bodies with two eyes instead of just one?
- How does having two eyes help with a 3-dimensional image?
- Since you have a blind spot, how can you see what is in that spot?

Taking it further

- Name some ways that the eye is protected from harm.
- Why do some people have to wear glasses or contact lenses?
- Why can you fool your eyes or your brain into thinking you saw something you didn't actually see?

Fooling your eyes

Purpose: To better understand how your eyes work

Materials: paper tube, piece of paper, pencil, marker

Activity 1—Procedure:

1. Hold a paper tube to one eye and place your other hand beside the tube with the palm facing you.

2. While looking straight ahead with both eyes, slowly move the hand closer or farther away from your face.

Conclusion: You should be able to see a "hole" through your hand. This is because each eye sees a different image. Your brain takes the images from both eyes and combines them into one image.

Activity 2—Procedure:

1. Hold your arm straight out with one finger sticking up.

2. Close one eye and focus on something on the wall across the room.

3. Alternate which eye you have open and which you have closed.

Conclusion: You should see your finger "jump" back and forth with respect to whatever you are focusing on. The finger appears to move even though it is stationary because each eye views the finger and the wall from a different position. This blending of images from different perspectives is what allows you to have depth perception.

Activity 3—Procedure:

1. Take a 3-inch by 6-inch piece of paper and draw a small star ½ inch from the left edge and draw a small circle ½ inch from the right edge. Color in both shapes so they are easy to see.

2. Hold the paper at arm's length and close your left eye.

3. While looking at the star with your right eye, slowly bring the paper closer to your face. Notice at what point the circle disappears.

4. Repeat by using your left eye to look at the circle and see where the star disappears.

Conclusion: The shape disappears because your eye has a blind spot where the optic nerve attaches to the back of the eyeball. Your brain fills in the blanks from what it sees around the blind spot. At a certain point the brain only sees the blank paper and cannot fill in the circle or star. As you bring the paper closer or farther away, your eye can detect enough of the image for your brain to fill in the rest.

Activity 4—Procedure:

1. Look at the image below. What figure do you see in the center?

2. If you looked from left to right you probably thought it was a B, but if you read it from top to bottom you probably saw a 13. Your brain associates images with those around it to determine what you are seeing.

Liquid in your eyes

In order to work properly, your eyeball must maintain its general size and shape. Your eyes have two different liquids that help it to do this. First, the aqueous humor is a liquid between the cornea and the lens. This liquid keeps the front of the eye firm. It also serves the function of blood by providing nutrients to the front of the eyeball. However, unlike blood, the aqueous humor is clear so it does not interfere with the light passing through the eye.

The second liquid is in the center of the eyeball. This liquid is called the vitreous humor. It is a clear jelly-like substance that helps to keep the eyeball firm.

Using the drawing on the previous page or an anatomy book, draw a detailed diagram of the eye. Be sure to label each of the following parts of the eye. Below your drawing, briefly describe the function of each part.

- Lens
- Pupil
- Iris
- Cornea
- Rods
- Cones
- Retina
- Optic Nerve
- Vitreous humor
- Aqueous humor

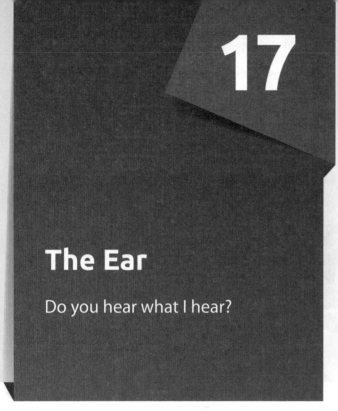

17

The Ear

Do you hear what I hear?

How does the ear detect sound?

Words to know:

auditory canal   frequency

cochlea   amplitude

Challenge words:

eustachian tube   semicircular canals

What is a sound and how do you hear it?

Sounds are vibrations of the air that travel in waves. These waves of vibrating air enter your ear through the opening of the ear, called the auditory canal, and hit your eardrum, causing it to vibrate. Those vibrations are passed on through three tiny bones in your middle ear, called the malleus, incus, and stapes, to the cochlea, which is a snail-shaped tube filled with liquid. The waves are then converted into electrical impulses and sent by the auditory nerve to the brain. The brain then interprets these signals as sounds.

Sound waves have two parts: frequency (pitch) and amplitude (loudness). The closer together the waves are, the higher the pitch. The peaks of a sound wave from a whistle would be much closer together than those from a bass drum. The bigger the waves are, the louder the sound. Sound waves from a loud sound are very tall, whereas a whisper produces very short waves. The differences in waves allow us to hear a large variety of sounds. Most sounds that we hear are not just one pitch but are some combination of pitches.

Some people have difficulty hearing or cannot hear at all. These people must learn to communicate differently than hearing people. Many deaf people communicate using sign language. Many also learn to read lips by watching the speaker's lips, tongue, and throat muscles. Generally, lip readers can read about half of the words and must guess at the rest.

Some people are born deaf; others have diseases that destroy their hearing. But many people become partially or completely deaf by being exposed to very loud noises. We can protect our hearing by wearing earplugs or other ear protectors when we must be around loud noises. We can also try to avoid loud noises that might damage our ears. God has given us wonderful senses to interact with our world, and we must take care of them.

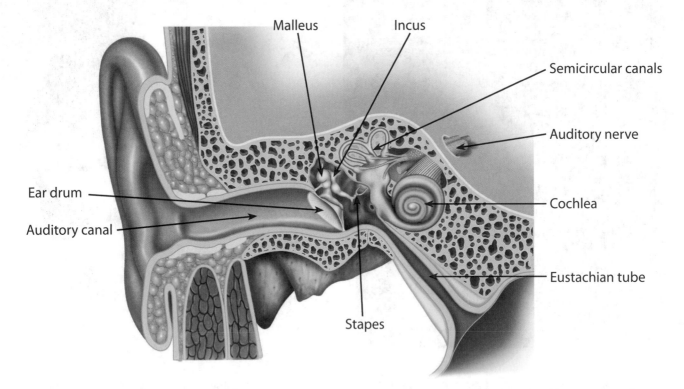

Malleus · Incus · Semicircular canals · Auditory nerve · Cochlea · Eustachian tube · Stapes · Ear drum · Auditory canal

🧠 What did we learn?

- What characteristic of a sound wave determines how high or low a sound will be?
- What characteristic of a sound wave determines how loud or soft a sound will be?

🚀 Taking it further

- Why do two different instruments playing the same note at the same loudness sound different?
- Name several ways to protect your hearing.
- How do you suppose deaf children learn to speak?
- How do you think a CD player or a telephone makes sounds?

🧪 Do you hear what I hear?

Complete the "Do You Hear What I Hear?" worksheet.

Loudness is measured in decibels. The quieter the sound, the lower the decibels. Falling snow is so quiet it has a loudness of 0 decibels (dB). A jet engine is so loud it is about 140 dB. Most people watch TV at a level of about 70 dB, but a whisper is much quieter.

Ear anatomy

The ear is divided into three areas. The outer ear is the stiff part on the side of your head. The outer ear is made of cartilage, which gives it its shape and stiffness. The purpose of the outer ear is to catch and direct sound waves down the auditory canal to the ear drum. Although the auditory canal is inside the head it is usually classified as part of the outer ear.

From the eardrum to the cochlea is considered the middle ear. The middle ear contains the ear drum and the three bones mentioned earlier in the lesson as well as the eustachian tube. The eustachian tube is a tube that goes from the ear to the throat. This tube helps regulate the pressure on your eardrum and middle ear. If you have ever been on an airplane or driving in the mountains you have probably experienced the urge to yawn and then had your ears "pop." This occurs because the pressure outside your ear was different than the pressure inside your ear. By yawning, you opened up the eustachian tubes allowing the pressure to equalize. The purpose of the middle ear is to move the sound waves from air to liquid.

Your inner ear contains the cochlea where sound vibrations are converted to electrical impulses and sent by the auditory nerve to the brain. The inner ear also contains what are called the semicircular canals. These canals are three tiny tubes filled with liquid. The liquid in these tubes indicates to your brain what direction you are moving. One tube detects forward and backward movement. One detects up and down movement. The third detects movement right or left. These tubes are responsible for helping you keep your balance.

Close your eyes and stand in one place. Were you able to do it? You probably had very little trouble keeping upright even with your eyes closed because your inner ear helps you keep your balance. Now, with your eyes closed, have someone spin you around several times. Keep your eyes closed and try to stand in one place. You probably had trouble doing this. This is because the liquid in your inner ear keeps moving even after your body stops so your brain is confused for a few moments about how your body is moving.

Nerves & Senses

18

Taste & Smell

What's for dinner?

How many different things can you taste?

Challenge words:

papillae

olfactory hairs

gustatory receptor cells

odorant

Your tongue and your nose work together to help you decide which foods are safe and good to eat. Things that are bad for you generally taste pretty bad, though not always. Most things that are good for you are pleasant to taste, although those of you who dislike vegetables may not agree. Your tongue determines taste and your nose determines smell. However, one without the other does not give you the full flavor of the food.

Fun Fact

Smells are often linked to memories—sometimes pleasant and sometimes unpleasant. When you smell a particular scent again a memory comes back to you. Can you describe a time when a smell triggered a memory?

You taste various flavors with your taste buds. A taste bud is a bump surrounded by a trench that traps saliva. The taste receptors in the trenches convert tastes into electrical signals that go to the brain. Most tastes buds are located on the surface of your tongue, but you also have some taste buds on the roof of your mouth and even a few in your throat. If you look closely in a mirror, you can see the taste buds on your tongue.

Your taste buds can detect four basic tastes: sweet, salty, sour, and bitter. Some scientists include a fifth taste called umami. This is a flavor that is common in Asian foods, and is found in a chemical called MSG.

However, a combination of these four or five tastes cannot account for the wide range of flavors we experience. The nose has smell receptors inside the nasal cavity that send signals to the brain at the same time the taste buds are sending taste signals. The brain uses all this information to allow you to taste the food. This is why sometimes when you smell something, like chocolate chip cookies in the oven, you can almost taste them, too. Scientists used to think there were only four basic smells: fragrant, fresh, spicy, and putrid. Other scientists have classified smells into seven categories: minty, floral, ethereal, musky, resinous, foul, and acrid. More recent studies have revealed that there may be hundreds

Fun Fact

You have almost 10,000 taste buds inside your mouth—even some on the roof of your mouth.

or even thousands of smells. This is an area in which more research is being done.

The tongue responds to chemicals dissolved in saliva. The nose responds to chemicals in the air. Together, these chemical messages are changed into electronic messages that are interpreted by the brain. This allows you to enjoy your meal, sometimes even your veggies.

What did we learn?

- What four flavors can your tongue detect?
- How does your tongue detect flavors?
- How does your nose detect fragrances?

Taste without saliva?

Purpose: To determine whether saliva is necessary for taste

Materials: Paper towels, salt, sugar

Procedure:

1. Dry your tongue with a paper towel to remove as much saliva as possible.

2. Sprinkle a small amount of salt on your tongue. Can you taste the salt? You won't be able to taste it if your tongue is dry, because the salt must be dissolved in saliva before your taste buds can detect it.

3. Rinse your tongue off with water.

4. Repeat steps 1–3 with sugar instead of salt. Again, you won't be able to taste the sugar if your tongue is dry.

Taking it further

- Can you still taste foods when you have a stuffy nose?

- Smells are used for more things than just enjoying food. List some other uses for your sense of smell.

- Oranges and grapefruits are both sweet and sour. Why do they taste different?

- Cocoa is very bitter. Why does chocolate candy taste so delicious?

Smell detective

Collect several items with distinctive odors. Close your eyes and have someone hold each item for you to sniff. How many you can identify just by smell?

Taste without smell

Peel a potato, apple, and carrot and cut each into the same size cubes. Close your eyes and plug your nose and then have someone feed you one cube of each item. How difficult was it to tell the difference between the foods without using your nose? Repeat this activity without plugging your nose. Was it easier for you to tell which food was which? It should be.

🎖 How we taste and smell

Let's take a closer look at how tastes and smells actually get to your brain. Taste and smell are both chemical reactions. In order to taste something the food must be dissolved in the saliva in your mouth. Your tongue is covered with taste buds called papillae, which are bumps with special cells that react with the chemicals in saliva. These special cells are called gustatory receptor cells. As the saliva passes over the gustatory receptor cells on the papillae, a chemical reaction takes place in these cells, which sends an electrical signal to your brain so that you can taste the flavor that particular cell can detect.

A similar process takes place in your nasal cavity. When you sniff air into your nasal cavity it passes over olfactory hairs, which are actually extensions of the dendrites of the olfactory nerves. These hairs bond with very light molecules called odorants. Food, flowers, perfume, and other items with distinctive scents have odorants, which are light molecules that easily evaporate. Items that have no scent do not have molecules that easily evaporate. When the olfactory hairs bond with the odorants, a chemical reaction takes place that then sends an electrical signal to your brain and you smell the odor.

Other things contribute to your sense of taste as well. In addition to taste buds, your tongue has

nerves that detect temperature and texture. This is why ground beef and steak taste different even though they are both the same food and why some people like hot tea and others like only iced tea. Also, your tongue can detect "coolness" from foods that are minty and "hotness" from foods that are spicy. These sensations are not technically flavors but they contribute to the overall experience of eating a particular food.

All of your senses take information from your surroundings and convert them into electrical signals that travel to your brain where they are processed. What is the input for each of your five senses? Aren't you glad your body knows how to process each of these inputs?

Nerves & Senses

UNIT 4

Digestion

19 The Digestive System

20 Teeth

21 Dental Health

22 Nutrition

23 Vitamins & Minerals

◊ **Identify** and **describe** the function of the parts of the digestive system.

◊ **Describe** the importance of proper nutrition.

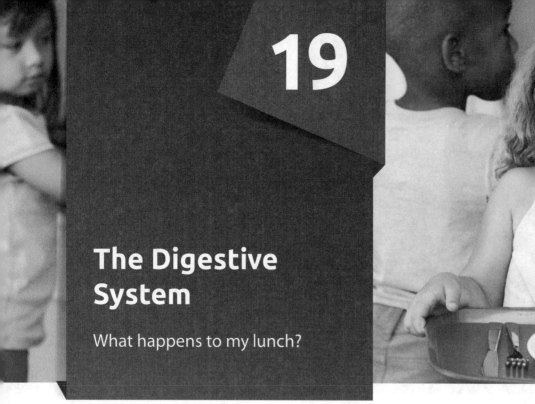

19

The Digestive System

What happens to my lunch?

Where does digestion begin and end?

Words to know:

digestive system

enzyme

esophagus

stomach

small intestine

villi

large intestine

Challenge words:

salivary amylase

gastric juice

bile

pancreatic juice

sodium bicarbonate

Your body needs energy to run and jump, to skate, and to ride a bike. It also needs nutrients to build strong bones and muscles and to help you grow. God designed your digestive system to give you the nutrients and energy you need.

The digestive system begins in your mouth, where your tongue and teeth work together to break food into small pieces that can be easily swallowed. Saliva glands squirt saliva into your mouth. Saliva contains various enzymes, chemicals that

help with digestion, to help begin the process of breaking down your food. The food then travels down the esophagus—a tube starting at the back of your throat that leads to your stomach.

In the stomach, water and hydrochloric acid break down the food particles and the stomach churns the food until it is a thin liquid consistency. Food spends from 30 minutes to 3 hours in your stomach, depending on what you ate. When it is broken down enough, it leaves the stomach and enters the small intestine.

The small intestine is a tube about 19 feet long that coils back and forth inside your body. It is lined with finger-like projections called villi. The food molecules pass through the villi membrane and into the blood stream where they are taken throughout the body and converted into energy. Then the nutrients are used to build up your body.

The parts of the food that cannot be used are passed on into the large intestine. This is a tube that

Fun Fact

The hydrochloric acid in your stomach is strong enough to eat through metal. Therefore, your stomach lining is protected by a layer of mucus and is constantly being renewed.

is wider but shorter than the small intestine. In the **large intestine** water is removed and the unusable parts of the food pass out of the body.

All of the parts of the digestive system work together to efficiently absorb the usable parts of the food and expel what cannot be used. Digestion is partly a mechanical process, with the teeth grinding the food, but it is mostly a chemical process. Chemicals are added to your food in your mouth, stomach, and intestines. These chemicals aid in breaking down the food into its basic nutrients.

There are several things you can do to keep your digestive system healthy. First, you need to eat the right foods. Eating a balanced diet helps keep your entire body working efficiently and helps you feel better. You need to eat foods from all the food groups including foods with fiber. Also, you need to drink enough liquids to ensure proper digestion. Exercise is also important to keeping your digestive system functioning properly. Finally, try and avoid negative feelings such as fear or anxiety near mealtimes. These can cause you to experience stomachaches and headaches.

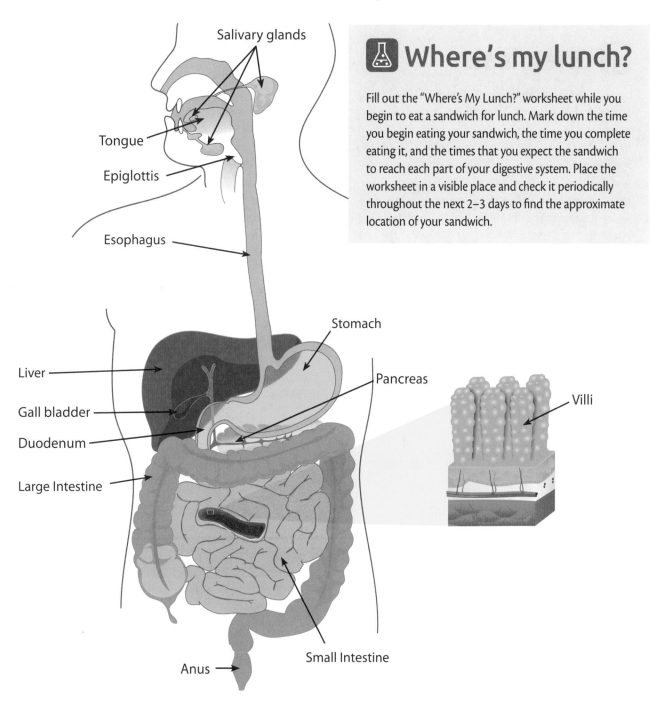

🧪 Where's my lunch?

Fill out the "Where's My Lunch?" worksheet while you begin to eat a sandwich for lunch. Mark down the time you begin eating your sandwich, the time you complete eating it, and the times that you expect the sandwich to reach each part of your digestive system. Place the worksheet in a visible place and check it periodically throughout the next 2–3 days to find the approximate location of your sandwich.

Salivary glands
Tongue
Epiglottis
Esophagus
Stomach
Pancreas
Villi
Liver
Gall bladder
Duodenum
Large Intestine
Small Intestine
Anus

Digestion

What did we learn?

- What are the main parts of the digestive system?
- What role do your teeth play in digestion?
- What role does your tongue play in digestion?
- Which is longer, your small intestine or your large intestine?
- Which is wider, your small intestine or your large intestine?

Taking it further

- Can you eat or drink while standing on your head?
- Why do some foods spend 30 minutes in the stomach while other foods spend 3 hours in the stomach?
- What makes you feel hungry?
- Why did God design your body with a way to make you feel hungry?

 # Chemicals

As we already mentioned, digestion is primarily a chemical process. Glands in the mouth add an enzyme called salivary amylase to the food that begins breaking down the starch molecules in your food even while it is still in your mouth. But the real chemical reactions begin in the stomach. The lining of the stomach secretes various enzymes as well as hydrochloric acid and mucus. These liquids combined together are called gastric juice. The gastric juice softens the food and breaks down the proteins into molecules that can be absorbed by the body.

Additional chemicals are added to the food as it enters the small intestine. Some of the chemicals are produced by the liver and stored in the gall bladder until they are released into the small intestine. This liquid is called bile and its main function is to break down fat molecules into tiny droplets. Other chemicals are produced by the pancreas and squirted into the small intestine. Pancreatic juices contain many chemicals that help digest fats, proteins, and carbohydrates. The pancreas also produces sodium bicarbonate, the same chemical as baking soda, which neutralizes the hydrochloric acid from the stomach.

Without all these chemicals, our bodies could not extract the energy we need from our food. Thankfully, God has designed a wonderful system that efficiently provides all the energy we need.

Using the diagram on the previous page or an anatomy book, label all of the parts of the digestive system on the "Digestive System" worksheet.

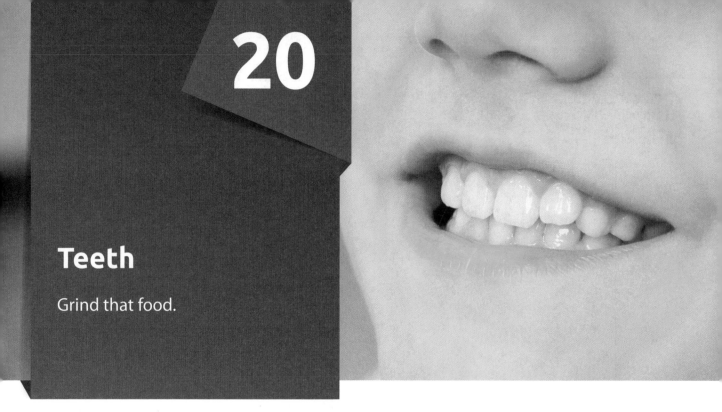

20

Teeth

Grind that food.

How many teeth do you have?

Words to know:

incisors

bicuspids

cuspids

molars

canine teeth

Challenge words:

crown

dentin

neck

enamel

root

cementum

pulp

periodontal ligament

root canal

gingiva

Teeth are an important part of the digestive system. Without good healthy teeth it is difficult to enjoy any but the softest foods. God designed our mouths to have two sets of teeth. The first set of teeth begins emerging when you are a baby. These teeth are relatively small because your

Fun Fact

Each person's set of teeth is unique—much like their fingerprints—even in identical twins.

mouth is small. In all, you will have 20 baby teeth.

As you grow, your mouth gets larger, making room for more and bigger teeth. When you are around 6 or 7 years old, you may start losing your baby teeth. A tooth will become loose and eventually fall out, making room for the larger permanent tooth. Also, as you continue to grow, additional teeth will grow in the back of your mouth that will not fall out. If all your teeth come in normally, you will have 32 teeth when you are an adult.

Fun Fact

If you're right handed, you will usually chew your food on your right side. If you're left handed, you will tend to chew your food on your left side.

Digestion

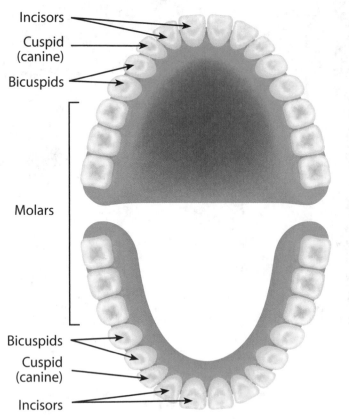

Incisors
Cuspid (canine)
Bicuspids

Molars

Bicuspids
Cuspid (canine)
Incisors

All of the teeth in your mouth are shaped differently and serve different functions. To the left is a chart showing the names of the teeth. In the front of your mouth are the incisors. **Incisors** have sharp straight edges for cutting and biting. On either side of the incisors are the **cuspids** or **canine teeth**. Canine teeth are pointed for tearing. Further back in the mouth are the bicuspids and molars. **Bicuspids** and **molars** are bumpy with a larger surface area for grinding.

What did we learn?

- What is the job of each kind of tooth?
- Why do people have baby teeth and why do they fall out?

Taking it further

- Why do we need to take care of our teeth?

Teeth molds

Purpose: To get a good look at your own teeth

Materials: modeling clay, tag board, plaster of Paris, aluminum foil

Procedure:

1. Form some modeling clay into a cookie shape about ¾ inch thick that will fit inside your mouth and around your teeth.

2. Press the clay onto your upper teeth up to the gums and then carefully remove the clay. Repeat this process for your bottom teeth.

3. Cut a two-inch wide strip of tag board, wrap it snugly around the clay, and tape the ends together. This should form a collar around the clay to hold the plaster. Repeat this for each piece of clay.

4. In a small bowl or cup, mix enough water with a small amount of plaster of Paris to form a creamy liquid.

5. Place the clay molds on a piece of foil and pour a small amount of plaster into each clay mold and shake the molds gently to fill in all the cracks.

6. Pour in enough plaster to fill the mold about half way up the collar.

7. Allow the plaster to dry for at least 8 hours.

8. When the plaster is dry, gently remove the tag board and the clay.

Conclusion: What you end up with should look something like the chart on the previous page though you probably have fewer teeth. Name each tooth and review its function in the eating process.

Digestion

🏅 Tooth structure

There are three parts to any tooth. The first part is the crown. This is the part of the tooth that you see. The crown is the part that helps you chew your food and allows you to have a beautiful smile. Below the crown is the part of the tooth called the neck. The neck goes down into your gums. Finally, the root of the tooth holds the tooth tightly in your jaw. When you lose your baby teeth, the roots of the teeth dissolve which is why they fall out.

If you look at a cross section of a tooth you see that the innermost part of the tooth is the pulp. The pulp contains nerves and blood vessels, which nourish the tooth and keep it healthy. These blood vessels enter the tooth at the tips of the roots and run up through the root canals. Surrounding the pulp is a substance called dentin. Dentin is a bone-like layer that gives the tooth its shape and size. Covering the dentin is a layer of enamel. Enamel is the hardest substance in the body and is comprised mostly of calcium and phosphorous.

The roots of the tooth are surrounded by a substance called cementum, which does exactly what it sounds like: it cements the tooth in place. Between the cementum and the jawbone itself is a fiber called the periodontal ligament, and above the jawbone is the gingiva, which you call your gums.

Although there is some controversy about whether fluoride should be added to drinking water, it is true that fluoride makes teeth stronger and more resistant to decay, and many cities add a fluoride compound to the water supply. Fluoride reacts chemically with the enamel in the tooth to make it more resistant to decay. Before a tooth erupts, fluoride reacts with the dentin and pulp as well as the enamel; however, after the tooth comes in only the enamel reacts with the fluoride.

Use three different colors of modeling clay to make a cross-section model of a tooth. Be sure to review the function and name of each part of the tooth.

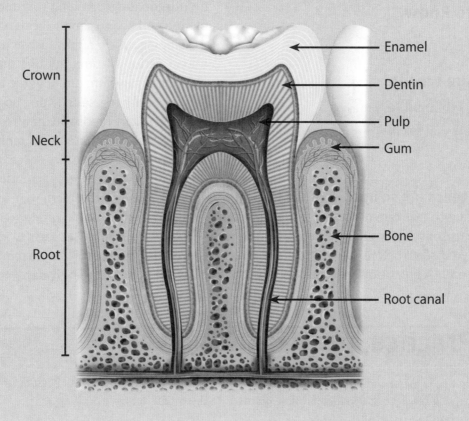

Crown · Neck · Root · Enamel · Dentin · Pulp · Gum · Bone · Root canal

Digestion

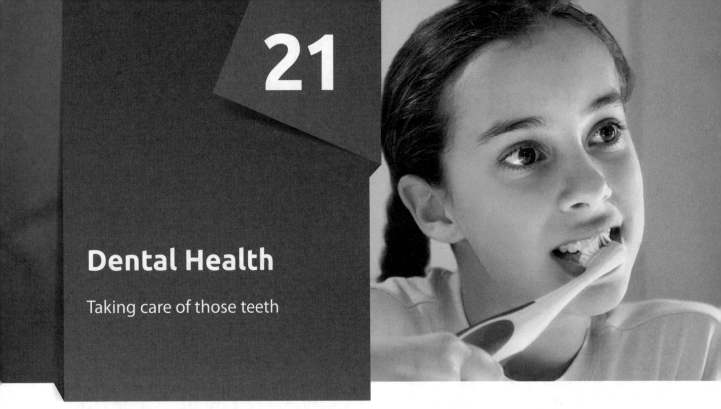

21

Dental Health

Taking care of those teeth

How do you properly care for your teeth?

Words to know:

plaque

Challenge words:

orthodontics   retainer

occlusion

Because teeth are so important to eating, it is important to take care of them. There are some very good reasons why your mom or dad makes you brush your teeth before you go to bed. Bacteria in your mouth break down sugars and form an acid. This is a natural part of the digestive process. However, these acids can attack the outside of your teeth and damage the enamel if they remain in your mouth too long. Brushing your teeth removes bits of food and helps keep the acids off of your teeth.

Sipping sugary drinks such as juice or soda over a long period of time, sucking on hard candy, or chewing sugary gum prolongs the time that sugar is in your mouth. These activities should be avoided. If you limit sugary foods and drinks to meal times, this helps reduce the amount of sugar in your mouth.

Also, a sticky substance called **plaque** builds up on the teeth. This not only traps the bacteria, sugar, and acid against the teeth, but it can also cause infection in the gums if it is not removed regularly. So, you should brush at least twice each day. You should also use dental floss to remove plaque from between your teeth each day. Finally, you should

 Practice, practice

Stand in front of a mirror and practice brushing your teeth. Have your teacher or parent demonstrate proper methods of brushing teeth. After you have adequately brushed, have them show you how to floss your teeth, and then get help flossing all your teeth. You may have already learned these things, but it never hurts to review these important skills.

If you are unsure how to brush or floss properly, you may contact a dentist (who will be happy to help teach you the proper methods for caring for your teeth).

visit your dentist twice a year to have your teeth cleaned.

Eating healthy foods such as fruits and vegetables, and foods with calcium help strengthen your teeth. Especially avoid eating sticky, chewy foods that stick to your teeth. If you do eat sticky foods, you should brush your teeth right away. Developing good dental habits while you are young will help you keep your teeth healthy throughout your life.

 ## What did we learn?

- What are three things you can do to have healthy teeth?
- How does brushing your teeth help keep them healthy?
- List some foods that are good for your teeth.
- List some foods that are bad for your teeth.

 ## Taking it further

- Since your baby teeth are going to fall out anyway, why do you still need to brush them and take care of them?

 ## Straight teeth

Many children and teenagers, and even some adults, have braces to help straighten teeth that do not come in straight or to correct jaw alignment. The practice of straightening teeth and correcting how they line up is called orthodontics. Attempts have been made to correct the way a person's teeth look for more than a thousand years; however, modern orthodontics began around 1850. To begin with, people attempted to correct poor tooth alignment by pulling teeth. Then in the 1890s they began replacing extracted teeth with false teeth to improve a person's appearance.

Also in the 1890s, Dr. Edward Angle developed a classification system for how teeth and jaws line up with each other. This system helped establish what would be considered a normal occlusion, or normal bite. Once orthodontists knew what was normal they developed ways to not only straighten the teeth but to also improve the alignment of the jaws.

Today, orthodontists use a variety of methods to correct crooked teeth and misaligned jaws. These methods include brackets attached to the teeth with wires between the brackets as wells as elastic bands, expanders, and headgear. A special plastic mouthpiece can sometimes be used to align teeth that are not too far out of place. Once a person's teeth and jaws are corrected, they usually wear a

retainer to hold the teeth in the proper position until the bones around the teeth grow solid. A proper bite not only improves a person's looks, but also improves dental health.

Orthodontics is much more common today than it was only 20 to 30 years ago. Do a survey to find out how many people you know have had braces. Ask 10 adults and 10 young people and find out how many of them have had or currently have braces. You will probably find that a higher percentage of the young people have had braces than of the adults.

Nutrition

What should you eat?

What does a healthy diet look like?

Words to know:

carbohydrate

The digestive system takes the food you eat and turns it into energy and nutrients for your body. But your body can only use what you feed it. Therefore, it is very important to eat the right foods and drink the right liquids so your body will have what it needs to grow strong and healthy. Eating too many sugary or high-fat foods can make you feel full and not willing to eat the foods that are better for you. Also, leaving out one of the food groups can prevent you from getting the vitamins and minerals your body needs. Thankfully, God has created a wide variety of foods. And people are very creative in preparing these foods so you can enjoy eating what your body needs.

To help you understand the different kinds of foods available, scientists have grouped foods together by the nutrients they supply to your body. The food groups include breads and grains, vegetables, fruits, dairy products, and meat and beans.

Breads and grains are high in **carbohydrates**, which are sugars and starches. Carbohydrates are a great source of energy. Foods in this category include whole wheat bread, oats, corn, cereals, rice, crackers, and pasta. You need to eat a significant amount of these kinds of foods each day.

Fruits and vegetables are probably the most important foods for you to eat. These foods are full of carbohydrates, vitamins, and minerals. Vegetables come in a wide variety of flavors, colors, and textures. Most can be enjoyed raw or cooked. Vegetables include broccoli, carrots, cucumbers, squash, green beans, peas, onions, tomatoes, lettuce, cabbage, beets, eggplant, and much more. Fruits are a sweet treat that can be eaten at any meal or as a healthy snack. Fruits include apples, pears, cherries, grapes, mangoes, strawberries, raspberries, pineapples, bananas, cranberries, grapefruit, lemons, oranges, and much more.

Many people, especially children, do not eat enough fruits and vegetables. You need to eat several servings of these healthy foods each day. Fresh or frozen fruits and vegetables almost always have more nutritional value than canned fruits and

Fun Fact

It can take more energy to digest celery than what you get from eating it, so a celery snack won't spoil your dinner!

vegetables. You should eat a wide variety of fruits and vegetables. Eating the same vegetable or the same fruit every day will not give you all of the nutrients that you need.

The next food group is the dairy group. This includes foods such as milk, cheese, and yogurt. These products provide calcium and protein for strong muscles and bones. Some people are concerned about getting too much fat from these products. You can limit the fat by drinking skim milk or eating low-fat cheese. But it is important to include dairy products so that you get the important nutrients that these foods provide.

The meat group includes beef, pork, fish, poultry, nuts, peanuts, and dried beans. All of these foods contain protein, which is needed for rapid growth and strong muscles. Again, variety is important so you receive all the different nutrients that your body needs.

If you look carefully through all the foods listed here, you will see that there are no cookies, potato chips, candy, soda, or other junk foods listed. These items are called junk food because they do not provide you with many nutrients and they are high in calories. They fill you up, but do not give you many of the building blocks that your body needs. You should limit the amount of sweets and fatty foods that you eat. It is okay to eat these foods in small amounts, but you should try to eat mostly foods that will help you grow strong and healthy. You are better off choosing a piece of fruit or some carrot sticks for a snack than a cookie or chips.

🧠 What did we learn?

- What are the five food groups listed in this lesson?
- What types of foods should you eat only a small amount of each day?
- Why is variety in your diet important?

🚀 Taking it further

- Can a vegetarian eat a balanced diet? Hint: What other foods contain proteins found in meat?
- Is it necessary to eat dessert to have a healthy diet?

⚗️ Eating a healthy meal

Plan a healthy lunch for you and your family. Be sure to select foods from all the different food groups. Arrange the food on each plate in a fun way. For example, you could make a face with the food by using broccoli pieces or carrot sticks to form a smile along the bottom of the plate, use apple slices for the ears, crackers with peanut butter for the eyes, and raisins for the nose. Add a glass of milk and you will have a creative and healthy meal.

🏅 Nutrition worksheet

Complete the "Nutrition Worksheet" to get a better idea of why some foods are good for you and why others are not so good for you. You can probably find the needed information on food labels in your kitchen or on the Internet.

Digestion

Florence Nightingale

1820–1910

The profession of nursing as we know it today owes much to one remarkable lady—Florence Nightingale. She is considered to be the first real nurse in England, and she became famous because she took other women to a war zone to help those who were wounded. But have you ever wanted to know why she did what she did? It was because God called her to do it.

Florence was born in Florence, Italy in 1820. She and her family returned to their home in England the next year. The Nightingales were a very wealthy family. Florence received most of her education at home from her father.

When Florence was almost 17 years old, she sensed God speaking to her, calling her to His service. But she was not sure how He wanted her to serve Him. From that time on she looked for ways to serve God. For several years Florence sought advice about how she could serve the poor and hurting people around her. In 1842 she learned about an orphanage and hospital in Germany where trained nurses were taking care of the poor in clean hospitals. This was a new idea to her, and she began to think about becoming a nurse.

After prayerfully considering her decision, Florence told her parents that she had decided to become a nurse. At this time, women of culture and education did not work as nurses. Nursing was only done by the poor and outcasts of society. Her parents were horrified. Her parents, hoping to change Florence's mind, encouraged her to go on a trip through Europe. But while on that trip, Florence studied what other countries were doing to help the sick and the poor, and she became an expert on hospitals and sanitation.

In 1851 Florence decided to begin formal nurse's training and went to Kaiserwerth in Germany. This

was the hospital she had heard about many years before. For four months she learned how to care for the sick and to treat many diseases. She then continued her education in Paris where Catholic nuns taught her more about nursing the sick.

In 1853 Florence felt that God wanted her to work serving the "sick poor" in England. She was offered the position as superintendent of The Institute for the Care of Sick Gentlewomen in Distressed Circumstances. This was a hospital in England that treated servants of wealthy people. Florence gladly accepted. Finally, she would be able to help in her home country.

The following year, England, France, and Sardinia came to the aid of Turkey in a war against Russia. The public heard of the needs of the wounded soldiers through the newspaper. They were outraged to find that their wounded soldiers were not being taken care of. Sidney Herbert, the Secretary of War, asked Florence to go help the wounded British soldiers, and she felt God calling her to this task. Florence put together a group of 38 nurses and went to Turkey. She was told that the hospital was a splendid facility and had an abundance of supplies. But what she found was quite different. She found a horribly dirty hospital where the wounded were surrounded by filth. There were no supplies, and the doctors were completely overwhelmed.

Florence went right to work. She instituted many changes to benefit the soldiers. Often the doctors opposed her changes. Many of them did not think women should be nurses and none of them liked taking orders from a nurse. But Florence insisted on implementing what she had learned and the results were spectacular. The death rate dropped from 42% to 2% in only five months. Florence and her nurses emerged from the war as heroines to both the soldiers and the people back home.

However, this victory was not without cost. Florence came down with what was called Crimean Fever. Some people believe this may have been Post Traumatic Stress Disorder. She was never strong physically again. She spent most of the rest of her life secluded and often in bed.

Her physical condition did not stop her desire to see improvements in the medical field, however. In 1859 she published a booklet entitled "Notes on Nursing." Millions of copies were sold, and the royalties from the book were the only wages Florence ever received.

Then, in 1860, the Nightingale Training School for nurses opened in London. Fifteen women began the one-year course and thirteen graduated. This school is considered the start of modern nursing, and completely changed the image of female nursing.

In 1861 Florence was asked to set up a plan to care for the sick and wounded of the American Civil War. She sent helpful information to the American Secretary of War and to Dorothea Dix, Superintendent of Nurses for Union forces.

Florence made many important changes to the hospital system in England as well. She set up separate wards for men, women, children, and the insane. She insisted that patients be given bells so they could ring for a nurse when they needed attention. She insisted on sanitary conditions. These changes spread throughout Europe and in 1872, Henri Durant, the founder of the Red Cross, said Florence's work had influenced him greatly.

When Florence was 76 years old, she was confined to bed permanently. At the age of 87, the King of England bestowed on her the "Order of Merit." She was the first woman to receive this high honor. She died in 1910, and at her burial six sergeants of the British Army carried her coffin.

Florence Nightingale followed God's calling on her life, and as a result millions of lives have been saved.

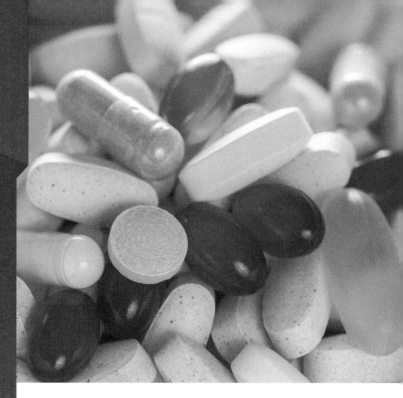

Vitamins & Minerals

Do I have to go to a mine to get minerals?

Where can you find the vitamins and minerals needed for a healthy body?

Foods contain energy in one of three forms: carbohydrates (sugars and starches), proteins, and fats. The digestive system breaks food down so your body can get energy from it. It uses different chemicals from the liver, pancreas, and gallbladder to break down these different forms of food.

Food also contains vitamins and minerals that your body needs. If you eat a wide variety of foods that have not been processed, you should get all of the vitamins and minerals you need. However, many processed foods no longer contain their original nutrients. Therefore, many foods have vitamins and minerals added to them.

Some of the vitamins you need and some of the foods that contain them include:

- Vitamin A—found in eggs, milk, dark green vegetables

- Vitamin B complex—found in wheat germ, brown rice, meat, milk, most vegetables

- Vitamin C—found in citrus fruits, tomatoes, broccoli, green peppers

- Vitamin D—found in milk, salmon, tuna, eggs

- Vitamin E—found in whole grain bread, cabbage, lettuce, yeast

- Vitamin K—found in yogurt, dark green leafy vegetables, cabbage, eggs

Your body also needs many minerals. Most of these are needed in very small amounts. Some of the minerals you need in slightly larger amounts include:

- Calcium—found in dairy products

- Iron—found in meat, dried beans, breads, cereals

- Magnesium—found in whole grains, potatoes, fruits

Fun Fact

Women are more likely to need vitamin and mineral supplements than men are. A woman's body needs more calcium and vitamin D to maintain healthy bones than a man's body does. So women, especially once they reach the age of 40, are often encouraged to take supplements to keep their bodies healthy.

Fun Fact

Your brain is composed of 70% water, your lungs are nearly 90% water, and 83% of your blood is water.

- Phosphorus—found in milk, cheese, dried beans
- Sodium—found in salt, milk, tomatoes, celery, meat
- Potassium—found in bananas and other fruits, soybeans, mushrooms, breads

By eating a wide variety of foods, you will get the vitamins and minerals your body needs.

Finally, one of the most important substances that you need for good health is water. Your body is about 60% water. Every cell contains water. Water is used in nearly every function of the body. So it is vital to restore the water in the body everyday. The amount of water needed varies depending on your size and activity level, the foods you eat, and the temperature outside. Some water comes from the foods we eat, but to be healthy most children should drink about six glasses of water every day. To avoid getting too much sugar and salt, water is a better choice than soda pop.

What did we learn?

- What are the three main forms of energy found in food?
- How can we be sure to get enough vitamins and minerals in our diet?
- Why is water so important to our diet?

Taking it further

- Can you drink soda instead of water?
- Are frozen dinners just as healthy as fresh food?
- Is restaurant food as healthy as home-cooked food?

Vitamin & mineral scavenger hunt

Purpose: To find as many of the vitamins and minerals listed in this lesson as you can

Materials: food containers

Procedure:

1. Take a look at several cans and boxes of food in your kitchen. By law, every package of food must be labeled with certain nutritional information. This includes serving size and servings per container, calories, grams of fat, carbohydrates and protein, and certain vitamins and minerals.

2. See how many of the vitamins and minerals listed in this lesson you can find in the foods on the shelves of your kitchen. Breakfast cereals almost always have added vitamins and minerals, so that is an easy place to start.

3. After checking out a variety of foods, write out a menu for at least three meals, including breakfast, lunch, and dinner.

4. For each meal record how many servings of each food group are included. Also, make a list of the vitamins and minerals that are included in each meal. When determining food groups, think about if a food fits into more than one category. For example, yogurt with fruit in it might give you a serving of dairy and a serving of fruit as well. A peanut butter and jelly sandwich contains a serving of bread, a serving of meats/nuts, and possibly a serving of fruit if the jelly actually has real fruit in it..

Health problems

A lack of a particular vitamin or mineral in your diet can lead to serious health problems. Scurvy is a disease caused by a lack of vitamin C. This disease used to be common among sailors, pirates, and soldiers who lived on a diet of salted meat and dried crackers for extended periods of time. Vitamin C is found in many fresh fruits including citrus fruits like oranges and lemons, and in vegetables like bell peppers and tomatoes. However, these foods tend to spoil quickly so were not taken on long voyages. The symptoms of scurvy include fatigue, spots on the skin, bleeding gums, and loss of teeth. If the disease becomes severe the person will eventually die. Many passengers and sailors on long ocean voyages died of scurvy.

Many people tried to find a treatment for scurvy, but the exact cause was not fully understood until 1932. Many navies were successful in treating the disease without knowing the exact cause by including lemon juice or vinegar in the daily rations. Today, scurvy is understood and quickly treated with a diet rich in vitamin C.

Another serious disease related to diet is rickets. Rickets is caused by a lack of vitamin D or a lack of calcium. Calcium is necessary for building strong bones and vitamin D is needed by the body to absorb calcium in the digestive tract. So even if a person eats foods containing calcium, they may not be able to absorb it if they do not have the necessary vitamin D in their bodies.

Because of a lack of calcium, people with rickets develop soft bones which often results in a deformed skeleton. This could include bowed legs, square skull, and other misshapen bones. The majority of the cases of rickets occur in children. Most of these children live in poor countries with limited diets. But recently several cases of rickets were diagnosed in England. These cases were caused by a lack of sunlight due to over use of strong sunblock. You may wonder what sunblock has to do with vitamin D. Well, sunlight is necessary to change inactive vitamin D in your skin into active useful vitamin D.

So if a child does not have any exposure to sunlight, his body will not be able to make useful vitamin D and will not be able to absorb and use the calcium needed for strong bones. Too much sunlight can damage skin, so it's important to limit exposure, but we should not completely avoid exposure to sunlight.

Most people can avoid rickets if they eat properly and get a few minutes of sunshine each day. Foods that contain vitamin D include butter, eggs, fish, and certain mushrooms. Dairy products such as milk, cheese, and yogurt are a great source of calcium and often have vitamin D added to them. So, if you eat well and spend some time outside, you should not have to worry about rickets.

Anemia is another serious disease caused by poor diet. Anemia is defined as a serious decrease in red blood cells or a lowered ability for the blood to carry oxygen to the cells in the body. Anemia can be caused by several different things, but the most common cause is a lack of iron and vitamin B12 in the body. People with anemia often feel weak or tired. They can experience shortness of breath and even pass out. In severe cases, they can even experience heart failure.

It is estimated that nearly one-fourth of the world population suffers from some form of anemia and that more than half of these people have anemia because of a lack of iron in their diets. Most of these people suffer from malnutrition, and over 180,000 people die each year from anemia. Most of these cases could be prevented with good nutrition. Foods that contain iron include most meats, tuna, eggs, shrimp, oatmeal, spinach and other green leafy vegetables, and peanut butter. People with severe anemia or with an increased risk of developing anemia are often given iron supplements to take in addition to the food they eat.

Most of you live in a part of the world where healthy food is abundant. When you think about all the great foods that are available, you can be thankful that they contain all the vitamins and minerals needed to keep you healthy.

Digestion

UNIT 5

Heart & Lungs

24 The Circulatory System

25 The Heart

26 Blood

27 The Respiratory System

28 The Lungs

◊ **Describe** the flow of blood through the heart, veins, and arteries.

◊ **Explain** the function of the different parts of blood.

◊ **Describe** the flow of air through the respiratory system.

◊ **Describe** how the circulatory and respiratory systems interact.

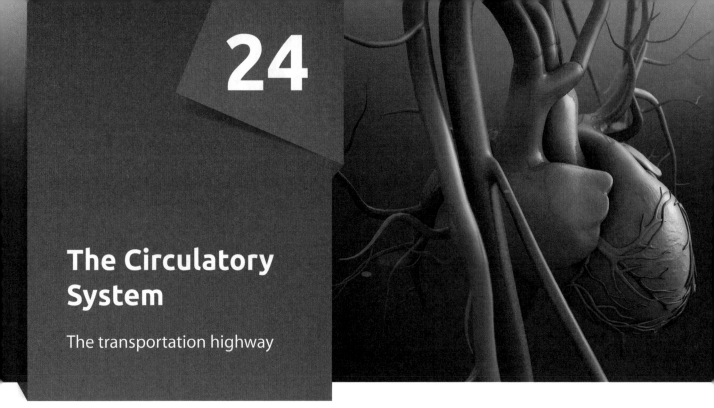

24

The Circulatory System

The transportation highway

How many directions does blood flow in your body?

Words to know:

circulatory system   vein

artery   capillary

Challenge words:

blood pressure   diastolic blood pressure

systolic blood pressure

The transportation highway of your body is the circulatory system. This system is made up of your heart, blood, and blood vessels. Your heart is really a magnificent pump, which pushes the blood throughout your entire body. This highway transports needed materials to each cell and carts away waste materials. The red blood cells are like trucks, the valves in the blood vessels are like traffic signals, and oxygen and carbon dioxide are some of the cargo that gets transported.

Blood is pushed out of the heart into the lungs where the red blood cells receive oxygen and give up carbon dioxide. This blood then returns to the heart where it is pumped throughout the body. As the blood passes through the digestive system, it absorbs food and nutrients to carry to the rest of the body. As it deposits nutrients and oxygen in the body's cells, it picks up carbon dioxide and other waste products that will be eliminated by the lungs and kidneys.

Each time the blood circulates from the heart out to the body, about 20% of it goes through the kidneys. The kidneys filter out some of the waste before the blood heads back to the heart.

Your heart pushes your blood 24 hours a day, 7 days a week, every day of the year, and you don't even have to think about it. Your blood makes about 600 round trips from your heart to the other parts of the body each day. If other body systems quit working, your body can often compensate. You can survive for many days without eating and some people live their whole lives without being able to see or hear. But you can only live a few

Fun Fact

The body contains approximately 25 trillion red blood cells. Each red blood cell lives about 120 days before it must be replaced. Therefore, the marrow in your long bones keeps very busy producing 2 million red blood cells every second!

Heart & Lungs

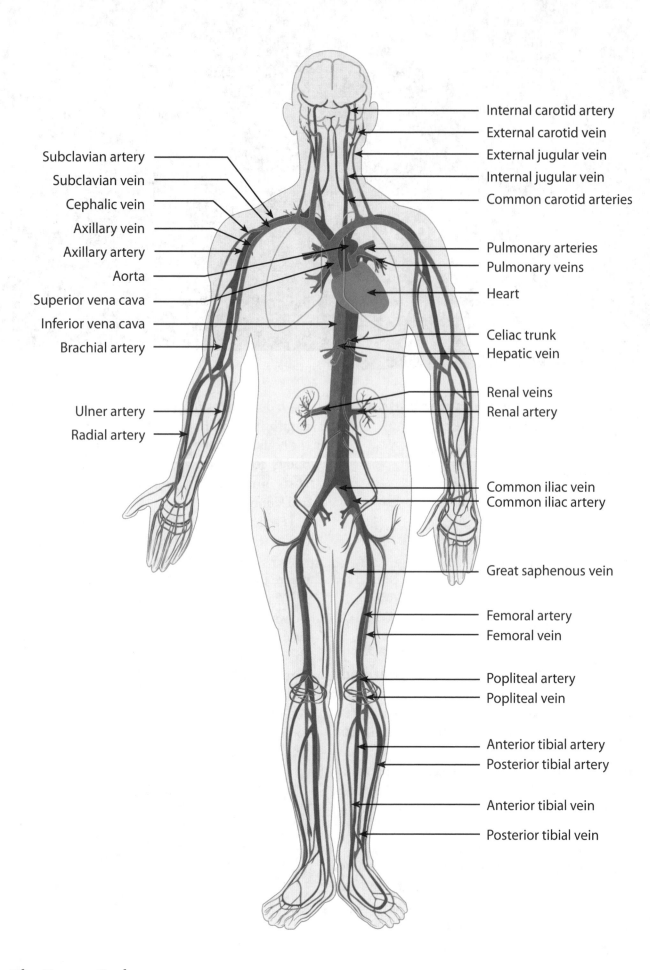

Internal carotid artery

External carotid vein

External jugular vein

Internal jugular vein

Common carotid arteries

Subclavian artery

Subclavian vein

Cephalic vein

Axillary vein

Axillary artery

Aorta

Superior vena cava

Inferior vena cava

Brachial artery

Pulmonary arteries

Pulmonary veins

Heart

Celiac trunk

Hepatic vein

Ulner artery

Radial artery

Renal veins

Renal artery

Common iliac vein

Common iliac artery

Great saphenous vein

Femoral artery

Femoral vein

Popliteal artery

Popliteal vein

Anterior tibial artery

Posterior tibial artery

Anterior tibial vein

Posterior tibial vein

Heart & Lungs

minutes without your heart pumping oxygen-rich blood throughout your body.

As blood travels throughout your body, it goes through three kinds of blood vessels. **Arteries** carry blood away from the heart. **Veins** carry blood toward the heart. **Capillaries** are the very small vessels connecting veins with arteries. This is where the blood exchanges oxygen for carbon dioxide. Capillaries are so small that the red blood cells must go through single file—one at a time. On the previous page is a diagram showing the major veins and arteries in your body.

Blood can only flow in one direction through the heart because valves inside it only open in one direction. When the heart contracts, blood is pushed through these valves, then when the heart rests, the valves close and the blood cannot flow back. God has truly created an amazing system for nourishing every cell in your body.

What did we learn?

- What are the three main parts of the circulatory system?
- What are two functions of blood?
- What are three types of blood vessels?
- Which blood vessels carry blood away from the heart?
- Which blood vessels carry blood toward the heart?
- What happens to the blood in the capillaries?

Taking it further

- How is the circulatory system like a highway?
- Why is exercise important for your circulatory system?
- List two other systems that depend on the circulatory system to function properly.
- Why does your pulse increase when you exercise?

🧪 Measuring your pulse

Your pulse is the number of times your heart beats each minute. There are several places where you can feel your pulse. The most commonly used location is on your wrist, just up your arm from your thumb joint. Another place is on your thumb. (Don't use your thumb to feel someone else's pulse, you just might be feeling your own instead.) A third place that you can easily feel your pulse is either side of your neck, just below your jaw. You can feel your pulse in these areas because these blood vessels are near the surface and are large enough for you to feel the surge of blood each time your heart beats.

Purpose: To test the effects of exercise on your heartbeat

Materials: stopwatch

Procedure:

1. Sit still for five minutes
2. Find your pulse and, using a stopwatch, count how many times your heart beats in 15 seconds.
3. Multiply that number by 4 to estimate your resting heart rate (beats per minute).
4. Next, exercise for 5 minutes by running in place or doing jumping jacks.
5. Now measure your pulse again.
6. Finally, rest for 5 minutes and measure your pulse again. What did you notice about your pulse?

🎖 Blood pressure

Have you ever heard someone say they have high blood pressure? You many not know what that really means. Blood pressure refers to the pressure placed on the walls of the blood vessels as they carry the blood throughout the body. This pressure is what keeps the blood moving.

The pressure in your blood vessels is not constant. If you are sleeping, your blood pressure will be lower than when you are exercising. The pressure also changes as your heart beats and then rests. When the ventricles in your heart squeeze the blood out, the pressure in your blood vessels goes up. This is called systolic blood pressure. When your heart rests, the pressure in your vessels goes down. This is called diastolic blood pressure. The ratio of the systolic over diastolic pressure is referred to as your blood pressure.

This blood pressure is measured in units called millimeters of mercury or mmHg. The normal range for systolic blood pressure is 110–140 mmHg and the normal range for diastolic pressure is 60–90 mmHg. So a normal blood pressure might be 120 over 80, written as 120/80. If either number is above the normal range, that person is said to have high blood pressure.

High blood pressure puts stress on the heart and can cause many health problems. Therefore, people with high blood pressure often have special diets and exercise programs to help lower their pressure, or they may take medication to keep their blood pressure under control.

If you have a chance, find out what your blood pressure is. You can have your blood pressure measured at a doctor's office or clinic.

Heart & Lungs

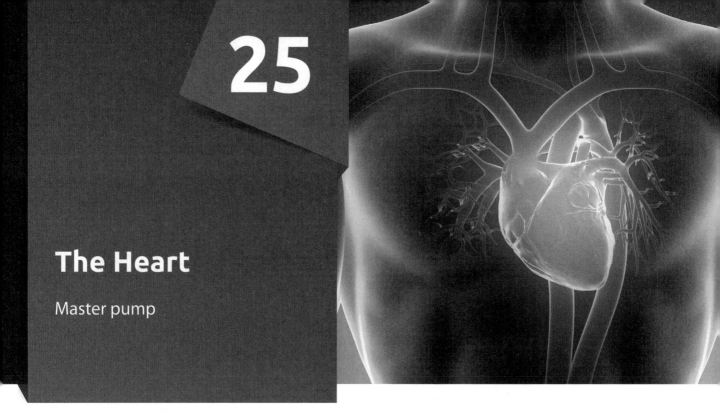

25

The Heart

Master pump

Why does your heart need valves and chambers?

Words to know:

atrium	superior vena cava
ventricle	inferior vena cava
pulmonary artery	aorta
pulmonary vein	coronary arteries
hemoglobin	

The heart is the major organ of the circu-latory system and one of the most important organs in your entire body. That is why God designed it to rest inside your rib cage surrounded by a layer of fat where it is protected from the outside world. The heart is a very strong muscle that contracts and relaxes about 70 times each minute for adults and more often for children. When the heart contracts it pushes blood out and when it relaxes it allows blood to flow into it.

The human heart is designed with four sections, or chambers. The upper chambers are the right **atrium** and the left atrium. The lower chambers are the right **ventricle** and the left ventricle. Blood from the body enters the right atrium

through the vena cava veins. The **superior vena cava** carries blood from the upper body and the **inferior vena cava** brings blood from the lower body to the right atrium. The blood moves from the atrium into the ventricle. When the heart squeezes, the blood is forced out of the right ventricle to the lungs through the **pulmonary artery**. In the lungs the blood gets rid of carbon dioxide and absorbs oxygen. The oxygen-rich blood now returns to the heart through the **pulmonary vein** which is connected to the left atrium. The blood moves from the left atrium into the left ventricle. Then when the heart contracts it forces the blood out of the heart through the **aorta**. The arteries on the top of the aorta carry blood to the upper part of the body and the lower part of the aorta

Fun Fact

Why do the veins on your arms and hands appear blue? Do you have blue blood? The blue color you see is due to an optical effect caused by the way in which light penetrates through the skin. This has led to a common belief that the oxygen-depleted blood in our veins is blue. The blood in your veins is not blue, it just appears that way. It is actually a dark red.

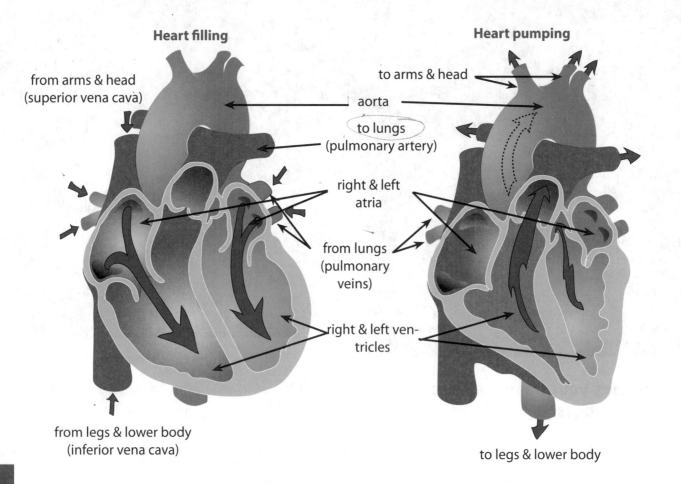

Heart filling

from arms & head
(superior vena cava)

aorta

to lungs
(pulmonary artery)

right & left
atria

from lungs
(pulmonary
veins)

right & left ven-
tricles

from legs & lower body
(inferior vena cava)

Heart pumping

to arms & head

to legs & lower body

carries blood to the lower body and legs.

Along the surface of the heart are several arteries called **coronary arteries**, which carry oxygenated blood to nourish the cells of the heart muscle. There is also a network of nerves throughout the heart that controls the contractions of the heart muscle so that it squeezes and relaxes at just the right times.

Between each atrium and ventricle is a special valve that prevents blood from flowing backward. On the right side the valve has three parts and on the left side the valve has two parts. These valves open when the heart is relaxed to allow blood to flow down from the atrium into the ventricle. Then when the heart contracts these valves close so the blood is forced out of the arteries.

Your heart pumps blood through about 60,000 miles (96,500 km) of blood vessels. Though your heart beats 24 hours a day, 7 days a week, it also gets to rest in between each contraction. So, it actually is working less than half of the time.

Since your heart is a muscle you can make it stronger by exercising it. Doing regular exercise a few times each week makes your heart stronger so it doesn't have to work as hard the rest of the time.

What did we learn?

- What are the four chambers of the heart?
- How many times does a blood cell pass through the heart on each trip around the body?

Taking it further

- What are some things you can do to help your heart stay healthy?
- Is your heart shaped like a valentine?
- Does Jesus live in your physical heart?

Blood flow in the heart

A chemical in red blood cells, called hemoglobin, is what makes these cells red. Hemoglobin turns bright red when it reacts with oxygen. When oxygen leaves the blood cells and enters the surrounding tissues, the red blood cells lose their bright red color and turn a dark red.

Fill out "The Heart" worksheet. Color blood containing oxygen red and blood containing carbon dioxide blue. Review the flow of blood through the heart.

Remember that blood flowing from the body into the heart and lungs should be colored blue even though your blood is never really blue (see Fun Fact), and blood flowing from the lungs and out of the heart to the rest of the body should be red.

Examine a heart

Mammals such as sheep and cattle have a four-chambered heart similar to a human heart. You can learn a lot about how the human heart looks and works by examining a cow's heart. You can obtain a cow's heart from your local grocery store or butcher. If you prefer, you can order a preserved cow's heart or sheep heart from a science supply store.

For those of you who are too squeamish to actually dissect a heart, you can view a dissection online at several different web sites. Even if you are not squeamish, you might want to watch a video to help you identify all of the parts of the heart and its attached blood vessels. There are several videos of both cow and sheep heart dissections on YouTube.

Purpose: To dissect a heart

Materials: cow or sheep heart, knife, anatomy book

Procedure:

1. Be sure to use gloves when handling the heart. Examine the outside of the heart. Look for the veins and arteries where the blood enters and leaves the heart.

2. Squeeze the heart and see if you can feel the chambers.

3. Carefully cut open the heart. Look for each of the four chambers. Look also for the valves that keep the blood flowing in the right direction through the heart. You can use an anatomy book or a dissection guide as a reference to help you locate all the various parts of the heart (also see the diagram on the previous page).

Heart & Lungs

26

Blood

Delivery trucks and policemen

How many different parts are found in your blood?

Words to know:

plasma

red blood cell

white blood cell

platelet

fibrin

Challenge words:

antigen

blood type

universal donor

universal recipient

If the circulatory system is a transporta-tion highway, then your blood cells are the delivery trucks, construction workers, and policemen. Blood is made up of four parts. Fifty-five percent of your blood is plasma. This is a yellowish liquid that carries the blood cells through the blood vessels. Red blood cells make up 44.5% of your blood. Red blood cells are the delivery trucks that carry oxygen and nutrients to your cells and carry away waste products. The last 0.5% is made up of white blood cells and platelets.

White blood cells are the policemen of the highway. If anything enters the body that does not belong, such as a germ, the white blood cells surround and eliminate it to help prevent infection and

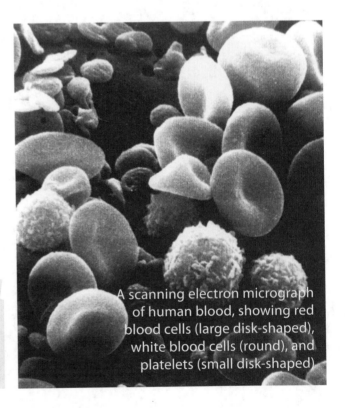

A scanning electron micrograph of human blood, showing red blood cells (large disk-shaped), white blood cells (round), and platelets (small disk-shaped)

Fun Fact

If all your red blood cells were laid side by side, they would make a line that went around the Earth four times!

illness. The platelets are the highway construction crew. If there is a break in the highway, like when you cut your finger or skin your knee, platelets go to the break and stick together to close the cut. Then a stringy substance called fibrin forms a web over the cut and traps red blood cells in the web. This hardens into a scab and protects the area until the cut is healed. This keeps blood from escaping and germs from entering.

The body has approximately 25 trillion red blood cells. These cells are very tiny and very efficient. As red blood cells age they become stiff and less efficient, so they must be replaced. New red blood cells are generated in the bone marrow found in the center of long bones. The spleen and liver break down the old red blood cells, and their parts such as hemoglobin and iron are recycled to be used in making new red blood cells. Blood, with its ability to bring oxygen to every cell in the body, is perhaps the most essential part of your body.

 # Blood cell game

Purpose: To model the role of blood cells

Materials: chairs, construction paper

Red blood cells—Procedure:

1. Set chairs in two rows to represent the blood vessel.

2. Have the chairs become closer at one end to represent a capillary.

3. Set pieces of blue construction paper on the capillary chairs.

4. Have several people pretend to be red blood cells by holding red pieces of paper.

5. Go through the capillary one at a time and set down the red paper and pick up a blue paper. This represents the exchange of oxygen and carbon dioxide.

White blood cells and platelets—Procedure:

1. Some of you pretend to be white blood cells and others pretend to be platelets. One person should pretend to be a germ.

2. The germ starts outside the chairs and, when a break is made in the line of chairs, the germ enters the blood vessel.

3. The white blood cells surround the germ and take it back outside the vessel while the platelets rush to the opening and form a wall to prevent other germs from entering.

 # Making "sample" blood

As you learned in the lesson, blood is made up of approximately 55% plasma, 44.5% red blood cells, 0.25% white blood cells, and 0.25% platelets. You can visualize this mixture by making your own sample blood.

Purpose: To make a "sample" of blood

Materials: corn syrup, red-hot candies, white jelly beans, candy sprinkles

Procedure:

1. Pour ½ cup corn syrup into a bowl. This represents the plasma.

2. Add ½ cup red-hot candies. This represents the red blood cells in your blood.

3. Add 1 tablespoon of white jelly beans, representing the white blood cells, and 1 tablespoon of candy sprinkles representing the platelets.

4. Mix these ingredients together and you have sample blood. What is the main color of your mixture? It should be red just like your real blood because of all the red blood cells.

🧠 What did we learn?

- What are the four parts of blood and the function of each part?
- What does your body do to help protect itself if you get cut?
- Do you have more red or white blood cells?

🚀 Taking it further

- What are some of the dangers of a serious cut?

🏅 Blood transfusions

If someone has a serious injury and loses a large amount of blood, it may be necessary to give that person a blood transfusion to save her life. However, though all blood contains the same basic ingredients, all blood is not the same. Red blood cells contain certain information that makes it so your body recognizes your own cells and distinguishes them from invaders. Blood that will be accepted by the person's body must be used in the transfusion. If the wrong blood type is used, the person's body will attack the blood cells and this could result in death.

The first recorded blood transfusion took place in the 1660s when a man named Richard Lower tried transfusing blood between dogs. He had some success so he tried transfusing lamb's blood into a human. The patient died and blood transfusions were outlawed for some time. Then in 1818 a man named James Blundell performed the first successful blood transfusion between a husband and a wife. However, some of his other patients died. Doctors and scientists did not really understand why. Finally, in 1901 Karl Landsteiner discovered that red blood cells carry antigens, which are like identification tags on the cells. These antigens are called antigen A and antigen B. The presence or absence of these antigens determines a person's blood type.

Someone with blood type A has blood that contains only antigen A. His blood contains antibodies (substances that attack and destroy invaders), which attack antigen B cells. Someone with blood type B has only antigen B and has antibodies that attack antigen A. Some people have both antigens A and B in their blood and do not have any antibodies against other blood types. These people have type AB blood. Other people have neither A nor B antigens and are said to have type O blood. These people have antibodies that will attack both A and B blood cells. It is vitally important to determine the blood type of both the donor and the recipient before a blood transfusion takes place, to ensure that there will not be a problem.

Approximately 43% of the people in the world have type O blood, 40% have type A, 12% have type B, and 5% have type AB blood.

In addition to the antigens that determine the four major blood types, blood can also contain another tag called the rhesus factor, or Rh factor. If the blood contains this antigen, the person is said to be Rh positive. If the blood does not contain it, they are said to be Rh negative. So a person's blood type could be O positive or A negative, or any other combination. People who are Rh negative have antibodies that fight cells that are Rh positive. So someone that is Rh negative must have blood that is Rh negative, but someone that is Rh positive can receive blood that is either Rh positive or Rh negative. Approximately 85% of the general population is Rh positive. There are other identification tags that vary from person to person, but other tags generally do not cause the serious problems that the ones mentioned here can cause when blood types are mixed.

Given what you just learned, fill out the "Blood Types 1" worksheet showing which type or types of blood can *donate* to each blood type and which type or types of blood can be *received* by each blood type.

Next, fill out the "Blood Types 2" worksheet where we incorporate the Rh factor.

Which blood type is the universal donor (can donate to anyone)? Which blood type is the universal recipient (can receive any type of blood)?

Heart & Lungs

Blood—Who Needs It?

Today we know that blood is one of the most important fluids in the body. It takes oxygen and nourishment to every part of the body, and removes waste products. The white blood cells also protect the body from infection. We also know today that without enough blood a person cannot live. However, people have not always understood this.

It has only been in the last 200 years that we have learned the importance of blood. Prior to that, blood was thought of as useless and in some cases harmful. Many illnesses were believed to be caused by "bad blood" or too much blood. In order to heal the person, the doctors would remove blood from the body. "Let out the blood, let out the disease," was a common motto for doctors until the nineteenth century.

The procedure known as bleeding (or blood-letting) was performed as a remedy for many different symptoms. Often the doctor would call in a barber to bleed the person. The barber would cut a vein or artery to let out the blood. Sometimes barbers would use leeches to suck out the bad blood. Barbers advertised their services with a red and white striped pole in front of their shops. Even though barbers no longer perform medical procedures, they have retained the red and white striped pole in many locations. The practice of using leeches to bleed people led to barbers, and sometimes doctors, being called leeches themselves.

Many patients were harmed and some even died as a result of being bled. George Washington, America's first president, is believed to have died because of blood-letting. President Washington originally had a cold. As he became more seriously ill, his doctors bled him. As he got worse they decided to let out more of the disease by bleeding him again. It is believed that this may have been the actual cause of his death. In the years prior to the 19th century, a person usually had a better chance of surviving using home remedies rather than seeing a doctor.

Understanding of the human body and the practice of medicine have improved dramatically in the last two hundred years. Today, you as a child might know more about the human body than doctors knew 200 to 300 years ago. And you certainly understand the importance of blood better than they did.

The Respiratory System

A breath of fresh air

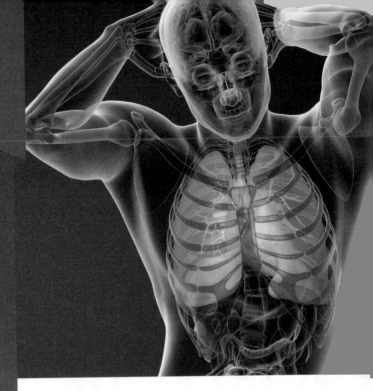

How does oxygen get into your bloodstream?

Words to know:

respiratory system	trachea
diaphragm	bronchi
pharynx	bronchial tubes
larynx	alveoli

Challenge words:

respiration	internal respiration
external respiration	cellular respiration

Although the respiratory system is con-sidered separate from the circulatory system, it is vitally connected to it. The circulatory system's main function is to get oxygen to the body. The respiratory system's main function is to get the oxygen to the blood. It does this through a series of "pipes" that go into the lungs and branch out like a tree's branches.

When you take a breath, a muscle below your lungs, called the diaphragm, contracts. This causes your chest to expand, drawing air into your lungs.

The air goes through your nose and nasal passage, or through your mouth, and into the back of your throat, sometimes called the pharynx. Then it passes through the larynx or voice box. Below the larynx is a tube called the trachea. The trachea splits into two tubes called bronchi, or bronchial tubes, which enter the lungs.

Inside the lungs the bronchial tubes split into many smaller tubes. At the end of each tube is a small sac called an alveolus. Capillaries surround the alveoli. Here, in these capillaries, the oxygen in the air is exchanged with the carbon dioxide in the blood. The oxygen enters the bloodstream to be taken throughout the body, and the carbon dioxide enters the air, which leaves your lungs as you exhale.

Breathing is an automatic function. You don't have to think about it. Your brain responds to the

Fun Fact

Women's vocal cords are generally shorter than men's so they vibrate faster. This gives most women a higher voice than most men. On the average, women's vocal cords vibrate about 220 times per second, whereas men's vocal cords vibrate about 120 times per second when they are speaking.

amount of carbon dioxide in your blood, causing the diaphragm to contract and allowing air to enter your lungs. When the diaphragm relaxes, air is pushed from your lungs. You can consciously control your diaphragm to some extent, but if you try to stop breathing too long, your brain will force you to begin breathing again.

The respiratory system is also an important part of speech. Air passing through the larynx is what allows you to talk and sing. Air causes the vocal cords in the larynx to vibrate, which in turn causes air molecules to vibrate. As you learned earlier, vibrating air produces sound waves. These sound waves leave your larynx and come out of your mouth. Muscles and nerves connected to the larynx are also important for making the proper sounds. These muscles can change the tension in your vocal cords to produce higher and lower pitched sounds. The diaphragm controls how forcefully the air passes to control the volume of the sound. Finally, you can control the muscles in your larynx, mouth, and tongue to produce the different words so you can sing beautiful songs and communicate with other people.

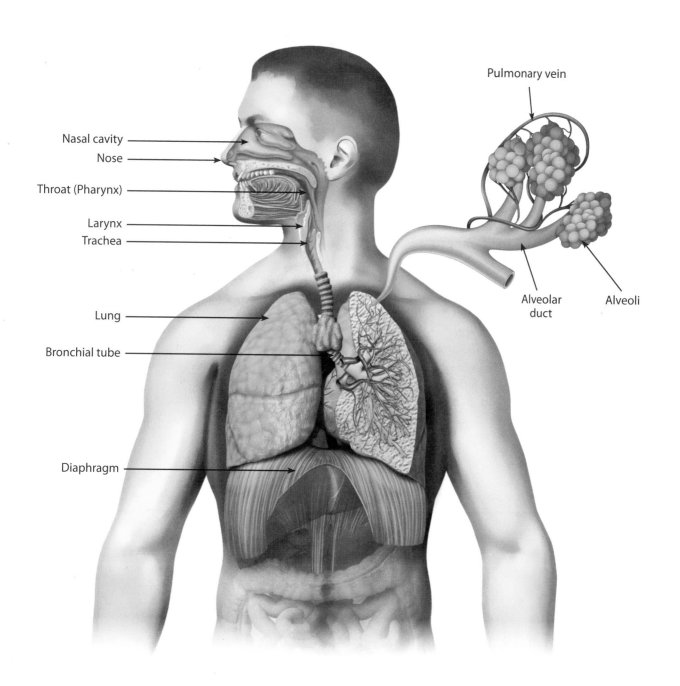

Nasal cavity
Nose
Throat (Pharynx)
Larynx
Trachea
Lung
Bronchial tube
Diaphragm

Pulmonary vein
Alveolar duct
Alveoli

Heart & Lungs

What did we learn?

- Describe the breathing process.
- How do the circulatory and respiratory systems work together?
- Where inside the lungs does the exchange of gases occur?
- What are the major parts of the respiratory system?

 # Taking it further

- How do you suppose your body keeps food from going into your lungs and air from going into your stomach when both enter your body in the back of your throat?
- How does your respiratory system respond when you exercise?
- How does your respiratory system respond when you are sleeping?

 # Respiratory system worksheet

Fill out "The Respiratory System" worksheet.

 # Respiration

When we think of respiration we think of breathing, and respiration definitely occurs when we breathe, but respiration does not always refer to breathing. Respiration is the exchange of oxygen and carbon dioxide. There are really several levels or types of respiration. The process of breathing is called external respiration. External respiration is the exchanging of oxygen for carbon dioxide in the lungs. This exchange occurs between the air and the blood in the lungs. Internal respiration occurs when oxygen and carbon dioxide are exchanged between blood cells and surrounding tissue cells. Finally, cellular respiration occurs when the gases are exchanged within a cell.

Cellular respiration is where the real action is. Inside the cell, oxygen is combined with food molecules to release the energy stored in the food molecules. The by-product of this chemical reaction is carbon dioxide. This is the process that provides energy for all living plants and animals.

We generally associate respiration with animals and photosynthesis with plants. Animals need oxygen, and plants produce oxygen through photosynthesis. However, plants also perform cellular respiration, especially at night when the sun is not shining, to get the energy they need to grow.

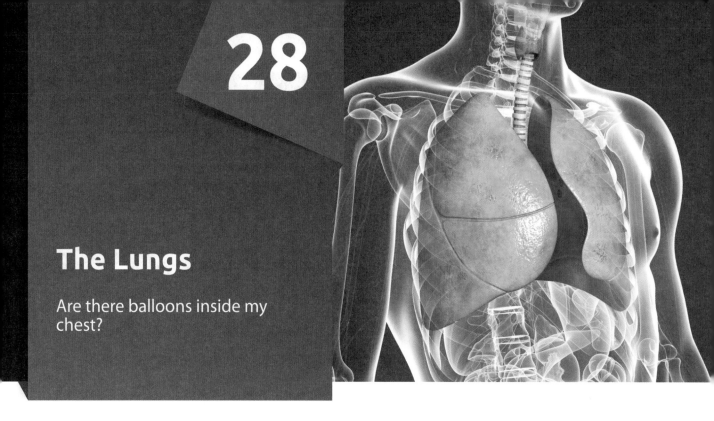

28

The Lungs

Are there balloons inside my chest?

What does the inside of a lung look like?

Words to know:

cilia

asthma

pneumonia

Because lungs inflate and deflate like a balloon, people often think their lungs are just like balloons—empty inside until you take a breath. But this is not the case. As we learned in the last lesson, when you take a breath, the air goes through your nose or mouth, through your trachea, and into your bronchial tubes. These tubes divide over and over again into smaller tubes inside your lungs. At the end of each tube is a small sac called an alveolus. Capillaries carrying blood to and from the heart surround the alveoli. It is in these capillaries that oxygen and carbon dioxide are exchanged. If you looked inside your lungs you would think they resembled a tree with hollow branches much more than a balloon.

The body has been designed to protect the lungs from elements in the air that might damage them. First, hairs in the nasal passage help to filter out dust particles and other debris. Next, special tissues in the back of the throat help kill bacteria before

they can enter the lungs. The bronchial tubes are lined with mucous that traps smaller dust particles that might pass through the nose or mouth. Tiny hairs, called cilia, sweep these particles out of the bronchi into the esophagus where they are eliminated in the digestive system. Finally, any particles or bacteria that do make it into the lungs are eliminated by special white blood cells that are found in the lining of the alveoli. This design by your Creator helps to keep your lungs healthy.

As we discussed earlier, keeping blood flowing continuously to get oxygen to the body is one of

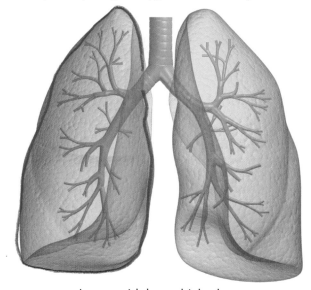

Lungs with bronchial tubes

the most essential functions of the body. This is why one of the first things you learn in a first aid class is how to help someone who has stopped breathing. But there are several things that can interfere with your ability to breathe well. These include sickness and lung disease. When you get a cold or flu, your lungs can become irritated and produce mucus, causing you to cough. **Pneumonia** is an illness that causes fluid to settle in the lungs. **Asthma** is when

Fun Fact

All of the alveoli in an adult's lungs together hold about the same amount of air as a basketball.

Many people use inhalers to treat asthma.

⚗ How big are my lungs?

Purpose: To see how much air your lungs can hold

Materials: balloon, cloth tape measure

Procedure:

1. Take a deep breath and blow as much air as possible into a balloon using only one breath. If you have trouble blowing up the balloon, ask your mom or dad to blow it up for you and release the air a few times first. This will stretch the balloon making it easier to inflate.

2. After you breathe into the balloon, tie a knot in it.

3. Use a cloth tape measure to measure the circumference of the balloon and compare it with others to see who has the biggest lungs.

⚗ Breath test

Purpose: To see how exercise affects our breathing rate

Materials: stopwatch

Procedure:

1. Sit still for several minutes.

2. Use a stopwatch to count how many breaths you take in one minute.

3. Exercise for five minutes by running in place or doing jumping jacks.

4. Count how many breaths you take in one minute.

5. Rest for 5 minutes and then count how many breaths you take in one minute. How did your rate of breathing change with your activities?

Conclusion: In lesson 24 you did a similar set of measurements with your pulse or heartbeat. Your heart beats faster when you exercise because your body needs more oxygen and your heart is pushing the blood around your body faster. If your blood is moving through your lungs faster, you need to get oxygen into your lungs faster, too. Therefore, you have to take more breaths when you exercise than when you are resting.

the bronchial tubes swell, reducing the amount of air that can pass. All of these conditions can be treated with medication to help ease the symptoms and allow you to breathe easily again. However, some illnesses cause permanent damage to the lungs and can permanently reduce a person's breathing ability.

One of the most damaging things people do to their lungs is smoke cigarettes. Smoking causes tar to build up inside the lungs and reduces a person's ability to breathe well. Smoking also causes cancer and other diseases that can kill the smoker. God told us that our bodies are the temple of the Holy Spirit (1 Corinthians 6:19–20) and we have an obligation to take care of that temple. Therefore, we should never do anything to knowingly harm our bodies.

 What did we learn?

- How does your body keep harmful particles from entering your lungs?
- How are your lungs similar to a balloon?
- How are your lungs different from a balloon?

 Taking it further

- What can you do to keep your lungs healthy?
- If you breathe in oxygen and breathe out carbon dioxide, how can you help someone who is not breathing by breathing into his or her lungs when you do CPR?

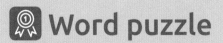 Word puzzle

You have learned many vocabulary words in this unit. Use those vocabulary words to create your own word puzzle or word game. Once you have the puzzle or game completed, give it to your teacher or classmate to see how much they remember.

Heart & Lungs

UNIT 6

Skin & Immunity

29 The Skin

30 Cross-section of Skin

31 Fingerprints

32 The Immune System

33 Genetics

34 Body Poster—Final Human Body Project

35 Conclusion

◊ **Identify** the source of skin color.

◊ **Describe** the three layers of the skin.

◊ **Describe** the parts of the immune system and their function.

◊ **Explain** how traits are inherited.

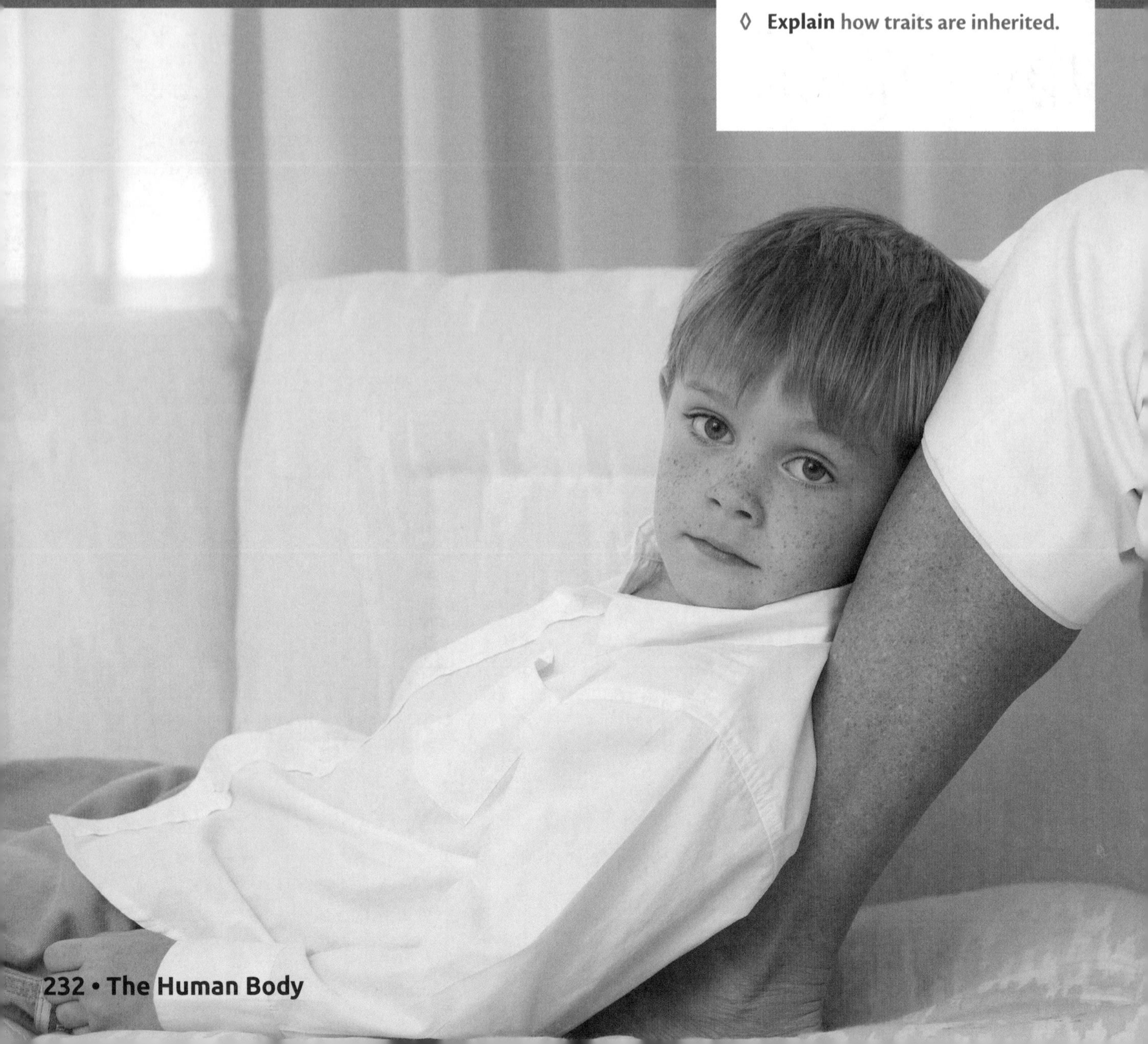

29

The Skin

Keeping your insides in

What are some of the unique things about your skin?

Words to know:

integumentary system
elastin

melanocyte
melanin

Challenge words:

carotene

albinism

The largest organ in your body is your skin. Your skin is part of the integumentary system, which includes your hair and nails as well. Your skin weighs about twice as much as your brain, and it serves several functions. First, it serves as a shield to protect the rest of your body from the outside world. Your skin protects you by keeping out things

Fun Fact

Your skin secretes a substance called keratin that hardens the top layer of skin cells to make them tougher and stronger. This is the same substance that your fingernails, toenails, and hair are made from.

that could harm you such as viruses, bacteria, and other foreign particles. It helps to protect you from hot and cold. Your skin also keeps out wind and rain and protects you from solar radiation.

Second, your skin keeps your insides in. It keeps your body from drying out by making a barrier between your moist body and the drier air. Your skin also helps you regulate your body temperature by opening and closing sweat glands, and by widening and narrowing blood vessels in your skin.

Finally, your skin works together with your nervous system as a communication network to your brain. The nerves in your skin collect information and send it to your brain continuously.

God designed your skin in amazing ways. It is stretchy and elastic, allowing you to move freely but not lose your shape. Your skin contains a substance called elastin, which lets your skin stretch and then contract back to its normal shape. Your skin allows your hand to grasp delicate items as easily as it grasps a hard rock. Skin is thickest on the soles of your feet and thinnest on your eyelids. It allows you to experience the whole world outside your body.

Melanocytes are cells located in the upper layer of your skin. These cells produce melanin, a pigment in the skin, eyes, and hair that gives them color. There are between 1,000 and 2,000 melanocytes per square

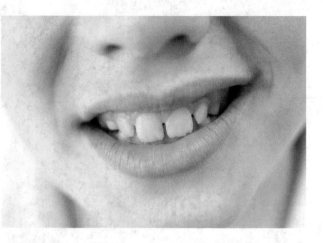

Our lips appear red because lip skin has fewer melanocytes, allowing the red blood vessels to show through.

millimeter of skin. They make up about 5–10% of all the cells in the skin. The difference in skin color between fair people and dark people is due not to the number of melanocytes in their skin, but to the melanocytes' level of activity. There are not different races of people, but merely people that have different facial features and different levels of melanin. All people on Earth are related, having descended from the first two people—Adam and Eve.

What did we learn?

- What are the purposes of skin?
- How does skin help you stay healthy?
- How does skin allow you to move without getting stretched out?

Taking it further

- Other than skin, in what other ways does your body keep out germs?
- What skin problems might you experience in a dry climate?
- What skin problems might you experience in a very moist or humid climate?
- What are the dangers of a serious burn?

Examining your skin

Purpose: To observe the skin on the various parts of your body

Materials: mirror, hand lotion

Procedure:

1. Compare the color, texture, and overall appearance of the skin in each area:
   - Back of your hand
   - Fingertips
   - Bottoms of your feet
   - Forehead (use a mirror)
   - Knee

   How is the skin different in each area? How is the skin the same in each area?

2. Apply lotion to part of your arm. Compare the lubricated skin with the skin on the other arm. How does lotion affect the texture and color of your skin? Your skin secretes oil that keeps your skin moist just like the lotion. Sometimes when the air is particularly dry or you wash your hands a lot, your skin becomes dry and you can help restore moisture by using lotion.

3. Examine your arm again. What do you notice besides skin? You also have tiny hairs all over your skin. The hair is thicker on some parts of the body than it is on other parts. This hair helps to keep you warm and to detect changes in your surroundings.

4. Try blowing gently across your arm. Sometimes this will cause you to get goose bumps as tiny muscles contract causing the hair to stand out from your arm.

🎖 Skin pigment

The pigment melanin plays many important roles in your body. The most important role is protecting your skin from the harmful ultraviolet radiation from the sun. Melanin absorbs UV light so that it does not damage the skin. Of course, if you spend hours in strong sunlight you can still damage your skin and get a painful sunburn. When the melanin absorbs UV light, it stimulates the melanocytes to produce more melanin. This produces a suntan. A suntan is the body's natural response to increased ultraviolet light.

Melanin also protects the eyes from ultraviolet light. Melanin is found in the iris and helps determine your eye color. People with dark colored eyes have melanin that is closer to the surface, while people with lighter colored eyes have melanin that is farther from the surface of the eye.

As you learned earlier, melanin plays a role in skin color. People with fair skin have melanin primarily in the upper layer of skin. People with darker skin have more melanin in all layers of their skin because their melanocytes are more active. Some people also have carotene, an orange pigment, in their skin, which can add a somewhat yellowish tint to the skin. Also, melanin is not always evenly distributed in your skin. Have you ever seen a freckle? A freckle is an area in your skin that has a higher amount of melanin than the areas around it.

Melanin plays an important role in hair color as well. All people have two kinds of melanin in their hair: eumelanin and pheomelanin. Eumelanin is black and brown while pheomelanin is red. The amount of eumelanin in hair determines the darkness of its color. A low concentration of brown eumelanin in the hair will make it blond, whereas more brown eumelanin will give it a brown color. Much higher amounts of black eumelanin will result in black hair, and a low concentration of black eumelanin in the hair will make it gray.

Some people's bodies do not produce melanin. This condition is called albinism. Someone with albinism will have very white skin and hair, and their eyes are very pale. This condition is very rare and is a genetic condition. It is not an infectious disease. Albinism can affect animals as well as humans. Albinism is not dangerous for humans except for the increased risk of skin cancer, but it can be fatal for a wild animal that cannot conceal itself from its predators.

An albino zebra

Skin & Immunity

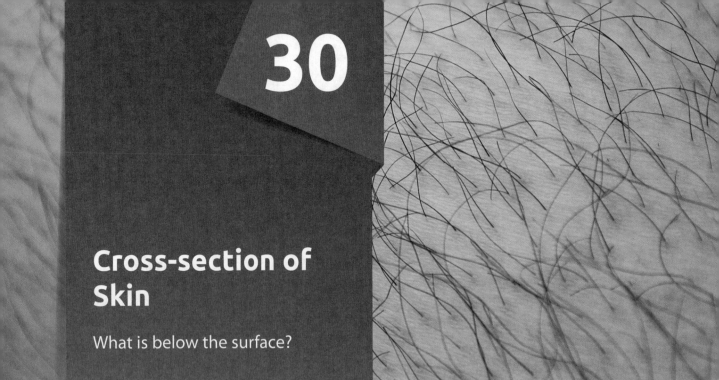

30

Cross-section of Skin

What is below the surface?

What is in each layer of skin?

Words to know:

epidermis	sebaceous gland
keratin	hair follicle
dermis	subcutaneous

Challenge words:

erector pili muscles

Although the skin may seem like a simple organ, it is actually quite complex. Skin is divided into three layers: the epidermis, the dermis, and the subcutaneous tissue. The epidermis is the top layer. The cells on the very top of the epidermis are dead cells that are shed as they rub against clothing and other objects. Just below the dead cells are cells that have keratin, a substance that makes them tough and strong. This layer of cells provides the watertight barrier of the skin. Melanocytes are located in the lower parts of the epidermis.

The second layer, the dermis, is where most of the functions of the skin take place. This layer contains sweat glands that secrete sweat to cool off the body when it gets too hot. It also contains sebaceous glands that secrete oil to keep the skin soft and flexible. Several types of nerve endings are also in the dermis. Hair follicles are located in this layer as well. The hair on your skin grows out of these follicles. Finally, blood vessels are found throughout the dermis. The blood vessels in the skin not only bring oxygen and food to the skin cells, but also help with regulating your body temperature. When you are over heated, these blood vessels dilate, or get wider. This allows more blood to flow near the surface of the skin where heat can escape from the body. When you are cold, the blood vessels constrict, or get narrower, keeping more of the blood away from the surface so less heat escapes.

The innermost layer of skin is the subcutaneous tissue. This is a fatty layer that connects the dermis to the tissues of the body. These fat cells provide insulation to protect the body from extreme temperatures and shocks, while allowing your hand to perfectly fit around whatever it is grasping.

Fun Fact

The average square inch of skin holds 650 sweat glands, 20 blood vessels, 60,000 melanocytes, and more than a thousand nerve endings.

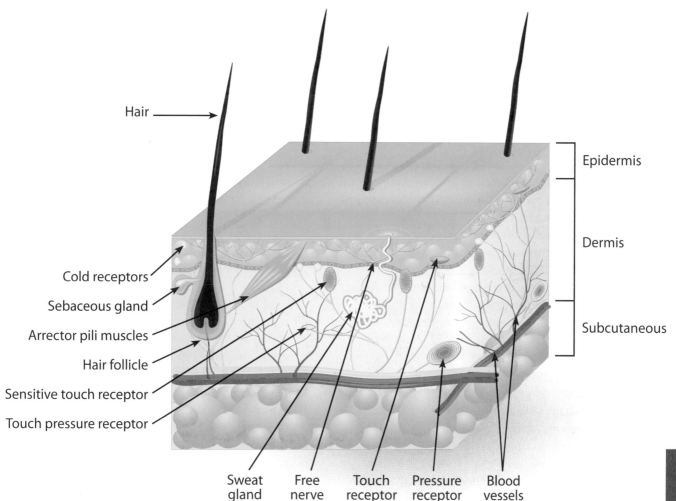

Hair

Epidermis

Dermis

Subcutaneous

Cold receptors

Sebaceous gland

Arrector pili muscles

Hair follicle

Sensitive touch receptor

Touch pressure receptor

Sweat gland

Free nerve

Touch receptor

Pressure receptor

Blood vessels

Your skin also contains elastic fibers called elastin, which allow your skin to stretch and then resume its normal shape. As people get older their elastin breaks down and the skin cannot spring back, thus it becomes more wrinkled.

Overall the skin is a very complicated organ, so, the next time you look at your skin, thank God for His great design.

What did we learn?

- What are the three layers of skin?
- What is the purpose of the sebaceous gland?
- In which layer are most receptors located?

Taking it further

- Explain what happens to your skin when you pick up a pin.
- How does your skin help regulate your body temperature?

Skin word search

Complete the "Skin Word Search."

🎖 Hair production

One of the more interesting functions of skin is the production of hair. Hair grows on many parts of your body including your head, arms, legs, and eyebrows. Hair in each location serves an important function. Hair on your head helps to keep heat in your body. It also helps define how you look depending on how you comb and style your hair.

Hair on your arms and many other parts of your body help you detect changes in your surroundings. As you learned in lesson 15, your hairs have nerves attached to them that detect breezes and cool temperatures. These nerves are connected to tiny muscles called the erector pili muscles. When your body feels cold, these muscles contract, causing goose bumps. This sudden movement helps to warm your body and to alert you that you need to take action to warm yourself up.

Your eyebrows and eyelashes serve to keep sweat and other substances out of your eyes. Even hair in your armpits serves a purpose. It reduces friction when you move your arms.

Hair grows from the hair follicles in your skin. People have between 100,000 and 150,000 hair follicles on their scalps. The Bible says that God cares enough about each of us that He even knows the exact number of hairs on our heads (Luke 12:7). A hair follicle is a vertical tube in the dermis. In the bottom of the follicle is the hair root. Cells in the root reproduce very quickly. They fill with keratin then die. As more cells are produced, the dead cells are pushed up. This is how hair grows. The dead cells form the shaft of the hair.

The shape of the follicle determines how the hair will look. If the follicle is round, the hair shaft will be straight and you will have straight hair. If the follicle is oval-shaped, you will have wavy hair. Sometimes hair follicles are kidney bean-shaped or very flattened. This shape of hair follicle produces very curly or kinky hair. What shape do you think your follicles are?

Hair on different parts of the body grows at different rates. On average, human hair grows about a half inch every month, but this varies from person to person. At any one time, about 90% of your hairs are growing and about 10% are resting. After a hair has grown for two to six years, it rests for about three months, and then usually falls out. So you are constantly losing hairs. You lose between 30 and 100 hairs every day. But don't worry; you won't be going bald anytime soon. Your body will grow new hairs to replace the ones that fall out.

Speaking of going bald, do some research and find out what causes baldness. Share what you find with your class or family.

31

Fingerprints

You are unique!

Do you have loops, arches, or whorls on your fingers?

Words to know:

arch   whorl

loop

Challenge words:

forensic science

God designed different types of skin for different parts of your body. The skin on your lips has no hair follicles and has a different color than your other skin. God also designed each person's skin to be unique. As you learned in lesson 10, you have special skin called friction skin on the palms of your hands and the bottoms of your feet. This skin has ridges and furrows that are like little hills and valleys. Friction skin helps you hold onto things with your hands and keeps your feet from slipping when you walk.

The patterns formed by these ridges and furrows are unique to each person. These patterns develop about 3–4 months before you are born and they never change throughout your lifetime. Your fingerprints are one thing that makes you different from every other person who has ever lived. Even identical twins have different fingerprints.

Although every person has unique fingerprints, fingerprints can be grouped into three different categories, as shown on the next page. Approximately 60% of all fingerprints are loops, 35% are whorls, and 5% are arches. Arches are designs that enter from one side and exit on the other. Loops are designs that enter and exit from

Fun Fact

The Federal Bureau of Investigation (FBI) maintains the largest biometric database in the world. The Next Generation Identification (NGI) system, which came online September, 2014, stores over 70 million entries in its Criminal Master File. These entries include fingerprints, mug shots, photos of scars and tattoos, criminal history, and physical descriptions. NGI has a new fingerprint matching algorithm that is 99.6% accurate. It also has facial recognition software, palm print matching algorithms, and is adding a pilot program to test out iris recognition as well. Over 18,000 law enforcement agencies use this system to aid in their investigations. NGI processes over 61 million requests each year.

| Arch | Loop | Whorl |

Skin & Immunity

Fun Fact

The word *forensic* comes from the Latin word that means forum. During Roman times, legal proceedings were held in the forum. Each side would present their case and the judge would decide the outcome. The person with the best forensic (forum) skills would win the case. This has led to some confusion with the use of the word forensics today. *Forensic science* involves evidence presented in court, whereas *forensic skills* usually refers to public speaking skills. A forensics club would teach speech and debate skills, not collecting and identifying of fingerprints.

the same side. **Whorls** are designs that form a circular pattern. In the past, fingerprints were collected using inkpads. Today optical scanners are used to take pictures of fingerprints, then computers are used to identify prints from hundreds of thousands of prints on file. This can be accomplished very quickly with computers.

Examine your fingerprints closely and see if you can identify which type of pattern you have on each finger. Remember, God made you special, even down to your fingertips.

What did we learn?

- Where can friction skin be found on your body?
- When are fingerprints formed?
- What are the three major groups of fingerprints?
- Can you identify identical twins by their fingerprints?

Taking it further

- What are some circumstances where fingerprints are used?
- Why do prints only occur on the hands and feet?
- Do children's fingerprints match their parents' prints?

Fingerprint identification

Pretend you are a police officer investigating a crime, and do the following activity.

Purpose: To collect and examine fingerprints

Materials: paper, pencil, clear tape, index cards

Procedure:

1. Trace each person's hand on a blank piece of paper and label the paper with his name.

2. Rub a pencil across a scrap piece of paper to make a very dark area about 2 inches square.

3. Have each person rub his or her fingertips, one at a time, across the dark area until the fingertip is black or dark gray. Recolor the paper as necessary to make it easy to get the prints.

4. Take a piece of clear tape and press it against the fingertip to "lift" the print.

5. Place the tape on the matching finger that was drawn on the blank paper.

6. Repeat for each finger on the hand. These pages are now your fingerprint file.

7. Now create "evidence" by lifting prints from each person and placing them on an index card.

8. Number each index card and have someone record which number matches which suspect, but don't let anyone else know.

9. Choose one card to be the guilty party and have each person try to match the evidence card to the correct page in the file. Be sure to look for arches, loops, and whorls to help you match the evidence to the right suspect.

10. After this card has been matched to a suspect, choose another card and repeat the process. See if you can match each card to the correct person.

In real life, detectives work with forensic scientists to help solve crimes. If you want to learn more about how crimes are solved using science, ask your teacher for permission to get books regarding the topic at your local library or to do searches online for additional information.

Skin & Immunity

🏅 Forensic science

Forensic science is the study of items related to legal proceedings. The information collected by a forensic scientist is usually used as evidence in a trial. Collecting and identifying fingerprints is only one area of forensic science. A forensic scientist might also collect shoe prints or even lip prints from a crime scene.

Forensic scientists also collect and type blood samples to use as evidence in a crime. Blood at a crime scene can tell a forensic scientist many things. Blood type can reveal if blood came from more than one person. It can tell if the blood was from the victim or the criminal. Also, a scientist can examine where and how the blood was splattered and determine what might have taken place.

A newer area of forensic science is the collection of DNA or genetic information. You will learn more about genetics and DNA in lesson 33, but it is important to know that every person has unique DNA stored in the cells of his body. So collecting some skin, hair, or blood gives the scientist a sample of the person's DNA. Careful comparison between the sample collected at the crime scene and the DNA of the suspect can yield important evidence.

Forensic scientists also collect fibers. Whenever two materials touch each other, very small fibers are left behind. These fibers can be collected and compared with clothing or other items to determine who or what may have been at the crime scene.

Finally, dental evidence is sometimes collected by forensic scientists. Each person has unique teeth. The bite patterns are unique for each person as well as the dental work that has been done. Using dental records, people can be identified by the work that has been done on their teeth.

Purpose: To practice forensics on "blood splatters"

Materials: light corn syrup, water, red food coloring, newspaper, white paper, eyedropper, "Blood Splatter Chart"

Procedure:

1. Make some sample "blood" by combining ¼ cup of light corn syrup with ¼ cup of water. Add several drops of red food coloring to this mixture. Now you are ready to start.

2. Cover the floor with newspaper and lay a sheet of white paper on top of the newspaper.

3. Fill an eyedropper with your "blood" solution.

4. Hold the dropper 2 cm above the paper and let one drop fall onto the paper.

5. Measure the diameter of the drop in millimeters and record your measurement on the "Blood Splatter Chart."

6. Next, hold the dropper at a height of 4 cm above the paper and let another drop fall onto the paper.

7. Measure and record this drop's diameter.

8. Repeat this process for all the heights listed on the chart. Replace the paper as often as necessary to avoid confusion about which drop to measure.

9. Once you have the chart completed, place a blank sheet of paper on the newspapers.

10. Have someone drop a drop of "blood" from some height between 2 cm and 100 cm without telling you that height.

11. Measure the diameter of the drop on the paper and use your chart to determine the height that you think the drop fell from.

Conclusion: This is a similar process to what a forensic scientist might go through in examining a crime scene. She must look at the pattern of blood or other liquid, and determine what direction and height it came from to help determine what actually happened at the crime scene.

32

The Immune System

Keeping you healthy

How does your body protect itself from foreign invaders?

Words to know:

immune system   antibody

lymph system   thymus

lymph   bone marrow

lymph nodes   spleen

Challenge words:

vaccine   antibiotics

Germs are everywhere! They are in the air, they are in the water, and they are in the food we eat. Viruses and bacteria, commonly called germs, are constantly trying to enter our bodies. If germs get into your body and begin to multiply, they can make you sick by producing toxins that cause inflammation or which damage or destroy cells. Thankfully, God designed our bodies to be able to deal with the multitude of germs around us. Your immune system works to keep germs from making you sick.

There are several ways that your body deals with germs. The first and most important thing your body does is to try to keep germs out of your body. Your skin is the largest part of your immune system and is the first line of defense against germs. As long as your skin is not broken, germs cannot pass through your skin. Also, your skin produces anti-bacterial substances that keep bacteria from growing on your skin.

But your skin cannot keep out all germs. Germs can enter through your nose, mouth, and eyes, as well as through cuts in your skin. Tears in your eyes and saliva in your mouth both contain enzymes which help to break down bacteria before they have a chance to do any harm. Also, mucus in your nasal passages and throat trap particles, including bacteria and viruses, so they can be eliminated in the stomach.

Even with these very effective measures, sometimes germs get inside your body and start to reproduce. So there is more to your immune system than just skin, tears, and mucus. Your lymph and circulatory systems are the other major parts of your immune system. The lymph system is similar to your circulatory system. It consists of vessels throughout your body that carry lymph, a clear liquid, to all the cells

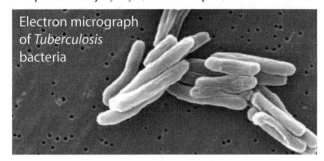

Electron micrograph of *Tuberculosis* bacteria

and tissues. This liquid picks up many germs and the lymph nodes, bean-shaped nodules containing white blood cells, filter them out. The lymph system can be considered the second line of defense against germs.

The third line of defense is in your circulatory system. White blood cells play a major role in defending against viruses and bacteria. There are many different types of white blood cells, but most of them serve a similar purpose. White blood cells detect any foreign object in the blood and quickly surround and eliminate it. White blood cells also generate proteins called antibodies. Antibodies are unique and can only attack one kind of bacteria or virus. Antibodies bind bacteria and help the white blood cells eliminate bacteria.

Other parts of your body play important roles in the immune system as well. An organ near your heart called the thymus produces specialized white blood cells called T-cells. Bone marrow, material in the center of long bones, produces most other white blood cells. And your spleen works as a filter for your blood and eliminates many of the germs that are not eliminated in other parts of the immune system.

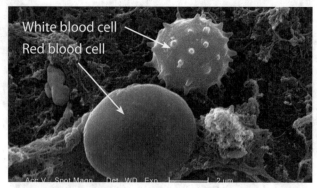
White blood cell
Red blood cell

Acc.V   Spot Magn   Det   WD   Exp   ⊢———————⊣   2 μm

Electron micrograph of red and white blood cells

Together your skin, lymph system, and circulatory system, as well as the parts just mentioned, form a very effective defense system to help keep you healthy.

Sometimes, however, all of these defenses are not enough and bacteria or viruses are still able to enter your body, reproduce, and make you sick. This is when your immune system kicks into high gear and really starts producing white blood cells and antibodies to overtake the invaders. Eventually your immune system overcomes the enemy and you get well if everything is working correctly.

🧪 How healthy are you?

Although God designed your body to be able to fight off germs and diseases, there are many things you can do to help ensure that your body can do its job. First, you can eat a well-balanced diet, full of fresh fruits and vegetables and other healthy foods, and you can limit the sweets that you eat. You can get enough rest every night. Most people need about 7 to 8 hours of sleep each night. And you need to exercise regularly. This will help your body be strong and healthy.

You can also limit your exposure to germs and prevent spreading germs. You should wash your hands with soap and water several times a day, especially after using the bathroom. You also need to keep your body clean by bathing regularly and brushing your teeth twice a day. Keeping your home clean helps to limit the germs you are exposed to. And if you do get sick, be sure to cover your mouth and nose when you sneeze or cough so that you don't spread the germs to other people in your home. Also, avoid going out in public when you are sick.

Purpose: to help you better see how well you are doing the things that keep you healthy.

Materials: Notebook paper

Procedure:

1. Write one of the headings below at the top of a sheet of notebook paper. Repeat until you have made a page for each healthy habit.:

   Healthy Diet   Clean Environment

   Exercise   Stop the Spread of

   Sleep   Germs

   Personal Cleanliness

2. At the end of each day write down what you did in the area listed at the top of each page. For example, write down how many times you brushed your teeth and if you took a shower on the page labeled "Personal Cleanliness," and write down how many hours you slept on the page labeled "Sleep."

3. At the end of one week, review how you are doing and decide what changes you need to make to keep your body healthy.

Conclusion: If you establish good habits when you are young, you are more likely to keep those good habits throughout your life, and you will be healthier because of it.

Taking it further

- Why are a fever and the itchiness from a mosquito bite both indications that your immune system is working?

 # What did we learn?

- What are the major parts of the immune system?

- What are the two major types of "germs" that make us sick?

- How do tears and mucus help fight germs?

Helping our immune system

Although your body is very good at fighting diseases, sometimes it needs a little help. So scientists have developed medicines that help your body when it is invaded by viruses and bacteria. Although there is no way to cure a disease that is caused by a virus, doctors have developed vaccines, which are substances that stimulate your immune system, causing it to produce antibodies against a certain disease. A vaccine contains a small amount of the disease that has either been killed or has been made non-toxic. When the vaccine is injected into your body it does not give you the disease, but your immune system recognizes it as an invader and produces antibodies to fight it. These antibodies stay in your body for a long time. So if the virus carrying that disease ever enters your body, your immune system is ready to fight it right away and you do not get the disease, or you get a milder case of it.

Some viral diseases, like the common cold, make you uncomfortable for a few days, but are not really serious. But other diseases such as mumps, measles, cholera, yellow fever, typhoid, hepatitis, polio, rabies, and tetanus can be deadly or have very severe effects on your body. Having an immunity to these diseases can save your life. Therefore, many people choose

to have themselves and their children vaccinated against diseases that they are likely to encounter in the future. There are potential side effects to vaccinations, and sometimes these are serious, so everyone should do research to make sure they understand the benefits and risks of vaccines.

Edward Jenner developed the first vaccine using cowpox to stimulate the human immune system against smallpox in 1776. Louis Pasteur built on this work and developed vaccines for anthrax and rabies in the 1870s and 1880s. Today there are hundreds of vaccines available. Some are used in the United States but many are only used in other countries where certain diseases are likely to occur. Some vaccines, like influenza (flu) must be administered each year because the viruses change quickly. Others, like tetanus and diphtheria, need to be updated about every ten years.

Not all diseases are caused by viruses. Many are caused by bacteria, fungi, or other microorganisms. Many of these diseases are treated with antibiotics, medicines that stop the growth of the bacteria or other invading germs. Antibiotics were first discovered by Alexander Fleming in 1928, somewhat by accident. Fleming found that bacteria in certain dishes were not growing where a particular mold was present. After much testing he developed penicillin from that mold. Penicillin was the first useful antibiotic. Today other types of antibiotics have been developed and are useful against many different bacteria including those that cause strep throat, bacterial pneumonia, many infections, and tuberculosis.

We can thank God for the men and women who have developed medicines like antibiotics. Because of them, many diseases that were once fatal are now almost unheard of. These medicines have saved millions of lives.

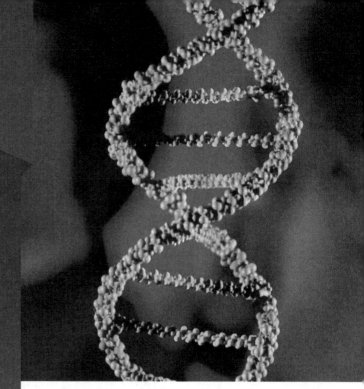

Genetics

Why you look like you do

How does DNA make your eyes brown?

Words to know:

genes   dominant gene

Challenge words:

DNA   thymine

double helix   guanine

deoxyribose   cytosine

base pairs   chromosome

adenine   mutation

Have you ever noticed brothers or sisters often look alike? And children usually resemble their parents. But you may look very different from your friend or neighbor. This is because how you look, and a lot of other things about your body, are determined by something called genes, and genes are something you inherit from your parents.

Genes are tiny bits of information contained in the DNA of each cell in your body. Half of your genes came from your mother and half came from your father. This information tells your body what color your hair and eyes should be, how dark your

Since identical twins come from a single egg, they have the same genetic information.

Fun Fact

Chromosome 1 in the human body is the largest molecule found in nature. It contains around 10 billion atoms.

Fun Fact

Even though the genes of the parents determine a child's eye color, most babies are born with blue eyes. It takes time for the melanin to be deposited in the iris of the newborn's eyes and thus reveal their permanent eye color.

skin will be, if you can curl your tongue, if your ear lobes are attached to your face, and thousands of other things about you.

What if your mom has blue eyes and your dad has brown eyes? What color will your eyes be? Some genes are dominant—they are "stronger"—so the **dominant gene** will determine your eye color. Brown eyes are dominant over blue, so you would probably have brown eyes. However, if one of your dad's parents (your grandparents) had blue eyes, your dad could pass on a blue eye gene to you and you might have blue eyes. But you would have a better chance of having brown eyes than blue ones.

God created Adam and Eve with a wide variety of genes. They had information for many different eye colors, hair colors, skin shades, etc., so their children could have looked very different from each other. Some of that information was lost as most of the people on Earth died in the Great Flood, but the wide variety we see in people today was preserved in the genes of Noah and his family.

After the confusion of languages at the Tower of Babel, people began to spread throughout the Earth by family groups. Since these groups became isolated from each other, the variety of the genes in one area became smaller. So some people had information for

some traits and not for others. People in a particular area shared certain traits and adapted to the conditions where they lived or moved to places that better suited them. Ultimately, we see that the groups that went to Africa ended up with mostly darker skin, while the people that went to Southeast Asia had mostly dark hair, etc. Still, all people have descended from Noah and his family (and thus from Adam and Eve) and therefore we are all special creations of God created in His image.

What did we learn?

- What are genes?
- Why do children generally look like their parents?

Taking it further

- If parents look very different from each other what will their children look like?
- In the past, evolutionists claimed that man evolved independently in different parts of the world and this is where the races came from. If this were true, how likely would it be that the different races could have children together?

Genetics quiz

Get a copy of "Genetics Quiz" and follow the instructions to see which traits you inherited from each of your parents.

DNA

God made each person unique. Your genetic code is like no one else's. But what exactly is this genetic code? All of the information needed to make a human being is stored in a very long molecule called DNA, or deoxyribonucleic acid. In 1953 James Watson and Francis Crick were the first to accurately describe the structure of DNA. They showed that DNA is a ladder-like structure with sides and rungs.

This ladder is then twisted and compressed. This structure is called a double helix.

The sides of the DNA ladder consist of sugar molecules, called deoxyribose, alternating with phosphate molecules. The rungs of the ladder are made up of pairs of chemicals called bases or base pairs. There are four kinds of bases that can be used to build the DNA ladder: adenine (A), thymine (T), guanine (G), and cytosine (C). Two bases connect together to form a rung, but only certain bases can be paired together. An A will always be paired with a T and a G will always be paired with a C. The shapes of the base molecules prevent them from pairing with the wrong bases.

Now that you understand the basic structure of the DNA molecule, you can begin to understand how this molecule contains information. If you stretched out a molecule of DNA so it looks like a ladder and looked at the base pairs from top to bottom you would get a list of letters. For example the first four rungs might be AT, TA, GC, GC. The pattern of bases provides information to the cells of your body. If the pattern were different, it would tell your body to do something different.

DNA is divided into sections called genes. Each gene in your body tells something about you, such as your hair color, height, or ability to curl your tongue. A gene contains about 100,000 base pairs, or rungs on the ladder, and each pair has to be in a specific order. Now that's a lot of information.

Beginning in 1990, a large group of scientists from around the world set out to map the complete sequence of base pairs in human DNA. It was called the Human Genome Project. The mapping was officially completed in 2003. They found that there are approximately 3.3 billion base pairs which are divided up into about 20,500 genes.

Thousands of genes are connected together to form a strand of DNA. A complete strand of DNA is called a chromosome. The cells in the human body contain 23 pairs of chromosomes for a total of 46 chromosomes. These chromosomes are stored in the nucleus of each cell. When the body needs

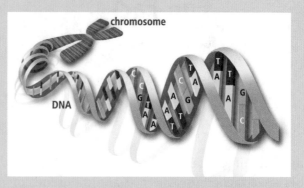
chromosome
DNA

information from the DNA, the correct chromosome is unwound and the section containing the information is passed through a special mechanism in the cell that reads the sequence of base pairs to get the information. Then the DNA is zipped back together and rewound. This is a very efficient way to store information.

If the information stored in the DNA were to get messed up, the body might not be able to do something that it should. This is why God created our bodies with two sets of chromosomes. One set is given to the baby by the mother, and the second set is given to the baby by the father. With two sets of code, it is unlikely that a mistake in the code would occur at the same location in both codes. Occasionally a problem will occur in the same location in both codes, and this usually results in a birth defect or a disease in the child. These mistakes are called mutations and are often harmful to the person. Evolutionists claim that millions of mutations in genetic codes are what has caused life to evolve; however, beneficial mutations are extremely rare; they are almost always neutral or harmful to the organism, and do not provide any new information.

Purpose: To better understand how DNA works by building a model

Materials: "DNA Puzzle Pieces," scissors, tape

(If you have an actual 3-D model, you can follow the directions included with your model to build the DNA strand.)

Procedure:

1. Make several copies of the "DNA Puzzle Pieces" and cut them out.

2. Tape the correct base pairs together. Be sure to only tape A's and T's together, and C's and G's together.

3. Once you have several pairs put together, arrange them vertically on the table to form a ladder.

4. Tape the sides of the ladder together. This will represent a very small section of one gene.

Gregor Mendel

1823–1884

Gregor Mendel was the first person to trace the characteristics of successive generations of living things. In other words, he was the first to show that many traits are passed on by parents to their children.

Gregor Mendel was the second child of Anton and Rosine Mendel, farmers in Brunn, Moravia (a part of the Austro-Hungarian Empire at that time).

Today, as we look back at his work, it would be easy to think of him as a world-renowned scientist of his day, but this is not the way it was. Gregor had done very well in school and his family wanted him to pursue higher education but they did not have much money. So Gregor entered a monastery to continue his education. There he also worked as a teacher and taught natural science to high school students.

Gregor Mendel had a real love for nature. He seemed to really enjoy his work. He said that he crossed different characteristics of peas over several generations just "for the fun of the thing." His initial work was inspired as he took frequent walks in the monastery's gardens. One day he found a plant with unusual characteristics. He moved it next to some other plants of the same type to see what would happen to the offspring. He found that some of the next generation of plants exhibited the unusual characteristics. This simple test gave him the idea of heredity. He also thought that some traits were dominant over others and were more likely to be inherited.

Mendel decided to test his theories on peas. So he spent the next seven years crossbreeding peas before he was able to prove the laws of inheritance. From this work, Mendel derived the basic laws of heredity, showing that hereditary factors do not combine, but are passed intact. This means, for example, that if one parent plant has rounded

seeds and the other has wrinkled seeds, the offspring will have either rounded or wrinkled seeds, but not something in between.

He also showed that one parent gives half the genes, or hereditary factors, with the other half coming from the other parent. And he proved that some characteristics are dominant over others. Finally, Mendel showed that different offspring of the same set of parents would receive different sets of hereditary factors. Two children from the same parents will not look identical (with the exception of identical twins who both developed from the same fertilized egg).

Because of Mendel's work, we now know that many diseases are inherited and can be traced along ancestral lines. This information can help unborn children by giving the doctors help in knowing what to look for. With this information today, some serious conditions can be treated before the baby is even born.

Mendel performed his experiments at about the same time that Darwin was developing his theory of evolution. Unlike Darwin, who based most of his theory on guesses and suppositions, Mendel performed his research very carefully and recorded exactly what he saw. He was able to demonstrate each of his ideas by showing the data from his experiments. In fact, the results Mendel achieved went against Darwin's idea of selective breeding resulting in new kinds of animals.

Mendel was able to demonstrate that the genes from the parents determine what the offspring will look like. Therefore, he showed that one kind of plant or animal will always produce that same kind of plant or animal. Evolutionists have had to "update" Darwin's theory by saying that mutations (mistakes) in the genes are what caused the changes from one kind of animal to another. However, all mutations that have been observed have only resulted in a loss of genetic information, not a gain as would be required for one creature to change into another kind of creature.

Although Mendel was not recognized as a great scientist in his lifetime, his work has had a profound impact on science today. Mendel's love for nature, his awareness of small differences around him, and his careful approach to experiments enabled him to make many important discoveries that laid the foundation for the field of genetics today.

34

Body Poster: Final Human Body Project

Putting it all together

Now that you have learned about each of the major systems of the human body, it is time to put what you have learned all together to better understand how your body works. Each system cannot function independently. They all have different but complementary jobs to do. They all work together.

For example, the brain and the rest of the nervous system control all of the other systems. Without your brain, nothing else would work. Your digestive system works together with your circulatory system to provide energy to your body. Your respiratory system works with your circulatory system to move oxygen and carbon dioxide around your body. God has created a marvelous and complex body for you so you can enjoy the world He made.

What did we learn?

- Name the eight body systems you have learned about.
- How do some of the different systems work together?

Taking it further

- What other systems can you think of that are in your body but were not discussed in this book?
- How do you see evidence of God the Creator in the design of the human body?

Skin & Immunity

Body poster

Purpose: To make a full-size drawing of your body systems

Materials: large piece of paper, pen or marker, anatomy guide

Procedure:

1. Lie down on a piece of large paper such as a roll of newsprint.

2. Have someone trace around your body with a pen or marker.

3. Draw in each of the systems studied in this unit. You might draw the nervous system on the left side of the body and the skeletal and muscular systems on the right side. Add the circulatory system to both sides.

4. Draw the lungs and heart on separate pieces of paper and tape them on the body so that they can be lifted to see what is underneath. Do the same thing for the digestive system.

5. Explain to your teacher or parent how each of these systems works individually and how the systems work together.

 # Body research

Although you have learned a lot about the body, there is still much more you can learn. Choose one (or more) of the topics below and do research to learn all you can about it. Create a presentation for your family or class.

- What role does the appendix play?
- What are the functions of the liver?
- Why is the left lung smaller than the right lung?
- What are adrenal glands, and what do they do?
- Why are bacteria and other microbes necessary in your body?
- What is color blindness, and why are men more likely to be color blind?
- Is "junk" DNA really useless? What does it do?
- Why do you dream?
- How fast do hair and nails grow, and what affects their growth?
- How does your stomach deal with all the acid in it?
- What parts of your body never stop growing even after you reach adulthood?

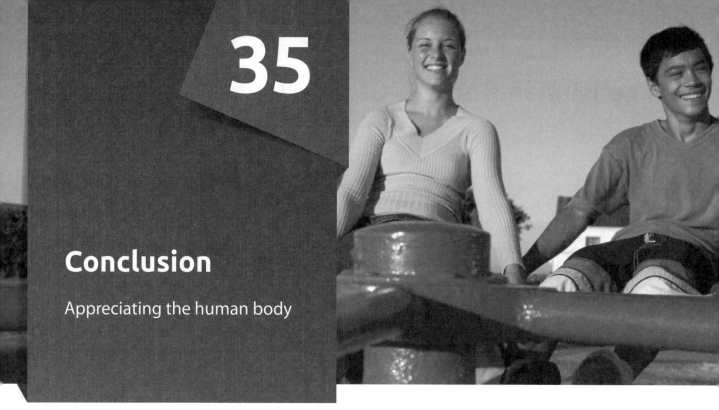

35

Conclusion

Appreciating the human body

God created Adam and Eve with amazing bodies. Because of the Fall of man, however, our bodies no longer work as well as they used to, and are now subject to disease and death.

Scientists and doctors are learning more about the human body every day. And the more they learn, the more they are amazed at the complexity and beauty of its design. There is no way that such complexity and organization could come about through naturalistic evolution. No, God created us.

Not only did God create your wonderful body, but He also cares deeply for you. Read the following Bible verses with your teacher or your mom or dad. Discuss the kind of relationship God wants to have with each of us.

*   Matthew 10:29–31
*   Isaiah 44:24
*   Psalm 24:1
*   Psalm 139:13–18

Using a concordance, look up verses in the Bible that talk about the body. What does the Bible say about the body? Discuss these verses with your teacher or parents and write a thank you note to God, thanking Him for making you special.

Skin & Immunity

The Human Body — Glossary

Alveoli   Sacs where exchange of gases takes place in the lungs (singular is *alveolus*)

Amplitude   How high waves are; in sound this determines loudness

Antibodies   Proteins that attack and destroy invading substances

Aorta   Artery taking blood from the heart to the body

Arteries   Blood vessels that carry blood away from the heart

Asthma   Swelling of the bronchial tubes

Atrium   Upper chamber in the heart that receives blood (plural is *atria*)

Auditory canal   Opening of the ear

Ball and socket joint   Moves in two planes, rotates in place

Bicep and tricep   Muscle pair in upper arm

Bicuspids   Bumpy teeth for grinding, next to canine teeth

Bone marrow   Material in the center of long bones that produces blood cells

Brain stem   Connection between the rest of the brain and the spinal cord, regulates automatic functions

Bronchi/Bronchial tubes   Tubes entering the lungs

Capillaries   Blood vessels that connect arteries and veins

Carbohydrates   Sugars and starches

Carpals   Bones of the wrist

Cartilage   Smooth, slippery material forming cushion between bones

Cell membrane   Protective shell or "skin" of the cell

Cell   Smallest part of the human body that can function on its own

Central nervous system   Brain and spinal cord

Cerebellum   Lower part of the brain, controlling balance and muscle movement

Cerebral cortex   Outermost layer of the cerebrum

Cerebrum   Upper part of the brain, controlling thought and memory

Cilia   Tiny hairs covering many body tissues

Circulatory system   System of heart, blood, and blood vessels that carry oxygen and nutrients throughout the body.

Clavicle   Collarbone

Cochlea   Fluid-filled part of the ear that changes vibrations to electrical signals

Cones   Special cells in the retina to detect color

Cornea   Front of the eye

Coronary Arteries   Blood vessels carrying oxygen-rich blood to the heart muscle

Corpus callosum   Large bundle of nerves connecting two sides of the cerebrum

Cranium   Skull

Cuspids/Canine teeth   Pointed teeth for tearing

Cytoplasm   Liquid inside the cell

Dermis   Middle layer of skin containing nerves, sweat glands, and other functions

Diaphragm   Muscle below lungs that expands the chest cavity when it contracts

Digestive system   System of organs that removes nutrients from food you eat

Dominant gene   "Stronger" gene, or predominant characteristic that is passed down from parent to child

Elastin   Elastic-like fibers that allow skin to stretch

Ellipsoid joint   Moves in two planes without rotating

Enzymes   chemicals that help with the digestion process

Epidermis   Top layer of skin

Esophagus   Tube connecting your mouth with your stomach

Femur   Large bone in upper leg

Fibrin   Stringy substance that helps form scabs

Fibula   Smaller bone in lower leg

Flat bones   Scapula, cranium, ribs, and pelvis

Frequency   How close waves are together; in sound this determines pitch

Friction skin   Ridged skin found on feet and hands, for gripping

Genes   Tiny bits of information contained in the body's cells, stored in DNA

Gliding joint   Bones slide over each other

Gluteus maximus   Muscle in rear

Hair follicle   Area in skin where hair is formed

Malleus, incus, and stapes   Tiny bones in the middle ear

Hemoglobin   Chemical in red blood cells that turns bright red in the presence of oxygen

Hinge joint   Moves in only one direction

Hippocampus   Part of the brain that stores and retrieves short-term memory

Humerus   Bone in upper arm

Immune system   System of organs that work together to fight off infection

Incisors   Sharp straight teeth for biting

Inferior vena cava   Vein bringing blood to the heart from the lower body

Integumentary system   System of organs including the skin, nails, and hair

Involuntary muscles   Muscles that are controlled without conscious thought

Iris   Colored part of the eye, controls size of pupil

Irregular bones   Bones that don't fit into any other category for shape

Keratin   Substance that makes skin tough

Large intestine   Tube where water is removed from unusable material

Larynx   Voice box

Lens   Part of the eye that focuses the image

Long bones   Arm and leg bones

Loops, whorls, and arches   Patterns formed by fingerprints

Lymph nodes   Bean-shaped organs in the lymph system containing white blood cells

Lymph system   System of vessels and lymph nodes that help eliminate invading substances

Lymph   Clear liquid in the lymph system that collects germs to be carried to the lymph nodes for elimination

Mandible   Jawbone

Medulla oblongata   Lowest part of the brain stem

Melanin   Pigment cells in the skin

Melanocytes   Cells which produce melanin

Metacarpals   Bones in the hand

Mitochondria   Break down nutrients to provide energy for the cell

Molars   Large bumpy teeth for grinding, in back of mouth

Muscular system   System of muscles that move the bones and other parts of the body

Nervous system   System of nerves that control the body

Neuron   Nerve cell

Nucleus   Brain of the cell

Optic nerve   Nerve that transmits image to the brain

Organ   Many tissues working together to perform a function

Patella   Kneecap

Pectoral   Muscles in upper chest

Peripheral nervous system   Nerves and other sensory organs

Phalanges   Small bones in your fingers and toes

Pharynx   Back of the throat

Pituitary gland   Part of the brain that controls growth

Pivot joint   Rotates only

Plaque   Sticky substance that builds up on teeth

Plasma   Yellowish liquid that transports blood cells

Platelets   Cells that help to close a wound

Pneumonia   Illness causing fluid in the lungs

Pulmonary artery   Artery carrying blood from the heart to the lungs

Pulmonary veins   Veins carrying blood from the lungs to the heart

Pupil   Opening in the eye that allows light to enter

Radius   Bone in the lower arm on the side with your thumb

Red blood cells   Cells that carry oxygen and nutrients to the body

Reflex   Automatic reaction that does not require a signal to go to the brain

Respiratory system   System of organs including the lungs whose main function is to get oxygen to the blood

Retina   Back of the eye that detects the image

Rods   Special cells in the retina to detect differences in light

Saddle joint   Moves in two planes, shaped like a saddle

Scapula   Shoulder blade

Sebaceous gland   Gland in the skin that secretes oil

Short bones   Bones of the fingers, toes, hands, and feet

Skeletal system   System of bones that provides strength and gives the body its general shape and size

Small intestine   Tube where nutrients are absorbed

Smooth muscle   Muscles that line the digestive tract and other internal organs

Spleen   Organ that filters dangerous organisms from the blood

Sternum   Bone in central chest connecting ribs

Stomach   Organ where food is broken down into smaller molecules

Subcutaneous   Lowest layer of skin, connecting skin to the body tissues

Superior vena cava   Vein bringing blood to the heart from the upper body

Tendon   Cord-like structure connecting muscles to bones

Thalamus   Part of the brain that routes messages within the brain

Thymus   Organ producing special white blood cells called T-cells

Tibia   Larger bone in the lower leg

Tissue   Many cells working together to perform a function

Trachea   Tube leading to the lungs

Trapezius   Muscles in upper back

Ulna   Bone in the lower arm on the side away from your thumb

Vacuole   Food storage area in the cell

Veins   Blood vessels that carry blood toward the heart

Ventricle   Lower chamber in the heart that pushes out blood

Vertebrae   Bones in the spine

Villi   Small finger-like projections inside the small intestine that absorb nutrients

Voluntary muscles   Muscles that move when you actively think about movement

White blood cells   Cells that help fight infection

The Human Body — Challenge Glossary

Adenine   Base used in DNA, must be paired with thymine

Albinism   Condition where the body does not produce melanin

Antibiotics   Chemicals that inhibit the growth of bacteria and other microorganisms

Antigens   Identification tags on cells

Appendicular skeleton   Outer bones including arms, legs, hips, shoulders, feet, and hands

Aqueous humor   Liquid between the cornea and the lens

Axial skeleton   Central bones including skull, face, neck, spine, and ribs

Axon   Part of the neuron that carries signal away from the cell body

Base pair   Two bases connected together to form a rung of the DNA molecule

Bile   Chemicals produced by the liver and stored in the gall bladder to be released into the small intestine and used for digestion

Blood pressure   Pressure placed on the walls of the blood vessels

Blood type   Determined by the absence or presence of certain antigens in the blood

Braille   System of raised dots to represent letters and other symbols

Cardiac muscle tissue   Tissue of the heart

Carotene   Orange pigment

Cellular respiration   Combination of oxygen with food molecules to release the energy

Cementum   Material next to root that secures tooth in the jaw

Chromosome   A complete strand of DNA

Collagen   Flexible protein that builds the structure of bones

Compound fracture   One in which the bone punctures the skin

Connective tissue   Connects body parts

Crown   Visible part of the tooth

Cytosine   Base used in DNA, must be paired with guanine

DNA   Deoxyribonucleic acid, molecule containing genetic information

Dendrite   Part of the neuron that receives input

Dentin   Bonelike material surrounding pulp of the tooth

Deoxyribose Sugar molecule forming the sides of the DNA molecule

Diastolic pressure Blood pressure when the heart is as rest

Double helix Shape of DNA; ladder that is twisted and compacted

Enamel Hard protective covering on teeth

Endocrine system Produces hormones

Epithelial tissue Lines all body parts

Erector pili muscles Tiny muscles in the skin attached to hairs

Eustachian tube Opening between the middle ear and the throat

Excretory system Removes wastes from the body

External respiration Exchange of gases in the lungs

Forensic science Study of items used in legal proceedings

Fracture A break in a bone

Gastric juice Enzymes and other chemicals secreted by the lining of the stomach

Gingiva Gums

Guanine Base used in DNA, must be paired with cytosine

Gustatory receptor cells Cells that react with food molecules to produce electrical signals

Hormones Chemical messengers to regulate body functions

Internal respiration Exchange of gases between blood cells and tissue cells

Interneuron/Association neuron Nerve cell that interprets input and generates output

Kidneys Main organs of the excretory system

Ligament Flexible cord-like material that connects bones together

Motor neuron Nerve cell that carries a signal from the brain to a muscle

Muscle tissue Contracts, for movement

Mutation A mistake in the genetic code

Myelin Material produced by the Schwann cells that provides insulation

Neck Part of tooth entering the gums

Nerve tissue Controls body activities

Occlusion Correct teeth and jaw alignment or normal bite

Odorants Light molecules that produce smell

Olfactory hairs Dendrites of the nerves in the nasal cavity that chemically react with smell molecules

Orthodontics The dental practice of straightening teeth and correcting jaw alignment

Pancreatic juice Enzymes and other chemicals produced by the pancreas for digestion

Papillae Taste buds

Periodontal ligament Fiber between cementum and jawbone material

Pulp Center of tooth containing nerves and blood vessels

Reproductive system Produces children

Respiration The exchange of oxygen and carbon dioxide

Retainer Device to hold teeth in proper position

Root canals Channels containing blood vessels in the tooth

Root Part of tooth anchoring the tooth in the jaw

Salivary amylase Enzyme that breaks down starch molecules

Schwann cells Cells that cover and insulate the axon

Semicircular canals Fluid-filled tubes that help determine balance

Sensory neuron Nerve cell that receives input and carries it toward the brain

Simple fracture One in which the bone does not puncture the skin

Smooth muscle tissue Tissue designed for long strong contractions

Sodium bicarbonate Chemical produced by pancreas to neutralize stomach acid

Striated muscle tissue Skeletal muscle tissue with striped appearance

Synovial fluid Slippery fluid in the joint to facilitate smooth movement

Systolic pressure Blood pressure when the ventricles of the heart contract

Thymine Base used in DNA, must be paired with adenine

Universal donor   Blood type that can be donated to all other types

Universal recipient   Blood type that can receive all other types

Uterus   Womb

Vaccine   A substance that stimulates the immune system against a certain disease

Vitreous humor   Jelly-like substance in the middle of the eyeball

The World of Animals

UNIT 1

Mammals

1 The World of Animals

2 Vertebrates

3 Mammals

4 Mammals: Large & Small

5 Monkeys & Apes

6 Aquatic Mammals

7 Marsupials

◊ **Distinguish** between vertebrates and invertebrates.

◊ **Identify** the five characteristics of mammals.

◊ **Distinguish** between apes and monkeys.

◊ **Distinguish** between marsupials and other mammals.

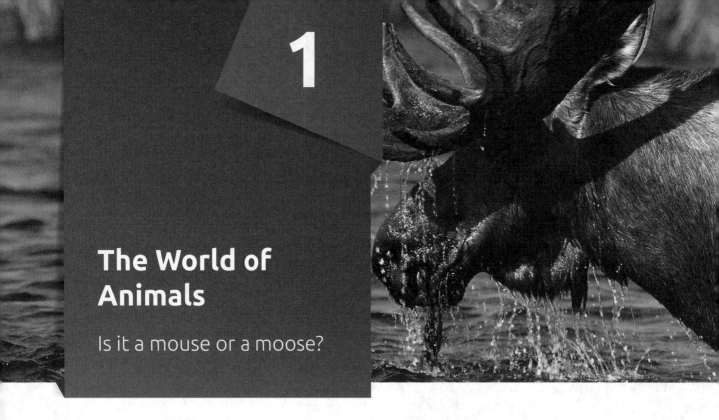

1

The World of Animals

Is it a mouse or a moose?

What is the difference between vertebrates and invertebrates?

Words to know:

vertebrates   invertebrates

Animals and plants are the two largest and most familiar groups of living things. The most distinguishing difference between plants and animals is that plants can make their own food and animals cannot. Animals (and man) were originally created to eat plants to obtain energy (Genesis 1:28–30). Since the Fall of man in the Garden of Eden, many animals still eat plants but others eat animals to obtain energy. Because animals must obtain their own food, they are mobile. They can move about to find plants or other animals to eat.

Animals come in all shapes and sizes. Some are so tiny you can only see them with a microscope. Others are as huge as a car or even a house. God originally created various animal kinds, like the cat kind, horse kind, and elephant kind. Since the Flood of Noah's day, these animal kinds have spread around the world and have adapted to different environments, so that today there are many different species of animals within each kind. Scientists have classified over 1 million different species of animals, and there may be millions more that have not been classified.

In order to study so many different types of animals it is convenient to group them together by their similar characteristics. The first grouping that scientists make is to divide animals by whether they have backbones or not. Animals with backbones are called vertebrates. Animals without backbones are called invertebrates.

Although only 3% of all animals are vertebrates, they are the animals we are most familiar

The African elephant is the largest living land animal.

Squids are some of the largest invertebrates.

Vertebrates are divided into five different groups: mammals, birds, fish, amphibians, and reptiles. We will explore each of these groups in more detail.

Invertebrates are animals without spinal cords. They are very diverse and account for nearly 97% of all animals. Invertebrates do not have internal skeletons. Invertebrates include sponges, jellyfish, worms, insects, and many more creatures. We will also study each group of invertebrates in more detail.

with. Vertebrates are the animals we see around us every day. Every vertebrate has a backbone. The backbone protects the spinal cord that passes through it. Vertebrates have the same major systems that humans have, including skin, skeletal, muscular, nervous, respiratory, and digestive systems. Although all of these systems occur in all vertebrates, they vary considerably among the different kinds of animals.

 What did we learn?

- What are the two major divisions of animals?
- What are two similarities among all animals?

Taking it further

- When did God create the different animal kinds?
- How is man different from animals?

Animal charades

This can be a fun family game. Pretend to be an animal and have everyone else guess what animal you are. Whoever guesses the animal correctly gets to be the next animal. Choose animals other than mammals, with which you are most familiar.

Unusual animals

There are many animals that you are familiar with. But with over a million different species, there are bound to be many that you are unfamiliar with as well. Below is a list of unusual animals. See what you can find out about each of these animals from an animal encyclopedia or other source, and prepare a short report to share with your class or family.

Three of them are shown below. Can you identify them?

- Pangolin
- Common snipe
- Echidna
- Queen Alexandra's Birdwing
- Grouper
- Liver fluke
- Common whelk

2

Vertebrates

Does it have a backbone?

What makes a vertebrate a vertebrate?

Words to know:

vertebrae

The animals we are most familiar with are vertebrates. A vertebrate is an animal that has a backbone. The backbone protects the spinal cord that runs inside of it. Vertebrates can be classified into five categories: mammals, birds, fish, amphibians, and reptiles. These are the animals we notice most around us because, in general, they are the largest animals. Although each of these groups of animals has unique characteristics, they have some common characteristics as well.

All vertebrates have spinal cords and brains. These are the major parts of each vertebrate's nervous system. The spinal cord is protected by a backbone, which is really a series of smaller bones called **vertebrae**, hence the name vertebrates. Messages travel from the animal's brain down the spinal cord to the various parts of the body to tell the animal how to move and what to do. Messages also travel from the various parts of the body along the spinal cord to the animal's brain. Vertebrates have some of the most complex nervous systems of all the animals.

Another common trait that is unique to vertebrates is an internal skeleton. This skeleton is what allows vertebrates to be much larger than most other animals. God gave vertebrates the internal structure needed to support the weight of a large body. Not all vertebrates are large, but nearly all large animals are vertebrates. A few exceptions are the octopus and giant squid. These creatures can be large without an internal skeleton because the water in which they live helps to support their weight. For the most part, vertebrates also have more complex muscular, digestive, and respiratory systems than invertebrates.

Dogs are mammals; they are warm-blooded and nurse their young.

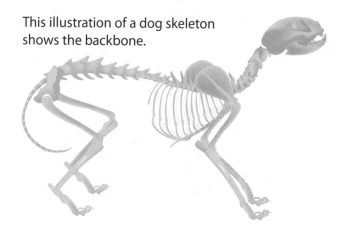

This illustration of a dog skeleton shows the backbone.

We will discuss each group of vertebrates in more detail in the following lessons, but here is a quick overview of the major types of vertebrates. Mammals are vertebrates with hair or fur. They are warm-blooded, and they nurse their young. Birds are warm-blooded animals with feathers. The other vertebrates are all cold-blooded animals. Amphibians are unique because they begin life in the water and as they mature their bodies change and they begin to breathe air through lungs. Reptiles are animals that have scales and breathe air. And fish are aquatic animals that have gills that extract oxygen from the water in which they live. Vertebrates are easy to find and fun to study. Enjoy learning more about God's wonderful creatures.

What did we learn?

- What are the two major divisions of the animal kingdom?
- What characteristics define an animal as a vertebrate?
- What are the five groups of vertebrates?

Taking it further

- Think about pictures you have seen of dinosaur skeletons. Do you think dinosaurs were vertebrates or invertebrates? Why do you think that?

Animal notebook

As you study the world of animals you will be making a notebook that will include your projects. Today, start your notebook by making dividers for each part of the animals we will study. Use the dividers with tabs that are designed for three ring binders. Make labels for each tab in the notebook. Tabs should be labeled as follows:

Mammals, Birds, Fish, Amphibians, Reptiles, Arthropods, Mollusks, Cnidarians, Echinoderms, Sponges, Worms, Protists, and Monerans (you may combine Protists and Monerans if you wish).

These are the various parts of the world of animals that you will be studying. Name as many animals in each category above as possible. Some, like mammals, will be very easy, but you may have no idea what animals belong in some of the other categories. As you go through the lessons in the book you can include anything in your notebook that you wish. Some ideas include the projects from this book, photos of projects or activities that you do, photos from field trips, photos cut from magazines, or coloring books and drawings. Use your imagination.

Notebook title page

Use your artistic, computer, and literary skills to create a title page for each section of your animal notebook. If you don't know what kinds of animals belong in some of the sections, look them up in an encyclopedia or on the Internet

3

Mammals

The fuzzy creatures

What makes an animal a mammal?

Words to know:

mammals

warm-blooded

mammary glands

Challenge words:

stance

digitigrade

unguligrade

plantigrade

ungulates

The most familiar vertebrates on earth are mammals. How can you tell if an animal is a mammal? There is great variety among mammals. Some are tiny such as mice; others are very large such as the giraffe or the elephant. Most live on land but a few, dolphins and whales for example, live in the water. To identify an animal as a mammal, however, we must examine their similarities. Mammals have five common characteristics. They are warm-blooded, they have hair, they give birth to live young, they feed milk to their young, and they breathe air through lungs.

First, mammals are warm-blooded. This means that their bodies stay about the same temperature regardless of the temperature of the air around them. A mammal's body regulates, or controls, its body temperature. To produce heat for the body, mammals must eat a lot of food.

Second, most mammals give birth to live young. Two exceptions are the spiny anteater (echidna) and the platypus, both of which lay eggs. Yet, even these animals feed their young milk from special glands in their bodies. These glands are called mammary glands, hence the name mammal. The major deciding factor in an animal being a mammal is whether it nurses its young or not.

Dolphins are not fish; they are mammals.

Zebra stripes help the animals hide in their environment.

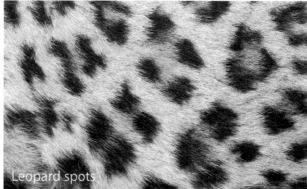
Leopard spots

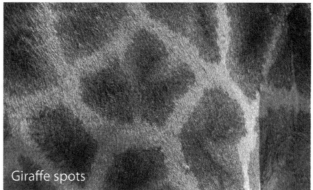
Giraffe spots

In addition to these common characteristics, all mammals have hair or fur on their bodies. Some mammals seem completely covered with hair while others have just a little hair. Most hair provides protection from the cold. Hair also helps with the sense of touch. And the color and pattern of hair helps many mammals hide from their enemies.

Finally, mammals breathe air through lungs. Even whales and dolphins have lungs and they must surface periodically to get a breath of fresh air, unlike fish that get oxygen from the water itself through their gills.

After looking at mammal characteristics, you might wonder if humans are mammals. Physically, humans share these same characteristics with mammals, and most scientists would classify humans as mammals. However, we know that man is not an ordinary animal. Man is a spiritual and moral creature who can have a relationship with God. Man alone was created in God's image (Genesis 1:26–27).

What did we learn?

- What five characteristics are common to all mammals?
- Why do mammals have hair?
- Why is a platypus considered a mammal even though it lays eggs?

Taking it further

- Name some ways that mammals regulate their body temperature.
- What are some animals that have hair that helps them hide from their enemies?

Mammals have fur

Complete the "Mammals Have Fur" worksheet. Use pictures of mammals to describe the fur for animals that you do not have access to. Although people are set apart from animals, compare a sample of your hair to that of some mammals. Add the worksheet to your animal notebook.

Mammals

🎖 Mammal feet

As you will learn in the following lessons, mammals can be grouped together in many different ways. One way that they can be grouped is by how their feet are designed; this is called the animal's stance. The design of an animal's feet determines how that animal will walk. A few mammals, such as whales and dolphins, do not have feet. But most mammals are land dwelling and walk on their feet.

One group of mammals has an unguligrade stance and are referred to as ungulates. Ungulates walk on the very tips of their toes. This may sound very painful, and for a human this would not be a normal or healthy way to walk. But ungulates have hooves which protect their toes so it is natural for them to walk on the tips of their toes. Horses, sheep, and goats are all ungulates. Animals with an unguligrade stance have extended strides and can often move very fast.

Many other mammals walk on the flats or undersides of their toes. These animals are said to have a digitigrade stance. These animals can also move very quickly. The cheetah, considered to be the fastest land animal, has a digitigrade stance. Dogs and cats also fit into this category of mammals.

The third way that mammals walk is with a plantigrade stance. These are animals that walk on the soles of their feet. Bears and raccoons have a plantigrade stance. Most animals that walk on their whole foot are not as fast as other animals. The ankle bones and toe bones are very different in the different stances, yet each was designed perfectly for the way each animal moves.

Think about how each of the following mammals walks. Decide which kind of stance that animal has. It might help if you look at pictures of the animals to see how they stand on their feet.

- Deer
- Rabbit
- Giraffe
- Wolf
- Skunk
- Elephant
- Opossum
- Chimpanzee
- Fox

Horses are unguligrade.

Cheetahs are digitigrade.

Raccoons are plantigrade.

4

Mammals: Large & Small

Armadillo to zebra

What are the largest land mammals?

Challenge words:

ruminants	cud
rumen	omasum
reticulum	abomasum

The variety of mammals is astounding. God created hundreds of different kinds of mammals. Mammals live in nearly every part of the world including the oceans. We cannot possibly cover every kind of mammal in this book, but we will look at a few of the more interesting ones.

Among the largest land mammals are the elephant, the giraffe, and the brown bear. Elephants are the largest of the land mammals. Adult elephants can weigh as much as 6 tons and stand up to 10 feet (3 m) high at the shoulder. They have only a little hair around their ears and eyes, but they are still

mammals. Female elephants, called cows, and baby elephants, called calves, travel in herds. The oldest female is usually the leader of the herd. Male elephants, called bulls, usually travel alone or with other bulls and only join the herd during mating season. Elephants have long trunks, which they use for drinking and for putting food into their mouths. They also

Fun Fact

Both male and female African elephants have tusks, but only male Asian elephants have them.

live in the African savanna or grassland. One of the most fascinating features of a giraffe is its long tongue, which can be up to 21 inches (53 cm) long!

Bears are another interesting group of land mammals. Grizzly bears are a type of brown bear. They live in parts of the northern United States and Canada. A grizzly can be up to 8 feet (2.4 m) long from head to rear and weigh about 800 pounds (360 kg). The Alaskan brown bear can be up to 10 feet (3 m) long and weigh as much as 1,700 pounds (770 kg). Bears usually live by themselves after they are about two years old. Bears will eat nearly anything. Although most of a bear's diet consists of plants and berries, it will also eat small animals and fish. When the salmon are swimming upstream, many bears will gather at the edges of the rivers to catch and eat the fish.

have long teeth called tusks that can be used to dig for roots and to remove bark from trees. Elephants are very strong and are sometimes trained by people to carry heavy burdens.

Giraffes are the tallest land mammals. They can grow to be nearly 19 feet (5.8 m) tall. This allows giraffes to eat leaves from trees that other animals cannot reach. Being so tall also allows giraffes to see long distances so they can watch for danger. Giraffes can also run very quickly, up to 35 miles per hour (15.6 m/s), for a short period of time. Giraffes

Pika

Mammals

Bears are very active during the spring, summer, and fall, but they sleep most of the winter. During the fall, bears eat nearly constantly to store up enough fat to keep them alive during the winter. They also prepare a den where they will be sheltered from the harsh winter weather. Then they will sleep during the cold weather. When spring arrives, a very hungry bear emerges from its den and begins eating again.

In contrast to the large mammals are some very interesting small mammals. The pika is a small animal that lives on rocky mountain slopes.

It grows to be about 8 inches (20 cm) long and is similar to rabbits and hares. Other small mammals include mice, voles, hamsters, and gerbils.

Bats are some of the most unusual mammals. These flying mammals might be confused with birds, but a closer examination will show that bats are very different from birds. Bats have hair, not feathers. And what appear to be wings are actually long fingers connected by a membrane that allows bats to fly. Bats are unusual also because they can detect objects by sending out high-pitched sound waves and sensing their reflections, somewhat like sonar.

Most mammals give birth to live babies, but two, the echidna (spiny anteater) and the platypus, are the only mammals that lay eggs. These animals are still considered mammals because they have mammary glands and nurse their young. They are warm-blooded, breathe air through lungs, and have hair as well.

God has created a wide variety of mammals. Many are cute and cuddly. Others are large and scary. But they are all part of the amazing world of animal.

What did we learn?

- What is the largest land mammal?
- What is the tallest land mammal?
- What do bears eat?

Taking it further

- What do you think is the most fascinating mammal? Why?

Investigating mammals

Choose a mammal that you want to learn more about. Then draw a picture of that mammal to include in your animal notebook.

For older children, research the animal you have chosen and write a report that answers as many of the following questions as possible.

1. What is this animal's habitat—where does it live?
2. How large does this animal grow to be?
3. What does this animal eat?
4. What enemies does this animal have?
5. How quickly does this animal reproduce? How many offspring does it have? How long is the mother pregnant? How long does the baby stay with the mother?
6. What other interesting things did you find out about your animal?

Add your picture and report to your animal notebook.

🏅 Ruminants

Another very interesting and important large mammal is the cow. Cattle are very important because of the milk and beef we get from them. Cattle are ruminants. Ruminants are animals that quickly eat their food without chewing it well. They later regurgitate their food and chew it very thoroughly before swallowing it again.

Ruminants have a four-chambered stomach. The first chamber is called the rumen. Here bacteria begin the process of digestion by beginning to break down the cellulose in the food. Some nutrients from the food are absorbed by the walls of the rumen. The food is then passed into the second chamber called the reticulum. The reticulum returns the food to the mouth for more chewing. At this point the food is called cud and the cow is said to "chew the cud" as it slowly chews up the food.

The cow then swallows the food for the second time. This time the food enters the third chamber of the stomach called the omasum where digestion continues. Much of the volatile fatty acids in the food is absorbed in the omasum. Water is also absorbed here.

The food finally enters the fourth chamber of the stomach called the abomasum, which is considered the true stomach. Here more digestive juices such as hydrochloric acid and enzymes are added and the

Fun Fact

Camels are ruminants, but they aren't true ruminants. They only have three chambers—rumen, reticulum, and abomasum.

food is further broken down.

Once the food leaves the stomach it enters the small intestine. Remaining nutrients are absorbed by the small intestine. What is not absorbed is passed into the large intestine where water is removed. Finally, the waste is expelled from the cow's body.

Ruminants have a very extensive digestive system because they have been designed to digest food that many other animals cannot eat. Grass, hay, and other feed are very difficult to digest, but the processes of chewing twice and fermenting in the rumen allow cattle and other ruminants to eat these foods. Other ruminants include goats, sheep, camels, oxen, and deer. Their digestive systems are another example of God's great design.

Draw a diagram of the ruminant digestive system. Be sure to label all the parts. Include this drawing in your notebook.

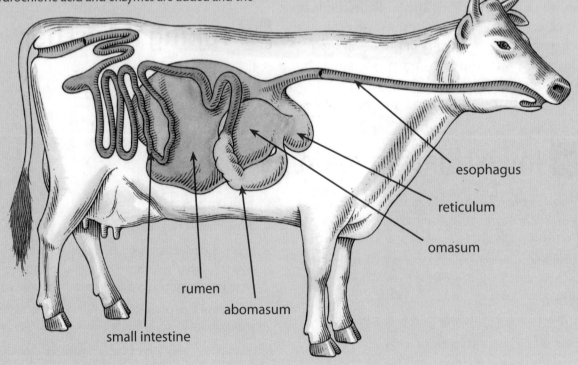

esophagus

reticulum

omasum

rumen

abomasum

small intestine

5

Monkeys & Apes

Primates

What animals are classified as primates?

Words to know:

primates	prehensile tail
binocular vision	Old World monkeys
New World monkeys	apes

One group of mammals that everyone enjoys watching at the zoo is the primates. Most people call these animals monkeys, but there are actually three different types of primates. Monkeys are the largest group of primates, but apes and pro-simians are also primates. All primates share several common characteristics. First, they have ten fingers and ten toes. Also, primates have eyes on the front of their faces so they have binocular vision. Many other animals have eyes located more on the sides of their heads and therefore do not have the good depth perception that primates have.

There are around 160 different species of monkeys. Some are very small like the pygmy marmoset, which weighs only 8 ounces (225 grams). The largest monkey is the mandrill, which can weigh as much as 100 pounds (45 kg). Monkeys live in Central and South America, Africa, and southern Asia. The monkeys that live in the western hemisphere are called New World monkeys. These monkeys are small to medium sized and have prehensile tails. A prehensile tail is one that is able to grasp onto things and can be used for climbing or swinging. Old World monkeys live in Africa and Asia. These monkeys are usually larger than the New World Monkeys and do not have prehensile tails.

Monkeys are excellent climbers, using their feet like a second set of hands. Monkeys spend most of their lives in trees and feed on leaves, fruit, flowers, and insects. A few monkeys prey on smaller animals.

Mandrill

Gorilla

Chimpanzee

The second group of primates is the apes. **Apes** are very similar to monkeys in appearance with one notable exception: apes do not have tails. Also, apes have arms that are longer than their legs. Common apes include gorillas, chimpanzees, orangutans, and gibbons. Apes live in the tropical forests of Africa and Southeast Asia. Unlike most monkeys, many apes spend a significant amount of time on the ground, although orangutans spend much of their time in the trees.

Gorillas are the largest apes. An adult male gorilla weighs about 350 pounds (160 kg) and an adult female weighs about 200 pounds (90 kg). Gorillas live in groups of 10 or fewer animals with one dominant male, several females, and several young gorillas that are not yet ready to live by themselves. When gorillas are mature they usually leave the group. A male will live by himself until he can find an unattached female to join him and begin a new group. A female will leave and join another group or a lone male.

Chimpanzees are very social apes. They live in groups of at least 12 and up to 100 members. They are mostly herbivorous and eat many different plants. However, they also eat termites and have even been known to eat other monkeys and small antelope. Chimps are very creative and use sticks and leaves to help collect termites and water. Other apes, such as orangutans, are less social and live more solitary lives.

The third group of primates is the prosimians. At first glance, prosimians may not seem to belong in the same category as apes and monkeys; however, they share the common characteristics of ten fingers and toes and binocular vision. Prosimians live mostly on the island of Madagascar, but some species live on mainland Africa and in southern Asia. There are 61 species of prosimians, including lemurs, tarsiers, lorises, and bushbabies. Most prosimians have very large eyes. This is helpful for hunting and seeing at night, which is when most prosimians are active.

Bushbaby

Lemur

Mammals

What did we learn?

- What are two common characteristics of all primates?
- What are the three groups of primates?
- What is one difference between apes and monkeys?
- Where do New World Monkeys live?
- Where do Old World Monkeys live?
- What is a prehensile tail?

Taking it further

- If a monkey lives in South America is it likely to have a prehensile tail?
- Are you more likely to find a monkey or an ape in a tree in the rain forest?
- Why do most prosimians have very large eyes?

Mammals word search

Complete the "Mammals Word Search." Put the word search in your animal notebook.

Ape intelligence

Many people claim that man and primates such as monkeys and apes are close relatives because they have so much in common. They also point out that primates, and especially apes, are very intelligent so they must be related to humans.

Several tests have been done to see just how intelligent apes are. In one test, a chimpanzee was given a stick to play with. Later a banana was placed just out of reach of the chimp. At first the chimp expressed frustration and shook the bars of its cage. But eventually, the chimp used the stick to bring the fruit closer, thus showing the ability to reason and solve problems. Other animals have been shown to have similar reasoning abilities.

Apes have also been taught sign language. Several studies have been conducted with various apes including chimpanzees, orangutans, and gorillas. These apes have been taught to make signs to represent various objects, feelings, and ideas. Although they use these signs for communication, there is great disagreement about whether this is real language. Several of the studies have been shown to be flawed, revealing that the apes were really just making signs to receive some sort of compensation. Other studies claim that the apes truly communicate original ideas with their signs. However, the apes fail to develop true language with grammar structure. This ability is limited to humans only. René Descartes, the famous philosopher/mathematician, believed that language was what separated humans who have souls from animals who do not.

It is true that animals have intelligence. God designed them that way. This is one thing that makes animals so interesting. However, there is a fundamental difference between animals and humans as pointed out by Descartes. Humans have souls and can commune with God. So even if your ape can say hello in sign language, that does not make him your brother.

God designed animals to be intelligent, to even reason and solve problems to a limited extent.

Man & Monkeys

Did man descend from the apes?

Nearly every library book you pick up about monkeys says that they are relatives of man or that man and monkeys descended from a common ancestor. They point out that humans and apes have many common characteristics so it makes sense that they have common roots. However, the Bible tells a very different story. The Bible says that God formed man from the dust of the ground and woman from man's rib (Genesis 2:7, 22). It also states that people are made in God's own image (Genesis 1:26–27). Humans are a result of God's miracle of creation, not an accident of nature or a series of genetic mutations.

For many years evolutionists have been trying to find the "missing link" between apes and humans. If a fossil of a creature that was partway between a man and an ape could be found, they say, it would be very powerful evidence for the theory of evolution. And several claims have been made that the "missing link" has been found. However, when each of these claims has been carefully examined, none has been shown to be something that is half ape and half man. Many examples have been shown to be either just an ape or just a human. Sadly, some examples have been shown to be frauds. Let's look at the most famous examples of "missing links."

One of the earliest supposed examples of an ape-man was the Neanderthal Man. In 1856 a few fragments of fossils were discovered in Neander Valley, Germany. Then, in 1908, a nearly complete skeleton of a Neanderthal was discovered in France. This skeleton was of a creature with a skull very much like a human (but with a larger brain case), but who did not walk completely upright. From this discovery, many scientists claimed that Neanderthal Man was subhuman. However, later it was discovered that this skeleton and other bones found in the same area showed that the people suffered from arthritis and from rickets, a disease that causes bones to become

deformed. Other Neanderthal skeletons have been discovered that indicate they walked upright and have completely human characteristics, and it has been shown that they made musical instruments, buried their dead, and had language capabilities.

Neanderthal Man has been shown to be just a man. Most biblical creationists believe Neanderthal Man was a unique variant of modern man who lived in Europe and adjacent Asia and North Africa after the Babel dispersion during the Ice Age.

In 1912 some fossils were discovered near Piltdown, England. These bones included pieces of a jawbone and a skull. Scientists examining the bones declared that the bones were all from one creature that had both human and ape characteristics. This sample was called the Piltdown Man. However, in 1950 scientists declared Piltdown Man to be a hoax. Someone had taken a human skull bone and an ape jawbone and stained them to make them look old. They had also filed the teeth in the jawbone to make them look more human. These "fossils" were then planted in a gravel pit where they were sure to be discovered. Piltdown Man was a fraud.

Nebraska Man was discovered in 1922 in western Nebraska. This discovery consisted of a single tooth, yet scientists declared that it proved the existence of an ape-like man or a man-like ape. The *Illustrated London News* even published a picture of Nebraska Man along with his wife and the tools they used. However, later expeditions unearthed other bones of the supposed ape-man and scientists discovered that the tooth actually belonged to a pig. Nebraska Man was just wishful thinking and bad science.

One of the most famous supposed "missing links" is Lucy. Lucy was discovered by Dr. Donald Johanson in Ethiopia in 1973. This skeleton supposedly shows an ape-like creature that walked upright and thus was an ancestor, or relative, of humans. However, there is great controversy surrounding Lucy. First, Lucy has a lower jaw bone (mandible) that closely resembles that of a gorilla—not that of a human or even a chimp. Second, Lucy's wrist structure has been shown to be consistent with other apes that walk using their knuckles for balance. And third, other skulls that are of the same species as Lucy have been tested and show inner ear characteristics of creatures that do not walk upright.

People are often misled by inaccurately reconstructed statues and images of Lucy displayed at museums and in textbooks, as her feet and hands are often portrayed as being very human-like. Lucy, however, had long curved fingers and toes, similar to modern apes, and a big toe that sticks out to the side, as in chimpanzees. Most scientists now believe that Lucy is simply the skeleton of an extinct species of ape.

Another possible "missing link" was discovered in 2003 when a nearly complete skeleton was discovered on the Indonesian Island of Flores. It has been given the name Flores Man. It has also been nicknamed the Hobbit because the bones indicate that this creature was very small compared to humans, only about three and a half feet tall. Additional excavation has uncovered bones belonging to seven other individuals who were equally small. There is considerable debate among secular scientists about whether this is a new species or just a collections of very small human remains.

Only one nearly complete skull has been recovered, and because it is so small, many scientists claim that these people had to have been related to apes instead of to humans. However, other scientist have shown that it is likely that the skull belonged to someone with Down Syndrome. In addition, despite its overall small size, the area of the brain most associated with intelligence, is about the same size in the Flores Man as in modern humans, which would explain the other things that were found in the same cave as the bones. There were indications of fire, tools, and hunting implements. There were also bones of a very small elephant species that lived on the island. So it is obvious that these people hunted and acted just like humans.

Other than their small size, there is nothing to indicate that these people were anything other than human. So it is believed by creationists that these bones belong to humans and not to apes or anything in between.

No discoveries have been made that show a direct link between apes and humans. The missing links are still missing and will remain missing because God created man and apes separately. So, the next time you pick up a book that says that man is a descendant of an ape, you can ask where the evidence is for that idea. Because the real evidence clearly indicates that apes are apes and humans are humans. You can believe the Bible.

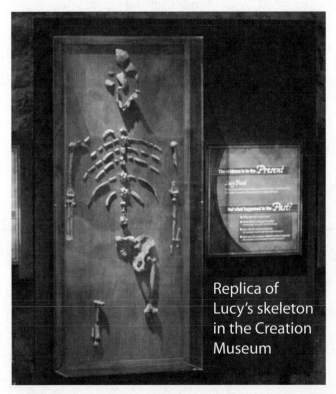

Replica of Lucy's skeleton in the Creation Museum

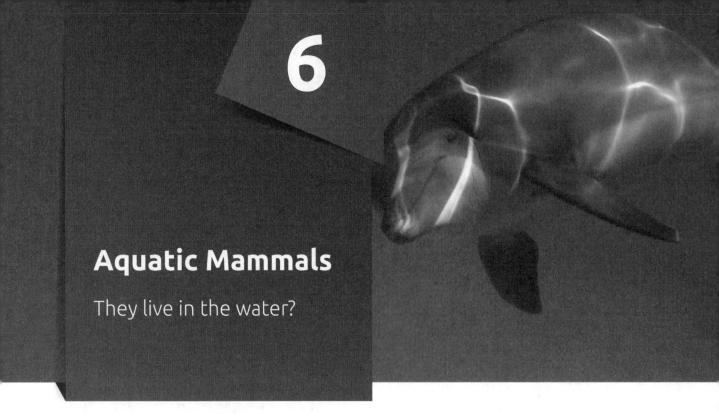

6

Aquatic Mammals

They live in the water?

How are whales and dolphins different from fish?

Words to know:

fluke   keratin

blowhole   rostrum

baleen

Challenge words:

rorqual

echolocation

When people think of mammals they generally think of furry animals that live on land. They think of monkeys, mice, and tigers. However, not all mammals live on the land. There are several mammals that live in the ocean. These include dolphins, porpoises, and whales. These animals are often thought of as large fish. However, whales, porpoises, and dolphins all breathe with lungs and must come to the surface for air on a regular basis. Also, they give birth to live young and nurse their young. Fish cannot do any of these things. In addition, dolphins, porpoises, and whales are warm-blooded while fish are cold-blooded.

Dolphins, porpoises, and whales all have bodies that were designed for living in the water. God gave these mammals sleek bodies that easily glide through the water as well as powerful tail fins, called flukes. The fluke moves up and down, instead of side to side like a fish's tail, allowing the animal to dive deep into the water and then resurface quickly for breathing. Because they are designed by God to live in the water, whales, porpoises, and dolphins do not breathe through a nose like most land animals. Instead, each has an opening on the top of its head called a blowhole through which it breathes. When the animal surfaces, it exhales the air in its lungs causing a spurt of air and a small amount of water to shoot into the sky before the animal takes a new breath.

Whale fluke as seen above water

Dolphins have a rostrum and a wave-shaped dorsal fin.

There are about 90 species of whales, porpoises, and dolphins. Dolphins, porpoises, and many species of whales have teeth. Other species of whales have large comb-like structures in their mouths that they use for straining food from the water. These structures are called baleen and are made from keratin, the same material that your hair and fingernails are made from. Some whales use their baleen to strain out fish and other animals. But the blue whale, which is the largest animal on earth, eats krill, tiny shrimp-like creatures, which are some of the smallest animals on earth. Of course, a blue whale eats about 8,000 pounds (3,600 kg) of krill each day!

What is the difference between dolphins and porpoises? In comparison to dolphins, porpoises are very small. Porpoises seldom exceed 7 feet (2 m) in length, whereas many dolphins can be more than 10 feet (3 m) in length. Dolphins have a lean sleek body, whereas porpoises often appear chubby. The dorsal fin (the fin on the animal's back) in porpoises is triangular, looking more like a shark, while the dorsal fin of the dolphin is shaped like a wave. Porpoises are blunt-nosed, lacking a rostrum, or beak, which is very prominent in dolphins.

Another mammal that spends its entire life in the water is a manatee. Manatees, which somewhat resemble seals or walruses, live in areas with warm

Mammals

Manatee

water such as the Florida Everglades and many of the rivers of South America. The manatee, and its relative the dugong, is a gentle, slow moving creature that grazes on sea grasses. This grazing habit is often compared to cattle grazing and the manatee is often called a sea cow. Manatees spend most of the time eating and can eat a pound of grass for every ten pounds of their weight each day. That means that a 600-pound (270 kg) manatee would eat 60 pounds (27 kg) of plants a day! Like the whales and dolphins, the manatee also has a tail that moves up and down to help it swim and dive. And although the manatee does not have a blowhole, God gave it nostrils on the top of its head so it can surface for air while keeping the majority of its body submerged in water.

Fun Fact

Some people believe that the legend of mermaids swimming in the ocean may have come from sailors who saw manatees slowly swimming below the surface of the water.

God designed most mammals to live on land, but a few were designed to live in the water. The next time you go to the ocean, keep your eyes open for mammals as well as fish.

What did we learn?

- Why are dolphins and whales considered mammals and not fish?
- What is the main difference between the tails of fish and the tails of aquatic mammals?
- What is another name for a manatee?
- Why are manatees sometimes called this?

🚀 Taking it further

- How has God specially designed aquatic mammals for breathing air?
- What do you think might be one of the first things a mother whale or dolphin must teach a newborn baby?

Acting like a whale

Activity 1

Aquatic mammals live their entire lives in the water, yet they breathe air so they must surface periodically to get a fresh breath. A porpoise can hold its breath for about 4 minutes. Manatees can stay submerged for up to 6 minutes at a time. A bottlenose dolphin can stay underwater for up to 15 minutes. But when it comes to staying submerged, the king of underwater mammals is the sperm whale, which can hold its breath for an hour or more. How long can you hold your breath?

Purpose: To appreciate how long animals can hold their breath

Materials: stopwatch

Procedure:

1. Use a stop watch to time how long you can hold your breath.

Activity 2

Baleen whales do not have teeth. Instead, they have comb-like ridges, called baleen, that trap food from the water.

Purpose: To understand how baleen whales get their food

Materials: nuts, fruits, vegetables, knife, toothbrush, two cups, water

Procedure:

1. Chop some nuts, fruits, or vegetables into tiny pieces.

2. Add the pieces to a cup of water. The chopped food represents the tiny creatures that live in the ocean.

3. Hold a toothbrush sideways over an empty cup and slowly pour the water and food mixture through the bristles of the toothbrush. The bristles will catch some of the food pieces.

4. Pull the pieces out of the toothbrush and eat them just like the whale pulls food out of its baleen with its tongue.

🏅 Amazing whales

Whales are some of the most amazing creatures in the world. When you learn about whales you see that God designed them with many special features. For example, land mammals have a connection between their mouths and their noses, but there is no connection between a whale's blowhole and its mouth. God designed the whale this way so that it can open its mouth to feed and not have a chance of water entering its lungs.

The blue whale is the largest creature ever created. Even the largest dinosaurs were small compared to the blue whale. A blue whale can be up to 100 feet (30 m) long and weigh up to 300,000 pounds (135,000 kg). The fin whale is the second largest creature reaching lengths up to 80 feet (24 m). These whales, which are part of the rorqual family of whales, have special grooved throats that expand as they eat, allowing these giant mammals to eat tons of tiny krill (small shrimp-like animals) each day.

Many whales use echolocation, or sonar, for communication. They send out sound waves. When these sound waves bump up against something they bounce off. The whale can detect the bounced waves and determine where the object is. Whales use their echolocation to communicate with other whales. They also use this process to find prey. This is similar to how bats locate prey.

Sperm whales are the deepest diving whales. They can dive up to 10,000 feet (3,050 m) below the surface and can dive up to 550 feet per minute (2.8 m/s). The water pressure increases one atmosphere for every 33 feet (10 m) that you go below the surface of the water, so as they dive, the water pressure on their bodies quickly increases. Sperm whales can experience a change of 15 atmospheres of pressure in less than a minute, and the pressure on the whale's head can be two or three times the pressure on its tail. You might expect this to be a problem for the whale. It is certainly a problem for humans who dive quickly and then resurface quickly. But God designed the sperm whale's body to compensate for these extreme pressure changes. The sperm whale can shut down parts of its circulatory system to send extra blood to areas that need higher pressure, and it can closely regulate the pressure in various blood vessels throughout its body.

The sperm whale can hold its breath for an hour or more. This allows it to dive deeply to find its main food, the giant squid. Once it reaches the bottom where the squid live, the sperm whale can shut down nearly every body function while it eats so that it can stay submerged long enough to eat its fill before needing to surface for more air.

Humpback whales also have interesting design features. The fins of a humpback whale have many blood vessels close to the surface. This allows the whales to use their fins to help control their body temperature. They move their fins back and forth in the water and sometimes in the air to cool their bodies.

Whales are truly designed by God to be well suited for their environment. See what other interesting things you can find out about whales that demonstrate God's special design.

Humpback whale

7

Marsupials

Pouched animals

How are marsupials different from other mammals?

Words to know:

marsupial   nocturnal

joey

Of all the mammals in the world, one of the most entertaining is the kangaroo. Kangaroos hop faster than many animals can run. Kangaroos box each other in a fight for a mate. And kangaroos are often seen with the head of a baby poking out of a pouch. These entertaining animals that God created are part of a group of mammals called marsupials.

Marsupials are mammals that give birth to babies that are not fully developed. These tiny babies, depending on the species, can be as small as a grain of rice or as big as a bumble bee. A newly-born baby is called a joey and is naked and blind. It uses its sense of smell to crawl along its mother's belly searching for the pouch that will protect it until it is fully developed. Once the joey reaches the pouch, it crawls inside and attaches itself to its mother's mammary gland where it will remain, nursing and growing, for several months.

Kangaroos are the most famous marsupials, but there are many other ones as well. Koalas, numbats, mulgaras, and Tasmanian devils are some of the over 260 species of marsupials. Nearly all marsupials live in Australia, Tasmania, and

Kangaroo

Fun Fact

A red kangaroo can hop up to 30 feet (9 m) in one leap.

Mammals

The opossum is North America's only marsupial.

Tasmanian devil

New Zealand. The only marsupial known to live in North America is the opossum.

Red kangaroos are the largest of the kangaroos and can be up to 8 feet (2.4 m) tall. They are the largest hopping animals on earth. Yet some breeds of kangaroos are very small. The musky rat kangaroo is only 10–12 inches (25–30 cm) high. But big or small, all kangaroos have large hind legs with big hind feet. The middle toe of each hind foot is longer than the others and is used for pushing off when hopping. Also, all kangaroos have large tails that help them keep their balance.

Large kangaroos can hop at speeds up to 30–35 mph (13–16 m/s). God designed the kangaroo to be a hopping machine. The large legs and tail are ideal. And at the back of each leg is a long stretchy tendon attaching the muscles of the leg to the ankle bones. This tendon stores up energy between hops that is released when the feet hit the ground. When a kangaroo is hopping, its body remains at about the same height, while its legs stretch out and then fold up as it hops. God designed the kangaroo so well for hopping that it uses up about the same amount of energy when it is hopping slowly as when it is hopping quickly.

Kangaroos are generally nocturnal, meaning they are active at night. They spend most of the day sleeping and resting. Then, when the sun goes down and the temperatures cool off, kangaroos begin eating, which they continue doing almost the entire time they are awake. Kangaroos are plant eaters, and like many other plant eaters, they chew their food and swallow it, then later, they spit the food back up and chew it some more. Kangaroos also have special bacteria living in their digestive tracts that eat the cellulose in the plants and help the kangaroos digest the plants.

Koalas, opossums, and kangaroos are all plant eaters. But many other marsupials are insect or meat eaters. The numbat is a marsupial that eats ants and termites. The numbat uses its sharp claws to tear open trees or termite hills. Then it uses its sticky 4-inch (10 cm) long tongue to pick up termites or ants for a tasty meal. A hungry numbat can eat as many as 20,000 termites in one day.

The most famous meat-eating marsupial is the Tasmanian devil. Thanks to its sharp teeth and tendency to growl, it has earned a reputation as a very fierce animal. However, recent studies have shown that it is not as fierce as once believed. Tasmanian devils live only on the island of Tasmania near Australia. These animals are nocturnal and live in brushy, wooded areas. They hunt wallabies, wombats, sheep, and rabbits. But they prefer to eat animals that are already dead instead of hunting.

Fun Fact

A female kangaroo is ready to mate at about two years old. From that time on she will be nearly always pregnant. In fact, she will often have a baby in her womb, a baby in her pouch, and a youngster at her side all at the same time.

Mammals

Making a pouch

Purpose: To make your own marsupial pouch

Materials: tag board, zipper bag, scissors, pencil, glue, fake fur or felt

Procedure:

1. On a sheet of tag board or construction paper, draw the belly of a kangaroo.

2. In the center of the sheet, glue a plastic zipper bag with the zipper side up.

3. Now glue fake fur or felt across the outside of the zipper bag. Be sure that the fur completely covers the sides and bottom of the zipper bag, but does not block the top of the bag. You now have a pouch.

4. If you have enough fur, you can glue it on the rest of the paper to make the pouch blend in with the belly of the kangaroo.

5. Next, use tag board or construction paper to make a baby kangaroo. You can zip and unzip the pouch just like a mother kangaroo tightens and loosens the muscles of her pouch to protect her baby. You many even want to make various sizes of babies. When a joey first enters the pouch it is smaller than a bumblebee, has no hair, and its eyes are sealed shut. It grows and develops in the pouch. When it is big enough, it leaves and reenters the pouch until it is too big to crawl back inside. Add your pouch and joey to your animal notebook.

While the name marsupial means "pouched" animal, there are marsupials that don't have pouches. These include the numbat and the brown antechinus.

From numbats to opossums, marsupials are very interesting creatures. See what else you can learn about these pouched animals.

What did we learn?

- What is a marsupial?
- Name at least three marsupials.
- How has God designed the kangaroo for jumping?

Taking it further

- About half of a kangaroo's body weight is from muscle. This is nearly twice as much as in most animals its size. How might this fact contribute to its ability to hop?

- How do you think a joey kangaroo keeps from falling out of its mother's pouch when she hops?

Fun Fact

Kangaroos keep cool by panting like a dog. When it is really hot, a kangaroo will lick its forearms and the evaporation of the saliva will help to cool down the kangaroo.

 # Koalas

Koalas are one of Australia's most famous animals and they are marsupials. See how much you can find out about koalas from an animal encyclopedia or from an online source. Then fill out the "Koala Fun Facts" worksheet.

Mammals

UNIT 2

Birds & Fish

8 Birds

9 Flight

10 The Bird's Digestive System

11 Fish

12 Fins & Other Fish Anatomy

13 Cartilaginous Fish

◊ **Explain** how birds were designed for flight.

◊ **Describe** the unique characteristics of birds and fish using examples.

◊ **Distinguish** between warm-blooded and cold-blooded animals.

8

Birds

Fine feathered friends

What features make birds different from all other animals?

Words to know:

talon

Birds are some of the most interesting and easy to watch animals in God's creation. These warm-blooded, feathered vertebrates can be found in every region of the world. There are approximately 9,000 different species of birds (but far fewer created "kinds" of birds). Birds lay eggs and breathe with lungs. Most birds are excellent flyers, although some birds do not fly. God designed birds' bodies to be efficient flying machines. Birds have strong yet lightweight bones; many bones have hollow spaces to make them lighter. Birds also have rigid or stiff backbones that support the strong muscles used to move the wings.

With 9,000 different species of birds, it is helpful to group the birds by some common characteristics. Birds are often grouped as perching birds, birds of prey, water birds, game birds, tropical birds, and flightless birds. The shape of the feet and beaks of these different groups reflects the different ecosystems or environments in which they live.

Perching bird

Fun Fact

There are between 100 and 200 billion birds on the planet.

Birds & Fish

286 • The World of Animals LESSON 8

Bird of prey

Approximately 60% of all birds are perching birds. Songbirds such as the thrush, robin, bluebird, and sparrow are just a few of the many perching birds. Only a few perching birds, such as the hummingbird and woodpecker, do not have songs. Perching birds have feet with 3 toes facing forward and 1 toe facing backward for grasping branches. Many have triangular-shaped pointed beaks for eating seeds and insects. Some of these birds, such as hummingbirds, have long narrow beaks for sucking nectar from flowers.

Birds of prey like eagles, hawks, falcons, and owls catch small animals such as rodents. They have very sharp eyesight, as well as hooked beaks and sharp talons, claw-like feet that allow them to catch and kill their prey. Many birds of prey, particularly owls, also have very keen hearing that allows them to pinpoint prey in the dark.

Water birds, such as ducks, swans, and geese, are specially designed for life on and near the water. They have rounded beaks for catching fish and other food in the water, and they have webbed feet for swimming. They also secrete oil that helps make their feathers water resistant.

Game birds are birds that are often hunted for meat. They have very strong flight muscles making them difficult to catch but good to eat once they are caught. These include wild turkey, quail, and pheasant. Although ducks and geese are considered water birds, they are game birds as well.

Tropical birds include parrots, parakeets, and toucans. These birds live in the tropical rain forests. Most are very brightly colored and have large hooked beaks. They have similar feet to perching birds since they spend most of their time in the trees.

Water bird

Game bird

Birds & Fish

Tropical bird

Finally, a few birds are flightless. These birds have wings but are not able to fly. Flightless birds include ostriches, emus, and penguins. These birds are designed for their lifestyle, being able to run or swim very swiftly.

🧠 What did we learn?

- How do birds differ from mammals?
- How are birds the same as mammals?

🚀 Taking it further

- How can you identify one bird from another?
- What birds can you identify near your home?
- Why might you see different birds near your home in the summer than in the winter?

Fun Fact

The smallest bird is the bee hummingbird from Cuba, which weighs only 0.056 ounces (1.6 g)— less than a penny.

Fun Fact

The largest bird is the ostrich, which can be up to 9 feet (2.7 m) tall and weigh as much as 300 pounds (136 kg).

🧪 Bird beaks & bird feet

Examine the pictures in this lesson as well as pictures of birds in other books to get a better idea of how different birds' beaks and feet look. Then fill out the "Bird Beaks and Feet" worksheet by drawing the different types of beaks and feet that birds have.

Notice the various uses of the different shaped beaks and feet and how they help the birds to survive in their environment. Add this page to your animal notebook.

Other Optional Activities

1. Put up a bird feeder and enjoy watching the birds come close on a regular basis.

2. Find abandoned nests and dissect them to find out what birds use to build their nests.

🏅 Birds vs. reptiles

Studying birds' beaks can be very interesting. In fact, one scientist, Charles Darwin, became famous when he made some detailed observations about the beaks of finches in the Galapagos Islands. Darwin observed that finches in one area had beaks that were larger and a different shape than ones in a different area. The size and shape of beaks of the various types of finches seemed related to the food available where the birds lived. Darwin concluded that this was a result of natural selection; the birds with the beaks that were well suited for their environment survived better than the others so they became the dominant species in that area.

This part of Darwin's theory is well supported by what we observe today. We see an animal with a particular trait surviving better than the same kind of animal without that trait. However, Darwin, and many scientists that have followed him, extended this observation to conclude that one kind of animal can change into another kind of animal by natural selection. We do not observe this happening today and there is no conclusive evidence in the fossil record that it has happened in the past.

Many evolutionists claim that the birds we see today have evolved from reptiles, possibly dinosaurs, in the past. Let's look at what kinds of changes would be needed for that to happen. First, birds are warm-blooded and reptiles are cold-blooded. A system would need to be developed to allow the animal in between a bird and a reptile to regulate its body temperature. But it is unknown how this could

happen in small progressive steps that are required by Darwin's theory. A system that was not fully functional would be useless and would not provide any known benefit.

Second, the animal would have to develop a much larger brain. On average, birds' brains are much larger than reptiles' brains. Also, the circulatory and respiratory systems are very different between birds and reptiles. We will look at this in more detail in lesson 10.

Finally, feathers and scales are very different. There is no known way to change a scale into a feather through small changes. So we see that it is very difficult to believe that a reptile changed into a bird, even given the supposed millions of years.

Instead of thinking about evolution when we see variety among birds' beaks, we need to think of God's wonderful creativity that made such variety. We see this variety among many kinds of birds. There are many different sparrows, each with distinct coloring, songs, and habits, yet they are all sparrows that came from the sparrows that were on Noah's ark. They look different because God created the original animals with the information to produce many different looking offspring, but their offspring are all still sparrows.

List some characteristics that may vary among an animal kind due to natural selection. Look through an animal encyclopedia to see examples of these characteristics. Notice that none of these various characteristics has resulted in a new kind of animal.

Charles Darwin

1809–1882

The name Charles Darwin can evoke strong emotions. Some people view him as one of the greatest scientists of the 19th century. Others see him as the man who destroyed our belief in God. Regardless of how you feel about evolution and creation, it is important to know what Darwin did and to examine his findings in light of the Bible and in light of modern science. Charles Darwin was born in Shrewsbury, England in 1809. His father was a doctor and his mother was the daughter of the famous china maker, Josiah Wedgwood.

After earning a degree in theology in 1831, Darwin was selected to be part of a nature tour around the world. From 1831–1839 he sailed from place to place on the ship HMS *Beagle*. At each place he visited, Darwin carefully studied and collected plants, animals, rocks, and fossils. He is most famous for his study of the finches of the Galapagos Islands. He discovered that different species of finches on each island had different beaks depending on the type of diet available there. This led him to seek an explanation for how such variety could occur.

In 1859, after years of study, Darwin published his most famous work, *On the Origin of Species*. In this work, Darwin suggested that changes within species were a result of natural selection—survival of the fittest. This idea was taken further to suggest that over time these small changes could result in a completely new kind of animal. Later, in 1871, Darwin published a book called *The Descent of Man*, in which he suggested that man evolved from ape-like ancestors.

It is important to note that Darwin knew nothing about genetics or how traits were passed from one generation to the next. We know today that animals have a wide variety of traits that are passed on through their genes. We can see this variety in the many species of dogs that exist today (wolf, fox, coyote, domestic dog, etc.). However, we also know that there is a limit to the amount of change that can occur genetically. Evolutionists claim that mutations in the genes can result in new information for new structures and organs, and that if these mutations help the organism survive, they are passed on to their offspring. However, no one has ever observed a mutation that added new information to the genes. All observed mutations have been determined to be harmful or neutral to the animal, and result in a loss of information.

We can observe adaptation, such as Darwin observed with his finches, but we do not see changes that change one kind of animal into another. Furthermore, no fossil evidence has been found to show a progression of changes from one kind of animal into another. What we observe in both nature and in the fossil record is that a finch is still a finch and a dog is still a dog. God created each type of animal with a wonderful capacity for variety within its kind, but there is no evidence of evolution from one kind to another.

9

Flight

How do those birds do that?

How are feathers used by birds?

Words to know:

airfoil

down feathers

contour feathers

flight feathers

preening

Challenge words:

casque

Although some birds are flightless, most birds are designed for flight. To watch a bird soaring into the sky is a marvelous thing. For centuries man sought to imitate birds, but only in the last 100 years or so has man truly begun to understand how perfectly designed the bird's body is for flight.

Birds have very strong breast muscles attached to wide sternums, and they have stiff backbones to withstand the forces of flight. The muscles help move the wings smoothly and efficiently. Birds also have a special respiratory system that allows them to breathe air through lungs into a system of air sacs that extract much more oxygen than any other animal's respiratory system can. Birds have hollow spaces in their bones, making them extremely light for their size. These and many other special features aid birds in flying.

By far the most important feature to help birds fly is the design of their wings and feathers. Their wings are shaped like an **airfoil**, forcing air to flow more quickly over the wings than under them. This creates lower pressure over the wings, thus creating lift.

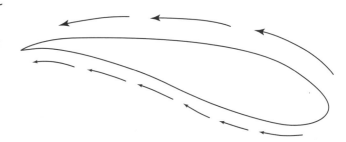

Birds & Fish

Fun Fact

Hummingbirds have the fastest wing-beat of all birds. Their wings can complete more than 75 up and down movements in a second.

Fun Fact

The peregrine falcon is perhaps the fastest animal on earth. In a stoop, or dive, the peregrine has been clocked at speeds of over 180 mph (80.5 m/s).

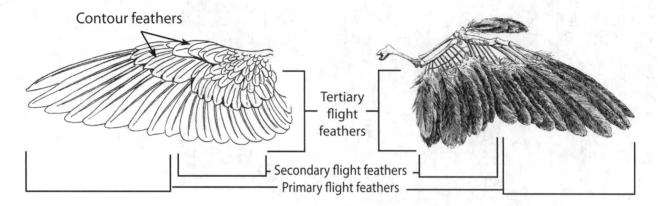

Contour feathers

Tertiary flight feathers

Secondary flight feathers

Primary flight feathers

Wing covered with feathers

Wing showing bone structure

Birds have three kinds of feathers, each with a different function. Soft fuzzy **down feathers** provide insulation near the bird's body. Over these are the **contour feathers** that cover the bird's body. All contour feathers point toward the tail, making air flow smoothly over the bird's body. **Flight feathers** give the wing the needed shape for flying. Feathers are designed with a hook and barb system to help the feather maintain its shape. If a feather gets pulled apart the bird can zip it back up with its beak. This is called **preening**.

A bird's wing has three sets of flight feathers. The primary feathers are attached near the end of the wing; the secondary feathers are attached in the center; and the tertiary feathers are attached to the upper wing, close to the body. Movement of the flight feathers makes tiny changes in the shape of the wing to compensate for changing air conditions. Contour feathers on the front of the wing make a smooth surface over which the air can easily flow.

Finally, the bird's tail serves as a rudder. By moving the tail from side to side, the bird can steer or change direction in the air. God designed every part of the bird for efficient flight.

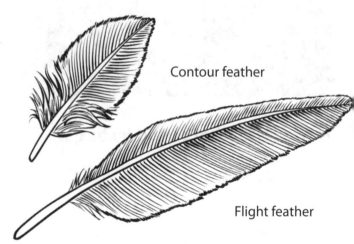

Contour feather

Flight feather

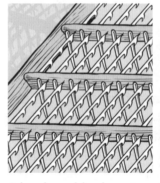

A hook-and-barb system holds the feather together.

🧠 What did we learn?

- What are some ways birds are designed for flight?

- What are the three kinds of bird feathers?

- How does a bird repair a feather that is pulled open?

- How does a bird's tail work like a rudder?

🚀 Taking it further

- Why can't man fly by strapping wings to his arms?

- How do you think birds use their feathers to stay warm?

- How is an airplane wing like a bird's wing?

Birds & Fish

Examining a bird's feather

Examine a bird's feather with a magnifying glass. Notice the barbs that hold the feather together. A bird can "zip up" its feathers with its beak if they get pulled open. This is called preening. Birds spend some time every day fixing or preening their feathers.

God designed birds to fly

Fill out the "God Designed Birds To Fly" worksheet by drawing an airfoil, labeling the feathers on the bird's wing, and drawing an example of the structure of a feather. Glue the bird's feather to the sheet. Add this page to your animal notebook.

Flightless birds

Although most birds were designed to fly, about one percent of all birds are flightless. Probably the most well know flightless bird is the ostrich. The ostrich is the largest bird in the world. Although it cannot fly, it can run up to 45 mph (72 km/h). The ostrich has the largest egg of any bird with eggs measuring up to eight inches (20 cm) long. Ostriches live in Africa. Because the ostrich is up to nine feet tall, it can see a long distance which helps the bird spot danger.

Several other flightless birds are related to the ostrich. The rhea looks much like a small ostrich. It grows up to five feet (1.5 m) tall. It lives on the plains of South America. The emu lives in Australia and also looks very much like an ostrich but is only about six feet (1.8 m) tall. Another large flightless bird somewhat resembling an ostrich is the cassowary, which also reaches heights of about six feet. The ostrich, rhea, and emu all have primarily gray or brown feathers. The cassowary is mostly black, but has a bright red and blue neck and head. The cassowary also has a large bony shield on its head called a casque. Cassowaries live in New Guinea and northern Australia. It is likely that all of these birds came from the same ostrich "kind" that was on the Ark.

The kiwi is another flightless bird that lives in New Zealand. The kiwi is much smaller than the ostrich-type birds mentioned above. It is only about 20 inches (51 cm) long. It has a very long beak with nostrils on the end. The kiwi uses these nostrils to sniff out food, which often includes earthworms and other small animals. Although the kiwi is about the size of a

Ostrich

Emu

Cassowary

Kiwi

King penguin

chicken, it can lay an egg that is nearly four times the size of a chicken egg. A kiwi has long thin feathers that from a distance could be mistaken for hair.

A very different group of flightless birds is the penguins. There are many different species of penguins, but they all have some common characteristics. Penguins live along coastal areas and spend much of their time in the water. They have webbed feet and wings which work as flippers to propel the bird through the water. Penguins are only found in the southern hemisphere.

Some penguins, such as the Galapagos penguin, live in tropical areas, primarily on tropical islands with few land predators. Other penguins, such as the

emperor penguin, live in Antarctica and are able to survive very harsh conditions. The emperor penguin is the largest penguin reaching heights up to four feet (1.2 m) tall. The little blue penguin is the smallest penguin at only 12 inches (30 cm) high.

Some people say that flightless birds are evidence for evolution, that they evolved from ancestors that could have flown in the past, and that their useless wings are just leftovers. However, is this really proof for evolution? It is not.

The "uselessness" of their wings is open to debate. These flightless birds still have muscles that control their wings and use them for various purposes. Some birds frighten away enemies by charging at them and flapping their wings. Other birds use their wings to shelter their young. And a penguin's wings are anything but useless. Their wings help them swim very quickly and dive deeply into the ocean for food. So even though these birds' wings do not help them fly, they are not useless.

The Bird's Digestive System

They sure eat a lot.

How is a bird's digestive system different from yours?

Words to know:

crop   esophagus

gizzard   cloaca

Challenge words:

counter-current
   exchange

Have you ever noticed that when birds are not flying they are almost always eating? This is because flying requires a lot of energy. In addition, warm-blooded animals need a lot of food to keep their bodies at a constant temperature. God created birds with a special digestive system to help them be able to fly and regulate their temperature.

First, a bird's digestive system works very quickly. A bird can digest its food in as little as 30 minutes to 3 hours. The human body takes several hours to as much as two days to completely digest its food. Second, a bird's digestive system is very efficient at extracting the nutrients it needs.

Birds do not have teeth, so God designed them with digestive systems that digest food that has not been chewed. A bird swallows its food, which enters its **esophagus**, the tube connecting the mouth to the stomach. The food is then held in a sac in the middle of the esophagus called a **crop**, to be released into the stomach at a constant rate. This allows a bird to eat quickly then fly away. The food is released at a constant rate so that energy is available continuously, even if the bird is flying for a long time, or sitting on the eggs in its nest.

This special digestive system helps birds have the necessary energy for flight.

Birds & Fish

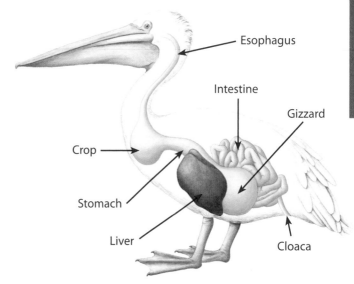

Esophagus

Intestine

Gizzard

Crop

Stomach

Liver

Cloaca

The food then goes into a small stomach where digestive juices are added. The food then enters the gizzard. This organ is very rough inside and grinds up the food. The gizzard compensates for the bird's lack of teeth. This ground up mixture then passes into the intestine where the nutrients are extracted. A bird's intestine is very efficient at extracting these nutrients so the energy from the food is available very quickly. A bird does not have to wait hours to get energy from the food it eats. Finally, what is not used by the bird passes into the cloaca and is eliminated as waste.

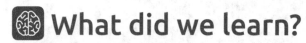 What did we learn?

- How does a bird "chew" its food without teeth?
- What purposes does the crop serve?

 Taking it further

- How is a bird's digestive system different from a human digestive system?
- How does a bird's digestive system help it to be a better flyer?

Digestive system worksheet

Draw and label the parts of the bird's digestive system on the "God Designed the Bird's Digestive System" worksheet. This can be added to your animal notebook.

Dissect an owl pellet

Owl pellets can be ordered from many science supply stores. An owl swallows its prey whole and later spits up a pellet of indigestible fur and bones. You can obtain pellets that have been sterilized and dissect them to see what the owl had for dinner by matching the bones to a chart that can also be purchased. This is a fascinating project.

Birds & Fish

Respiratory system

God not only designed birds to have a special digestive system, He also designed them with a special respiratory system that allows them to get a higher percentage of oxygen out of the air than most other animals. This is a very efficient system, which allows birds to fly for extended periods of time without tiring, and enables them to fly at high altitudes where there is less oxygen in the air.

In most animals with lungs, including mammals and reptiles, the chest cavity expands drawing air into the lungs. The air passes through smaller and smaller passages in the lungs until it reaches tiny sacs that are surrounded by blood vessels. Oxygen passes into the blood and carbon dioxide leaves the blood and enters the air in these sacs. The chest cavity then compresses, forcing the air out of the lungs. This is a bellows type of process.

The bird's respiratory system is very different, however. The bird's lungs do not expand and contract. When a bird inhales, the air passes through the lungs into rear air sacs. As the bird exhales, the air passes through small tubes in the lungs where the exchange of oxygen takes place. When the bird inhales again, the air in these tubes is forced into forward air sacs. Finally when the bird exhales again the air in the forward air sacs leaves its body. Thus the bird inhales and exhales twice for each breath of air.

The blood flow through the lungs is in the opposite direction as the air flow. Blood is always exposed to air that has a higher concentration of oxygen. Thus, this opposite flow allows for the greatest amount of oxygen to be exchanged within the lungs. This is called counter-current exchange.

In addition to being very efficient in exchanging oxygen, the bird's respiratory system also serves another vital function. Air flowing through the air sacs also flows through small tubes inside the hollow spaces in the bird's bones. This removes heat from the bird's body as the cool air moves through the sac and out of the body again. This is a very efficient way to cool the bird while it is flying for long periods of time.

Earlier we examined some of the ways that birds are different from reptiles. Their respiratory system is one of the biggest differences. It is impossible to conceive of a way that the bellows type of respiratory system of a reptile could slowly change into the counter-current exchange system of a bird with slow gradual changes proposed by evolution. Again, we see that God created the different kinds the way they are for His glory.

Bird's respiratory system

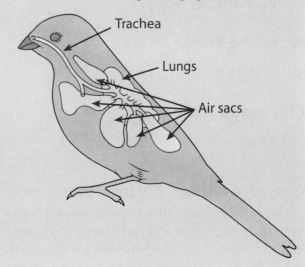

Trachea

Lungs

Air sacs

11

Fish

Do fish go to school?

What features allow fish to survive underwater?

Words to know:

cold-blooded   gills

Challenge words:

placoid scales   leptoid scales

One of America's favorite pastimes is fishing. Fish can be found in the smallest ponds and streams, in large lakes, and throughout the oceans. There are over 22,000 species of fish, making them the most diverse group of vertebrates. Fish are vertebrates that live in the water. They have scales and they breathe oxygen from the water using gills, special organs that remove oxygen from the water. Fish are cold-blooded, which means that their bodies do not stay the same temperature all the

time, but become the same temperature as their surroundings. This allows them to survive even in very cold climates. Most fish reproduce by laying eggs, although a few give live birth. Most fish live in either salt water or fresh water, but a few can survive in both salt and fresh water environments.

Most fish are bony fish, meaning they have bony skeletons. Bony fish have fins and tails that make them excellent swimmers. When you think of a fish, you probably think of a trout, bass, or goldfish. But about 5% of all fish do not have rigid bones. Instead, they have flexible skeletons made from cartilage. Cartilaginous fish include sharks, rays, and lampreys.

Even though dolphins and whales appear to be a lot like fish, recall that there are a few very important differences. One of the most distinct

Fish breathe using their gills.

Fun Fact

Aquarium fish are the most popular pet in America, with nearly 12 million households owning more than 158,600,000 fish.

Birds & Fish

differences is in how they breathe. As we already learned, dolphins, whales, and other aquatic mammals must periodically go to the surface for fresh air, which they take into their lungs. Fish, on the other hand, get their oxygen from the water. Water enters the fish's mouth, is forced over the gills, and then exits the fish's body. As the water passes over the gills, oxygen moves from the water into the fish's blood stream.

If a fish swims with its mouth open, there is a constant flow of water through the gills. If a fish is not swimming, it can force the water through the gills by contracting its throat. Some sharks cannot do this so they must continually stay in motion.

What did we learn?

- What makes fish different from other animals?
- How do fish breathe?
- Why do some sharks have to stay in motion?
- What is the difference between warm-blooded and cold-blooded animals?

Taking it further

- Other than how they breathe, how are dolphins different from fish?
- How are dolphins like fish?

Name a group game

Have one person name an animal, then have another name what a group of that type of animal would be called. Here are a few to get you started:

A school of fish, a flock of birds, a gaggle of geese, a herd of elephants, a pride of lions, a pack of wild dogs, a flock of sheep, a brood of vipers, a swarm of flies. For a large list, check the related activity in the teacher guide for this course.

Fish school

A group of fish is called a school just like a group of birds is called a flock. Create an underwater picture. Try to include seaweed, sand, rocks, or other sea life. Then glue a group of goldfish snack crackers on the picture to show

a school of fish. Take a picture of your creation to include in your animal notebook. It can also be fun to eat some of the fish.

🏅 Designed for speed

God designed fish to live in the water. You already learned that fish are cold-blooded and have gills to remove oxygen from the water. But there are many other features that allow the fish to survive in this wet environment. One of the most obvious features of fish is their scales.

Most fish are covered with scales from head to tail. These scales can have very different shapes and fit together in different ways, but they all point backward toward the tail, allowing water to flow smoothly over them. Also, glands under the scales secrete a slimy mucus. This makes the fish very slick, which also allows the water to flow smoothly. Thus scales allow fish to move easily through the water so they need to exert less energy and can move more quickly as they swim.

Sharks and other cartilaginous fish have flat tooth-shaped scales called placoid scales that are supported by tiny spines. These scales feel very rough if stroked from tail to head, but lay very flat when water moves from head to tail. These scales do not grow, so as a shark grows, more scales develop and fill in the gaps.

Bony fish, on the other hand, have very different kinds of scales from the kind that sharks possess. They have leptoid scales which grow as the fish grows by adding material to the outer edge of each scale. Thus the scales have growth rings, somewhat like the rings inside a tree trunk. These scales overlap each other from head to tail like shingles on a roof. Again, this design allows the water to flow easily over the fish as it swims. Scales are another example of God's provision for life on earth.

Placoid scales as viewed through an electron microscope.

Leptoid scales overlap like shingles.

12

Fins & Other Fish Anatomy

Designed for efficiency

How are fins used by fish?

Words to know:

swim bladder

pectoral fin

pelvic fin

dorsal fin

anal fin

caudal fin

Challenge words:

olfactory lobe

lateral line

optic lobe

Most fish have a similar body shape that is long, thin, and somewhat flat. God designed a fish's body to be very efficient in the water. First, gills are designed to remove up to 80% of the oxygen from the water. By comparison, lungs usually remove only about 25% of the oxygen from the air.

To be efficient swimmers, God designed fish with long narrow bodies that glide easily through the water. The fish's body produces slimy mucus that coats the body and helps it swim more easily. To stay afloat, most fish have **swim bladders**. These are balloon-like sacs that can be inflated with air to help the fish rise in the water, or can be deflated to help the fish sink or go deeper in the water.

Finally, fish were designed with several different fins to help them be great swimmers. Fish have two pairs of fins toward the front of their bodies. **Pectoral fins** are located on the sides behind the mouth. The **pelvic fins** are lower down on the body. Pectoral and pelvic fins allow the fish to angle up or down when swimming. They can also act as brakes to slow the fish down. And they can even be used to slowly move the fish backward. These fins also help the fish swim in a straight line.

Fish usually have one or two fins that stick up on their backs. These are called **dorsal fins**. They also have a fin pointing down from the bottom called an **anal fin**. Dorsal and anal fins keep the fish from tipping sideways and give it stability.

The final fin is the tail, called the **caudal fin**. This is also called the tail fin. It provides the main power for forward movement in fish.

All of these designs, along with strong muscles, make the fish one of the most efficient swimmers in creation. God's great design is very evident in the fish's body.

One of the few exceptions to the fast-swimming fish is the seahorse. This tiny creature may not even seem like a fish, but it is cold-blooded, has fins, scales and gills, and lays eggs like other fish. This tiny fish has a dorsal fin that moves it forward in an upright position at a rather slow speed.

Birds & Fish

Spiny dorsal fin   Soft dorsal fin

Pectoral fin   Pelvic fin   Anal fin   Caudal fin

However, just because it is slow does not mean it was not well designed.

A protective bony armor cleverly protects the seahorse from imminent danger. Its tough skeleton makes it unappetizing for predators, so sea horses are usually left alone.

A seahorse has a prehensile tail allowing it to grip plants and other objects.

The seahorse is unique among fishes in that its head is set at right angles to its body. It swims with its body held upright. It can bend its head down or up, but not from side to side. The inability to move its head from side to side would create problems in other creatures, but God in His wisdom has designed the seahorse's eyes to move independently, swiveling about to watch each side.

What did we learn?

- What is the purpose of a swim bladder?
- How did God design the fish to be such a good swimmer?

Taking it further

- How does mucus make a fish a more efficient swimmer?
- How has man used the idea of a swim bladder in his inventions?
- What other function can fins have besides helping with swimming?
- What similar design did God give to both fish and birds to help them get where they are going?

 # Fish fins

Cut fins from construction paper and glue them in the correct places on the "Fish Fins" worksheet. Label the fins and color the fish. This page can be included in your animal notebook.

 # Nervous system

Fish are designed with an amazing nervous system. It is similar to the nervous system of other vertebrates in many ways, but in other ways it is very different. Like all vertebrates, a fish has a brain that is connected to a spinal cord and a series of nerves throughout its body. However, a fish can sense things that mammals cannot.

Most fish have a highly developed sense of smell and can find their food by smelling the water. The section of the brain responsible for smell is the olfactory lobe; this is one of the largest parts of the fish brain. This sense of smell also helps them sense predators in the area. Pacific salmon have such a good sense of smell that they can find their way from the ocean to the stream in which they hatched. It is believed that they can sense the smell of the particular water plants in that area or the soil run-off from the streams and these scents help to guide them home when it is time for them to reproduce.

Fish are very sensitive to even slight changes in ocean currents because of their lateral line. The lateral line is a series of special nerves that cover the head and sides of the fish. These nerve endings are protected by a row of pitted scales. The lateral line allows the fish to detect very low frequency vibrations, changes in pressure, and even slight turbulence in the water. Some fish use this information to detect prey and move toward the vibrations. Others use this information to detect danger and move away from the vibrations.

Sight is also very important to fish. The optic lobes, the parts of the brain responsible for sight, are often larger than the cerebrum and cerebellum combined. In proportion to its brain, a fish's eyes are quite large. Thus fish generally have very good eyesight.

Finally, fish can often sense things that most other animals cannot. Some fish can sense the electrical fields that are generated by the nervous systems of other animals. This is how some fish find their prey. Other fish can sense magnetic fields. This allows fish to navigate using the earth's magnetic field. The nervous system of fish is a design marvel, given to them by their Creator.

Birds & Fish

13

Cartilaginous fish

No bones about it

What sets sharks apart from most other fish?

Words to know:

cartilage

scavenger

parasite

About 5% of all fish do not have bony skeletons. These fish have cartilage structures instead. Cartilage is a tough yet flexible material that provides shape and structure without being stiff. Cartilage is what gives your nose and ears their shape. The most well-known cartilaginous fish is the shark (pictured above). These fearsome fish can be as small as 6 inches (15 cm) or as big as 50 feet (15 m) long.

Like all animals, sharks were originally created to eat plant material, but today they are meat-eaters. They can be found in most parts of the ocean. Most sharks have several rows of razor-sharp teeth. When one row of teeth wears out, the next row moves up to take its place.

Most sharks have the same general shape as the bony fish. However, their internal structure and function are quite different. First, sharks do not have swim bladders. If sharks quit swimming, they sink to the ocean floor. Also, many sharks cannot force water out of their throats, so they must remain in constant motion to keep water flowing over their gills. Sharks do not have covers over their gills. Instead, they have several gill slits that are easily visible on the sides of their bodies. Finally, many sharks give birth to live young instead of laying eggs.

Shark babies are born ready to care for themselves and leave their mothers right away. Sharks that lay eggs usually place their eggs in a thick egg sac and then never return. The young are on their own when they hatch.

Another type of cartilaginous fish is the ray (pictured on page 306). Rays do not have slim,

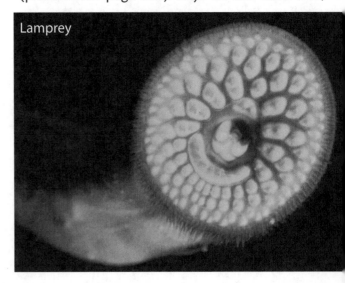

Lamprey

tapered bodies; instead, they are wide and flat. They glide through the water using their pectoral fins like wings. Rays are generally harmless to man—except for the stingray. The stingray has a whip-like tail that can inject venom into its enemies or cause a painful sting and sometimes death in humans.

Other cartilaginous fish that are not shaped like most fish are the lampreys and hagfish. These fish resemble snakes with their long round bodies. They do not have jaws like other fish. Instead, they have a sucking type of mouth (see photo on previous page). Lampreys are parasites—animals that take nutrients from a living host, often harming the host. They attach themselves to other fish and suck nutrients from their bodies. Lampreys are similar to eels. However, eels have bony skeletons and jaws, while lampreys have cartilaginous skeletons and no jaws. Hagfish are generally scavengers—animals that eat dead plants or animals.

Hagfish

🧠 What did we learn?

- How do cartilaginous fish differ from bony fish?
- Why is a lamprey called a parasite?
- Why can sharks and stingrays be dangerous to humans?

🚀 Taking it further

- Why are shark babies born independent?
- What do you think is the shark's biggest natural enemy?

🧪 Clay models

Use modeling clay to make models of cartilaginous fish such as sharks and rays. When you are done, take pictures to put in your animal notebook.

🏅 Manta rays

There are over 600 species of cartilaginous fish including sharks, rays, and kites. Rays are fish with flat bodies and triangular shaped pectoral fins. They smoothly "fly" through the water by moving these fins up and down like wings. Rays easily hide from their predators by lying on the ocean floor and moving back and forth to cover themselves with sand.

The largest ray is the Manta ray. The largest species of Manta ray can be up to 23 feet (7 meters) wide and can weigh up to 3,000 pounds (1,350 kg). Mantas are generally black on their back/top sides with white markings on their "shoulders" and white on the bottom side. They also have distinctive fins that protrude forward on either side of their mouths.

Mantas are eagle rays which are a family of sting ray. Most rays have beaklike mouths pointing downward used for breaking open shells of clams, crabs and other small animals. But mantas have mouths that face forward. This is an ideal design since they eat large amounts of plankton including tiny shrimp and krill as they swim with their mouths open. When feeding, a Manta will slowly swim around a plankton-rich area, herding the tiny creatures into a ball. It then swims quickly through the area with its mouth open. The fins on the sides of its mouth help to funnel the food into its mouth. Mantas eat up to 13% of their body weight each week.

Mantas, as well as other rays, give birth to live young called pups. A female carries one or two young in her body for about a year. When the baby is fully developed it is expelled from the body and is left to fend for itself. The mothers do not care for the young once they are born. Manta babies weigh at least 150 pounds (70 kg) and are 6 feet wide (1.8 meters) at birth. Little is known about Manta reproduction because they are difficult to follow in the wild, and only 2 or 3 babies have ever been born in captivity.

Periodically, manta rays breach, which means they jump out of the water. It is unclear why they do this. But mantas have been seen jumping several times in a row. Sometimes they leap forward and enter the water head first. Other times they jump up and come back down tail first. They have even been observed to do somersaults in the air.

Another unusual activity is the manta's visit to a cleaning station. Mantas frequently swim near coral reefs and then stay relatively still while smaller fish eat any parasites off of the manta's body. This is a beneficial situation for both the ray and the cleaner fish that is provided with a free meal. Manta's often visit the same cleaning station over and over.

Manta rays live in tropical and subtropical oceans but have been seen as far north as North Carolina and as far south as New Zealand. It is believed that Manta rays live for up to 50 years.

UNIT 3

Amphibians & Reptiles

14 Amphibians

15 Amphibian Metamorphosis

16 Reptiles

17 Snakes

18 Lizards

19 Turtles & Crocodiles

◊ **Describe** the unique characteristics of reptiles and amphibians using examples.

◊ **Distinguish** between reptilian and amphibian life cycles.

◊ **Describe** how reptiles defend themselves.

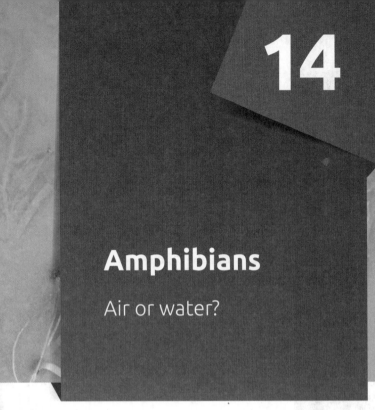

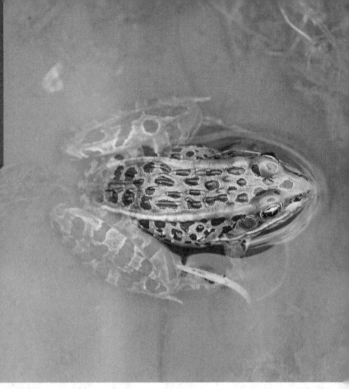

14

Amphibians

Air or water?

Which animals are classified as amphibians?

Words to know:

amphibian   larval stage

As we have learned, there are five groups of vertebrates (animals with backbones). The first two groups we studied, mammals and birds, are warm-blooded. Their body temperature remains constant. The others—amphibians, reptiles, and fish—are cold-blooded. This means their body temperature goes up when the temperature around them is warm and down when their environment gets colder.

Amphibians are cold-blooded animals that have smooth moist skin. They generally live in very moist areas or near the water to keep their skin

from drying out. They lay eggs. But the unique thing about amphibians is that they spend the first part of their lives in the water using gills to breathe. Then their bodies change and they develop lungs that allow them to breathe air. The word amphibian means "on both sides of life," reflecting this change.

The three major groups of amphibians are frogs and toads, salamanders, and caecilians (seh-SILL-yen). The vast majority of amphibians are frogs and toads. Frogs and toads come in many sizes and colors. Frogs usually have smooth moist skin and toads usually have more dry bumpy skin. Aquatic frogs live in or near the water. Many tree frogs live in the trees in tropical forests. Tree frogs are usually much more colorful and are often poisonous. Tree frogs also have suction cups on the bottoms of their feet to allow them to climb trees very quickly. Toads often live farther from the water but most must return to the water to reproduce.

Frog

Toad

Poison dart frog

A salamander

Bombay caecilian

Salamanders have long thin bodies and tails. They might be confused with lizards, but their skin is smooth and moist, unlike a lizard's skin, which is dry and scaly. Also, as babies, salamanders look very different from lizards. They spend the first part of their lives in the water in a larval stage, an immature form, before they change into the more familiar adult form.

The smallest group of amphibians is the caecilians. Caecilians are legless amphibians that resemble worms. They are long and thin and usually burrow in the ground. Caecilians live in the tropical forests of South America, Africa, and Southeast Asia. Because they spend most of their lives underground, people seldom see them.

What did we learn?

- What are the characteristics that make amphibians unique?
- How can you tell a frog from a toad?
- How can you tell a salamander from a lizard?

Fun Fact

Many frogs can breathe not only with their lungs, but also through their skin. A frog's skin is thin and contains many mucous glands that keep it moist. Oxygen can be absorbed through this thin, damp skin.

Amphibians & Reptiles

Warm-blooded/cold-blooded

Have one child pretend to be a warm-blooded animal such as a dog and have another child pretend to be a cold-blooded animal such as a frog. Act out what your animal might be doing if the temperature around you was 15°F (−9.4°C). Remember that cold-blooded animals cannot be active in cold weather and they often go into hibernation.

Now act out what your animals might do if the temperature was 65°F (18.3°C), and again if the temperature was 95°F (35°C). Remember that warm-blooded animals must find ways to keep their bodies warm in the cold weather and cool in the hot weather. Also remember that cold-blooded animals must find shade when the weather is too hot or sunshine when it is too cold.

- What advantages do cold-blooded animals have over warm-blooded animals?

- What advantages do warm-blooded animals have over cold-blooded animals?

- Why are most people unfamiliar with caecilians?

Animal communication

Animals communicate with each other in many different ways and for many different reasons. Animals communicate to find a mate, to mark and protect their territory, and to warn enemies or predators to stay away. Animals use sounds, body markings, and chemicals to communicate.

Amphibians primarily communicate by sound. You have probably heard frogs and toads croaking on a warm summer evening. Male frogs and toads have inflatable air sacs or throat pouches that help amplify their calls. This allows them to talk to others of their species, primarily to find a mate.

But their communication goes far beyond simple croaking. Every species has a different call with a different frequency that it uses for communication. A female bullfrog for instance will only respond to a call from a male bullfrog. She will ignore calls from tree frogs or other types of frogs. In tests, a frog could distinguish between the calls of 35 different types of frogs and only responded to calls from the same species. Not only does each species produce a unique sound, but many species have ears that are particularly tuned to the call of their species. They have selective hearing.

There may be many species of frogs and toads living in a particular area, especially in rainforests or jungles. In order to make their communication more clear, these amphibians do more than just use different frequencies to communicate. Some amphibians use "time sharing," that is, certain species communicate only at particular times of the day or night. Frogs are also able to detect how often other frogs are croaking and time their croaks to be in between other croaks so they can be heard. Some species also increase their volume so that they can be heard above other species. One species of frog can make noises that are so loud they are near the pain threshold for humans.

Although amphibians primarily communicate by sound, they can also communicate in other ways. One unmistakable way that poison dart frogs communicate with their predators is with their bright colors. These brilliantly-colored amphibians produce a toxic chemical on their skin. Their bright colors warn predators to stay away. Natives to Central and South America where these frogs live have learned to imitate the calls of the poison dart frogs to capture them. They then collect the poison from the frogs' skins and dip their arrows in the poison. These arrows are then used for hunting. The poison instantly paralyzes a deer or other animal shot with the arrow. The poison is only effective when it enters the blood stream. It is broken down in the digestive system so the hunter can eat the animal without fear of poisoning himself.

Look for other ways that animals communicate with each other. Look for patterns on their bodies, listen to the noises they make, and even smell the scents they leave behind. These are all ways that animals talk to each other. For fun, get three friends or siblings together and try to practice communicating the way frogs do. Have one person make a short noise every second. Have a second person make a different noise in between the first person's noises. Then you try to carry on a conversation with a third person. The trick is that you and your partner can only talk when both of the other people are quiet. This is very difficult to do. Does this help you appreciate how well God designed frogs to communicate with each other?

15

Amphibian Metamorphosis

Making a change

What changes happen in metamorphosis?

Words to know:

metamorphosis   pollywog

tadpole

Amphibians do what no other animals do. They start out in life using gills to get oxygen from water. Then they slowly change into an adult with lungs to get oxygen from the air. The most familiar amphibian is the frog. Although most amphibians go through this metamorphosis, or change, we will examine the changes a frog experiences to better understand this process.

Most frogs go to the water to reproduce, even if they do not live in or near the water the rest of

the time. Their eggs are laid in a mass in the water. A jelly-like substance coats and protects the eggs until they hatch. Eggs usually hatch in 6–9 days.

What hatches from the egg is called a tadpole (or sometimes a pollywog). The tadpole is the larval stage in the frog's life cycle. This "infant" frog has a tail for swimming and looks a little like a small fish. It lives in the water and spends most of its time eating and growing. The tadpole has gills, which are organs that transfer oxygen from the water into the animal's blood stream.

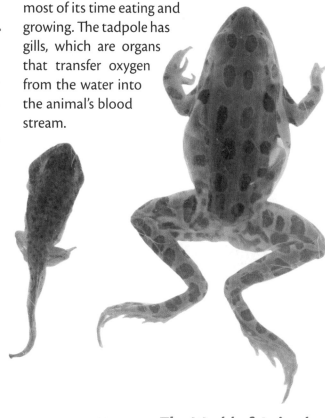

In a matter of weeks, the tadpole begins to change noticeably. This change is called metamorphosis. During metamorphosis, hind legs begin to grow at the base of the tail. The front legs begin to form. Eventually the tail shrinks away. At the same time the legs are forming, the frog begins to develop lungs. Lungs are organs that transfer oxygen from the air to the animal's bloodstream. Until the lungs are fully developed, the frog uses gills to extract oxygen from the water. Once the lungs are ready, the gills begin to disappear and the tadpole has transformed into a frog! Most adult frogs leave the water and spend the majority of their adult lives on land and return to the water only to lay eggs. A few types of frogs continue to live close to the water throughout their lives. This transformation from a water-dweller with gills to a land-dweller with lungs is what makes amphibians unique.

What did we learn?

- Describe the stages an amphibian goes through in its life cycle.

- What are gills?

- What are lungs?

Taking it further

- Does the amphibian life cycle represent molecules-to-man evolution? Why or why not?

Amphibian life cycle

After looking at pictures of a frog changing from a tadpole into an adult, draw a picture representing each stage of an amphibian's life cycle on the "Amphibian Life cycle" worksheet. Add this sheet to your animal notebook.

Optional—grow a frog

The best way to appreciate the metamorphosis of a frog is to get a tadpole and watch it change day by day. Science supply catalogs often sell kits that come with a live tadpole and pet stores sometimes sell tadpoles. Or if you live near a pond, you might be able to catch some tadpoles to raise and then release the grown frogs.

⓵ Unusual amphibians

Most amphibians lay their eggs in water where the tadpoles hatch and then grow into adults. However, some amphibians have unusual methods of reproduction. Some amphibians experience metamorphosis inside the egg; the tadpole changes from a water-breathing creature into an air-breathing creature before it hatches. It emerges from the egg looking like a miniature adult. A few species of salamanders and caecilians give birth to live young.

Some amphibians do not complete metamorphosis unless they experience unusual stress in their environments. The axolotl is a salamander that lives in lakes near Mexico City. It often remains in the tadpole stage its whole life and only develops into the adult form under unusual circumstances. It can reproduce by laying eggs while it is a tadpole.

The Surinam toad has a very interesting breeding process. The female lays eggs, then after fertilizing the eggs, the male uses his body to press them into the spongy skin on the female's back. The eggs hatch but the young tadpoles stay inside the skin on the mother's back until they change into fully formed toads. Then the tiny toads emerge from their mother's back, ready for life on their own.

Mouth-brooding frogs have an even more interesting method for raising their young. The female lays the eggs and the male fertilizes them. Then, as the eggs are beginning to hatch, the male swallows the eggs and keeps them in his voice sac.

There the tadpoles eat their own egg yolks and begin to develop. After about three weeks the tadpoles have transformed into frogs and the father spits them out into the water where they begin their independent lives.

Another father that plays an unusual role in the reproduction process is the midwife toad. The female lays her eggs on land. The male then fertilizes the eggs and wraps them around his hind legs. For about a month, the father carries the eggs around and frequently dips them in the water to keep them moist. After about a month, the eggs are ready to hatch and the father lowers them into shallow water and removes them from his legs. The tadpoles stay in the water until they complete metamorphosis, then they leave the water and live primarily on land.

Look at an animal encyclopedia or other source to find out about other unusual methods of amphibian reproduction. Although the methods may differ, they all still go through the stages of metamorphosis.

An axolotl

16

Reptiles

Scaly animals

Where are scales found on reptiles?

Words to know:

nictitating membrane   hibernation

Challenge words:

ceratopsian   theropod

plated dinosaur   sauropod

Ever since the serpent tempted Eve in the garden of Eden, reptiles have held a strange fascination and often fear for humans. Reptiles are vertebrates with dry, scaly skin. Most lay eggs (though some bear live young), breathe with lungs, and are cold-blooded. In addition to regular eyelids, most reptiles have additional clear eyelids called nictitating membranes that cover and protect their eyes. These membranes are needed so the animal can still see even if it is in harsh conditions such as in a desert windstorm or underwater.

The four major groups of reptiles are snakes, lizards, turtles, and crocodiles. In addition to these, there is one species of tuatara. Tuataras are similar to lizards but have a slower metabolism, a different bone structure, and mate differently than lizards. Scientists call these creatures "living fossils" because they are similar to fossil tuataras and supposedly have not changed for more than 200 million years. Mutations (genetic copying mistakes) are happening all the time, yet if one believed these imaginary long ages, this creature has gone through maybe a billion or more generations virtually unchanged. This is very unlikely to happen and is evidence against life on earth being millions of years old. In fact, there are hundreds of "living fossils" recognized today. For those who believe the Bible, however, there should be no mystery

Fun Fact

Since cold-blooded animals don't burn energy to heat their bodies, reptiles eat 30 to 50 times less food than do birds and mammals (warm-blooded animals) of similar sizes.

A tuatara

about these so-called "living fossils." We have an eyewitness account (God's Word) of how these creatures were created only a few thousand years ago to be fruitful and multiply after their kind. So the fact that modern creatures are similar to their fossilized ancestors is no surprise at all.

Of the 6,800 different kinds of reptiles, about half are lizards. Another 2,700 species are snakes. There are only about 240 kinds of turtles and only 21 kinds of crocodiles and alligators.

Fun Fact

Tuataras have a "third eye" on top of their heads, which cannot see, but is sensitive to light. Scientists are not sure of the function of this eye, but it may be for telling them when to hibernate, or for allowing young tuataras to soak up the sun to make vitamin D, giving them the nourishment they need to grow into mature adults.

Reptiles live in all parts of the world. Because they are cold-blooded, many reptiles in hot tropical climates are nocturnal so they can sleep during the hottest part of the day and hunt at night when it is cool. Reptiles can also live in very cold climates. But because their bodies slow down so much in the cold, they go into hibernation, a sort of sleep where the animal's body processes significantly slow down until the weather warms up.

 # What did we learn?

- What makes reptiles different from amphibians?
- What are the four groups of reptiles?

Taking it further

- How do reptiles keep from overheating?
- What would a reptile likely do if you dug it out of its winter hibernation spot?

 # Scaly picture

Draw an outline of a reptile, and then glue sequins wherever the creature would have scales on its body. Turtles only have scales on their legs, feet, tail, neck, and head. Alligators have very large scales on their bodies. Snakes have scales over their entire bodies. Include this picture in your animal notebook.

 # Dinosaurs

Although there is some controversy over whether dinosaurs should be considered reptiles, they were originally classified as reptiles so we will talk about them in this section. Since no known living dinosaurs have been found, everything we know about dinosaurs comes from fossil evidence, which is open to some interpretation, so there are disputes and disagreements about many aspects of dinosaurs. However, there are many ideas that are commonly accepted among both creationists and evolutionists concerning dinosaurs.

Dinosaur fossils have been found all over the world from Alaska to Africa to Australia. Many dinosaurs were small. *Compsognathus* was the smallest known dinosaur at about 6 pounds (3 kg).

It was probably about the size of a cat or a chicken. Other small dinosaurs include the *Podokesaurus*, which stood 3–5 feet (1–1.5 m) tall and the *Strithiomimus*, which was 6–8 feet (2– 2.4 m) tall. These small dinosaurs walked on two feet and ate small lizards, insects, and other small animals.

Another group of dinosaurs includes the horned dinosaurs called ceratopsians. *Triceratops* is probably the best known of the ceratopsians. These dinosaurs walked on all four legs and had massive skulls with various numbers of horns on their heads. God designed the horned dinosaurs' bodies to support their massive heads. The neck and shoulders of these animals are stronger than in other animals. Also,

Apatosaurus

the first several vertebrae in their necks are fused together to help support the weight of the massive skull. Other horned dinosaurs include the *Torosaurus, Styracosaurus, Chasmosaurus, Nonoclonius,* and the *Eucentrosaurus.*

Stegosaurus is one of the plated dinosaurs. Plated dinosaurs had rows of large plates down the sides of their backs. The grooves and spaces in the plate fossils suggest that there could have been significant blood flow through these plates. If this was true, the plates were likely used to cool the body of the dinosaur. Plated dinosaurs also have large spikes on their tails, which were likely used for self-defense. The *Kentrosaurus* and the *Tuojiangosaurus* were also plated dinosaurs.

Probably the most well known group of dinosaurs is theropods—meat-eating dinosaurs with large back legs and very small front legs. This group includes the *Tyrannosaurus rex,* the ceratosaurus, and the allosaurs. The *T. rex* is the largest known carnivore weighing in at 6 to 7 tons and measuring up to 50 feet (15 m) long. Its mouth was full of razor sharp teeth as long as a man's hand. The front arms of these meat eaters were short and not very strong.

The largest dinosaurs belong to the sauropod group of dinosaurs. Sauropods have long necks and tails and column-like legs. This group includes the

Diplodocus, the *Apatosaurus,* and the *Brachiosaurus.* These massive animals were up to 100 feet (30 m) long. Some think they were able to rise up on their hind legs so they could reach branches high up in the trees. The sauropods likely spent much of their time in the water.

Many controversies rage over the interpretation of dinosaur fossils and what they tell us about these fascinating creatures. One of the biggest controversies is whether the dinosaurs were cold-blooded or warm-blooded animals. Do a search on the Answers in Genesis web site (answersingenesis.org) to see what the latest research has to say about this controversy.

Create one or more pages on dinosaurs for your notebook. Include any interesting information you find.

Stegosaurus

Chasmosaurus

Ceratosaurus

When Did the Dinosaurs Live?

When did dinosaurs live? If you listen to many scientists, they will tell you that dinosaurs lived from 230 million to 65 million years ago—long before man walked the earth. But you must remember that fossils don't come with labels telling how old they are. The idea of millions of years of evolution is just a story about the past.

The Bible, our source for truth, tells us that land animals (which would include dinosaurs) were created on Day Six of Creation along with man about 6,000 years ago. God judged the world with a global Flood about 4,400 years ago, but representatives of all the kinds of air-breathing, land-dwelling animals survived on board the Ark with Noah and his family. What happened to the land animals that were not on board the Ark? They drowned. Most of the fossils around the earth today were formed as a result of the Flood. Therefore, most of the dinosaur fossils we find are about 4,400 years old, not millions of years.

Despite what some claim, there is abundant evidence that man and dinosaurs lived together:

- In Job 40:15–24, God describes to Job (who lived after the Flood) a great beast called *behemoth*. It is described as "the chief of the ways of God"—perhaps the largest land animal God created. Impressively, he moved his tail like a cedar tree! Although some Bible commentaries say this may have been an elephant or hippopotamus, the description actually fits that of a dinosaur like *Brachiosaurus*.

- Almost every culture has stories of dragons, and there are many very old history books in libraries around the world that have detailed records of dragons and their encounters with people. Surprisingly (or not so surprisingly for creationists), many of these descriptions of dragons fit how modern scientists would describe dinosaurs.

- In the North Atlantic during World War I, seconds after a German U-boat sunk the British steamer *Iberian*, there was an underwater explosion. The U-boat commander and some of his officers reported: "A little later pieces of wreckage, and among them a gigantic sea animal, writhing and struggling wildly, were shot out of the water. . . . It was about 60 feet [18 m] long, was like a crocodile in shape and had four limbs with powerful webbed feet and a long tail tapering to a point."

- The tomb of Bishop Richard Bell in Carlisle Cathedral (UK) shows engravings of animals, including a fish, an eel, a dog, a pig, a bird, a weasel . . . and a dinosaur! This man died in 1496 and these brass engravings attest to the possible existence of dinosaurs only 500 years ago.

- The Ica stones of Peru were found in a cave that was exposed in the first half of the twentieth century by the flooding of the Ica River. The cave proved to be a repository of more than 15,000 carved stones. These artifacts from South America depict dinosaurs and flying reptiles of all types and sizes. This stone art is believed to date from 500–1000 AD.

- Over the past 100 years, there have been many reports of sightings, in a remote area of central Africa, of a swamp-dwelling animal known to local villagers as "mokele-mbembe"—the "blocker-of-rivers." It is described as living mainly in the water, its size somewhere between that of a hippopotamus and an elephant, but with a squat body and a long neck. The creature is said to climb the shore at daytime in search of food. Witnesses' drawings show that mokele-mbembe resembles nothing recognizable as alive on earth today, but it does bear a startling likeness to a sauropod dinosaur known to us by its fossil skeletons—similar in shape to a small *Apatosaurus*.

- Stories of giant man-eating birds (similar to pterosaurs) are common among many Indian tribes of the American Southwest. The Yaqui Indians spoke of a giant bird that lived on the hill of Otan Kawi. Every morning it would fly out to capture its human prey. After many deaths, a young boy who lost his family to this bird killed the creature with a bow and arrows.

- In Utah there is other evidence that suggests man lived with pterosaurs. In the Black Dragon Canyon, there is a beautiful pictograph of a pterosaur. The Indians of the Swell apparently saw a bird-like creature with enormous wings, a tail, a long neck, a beak, and a vertical head crest.

- In 2005 scientists from the University of Montana announced that they had found *T. rex* bones that were not totally fossilized. Interior sections of the bones were like fresh bone and contained soft tissue. If these bones really were millions of years old, this organic matter would have totally disintegrated. More recently, other soft tissues have been discovered in fossils including a protein called keratin in fossilized lizard skin and a protein called collagen found in a fossilized bone from an ocean-dwelling reptile called a mosasaur. All of these soft tissues point to animals that were rapidly buried only a short time ago rather than millions of years ago.

So, what happened to the dinosaurs? If they were so big and powerful, why aren't they around today? After the Flood, the land animals, including dinosaurs, came off the Ark and lived alongside people. Because of sin, the judgments of the Fall and the Flood have greatly changed the earth. Post-Flood climatic change, lack of food, disease, and man's activities caused many types of animals to become extinct. The dinosaurs, like many other creatures, died out.

By looking at all the evidence, we see that it is explained by the biblical account that man and dinosaurs were created at the same time and lived together for much of history. For more information on dinosaurs, visit the Answers in Genesis website and search using the keyword "dinosaur."

Snakes

Those hissing, slithering creatures

How do snakes move?

Words to know:

Jacobson's organ

constrictor

colubrid

venomous

lateral undulation

rectilinear movement

concertina movement

side winding

The vast majority of reptiles are snakes and lizards. Snakes are the most common legless reptiles. Snakes all have the same general shape—long and round—but can be as short as 5 inches (12.5cm) or as long as 30 feet (9 m).

Snakes have eyes on the sides of their heads but no eyelids. Instead, they have clear scales that fit over their eyes. They do not have external ears. Instead, they sense vibrations and low noises through their lower jaw, which sends the vibration to an inner ear. Snakes have nostrils that help with smell but, in addition, each time they flick their tongues, they pick up scent particles. These particles are then touched to the Jacobson's organ in the top of the mouth. This organ is very sensitive to smell and allows the snake to follow the scent of its prey.

Snakes do not need to eat very frequently since they are cold-blooded. A warm-blooded animal eats frequently because it requires more energy to maintain its body temperature. Cold-blooded animals do not have to eat as often since they do not maintain a specific temperature—they do not need as much energy as a warm-blooded animal.

Snakes eat many different kinds of prey, from insects to large mammals, depending on the size of the snake. Snakes cannot chew or tear their food;

Cobra

instead, they swallow it whole. Snakes are able to do this because their lower jaws are not permanently attached to their skulls. They can disconnect their lower jaws and stretch their mouths around something much larger than the diameter of their own bodies. After swallowing its meal, the snake's strong muscles squeeze its prey as it begins digestion.

Most snakes fall into one of three groups: constrictors, colubrids, and venomous snakes. Constrictors are found mostly in tropical jungles. Constrictors overcome their prey by wrapping around and squeezing it. As the victim exhales, the constrictor squeezes tightly. After a few minutes, the prey has suffocated, and the snake then eats it. Pythons and boas are some of the most familiar constrictors.

Over two-thirds of all snakes are colubrids. Colubrids are found in most parts of the world. Most of these snakes are nonvenomous and many are useful for keeping down the rodent population. Bull snakes, rat snakes, and garter snakes are some common colubrids.

The most feared snakes are the venomous

Timber rattlesnake

snakes. These snakes have fangs that are used to inject venom into their prey. The venom attacks the nervous system, circulatory system, or both. The prey is usually paralyzed and stops breathing in a matter of minutes. Then the snake can eat its meal without a struggle. Many venomous snakes, but not all, are toxic to humans. Some well-known venomous snakes include rattlesnakes, coral snakes, and cobras.

To learn more about how snakes fit into God's design, see information in the teacher guide for this lesson.

What did we learn?

- How are snakes different from other reptiles?
- What are the three groups of snakes?
- How is a snake's sense of smell different from that of most other animals?
- What is unique about how a snake eats?

Taking it further

- How are small snakes different from worms?
- If you see a snake in your yard, how do you know if it is dangerous?

Fun Fact

Many people confuse the terms venomous and poisonous. Venom is injected, but poison is ingested. So, a good rule of thumb is that if it bites you and you get sick, it is venomous. If you bite (or touch) it and get sick, it is poisonous.

Boa constrictor

Slithering like a snake

Lie on the floor and try to move in the following ways. It may not be easy to match the movements of a snake, but you will have fun trying.

Snakes move in one of four ways.

1. Lateral undulation—Sideways waves

The most common way for a snake to move is in this S-shaped squiggling. The snake's body moves in curves from side to side. Snakes can move on land or in the water this way. Lie on your stomach, then try squiggling from side to side without using your arms.

2. Rectilinear—Straight line

Snakes that exhibit rectilinear movement stretch then contract their bodies in a straight line. They use their scales to help anchor one part of their bodies while they move another part. Lie on your stomach, pull your knees up to your chest and then stretch back out.

3. Concertina—Coiling

This is a slinky type of movement where the snake coils up then uncoils like a spring. Lie on your side, bend at the waist and knees, then push with your feet to spring forward.

4. Side winding—Angled

A sidewinder anchors its head and tail, moves its body sideways, and then moves its head and tail to match the body. The result is a diagonal movement to the direction the snake is facing. Lie on your stomach, move your hips sideways, move your head and shoulders to line up with your hips and then repeat this motion.

Snake research

There are over 2,300 species of snakes. We have only scratched the surface in this lesson. Use an animal encyclopedia or the Internet to find out more about snakes. Make a snake presentation to include in your animal notebook. Include pictures and interesting facts that you find about various kinds of snakes.

Rattlesnakes

It's a sound that puts fear in every heart: the gentle rattle coming from the grass. Rattlesnakes can be a frightening and dangerous sight. Yet, they are very interesting creatures. Rattlesnakes are the largest snakes that live in the United States. They can be found in nearly every part of North and South America.

Rattlesnakes are different from all other snakes because they have a rattle on the end of their tails. Each time a rattlesnake outgrows and sheds its old skin (a process called molting) its rattle gains another ring. These rings hitting each other as the snake shakes its tail are what give the rattlesnake its distinctive sound.

Rattlesnakes are vipers and are therefore venomous. They kill their prey by injecting it with venom. The snake bites its prey very quickly and then pulls back. The animal will run away but will soon die. The poison paralyzes the animal and then begins to break down its body before the snake even swallows it. The snake then uses its sense of smell to track down the animal and swallows it whole shortly after it dies.

Rattlesnakes seldom bite people. If someone approaches the snake, it usually gives a warning by shaking its tail to frighten them. If you should come upon a rattler, be sure to stay at least 10 feet (3 m) away. A snake can only strike about half the length of its body, so if you stay back it cannot bite you. A rattler will usually not bite someone unless that person persists in getting too close. Rattlers bite about one thousand people each year in the United States. Nearly everyone who is bitten survives if they go to a hospital for treatment. Doctors have developed a serum called antivenin (or antivenom), which is made from the venom of rattlesnakes and helps by breaking down the toxins in the venom.

Although rattlesnakes can be harmful to people, they can also be very helpful. Snakes are some of the best mice and rat hunters and are helpful in keeping down the pest population.

- There are 70 different kinds of rattlesnakes.

- A rattlesnake's rattle is made from keratin—the same material your fingernails are made of.

- Rattlesnakes hatch their young inside their bodies before giving birth.

- A rattlesnake can eat an animal as big as a five-pound (2.2 kg) rabbit.

- Rattlesnakes have no eyelids; in fact, no snakes have eyelids.

- The smallest adult rattlesnake is the pygmy rattlesnake, which grows to only 18 inches (46 cm) long.

- The largest rattlesnake is the Eastern diamondback, which grows up to 8 feet (2.4 m) long.

- The most venomous rattlesnake in the United States is the Western diamondback.

- If a rattlesnake loses a fang, it can grow a new one.

- About 10 people die each year in the United States from rattlesnake bites.

18

Lizards

Chameleons and
Gila monsters

How do lizards protect themselves?

Lizards are the largest group of reptiles. They have long thin bodies with legs that attach to the sides of their bodies. They have tapered tails. Their feet have claws, and they are covered with scales.

Lizards can be found in nearly every climate and ecosystem. They range in size from a few inches to 12 feet (3.7 m). Most lizards are not dangerous to humans, but the Gila monster is venomous, and Komodo dragons can cause infection if they bite a human.

Lizards have various ways to protect themselves from predators. The chameleon can change colors to match its surroundings. Some chameleons can change only their color, while others can change both their color and pattern. Lizards that cannot change color have other forms of self-defense. The horned lizard has sharp spikes on its head and back to protect it from its predators. The chuckwalla crawls into a crack in the rocks when it feels threatened, then fills its body with air, making it nearly impossible to get it out of the crack. Finally, some lizards have the ability to shed or break off their tails if a predator grabs on. Later, a new tail will grow in its place. The predator gets the tail but the lizard gets away.

A few lizards eat plants, but the majority of lizards eat insects. This makes them a welcome visitor in many homes, especially in the tropical areas. Komodo dragons, some of the largest living reptiles, eat dead animals. They have a keen sense of smell and will cross large distances to reach a decaying carcass.

Geckos are some of the most interesting lizards. They live in almost all warm environments. They can often change their color and many can shed their tails when caught by a predator. Geckos are also very social and communicate with chirps. Their

Gila Monster

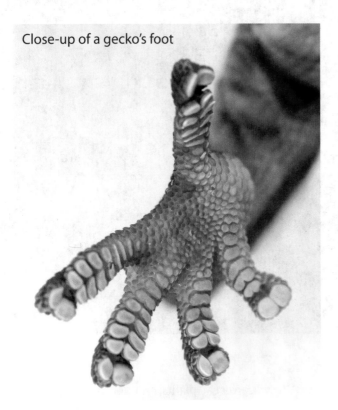

Close-up of a gecko's foot

of each foot. And each of these hairs splits into tiny pads that are so small that they are attracted to the surface on which the lizard walks on a molecular level. It is believed that the hairs on the feet of a 2.5 ounce (70 g) gecko have enough sticking power to hold up to 300 pounds (130 kg). Yet, the gecko can quickly peel his toes back, breaking the attractive forces and move on to the next step. This is an amazing design that only God could think of.

What did we learn?

- List three ways a lizard might protect itself from a predator.
- What do lizards eat?

Taking it further

- Horny lizards are short compared to many other lizards and are often called horny toads. What distinguishes a lizard from a toad?
- Why might some people like having lizards around?
- How does changing color protect a lizard?
- What other reasons might cause a lizard to change colors?

mating call can often be confused with a bird chirping. But the most interesting thing about geckos is their ability to walk on nearly any surface. They can even walk upside down on a smooth piece of glass. For years scientists could not understand how the gecko could do this. But research has revealed that the gecko has thousands of tiny hairs on the bottom

Animal camouflage

Draw or paint a picture showing how a chameleon can blend into its surroundings. For example, show a chameleon on a rock. Make the chameleon have a similar color and pattern to the rock, or show it sitting in a tree with similar colors to the leaves. If you have sequins left from the reptile project, you could glue them on the chameleon if they are similar colors to the surroundings. Add this page to your animal notebook.

People camouflage

Discuss how soldiers use camouflage paint to cover their skin and camouflage clothing to help them blend in with their surroundings. Use face paint to cover your skin to help you blend in with the trees and bushes or other environment you may choose. If you like, someone can take a picture of you in camouflage and you can include it in your animal notebook.

🏅 Large lizards

Iguanas are one of the largest lizards in the world. They can grow up to six feet (2 m) long. Although these lizards may look intimidating, they are harmless and only eat plants. Iguanas spend most of their time in trees and are green mottled with brown, which makes them very hard to spot when they are lying in tree branches. God has designed these animals with powerful feet and sharp claws to enable them to easily climb trees. Common iguanas live throughout Central and South America.

Marine iguanas are found only in the Galapagos Islands off the coast of Ecuador. They are the only lizards that spend a significant amount of time in the water. Although the common iguana may leap from a tree into the water to escape an enemy, it primarily lives on land. However, the marine iguanas live along the coast of the islands and spend much of their time in the ocean eating seaweed and algae that grow on the rocks near the shore.

These animals are well suited for swimming in the cold waters around the Galapagos Islands. Since the iguana is a cold-blooded animal it would ordinarily lose much of its body heat as it swims in the cold water. However, the marine iguana's heart rate slows significantly when it dives into the water. This slows down the flow of blood through its body and reduces the amount of heat that it loses. After it is done swimming, the iguana spends much of its time lying in the sun to warm its body back up.

The marine iguana is designed for swimming. Its wide head and flat tail work to propel it through the water. The marine iguana can stay submerged for up to 20 minutes or more. Although the marine iguana and the common iguana have many different characteristics, they are both the same kind of creature and show that God gave the original iguanas a wide variety of genetic traits.

The largest meat-eating lizard is the Komodo dragon. Do some research and see what you can find out about these interesting creatures. Make a Komodo dragon page for your animal notebook.

Marine iguana

19

Turtles & Crocodiles

Turtle or tortoise, crocodile
or alligator—how do you tell?

What special design features do turtles and crocodilians have?

Challenge words:

carapace   plastron

Turtles are the only reptiles with shells.
Unlike many sea creatures such as crabs, which can be removed from their shells, turtles' shells are an integrated part of their bodies, not just a home they live in. The shell provides protection for the turtle's internal organs. Also, many turtles can pull their heads, tails, and legs inside their shells when they feel threatened.

Like all reptiles, turtles have scales covering their skin, are cold-blooded, and lay eggs. Turtles can be found in most warm climates. In some areas with cold winters, turtles will burrow underground and hibernate until warmer weather arrives. The term *turtle* is a general term often used to refer to turtles, terrapins, and tortoises.

True turtles live in the water. Sea turtles live almost permanently in water only coming to land to lay eggs. Fresh water turtles will sometimes bask in the sun on land but spend the rest of their days in the water. Fresh water and sea turtles are equipped with webbed feet or flippers for swimming.

Tortoises live completely on land. They have claws instead of webbed feet, as well as short sturdy legs designed for walking on land. Both turtles and tortoises lay their eggs on land.

Terrapins are almost a combination of turtles and tortoises. They live in water, mostly in small ponds, however they can also live on land and often travel long distances between water sources.

Green sea turtle

Giant domed-
shaped
tortoise

Alligator

Crocodile

Even though they are good swimmers, terrapins don't have webbed feet or fins.

The group of reptiles with the smallest number of species is the crocodiles. This group includes crocodiles and alligators. These can be the largest reptiles alive today with bodies up to 25 feet (7.6 m) long. It is often difficult to distinguish a crocodile from an alligator. Alligators have wider snouts and all of their teeth are covered when their mouths are closed. Crocodiles have longer, narrower snouts and some of their teeth, usually one on the bottom on each side, stick out even when their mouths are closed.

Crocodiles and alligators are generally found in warm tropical climates. They live near water and have webbed feet and strong tails that enable them to be good swimmers. Their eyes and nostrils are located on the top of the head and snout, allowing the animal to float with most of its body underwater while it waits for prey to come close enough to attack. A floating crocodile resembles a fallen log floating in the water. When the prey is close, the crocodile snaps its jaws around the victim and drags it underwater, where it holds the prey until it drowns. Crocodiles generally eat turtles, fish, waterfowl, and other small animals. But some larger crocodiles will attack larger animals as well.

Like most reptiles, crocodiles lay their eggs on land. But unlike other reptiles, when the babies are about to hatch, the mother carries the eggs to the edge of the water in her mouth. After they hatch, the mother protects her young for several weeks. Adult crocodiles will eat young crocodiles, so after they leave their mother's protection, they stay away from adults until they are fully grown.

🧠 What did we learn?

- Where do turtles usually live?
- Where do tortoises usually live?
- How does the mother crocodile carry her eggs to the water?
- Why can't you take a turtle out of its shell?
- How do crocodiles stalk their prey?

🚀 Taking it further

- Why might it be difficult to see a crocodile?

Fun Fact

Have you ever heard of crying crocodile tears? Crocodiles often secrete a liquid from their eyes as they are wrestling with their prey. This gives the appearance that they are crying for their victims. Thus, "crocodile tears" refers to insincere sorrow.

🧪 How can you tell them apart?

Complete the "How Can You Tell Them Apart?" worksheet by drawing pictures showing how to tell turtles from tortoises and crocodiles from alligators. This worksheet can be included in your animal notebook.

Turtle feet—tortoise feet

Purpose: To better understand the difference in turtle and tortoise feet

Materials: tape

Procedure:

1. Tape all the fingers on one of your hands together to represent a turtle's flipper.

2. Make a claw with your other hand.

3. Fill up the kitchen sink with water (or try this in a bathtub or swimming pool) and try pushing the water with your flipper and your claw. Which hand was able to push the most water?

Conclusion: The flipper is much better for swimming. Since a turtle spends most of its time in the water, the flipper is a better design than a claw-like foot. God gave each kind of animal great variability to adapt and survive in its environment.

 # Turtle shells

As you just learned, the turtle is the only reptile with a shell. The shell has a special design which makes it very strong. The top part of the shell covering the turtle's back is called the carapace and the bottom of the shell, covering its belly, is called the plastron. The carapace and the plastron are connected together at the sides by joints called bridges.

The shell has two layers. The outer layer is made up of epidermal shields that are made of keratin, the same material that fingernails are made of. Below the epidermal shield is a layer of bony plates that are fused to the turtle's ribs and vertebrae.

The sections of the outer layer of the shell are called shields and are arranged in symmetrical shapes. As the turtle grows, new layers of keratin are added under the old layers, making the shell thicker and stronger as the turtle grows. The bony layer of the inner shell is also broken into sections called plates.

When a baby turtle hatches from its egg, it has a fully formed outer shell, but does not have a bony inner shell. As the ribs grow, they send out cells that invade the skin around them turning them into bone. Eventually, the whole area under the epidermal shields is turned into bony plates, creating the strong double-layered shell.

Some turtles can pull their legs, heads, and tails inside their shells. These turtles have hinged plastrons. Once the body is pulled inside the shell, the plastron is pushed up against the carapace, providing protection for the turtle. Turtles that do not have a hinged plastron cannot pull inside their shells.

The leatherback turtle has a unique shell. Instead of the scale-like shields that most turtles have, the leatherback has a rubbery or leathery skin covering its shell. The leatherback is the largest turtle in the world and can be up to 6 feet (1.8 m) long and 8 feet (2.4 m) from tip to tip of its flippers.

In general, tortoises have dome-shaped shells that provide protection from predators while sea turtles usually have flatter, more streamlined shells that are lighter and allow them to glide more easily through the water. God designed the turtle's shell to be strong and effective for its environment.

Amphibians & Reptiles

UNIT 4

Arthropods

20 Invertebrates

21 Arthropods

22 Insects

23 Insect Metamorphosis

24 Arachnids

25 Crustaceans

26 Myriapods

◊ **Identify** the characteristics of arthropods.

◊ **Describe** the five groups of arthropods using examples.

◊ **Distinguish** between complete and incomplete metamorphosis.

◊ **Describe** the body plan of insects, arachnids, crustaceans, and myriapods using models.

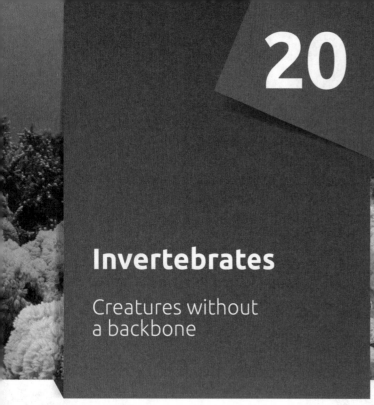

20

Invertebrates

Creatures without
a backbone

Which animals are invertebrates?

Challenge Words:

bilateral symmetry   spherical symmetry

radial symmetry   asymmetrical

Although most familiar animals are vertebrates, the vast majority (nearly 97%) of all animals are invertebrates—animals without backbones. Invertebrates do not have internal skeletons; therefore, most of them are small creatures. The squid and the octopus are the only large invertebrates.

The huge variety among invertebrates makes it difficult to group them together. However, scientists have grouped most invertebrates into six groups: arthropods, mollusks, cnidarians, echinoderms, sponges, and worms. In these groups are familiar creatures such as jellyfish, corals, starfish, crabs, shrimp, spiders, ladybugs, and butterflies.

Invertebrates can be found in every part of the world. Some, such as spiders and insects, may be found in your home. Perhaps you had invertebrates for dinner. You did if you ate shrimp or clams. Earthworms live in your garden. Many more invertebrates live in the waters of rivers, lakes, and oceans.

Many larger animals eat invertebrates for food. The largest creatures of the sea—whales—eat tons of small invertebrates each day. Also, invertebrates help to break down dead organisms to be recycled. We will find God's marvelous creativity all around us as we explore the world of invertebrates. ✺

Spiders like this bird-eating spider from Brazil are invertebrates.

Perhaps you had invertebrates for dinner.

What did we learn?

- What are some differences between vertebrates and invertebrates?

- What are the six categories of invertebrates?

 # Taking it further

- Why might we think that there are more vertebrates than invertebrates in the world?

 # Invertebrate repeat game

This is a simple memory game. Have the first person name an invertebrate. The second person repeats that animal and names a new and different invertebrate. The third person says the first two animals and adds a new one. The game continues until someone breaks the chain or cannot name a new invertebrate.

To help you recognize invertebrates, you can review the vertebrates: mammals, birds, amphibians, reptiles, and fish. Make sure the players understand that they are not to name any of these animals in the game. Think of a few invertebrates to get you started.

This game can be a lot of fun, and will help you realize that invertebrates are really more common than you thought.

 # Invertebrate pictionary

Draw a picture of an invertebrate on a white board or piece of paper. While you are drawing have other people guess what the animal is. The first person to guess the correct animal gets to be the next artist.

Symmetry

As we learn more about animals, it is useful to understand the concept of symmetry. Symmetry describes how an animal's parts are arranged. Many animals have bilateral symmetry. This means that if you drew a line down the middle of the animal the left side would look pretty much the same as the right side only flipped or mirrored. But there is only one way you can draw the line to divide something with bilateral symmetry. If you draw a line vertically down the middle of a bear from its head to its tail you get two sides that are pretty much the same. But if you draw the line horizontally through the middle of the bear around its torso the two halves would not be at all alike. Most vertebrates and many invertebrates have bilateral symmetry. You have bilateral symmetry, too.

But many invertebrates do not have bilateral symmetry. Several invertebrates have radial symmetry. Animals with radial symmetry are basically round in one direction. If you drew a line down the middle the two halves would be the same. That line can be drawn in any direction as long as it goes through the center of the circle. Think about a sea anemone. It is shaped like a cylinder with tentacles coming out the top. If you draw a line that goes through the center of the circle formed by the cylinder and down through its body you end up with

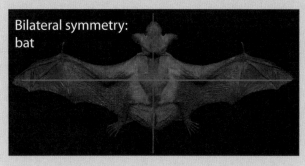

Bilateral symmetry: bat

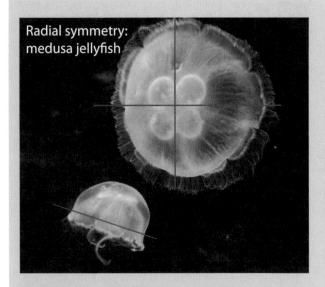

Radial symmetry: medusa jellyfish

Asymmetrical: sea sponge

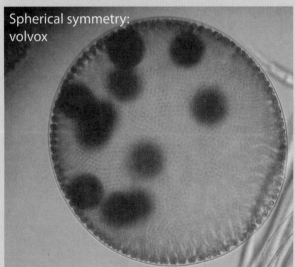

Spherical symmetry: volvox

two halves that are basically the same. But again, if you draw the line horizontally through its body the top half would not look like the bottom half. Jellyfish and starfish also have radial symmetry.

A few animals have spherical symmetry, which means you can draw a line through the center of its body in any direction and end up with two similar halves. These animals are shaped like a ball. A volvox has spherical symmetry.

Finally, some animals do not have any symmetry. No matter how you divide them you will never get two similar halves. Many sponges and amoebae have no symmetry. These animals are said to be asymmetrical. Understanding these various types of symmetry will help you better understand how different animals are classified.

21

Arthropods

Invertebrates with jointed feet

What do shrimp, spiders, and mosquitoes have in common?

Words to know:

arthropod

exoskeleton

segmented bodies

chitin

endoskeleton

The largest group of invertebrates is the arthropods. Over 75% of all animal species are arthropods. Arthropod means "jointed foot," so obviously all of the creatures in this group have jointed feet or jointed legs. In addition, all arthropods have segmented bodies, meaning they have two or more distinct body regions. Arthropods also have exoskeletons. Instead of an endoskeleton which is an internal skeleton of bones or cartilage like vertebrates, arthropods get their protection and structure from an external covering or exoskeleton. This outside skeleton is both strong and flexible. It is made of chitin, a starchy substance. Exoskeletons do not grow as the animal grows. Instead, the animal periodically sheds its exoskeleton and grows a new one.

Of the five groups of arthropods, the largest group is insects (90%). The other groups are arachnids (6%), crustaceans (3%), millipedes (0.8%), and centipedes (0.2%). There are approximately 1 million different species of insects that have been identified, and scientists believe there may be as many as 1 million more species that have not yet been classified. Some of the more common insects include flies, beetles, mosquitoes, butterflies, and ants. Arachnids include spiders, ticks, mites, and scorpions. Nearly all crustaceans live in the sea, and include shrimp, crabs, and lobsters. Centipedes and millipedes are similar creatures, both having multiple body segments and many legs.

As you study this large diverse group of invertebrates, look for evidence of God's design.

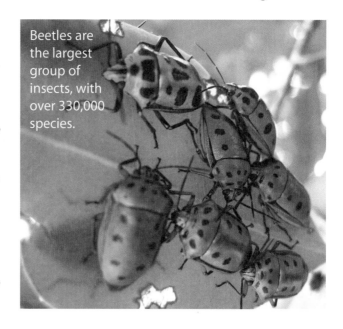

Beetles are the largest group of insects, with over 330,000 species.

🧠 What did we learn?

- What do all arthropods have in common?
- What is the largest group of arthropods?

🚀 Taking it further

- How are endoskeletons (internal) and exoskeletons (external) similar?
- How are endoskeletons and exoskeletons different?
- Why should you be cautious when hunting for arthropods?

Arthropod pie chart

A pie chart is a special type of picture or diagram that helps us quickly see how a group can be divided up. It is basically a circle that is divided into sections like pieces of a pie. The size of each piece shows how much of the group is made up of that particular item. Today you are going to make a pie chart of all arthropods. The circle represents all of the different arthropods. The circle is divided into pieces. Each piece represents one type of arthropod. So there will be a piece for insects, another piece for arachnids, and so on. Since insects are the largest group of arachnids the largest piece of the pie should be labeled with the word "Insects."

The smallest group of arachnids is the centipedes. So the smallest pie piece should be labeled "Centipedes." Use the following information to label the "Arthropod Pie Chart."

- Insects: 1,000,000 species
- Arachnids: 70,000 species
- Crustaceans: 30,000 species
- Millipedes: 10,000 species
- Centipedes: 2,800 species

Include this pie chart in your animal notebook.

Arthropods

Exoskeleton model

One distinctive characteristic of arthropods is their exoskeleton. The exoskeleton is made of a starchy material called chitin.

Purpose: To help you understand how an exoskeleton helps protect an animal's body

Materials: long narrow balloon, string, newspaper, flour, water

Procedure:

1. Fill a long narrow balloon with air and tie it closed.

2. Tie a piece of string around the middle of the balloon to make two or three body segments. If you do not have a long narrow balloon, you can fill two round balloons with air and tie their necks together to form two body segments.

3. Tear newspaper into strips.

4. Prepare your paste: combine 1 cup of flour with 2 cups of water. Mix to remove all lumps. Add more flour or water as needed to make a smooth paste.

5. Dip one strip of paper at a time in the paste. Slide your fingers along the strip to remove excess paste, then place the strip on your balloon. Be sure to smooth it out so there are no bumps.

6. Add more strips of paper to your model, making sure to overlap the strips. Keep adding strips until the balloon is completely covered.

7. Allow your creation to dry overnight.

8. Repeat the process so that there are two or more layers of paper over the entire model, allowing the strips to completely dry after each layer.

Conclusion: Once you are done, you can feel how the paper with the glue provides a strong covering for the balloons. Flour is made of starch, just like chitin. When it dries it becomes hard just like the chitin. The paper mâché is not as flexible as an arthropod's exoskeleton, but it should help you understand how something like starch can provide protection for insects and other animals.

22

Insects

Don't let them bug you.

How can you tell if something is an insect?

Words to know:

insect

head

thorax

abdomen

Challenge words:

compound eye

spiracle

open circulatory system

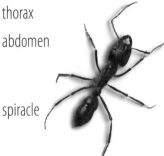

There are over 1 million species of insects. No wonder you have trouble keeping them out of your house. **Insects** are the largest group of arthropods. In addition to jointed legs and exoskeletons, insects have three distinct body parts. The **head** is the front segment, the **thorax** is the center segment, and the **abdomen** is the back segment. They also have a pair of antennae on their heads, as well as simple and compound eyes. Insects have six legs attached to their thoraxes and most have one or two pairs of wings.

Because there are so many different types of insects, scientists have grouped them into categories by similar characteristics. One group has straight wings. This includes grasshoppers and crickets. Half-wings are the true bugs such as the stinkbug. Butterflies and moths are in their own group. Flies and mosquitoes are in another. Beetles include the stag beetle, weevil, and June bug. There are many other groups of insects as well.

Many insects are pests. They can destroy crops and spread diseases. Insects can cause painful bites, or they can be annoying. However, insects play a very important role in the ecosystem. Birds, reptiles, amphibians, and many other animals depend on insects for food. Insects are also very important for pollinating flowers. And

Fun Fact

The bombardier beetle uses its rear-end "cannon" to fire a high-pressure jet of boiling irritating liquid at an attacking predator. The bombardier rapidly mixes two chemicals and injects them into a combustion chamber, which contains mainly water. The beetle then injects a third chemical, which greatly speeds up the normally mild reaction to explosive force. The jet of boiling liquid and gases fires repeatedly (up to 500 pulses per second) through twin "exhaust tubes" at his tail at a stunning 65 feet (20 m) per second.

some insects, such as butterflies, are very pleasant to have around. As much as we might like to get rid of them, insects are vitally needed.

What did we learn?

- What characteristics classify an animal as an insect?

- How can insects be harmful to humans?
- How can insects be helpful?

Taking it further

- How might insects make noise?

Insect models

Purpose: To make an insect model

Materials: three Styrofoam balls, toothpicks, paint, pipe cleaners, paper, scissors

Procedure:

1. Connect 3 Styrofoam balls together with toothpicks to form the body of the insect.

2. If desired, paint the balls the color of the insect; for example, paint it yellow and black if it is a bee or red or black if it is an ant.

3. While the paint is drying, cut pipe cleaners into eight equal-length pieces. You will use six of these pieces as legs.

4. Insert the legs into the center ball (the thorax), three on each side, and bend them to look like legs.

5. Insert the other two pieces of pipe cleaner into the head for antennae.

6. Cut two or four wings from paper. Use brightly-colored paper if you are making a butterfly. Many other insects have translucent wings so you could use white paper or make a frame from pipe cleaners and cover the frame with plastic wrap. If using paper, tape the wing pieces to additional pieces of pipe cleaner and insert them into the center ball.

Conclusion: Discuss each part of the insect as you put it together. Take pictures of the models and include them in your animal notebook.

Water skipper model

Purpose: To make a model of a water skipper

Materials: 3x5 inch index card, bowl of water

Procedure:

1. Fold an index card in half with long sides together.

2. Trace the pattern below onto the card and cut out the bug shape.

3. Fold the feet out and very carefully place the card in a bowl of water.

Conclusion: The card should float on the surface of the water. Water molecules are attracted to each other and create what is called surface tension. Things that are light enough can stay on the surface of water without sinking. Water skippers and other light insects can walk across the surface of the water without sinking because they are light enough not to break the surface tension.

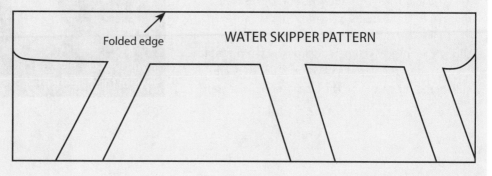

Folded edge WATER SKIPPER PATTERN

Optional activity

Playing the game "Cootie" from Milton Bradley is a fun way to review the parts of an insect.

 # Insect anatomy

The different segments of the insect's body each have special functions. The head serves as the communication center for the animal. The antennae, which are attached to the head, provide a sense of touch, smell, and taste. The antennae on most insects also have tiny hairs that detect sound waves or other vibrations providing a sense of hearing as well.

An insect has two compound eyes, one on each side of its head. Compound eyes have multiple lenses fitted together like a mosaic. Each lens can see only a small area, but the images from all the lenses are combined together to give the insect a good view of what is around it. In addition to compound eyes, many insects also have simple eyes, which can detect light and shadow and some movement.

Different insects have different abilities to see. Flies and mosquitoes are very near-sighted and can only see a few millimeters away from their heads, but can see a very wide area around them. Butterflies are very sensitive to color and find their food by the color of the plants. Other insects are completely color-blind. Dragonflies have very acute eyes and can detect and identify other flying objects while flying themselves.

The thorax is the center for movement. The legs and wings are both attached to this segment so walking and flying are both coordinated here. The thorax is divided into three sections and one set of legs is attached to each section. The wings are attached to the middle section as well.

The abdomen contains most of the insect's internal organs. Insects have most of the same internal systems that vertebrates have. Even though an insect's internal organs may seem simple compared to the systems of vertebrates, they are still incredibly complex. The insect digestive system is similar to a bird's digestive system in many ways. It contains a crop for holding food and a gizzard for grinding the food up before it enters the stomach. Nutrients are absorbed primarily through the stomach since insects do not have small intestines.

Insects have a very different circulatory system from most vertebrates. Insects do not have closed blood vessels to carry the blood throughout the body. Instead, the heart pumps blood into the head. The blood then flows toward the rear of the insect through its body chamber around all of the internal organs. This is called an open circulatory system. The heart is a tube-like organ that runs the length of the abdomen. It has many tiny valves all along its surface that allow blood to flow from the body into the heart to be pumped again toward the head.

Finally, insects do not have lungs or gills like vertebrates. Instead an insect has openings call spiracles in the sides of it body. Air flows through the spiracles into air sacs that run throughout the insect's body. Exchange of oxygen and carbon dioxide occurs in these air sacs. The insect's abdomen expands and contracts to force the air to move throughout its body.

If you look closely, you can see the compound eyes of this killer bee.

Arthropods

Insect Metamorphosis

Making a change

Do grasshoppers and butterflies undergo the same type of metamorphosis?

Words to know:

incomplete
  metamorphosis

complete metamorphosis

nymph

larva

chrysalis

pupa

Challenge words:

bioluminescence

All insects reproduce by laying eggs. However, what hatches out of the egg may or may not look anything like the parents. Most insects go through a metamorphosis, or change, between birth and adulthood.

Fun Fact

The firefly is the state insect for both Pennsylvania and Tennessee.

Some insects, such as grasshoppers, go through incomplete metamorphosis. This means the young resemble their parents when they hatch and gradually change into an adult. There are three stages to an insect's life if it experiences incomplete metamorphosis: egg, nymph, and adult. The nymph hatches from the egg, and then as it grows it molts or sheds its exoskeleton several times. As it gets bigger, the nymph begins growing wing pads. After its final molt, the insect has complete wings and is considered an adult. Dragonflies, crickets,

INCOMPLETE METAMORPHOSIS

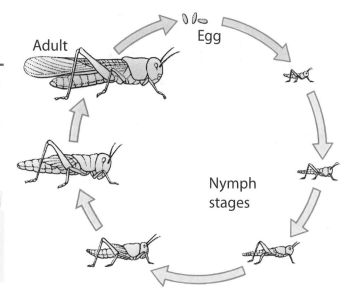

Adult

Egg

Nymph stages

termites, and grasshoppers are some of the insects that experience incomplete metamorphosis.

Most insects experience a 4-stage life cycle called complete metamorphosis. An insect that goes through complete metamorphosis starts out as an egg. When it hatches, it is called a larva (plural: larvae). The larva of the butterfly is a caterpillar. Other insect larvae also resemble caterpillars. The larva does not look much like the adult that it will become.

As the larva grows, it spends most of its time eating. Its exoskeleton cannot grow with it, so it sheds the exoskeleton several times as it grows. After a few days or weeks, the larva enters the third stage of its life, called the chrysalis or pupa stage. During this stage, the larva's body undergoes a tremendous change. This stage can last from a few days to a few months, depending on the type of insect.

COMPLETE METAMORPHOSIS

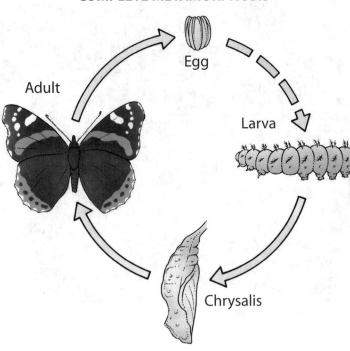

Adult
Egg
Larva
Chrysalis

Fun Fact

Monarch butterflies are one of the few insects that migrate with the changing seasons. Huge groups of monarchs can sometimes pass through an area for several days or even weeks as they migrate between the U.S. and Mexico. Monarchs have been known to migrate more than 1,500 miles.

When the change is complete, the insect breaks out of its chrysalis and is an adult. The most dramatic change to witness is the changing of a caterpillar into a butterfly, but other insects experience drastic changes as well. Witnessing this change is an amazing experience.

🧠 What did we learn?

- What are the three stages of incomplete metamorphosis?
- What are the four stages of complete metamorphosis?

🚀 Taking it further

- What must an adult insect look for when trying to find a place to lay her eggs?

🧪 Metamorphosis worksheet

Draw and color the different stages of metamorphosis on the "Stages of Metamorphosis" worksheet. Include this worksheet in your animal notebook.

Observe metamorphosis

The very best way to appreciate the changes that occur in complete metamorphosis is to actually observe them. Many science supply catalogs sell live caterpillars that can be kept and observed while they turn into butterflies (or you might be able to find a caterpillar in the fall, and keep it in a jar until it forms a chrysalis). The butterflies can then be released if the weather is favorable.

Fireflies

One insect that has an unusual characteristic throughout all stages of metamorphosis is the firefly (or lightning bug). Even though its name might imply that it is a fly, the firefly is really a beetle. This beetle has the ability to glow. It can glow inside its egg, it can glow as a larva, and it can glow as an adult.

The process by which a firefly glows is called bioluminescence. This is a chemical reaction that takes place inside the insect's body that produces a pale green light. A protein in the insect's abdomen reacts with a chemical called luciferase when air enters the chamber containing the two substances. This chemical reaction gives off light. The firefly can control the flow of air and thus controls the light that is given off.

The light that is produced by bioluminescence is a cool light because the process is very efficient. Nearly 96% of the energy is turned into light, so very little heat is produced. In an incandescent light bulb the majority of the energy is turned into heat. This is why some light bulbs get quite hot. But fireflies and other light-producing animals have the ability to produce light with very little heat.

Scientists are unsure why firefly eggs emit light. It is believed that larva emit light as a warning to predators since many species of firefly larva contain substances that are poisonous to predators. As adults the main purpose of emitting light is to attract a mate. Each species sends out a different series of flashes to identify itself. The male firefly emits light while flying and the female firefly answers with her own light from her location on the ground or in a tree. Thus the light guides the male to the female. In areas where there are many species of fireflies, each species emits light at a different time, similar to different frog species croaking at different times. This synchronized lighting allows more individual species to communicate with each other.

24

Arachnids

Spiders and such

How do spiders keep from getting caught in their own webs?

Words to know:

arachnid

cephalothorax

spinnerets

Challenge words:

urticating hairs

Many people wonder if spiders are insects. Despite some similarities in their looks, there are several differences between insects and spiders. Insects have three body parts, whereas spiders have only two body parts. Also, insects have six legs and spiders have eight. These differences place spiders in the class of arachnids.

Arachnids have two body parts. The front segment is called the cephalothorax and is essentially a head and thorax fused together. The rear segment is called the abdomen. Arachnids also have eight legs which are attached to the cephalothorax. Arachnids lack wings and antennae which is another difference between them and insects.

Spiders are the most common arachnids. They can be found throughout the world. Most spiders spin webs and kill their prey with venom. But only a few spiders are dangerous to humans. Spiders do not have mouth parts for biting or chewing. They can only suck liquids from their prey. Spiders have special organs at the back of their abdomen called spinnerets that produce the silk thread used in weaving webs. If you closely examine a spider's web,

A scorpion

you will find that some of the strands are smooth and some are sticky. The spider can move easily around its web by walking on the smooth strands. Also, spiders secrete an oily substance on their feet that keeps them from sticking to their own webs.

Spiders are not the only creatures in the arachnid family. Mites, ticks, and scorpions are also arachnids. Mites and ticks resemble small spiders. However, they do not spin webs or catch insects. Instead, like many other parasites, they attach themselves to other animals and suck their blood. For many creatures, mites and ticks are a nuisance. But for some, including humans, mites and ticks can carry and spread serious diseases. That is why it is always a good idea to check for ticks after hiking in the woods or other areas where ticks live.

At first glance, scorpions may not seem to fit in with spiders, ticks, and mites. But a closer examination shows that, like spiders, scorpions have eight legs attached to a cephalothorax, as well as

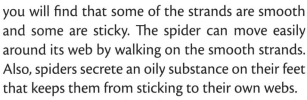

Spider and scorpion models

Purpose: To make a spider and scorpion model

Materials: marshmallows, toothpicks, pipe cleaners, marker

Spider model—Procedure:

1. Connect two large marshmallows with a toothpick. These are the two body parts.

2. Cut two pipe cleaners into four pieces each and insert them into the front marshmallow (four on each side).

3. Bend the pipe cleaners to resemble legs.

4. You can draw eyes on the front of the spider with a marker if you want to. Note the different parts as you assemble the model.

Scorpion model—Procedure:

1. You will use one large marshmallow for the cephalothorax.

2. Using a piece of flexible wire or pipe cleaner, string several small marshmallows together for the abdomen and attach them to the end of the large marshmallow.

3. Bend the wire up so the small marshmallows resemble a tail with a stinger.

4. Use pipe cleaners to make eight legs and stick them into the large marshmallow.

5. Twist a small piece of pipe cleaner onto the end of each of the front legs to make claws. Remember that scorpions are venomous.

Take pictures of the models to add to your animal notebook.

Optional—Spider Snacks:

For a fun snack, you can make edible spider snacks. Use a round cracker for the cephalothorax. Spread peanut butter on the cracker. Add raisins for eyes. Add eight pretzel sticks to the cephalothorax for legs. Add another round cracker to one edge for the abdomen. Spread peanut butter on this cracker as well. Yum!

Optional—Looking at a Web:

If you have the opportunity, closely observe a real spider's web. Use a magnifying glass to look at the individual strands. Sprinkle a light powder, such as powdered sugar, on the web. It will stick to the sticky strands but not to the non-sticky ones.

Arthropods

an abdomen. The scorpion's abdomen is jointed and curls behind it, ending in a stinger. Scorpions can inflict a painful sting and should be avoided. 🦂

What did we learn?

- How do arachnids differ from insects?
- Why are ticks and mites called parasites?

🚀 Taking it further

- Why don't spiders get caught in their own webs?

 Tarantulas

Tarantulas do not spin webs as most other spiders do. Instead, the tarantula will hide near its burrow waiting for an unsuspecting animal to walk near. Most spiders have poor eyesight and the tarantula is no exception. The tarantula senses its prey through vibrations and through feeling with its legs and feet. When an animal walks within range, it attacks with its fangs and injects venom into its victim. Once the animal is dead, the spider injects it with digestive juices, which liquefy the body and allow the spider to suck up its dinner. Although the largest tarantulas have been known to eat birds, lizards, mice, and other animals, most small tarantulas eat large insects such as crickets, grasshoppers, and beetles.

Tarantulas can be found in nearly every part of the world. The largest ones are found in South America. Most tarantulas are gray or brown, but some species have brightly-colored spots on their legs or abdomens. Their bodies are covered with fine hair. They are generally inactive during the day and hunt at night.

Although tarantulas are deadly to their prey, they are not considered to be dangerous to humans. Although people have been accidentally bitten by tarantulas, this usually results only in a swollen spot that is itchy but quickly heals. Tarantulas also protect themselves with special barbed hairs, called urticating hairs, that they can rub off their abdomen and kick toward an enemy. These hairs can cause itching and irritation in skin or eyes and encourages enemies to back off. Despite the very slight chance of being bitten, many people keep tarantulas as pets.

It takes several years for a tarantula to completely mature. Once a male matures, he searches for a female to mate with. After mating, the male quickly leaves because female tarantulas are known to eat males. Males usually live only a few months after mating. Females, on the other hand, can live for 10 to 20 years after becoming mature.

Arthropods

25

Crustaceans

Are they crusty?

Where do we find crustaceans?

Words to know:

crustacean

Have you ever chased a crawdad in a stream, or eaten shrimp or lobster? Have you ever watched a crab burrow in the sand or dug up a roly-poly? If so, then you are familiar with crustaceans. Most crustaceans live in the water with the notable exception of the woodlouse (sometimes called a pill bug or roly-poly).

All **crustaceans** are arthropods with jointed legs and exoskeletons. In addition, crustaceans have two distinct body parts or regions: the cephalothorax and the abdomen. They also have two pairs of antennae, two or more pairs of legs, and gills for breathing in the water.

The crawdad, or crayfish, is a very familiar crustacean found in many fresh water streams. Crayfish have two pairs of antennae on their heads that help them sense food or enemies. They also have five pairs of legs attached to the cephalothorax. The front legs end in pincers, or claws, which they use for catching prey or defending themselves. God put its mouth on the underside of its body, so a crayfish eats food from the bottom of the riverbed. Also, a crayfish can evade an enemy by darting backward very quickly.

You may be most familiar with the larger crustaceans such as crabs, shrimp, lobsters, and crayfish. But the majority of crustaceans are very

White speckled lobster

Crayfish

Arthropods

Many crustaceans, such as shrimp, are eaten for food.

small—mostly microscopic. Many sea creatures today depend on these tiny animals, such as brine shrimp and water fleas, for food. Many whales have special "teeth," called baleen, which they use to strain these tiny crustaceans from the water.

What did we learn?

- What do all crustaceans have in common?
- What are some ways that the crayfish is specially designed for its environment?

Taking it further

- Why might darting backward be a good defense for the crayfish?
- At first glance, scorpions and crayfish (or crawdads) look a lot alike. How does a scorpion differ from a crayfish?
- How can something as large as a blue whale survive by eating only tiny crustaceans?
- If you want to observe crustaceans, what equipment might you need?

Clay models

Make clay models of several different crustaceans. Note the similarities and differences between the animals. Take pictures of the models to add to your animal notebook.

Woodlouse exploration

If weather permits, search for a woodlouse. Because they breathe with gills, they must stay in moist areas, so they can usually be found under rocks or pieces of wood, or in other protected areas. If you find one, examine it carefully with a magnifying glass. Pay close attention to its jointed legs, antennae, exoskeleton, and segmented body.

Crustacean research

There are many interesting crustaceans that you may not be familiar with. Do some research in an animal encyclopedia, on the Internet, or other source and find out what you can about the animals listed below. Create one or more pages in your animal notebook using the information you find on the following animals:

- Krill
- Plankton
- Cleaner shrimp
- Barnacles
- Water slater

26

Myriapods

How many shoes would a centipede have to buy?

How do you tell the difference between a millipede and a centipede?

Words to know:

myriapod

centipede

millipede

Centipedes and millipedes are called myriapods. The word *myriapod* means "many feet." Centipede means "100 feet" and millipede means "1,000 feet." But, do centipedes and millipedes really have that many feet? Not necessarily, but they do have a lot of feet. Let's see just how many feet they have.

Centipedes usually have between 15 and 25 body segments. Each segment has one pair of legs, so a centipede has between 30 and 50 legs. Its first pair of legs has venomous claws that are used to kill its prey. Centipedes also have long antennae and a flattened body that is usually a few inches long.

Millipedes differ from centipedes in several ways. First, they have rounded bodies, not flat bodies. Also, they are not venomous. But the most

Fun Fact

Although most centipedes are small, some grow to be 12 inches (30 cm) long. These large centipedes are eaten in parts of China. They are skewered down the center and grilled.

Arthropods

Giant desert centipede

Millipede

distinctive difference is that they have two pairs of legs per body segment instead of only one pair. Millipedes usually have between 44 and 400 feet, but not 1,000. Millipedes tend to be bigger and slower than centipedes and have shorter antennae. Both centipedes and millipedes live in dark moist places.

Centipedes and millipedes are sometimes confused with caterpillars. However, caterpillars do not have legs on every body segment. Also, caterpillars experience metamorphosis and change into butterflies or moths. Centipedes and millipedes do not change into another form. Caterpillars are often fuzzy and live in the open on different plants, while myriapods are usually smooth and live in dark places such as under rocks or under the ground.

What did we learn?

- How can you tell a centipede from a millipede?
- What are the five groups of arthropods?
- What do all arthropods have in common?

🚀 Taking it further

- What are some common places you might find arthropods?
- Arthropods are supposed to live outside, but sometimes they get into our homes. What arthropods have you seen in your home?

Arthropod baseball

Set up a "baseball diamond" by assigning places such as chairs or pieces of paper on the floor to be home, first, second, and third base. Set a chair in the middle as the pitcher's mound. An adult gets to be the pitcher and each student gets to be a batter. The batter selects the difficulty of the pitch: single, double, triple, or home run. The pitcher selects an appropriate question about arthropods. For example, "Name the 5 groups of arthropods." The batter must answer the question. If the answer is correct, the batter advances to the appropriate base (e.g., 1 base for a single, 2 bases for a double; the harder the question, the more bases the question is worth). Then the next batter gets to answer a question.

If the batter cannot correctly answer a question, it is considered an out. After three outs, the adult gets to be the batter and the students get to ask the questions. See who can score the most runs.

Myriapod models

Myriapods have many similarities. They all have a very simple digestive system which consists of a single tube running the length of the body with salivary glands that add digestive juices to the food that is consumed. They also have simple open circulatory systems similar to that of insects that includes a heart that runs the length of its body. Also millipedes and centipedes breathe through spiracles in each body segment. But despite these similarities, there are several distinctive differences between millipedes and centipedes in addition to those already mentioned in the lesson.

One very important difference is in what they eat. Millipedes eat mostly plants and decaying matter. Millipedes play an important role in breaking down leaf litter in most forest areas. They are also slow moving and burrow into the ground. Millipedes have two main defense mechanisms against predators. They curl up into tight coils to expose only their exoskeletons to their enemies. Also, many can release chemicals for protection. Some of these chemicals have an unpleasant smell that causes predators to leave. Others are caustic and can eat through exoskeletons of ants or other pests or irritate the eyes of larger predators. These chemicals are sometimes used by other animals. Certain monkeys and lemurs have been observed to harass millipedes to force them to secrete their defensive liquids. These mammals then smear the liquid on themselves as a mosquito repellent.

Centipedes are carnivorous. They eat nearly anything that comes their way that is small enough for them to inject with their venom. It is believed that they primarily eat earthworms and insects, but larger centipedes have been seen eating small reptiles, amphibians, and mammals as well. A centipede's main defense mechanism is its speed. It can quickly run away from most enemies. It can use its venomous claws to defend itself as well.

Purpose: To demonstrate your understanding of the differences between centipedes and millipedes by making models of each

Materials: modeling clay, pipe cleaners or craft wire, camera

Procedure:

1. Use modeling clay to make each segment.

2. Flatten the body of the centipede and make sure the millipede is round.

3. Use pipe cleaners or craft wire to add legs to each segment. Be sure to add one set of legs to each segment of the centipede and two sets of legs to each segment of the millipede. Also add small claws to the first set of legs on the centipede.

4. Take a picture of each of your models to include in your animal notebook. Feel free to add drawings or photographs, too.

5. Add any interesting information you can find on these myriapods.

Arthropods

UNIT 5

Other Invertebrates

27 Mollusks

28 Cnidarians

29 Echinoderms

30 Sponges

31 Worms

◊ **Describe** the three groups of mollusks using examples.

◊ **Illustrate** the two-part life cycle of cnidarians.

◊ **Describe** the basic characteristics of echinoderms.

◊ **Describe** two ways that sponges reproduce.

◊ **Identify** three kinds of worms.

27

Mollusks

Creatures with shells

Do all mollusks have shells?

Words to know:

mollusk
mantle
bivalve
gastropod
cephalopod

Challenge words:

buoyant

As you walk along the beach you are likely to find a variety of sea shells. Most of these shells are the remains of mollusks. Mollusks are soft-bodied invertebrates. They have non-segmented bodies with no bones. A mollusk has one muscular foot for moving about, a hump containing the internal organs, and a mantle, which is an organ that secretes a substance that hardens into a shell in most species. Most, but not all, mollusks live in the water.

Although all mollusks have these characteristics, there is great variety among them. Mollusks that have two-part shells are called bivalves. Oysters, clams, scallops, and mussels are all bivalves. The shells of these mollusks are connected by a hinge at the back and are opened and closed by strong muscles. Many bivalves produce a pearly substance that protects the internal organs from irritants that get inside their shells. Oysters produce a shiny substance that, after a period of years, turns the irritants into pearls that are prized by people.

Many mollusks have only one-piece shells. These are called gastropods. Gastropods include

Bivalve

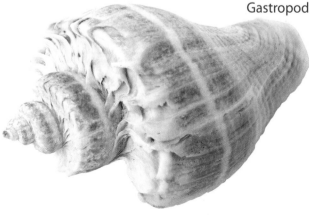

Gastropod

Other Invertebrates

Slug

snails, conchs, abalones, and slugs. With the exception of slugs, gastropods produce beautifully-spiraled shells. Each species produces a unique style of shell, so shells can be used to identify the animal.

The third group of mollusks is the **cephalopods**. This group includes squids, octopuses, and nautiluses. At first glance, this group may not seem to fit the characteristics of mollusks. However, a closer examination reveals a foot merged with the head, a hump containing the internal organs, and a mantle. In some cephalopods, the mantle produces an outer body wall and not a rigid shell.

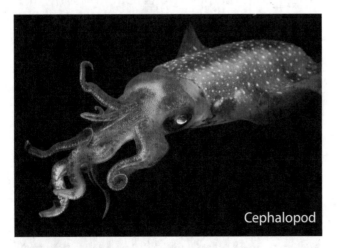
Cephalopod

Squids and octopuses can move quickly through the water by jet propulsion. They can shoot a stream or jet of water out the back of their bodies. This forces them to move forward very quickly. Also, both creatures can spray out an inky substance to confuse their enemies and get away when they feel threatened. Both squids and octopuses have complex eyes that are similar in design to the eyes of vertebrates. Evolutionists have a very hard time explaining how creatures with such supposedly different evolutionary chains as octopuses and humans, ended up with such similar and complex eyes. We know, however, that God designed them both.

The giant squid that lives in the Pacific and North Atlantic Oceans can grow to be 60 feet (18 m) long, weigh up to 1 ton, and is the largest invertebrate. Although they are large, they are often food for an even larger vertebrate—the sperm whale. Octopuses, though not as large as the giant squid, have a complex brain and are considered to be one of the most intelligent invertebrates.

What did we learn?

- What are three groups of mollusks?
- What body structures do all mollusks have?
- How can you use a shell to help identify an animal?

Taking it further

- How are pearls formed?

Shell identification

Collect as many different shells as you can. Each mollusk generates a unique shape of shell; therefore, you can tell what animal used to live in it if you have a guide to help you. Use a shell guidebook to help you identify what creature used to live in each of your shells. Which shells were bivalves (two parts)? Which shells were gastropods (one part—spiraled)?

Take pictures of your shells and include the pictures and identifications in your animal notebook.

⬤ The nautilus

A very interesting cephalopod is the nautilus. Like the octopus and squid, the nautilus has many tentacles. It uses these tentacles to grasp its food. The nautilus eats lobsters, shrimp, and crabs. After grasping the food, it then breaks open its food with its sharp beak. Also like the octopus, the nautilus is nocturnal. It hides during the day, usually in deep water, and hunts in shallower water at night.

Unlike the octopus and squid, the nautilus has a permanent shell. This shell has many chambers inside. It is believed that the first four chambers of the shell form while the nautilus is still inside the egg. As the nautilus grows, the shell grows and adds more chambers. The animal itself actually lives in the largest chamber of the shell. As new chambers are added to the shell, water is pumped out of the innermost chambers and gas takes its place. This allows the animal to remain buoyant, able to float, in the water even as its shell gets bigger and heavier. If the animal feels threatened, it can pull its body inside its shell and close a leathery flap over the opening.

Cephalopods move by sucking in water, then pushing the water out the back of their bodies in a powerful stream that shoots the animal forward. In the nautilus, the funnel which takes in the water contains gills, allowing the nautilus to breathe as water flows through its body.

Purpose: To demonstrate the type of propulsion used by cephalopods

Materials: water balloon, bathtub

Procedure:

1. Fill a bathtub with several inches of water.

2. Fill a small balloon with water but do not tie it closed.

3. Place the balloon in the tub and let go of the neck of the balloon.

Conclusion: The water will shoot out the neck of the balloon, forcing it to race through the water. Of course the balloon does not have any control over the flow of the water so it may move recklessly about the tub, but cephalopods can control the flow and are very agile in the water.

28

Cnidarians

Jellyfish, coral, and sea anemones

Why are cnidarians so dangerous to most animals?

Words to know:

coral

coral colony

coral reef

cnidarian

polyp

planula

medusa

symbiotic relationship

Challenge words:

siphonophore

What do jellyfish, coral, and sea anemones have in common? They all have hollow bodies and stinging tentacles, so they are grouped together as cnidarians. Cnidarian (ni-DARE-ee-un) means "stinging tentacles." Cnidarians spend at least part of

their lives in the form of a polyp. A polyp has a cylinder-shaped body with tentacles and a mouth on top.

This description of a polyp may not make you think of a jellyfish, but the jellyfish goes through many changes in its life cycle (see illustration on next page). It begins life as an egg. The egg hatches into a planula, which looks like a worm. The planula settles on the sea bottom and grows into a polyp. It may remain in the polyp stage for up to a year. Eventually, disks grow at the top of the polyp. When these disks break off they become medusas. When the medusas are mature, they have the jelly-filled bodies we consider to be adult jellyfish. Jellyfish inhabit nearly all

Fun Fact

Lion's Mane jellyfish are the world's largest jellyfish. In the Arctic, specimens can reach 8 feet (2.4 m) in diameter and their tentacles can reach up to 100 feet (30 m) long.

Polyp stage of a cnidarian

Coral colony feeding

Sea anemone

parts of the ocean. Jellyfish have stinging tentacles, so most creatures stay away from them. A few animals, such as the clownfish, have special protection from the stings and can live closely with jellyfish.

Coral may not appear to be similar to jellyfish but their design is very similar to the polyp stage of the jellyfish. A coral also begins life as an egg that hatches into a larva. The larva settles on the sea bottom and begins secreting a calcium-based substance. This substance hardens into a case around the larva. The larva then develops into a polyp.

Hundreds of thousands of polyps live together to form a coral colony. Millions of coral colonies create a coral reef. Coral polyps stay inside their hard cases when threatened, but when hunting, the polyps come out and shoot poison arrows at their prey. Then the polyps' tentacles pull the stunned food into their hollow bodies.

Sea anemones have a similar polyp body structure to jellyfish and coral. They are often brightly colored and catch their prey with their long stinging tentacles.

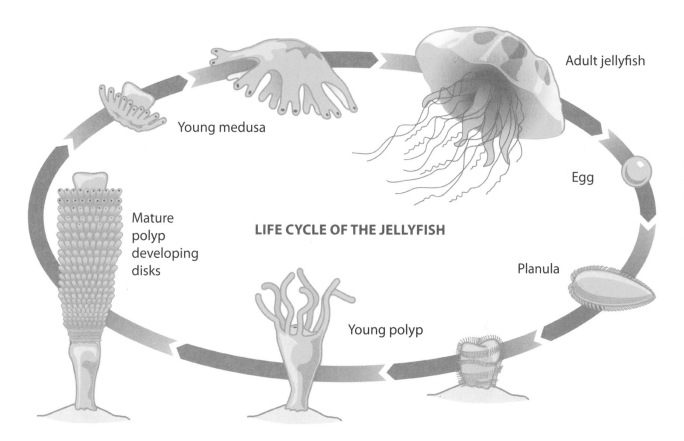

Young medusa

Adult jellyfish

Egg

Mature polyp developing disks

LIFE CYCLE OF THE JELLYFISH

Planula

Young polyp

🧪 Grow your own coral colony

Purpose: You can get a good idea of how coral colonies grow by doing the following project.

Materials: baking dish, copy of "Coral Pattern" worksheet, thin cardboard, food coloring, liquid bluing, salt, ammonia, water

Procedure:

Note: this activity should be done in a well ventilated area as ammonia has a very strong smell.

1. Trace the pieces of the coral pattern onto thin cardboard. Cut along the lines and assemble by sliding one piece over the other. You should end up with a 3-D form for your coral colony to grow on.

2. Combine 3 Tablespoons of liquid bluing, 3 Tablespoons of water, 3 Tablespoons of salt, and 1 ½ Tablespoons ammonia. Pour the solution into a baking dish.

3. Set the cardboard form into the dish and drip a few drops of food coloring on the form. Different colors should produce different colored crystals so use more than one color of food coloring.

4. Place in a location where the dish will not be disturbed for several days. Check the progress of your

crystals each day. You should see crystals growing in a day or two.

5. Take pictures of your coral colony each day and include them in your animal notebook.

Conclusion: The crystals slowly grow on top of and next to each other. Eventually they cover the form. This is similar to how coral colonies are built. Each tiny coral produces a hard shell around itself. Thousands of coral build next to each other. As coral die, new coral build their shells on top of the now empty shells. Over time, the colony can become quite large.

Several cnidarians have **symbiotic relationships** with other creatures, relationships where both benefit. For example, some corals have an algae living inside them. This algae produces food for the coral, while the coral provides protection for the algae.

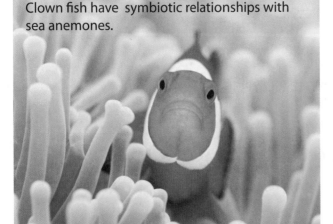

Clown fish have symbiotic relationships with sea anemones.

Also, some fish that are not harmed by jellyfish live near them. When a larger fish attacks the smaller fish, the jellyfish stings the attacker, then both the jellyfish and the smaller fish share the meal. 🐟

🧠 What did we learn?

- What characteristics do all cnidarians share?
- What are the three most common cnidarians?

🚀 Taking it further

- How do you think some creatures are able to live closely with jellyfish?
- Why do you think an adult jellyfish is called a medusa?
- Jellyfish and coral sometimes have symbiotic relationships with other creatures. What other symbiotic relationships can you name?

Other Invertebrates

🏅 Man O' War

The Portuguese Man O' War is a cnidarian that is often called a jellyfish; however, it is actually a siphonophore (sī-FON-u-for), not a jellyfish. A siphonophore is a collection or colony of cnidarians living together in a symbiotic relationship.

Each creature forming the Man O' War has a special purpose. One creature forms the float, which is an air-filled pouch that keeps the colony floating on the surface of the ocean. Other creatures form tentacles, which sting fish and other sea creatures for food. Some creatures in the colony provide digestion and others are in charge of reproduction. This is truly a group effort.

The Man O' War can have very long tentacles that dangle in the water. These tentacles can be up to 60 feet (18 m) long. These tentacles have a very powerful sting and have been know to kill people. They do not attack people, but swimmers have become tangled in the tentacles and have died from the stings.

The float on a Man O' War has a flat band across the top, which works like a sail to catch the wind and move the creature through the water. Another siphonophore that also sails through the water is called the by-the-wind sailor. A by-the-wind sailor has shorter tentacles than the Portuguese Man O' War and has a flatter float with a broader sail shape on top. These sailors often float together in large groups up to 60 miles (100 km) across. Sometimes the wind blows them to shore and thousands can be seen trapped on the beach.

Although you don't want to touch cnidarians because of their stinging tentacles, you can observe some pretty harmless creatures in this group. Hydras are tiny, often microscopic, cnidarians that live in fresh water. They have the familiar hollow body shape with multiple tentacles for catching food. You can order samples of live hydras from a science supply store and view them with a magnifying glass or microscope. They can be fascinating to watch. For a fun research project, find out how hydras reproduce.

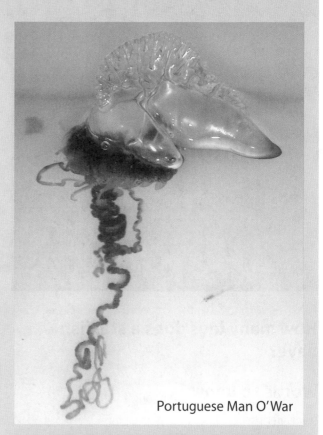

Portuguese Man O' War

A microscopic freshwater hydra

Echinoderms

Spiny-skinned creatures

How many legs does a starfish have?

Words to know:

echinoderm   regenerate

Challenge words:

water vascular system   ray canals

circular canal   tube feet

madreporite

Echinoderms (ee-KINE-o-derms) are spiny-skinned animals. These creatures have hard spikes made from calcium carbonate. Echinoderms also have a system of water-filled tubes that help them move. The most familiar echinoderms are starfish, sea urchins, and sand dollars. Most echinoderms have a central disk with five rays going out from the disk. This design is easily seen in starfish but can be observed in sand dollars as well.

Starfish (or sea stars) are the most well known echinoderms. These spiky creatures generally have five arms radiating from a central disk. However, some species have seven, ten, or even more arms. One species has fifty arms, but the vast majority have only five. They are flexible and can move quickly along the sea floor. Starfish mainly eat clams and oysters. A starfish can grip a clam or oyster and pull on its shell until the creature tires. If the clam opens its shell only a fraction of an inch, the starfish will turn its own stomach inside out through its mouth. Forcing its stomach into the crack, the starfish then digests the clam while it is still in its shell. When it is done eating, the starfish pulls its stomach back inside its body and moves on.

Starfish also have the ability to regenerate or grow back a missing body part. If one of its limbs is cut off, it can grow another one. In fact, if a starfish is cut in half, both halves will regenerate, producing two new starfish.

Sea urchins are another type of echinoderm. They are nicknamed sea hedgehogs because they often resemble the spiky mammals. Like starfish they have five body parts that radiate from a

Fun Fact

The largest starfish ever collected came from the southern Gulf of Mexico in 1968. It measured over 51 inches (1.3 m) from tip to tip of its long, thin arms, but its body disc was only about 1 inch (2.6 cm) in diameter.

Other Invertebrates

Sea urchin

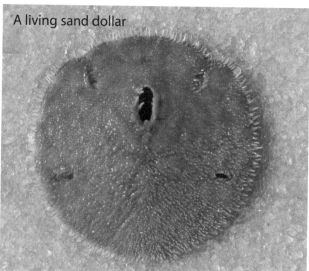
A living sand dollar

central core. This design is often not obvious while the creature is living since it is usually rounded and covered with long spikes, but the design becomes obvious when it dies and dries out. Like starfish, sea urchins also move using water-filled tube feet. Their mouths are on the underside of their bodies. They move slowly through the water eating mostly algae.

Sand dollars are special sea urchins that are mostly flat instead of round. They have a rigid endo-skeleton (internal skeleton) called a test. Over this form is skin covered in short velvety spines. These spines can be a variety of colors from brown to pink or purple.

Most echinoderms have a similar lifecycle. They begin life as an egg, hatch as a larva, and grow to become adults. They are also often very brightly colored. They are found in every ocean of the world from the tropics to the freezing waters of the Arctic. Because they live on the ocean floor and are spiky, you want to be careful not to step on one of these creatures when visiting the ocean.

🧠 What did we learn?

- What are three common echinoderms?
- What do echinoderms have in common?

🚀 Taking it further

- Why would oyster and clam fishermen not want starfish in their oyster and clam beds?
- What would happen if the fishermen caught and cut up the starfish and then threw them back?
- What purpose might the spikes serve on echinoderms?

🧪 Starfish model

Make salt dough by combining 1 cup flour, 1 cup salt, and ½ cup water. Use salt dough to form a 5-legged starfish on a piece of tag board or cardboard. Try to make the model thicker in the middle and thinner at the ends of the legs. Gently press mini-chocolate chips into the starfish to represent spikes. Take a picture of this model to include in your animal notebook.

Other Invertebrates

Observing echinoderms

If possible, obtain a real (dead) starfish or sand dollar. These are sometimes available at craft or novelty shops. Observe each creature with a magnifying glass. Look for five legs and spiny skin. A sand dollar does not have five legs, but does have markings for five sections.

Water vascular system

As you just learned, echinoderms move via a water vascular system, which is a series of tubes that are filled with water. Let's take a look at exactly how this works in a starfish. The starfish has a central disk that contains its internal organs. Around the circumference of this disk is a tube called the circular canal or ring canal. This tube is connected to the outside of the starfish through the madreporite, which is a porous, button-shaped plate that forms the intake for the water-vascular systems.

Water is pumped from the circular canal into each of the legs or rays of the starfish through a series of tubes called ray canals. The ray canals run the length of each ray and split off into two rows of tubes which go to the tube feet. Tube feet are rows of tubes that line the bottom of each ray.

When water is pumped into the tube feet, they expand. Then when the water is released into the ocean, this creates a vacuum causing the feet to become suction cups. This expanding and contracting movement allows the starfish to move quickly along the bottom of the ocean floor and to be able to grip its prey.

You can better understand the anatomy of a starfish if you actually dissect one or observe a dissection. You can order dissecting materials from a science supply store and follow the instructions that come with the specimen. Or if you prefer just to watch a dissection, you can find several sites on the Internet that show step-by-step photos of an actual starfish dissection.

Draw a diagram of the starfish water vascular system. Label all of the parts. Include this diagram in your animal notebook.

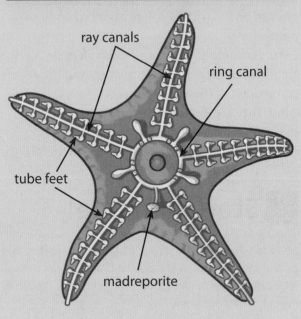

ray canals

ring canal

tube feet

madreporite

30

Sponges

How much water can a sponge hold?

Is a sponge really an animal?

Words to know:

sponge

pores

Challenge words:

biomimetics

fiber optics

One of the simplest multi-celled invertebrates is the sponge. Sponges attach themselves to the sea floor. They have tube-like bodies with no complex systems. It is believed that sponges do not even have nerve cells. What sponges do have is lots of holes.

Sponges come in all shapes and colors.

Water flows into pores, which are small openings or holes in the sides of the sponge. Oxygen and microscopic organisms are removed from the water as it flows through the sponge. Then the water and any waste products are released through an opening on the top of the sponge.

Like starfish, sponges can regenerate. If even a small piece is cut off of a sponge, it can grow into a new sponge. In fact, some sponge farmers grow sponges by cutting them up, attaching them to cement blocks, and lowering the blocks into the sea.

Sponges are often found in the same areas as coral. When an area becomes too crowded, a sponge may become aggressive and overgrow a colony of coral. Sponges are immune to the poison darts shot out by coral and can eventually overtake a coral colony.

For many years, sea sponges were harvested for use as cleaning tools. However, synthetic sponges are now much more popular and real sponges are used less frequently.

Scientists originally thought sponges were plants because they do not move. But studies have shown that sponges do not produce their own food so they cannot be plants. Also, sponges can reproduce with eggs and the larvae do move around before anchoring themselves to the sea floor, thus classifying them as animals.

What did we learn?

- How does a sponge eat?
- How does a sponge reproduce?
- Why is a sponge an animal and not a plant?

 # Taking it further

- Why can a sponge kill a coral colony?
- What uses are there for sponges?
- Why are synthetic sponges more popular than real sponges?

 # Sponge painting

Have your teacher help you cut synthetic sponges (the kind you get at the grocery store) into the shapes of jellyfish, coral, starfish, sand dollars, and other sea creatures. Create an underwater picture by dipping each sponge into paint and pressing it on a piece of paper. When it is dry, this picture can be added to your animal notebook.

If a real sea sponge is available, examine it closely. Compare and contrast a real sea sponge with a synthetic sponge. How are they alike? How are they different? Which one would you prefer for cleaning your house?

 # Biomimetics

Sponges are one of the simplest animals that exist, yet they amaze scientists with their design. Scientists at Lucent Technologies' Bell Labs are involved in the study of biomimetics, which is the study of living creatures to find ways to apply their designs to human technology.

One amazing discovery that these scientists have made is the discovery of fiber optic materials in sponges. Fiber optic applications use very thin glass strands to carry signals of light for telephone transmissions and other communications. The sponges being studied are called Venus Flower Basket sponges. These sponges have a crown of fibers at their bases made from silica, the same material that glass is made from. Although they are not clear enough for communication purposes, these strands can transmit light. What makes them so amazing, however, is that these fibers are much stronger than man-made fibers and resist breaking and cracking. Scientists are continuing to study these fibers to see how they can make man-made fibers stronger.

Another biomimetic project at Bell Labs is studying the eyes of the brittle star, an echinoderm similar to a starfish. The lenses on these brittle stars are very tiny crystals imbedded in their skin, which work together to form a compound eye. These microlenses are very good at reducing distortion. Scientists are developing similar crystals to use in electronic optical systems to achieve much clearer images.

A third project is studying a protein from jellyfish that glows. Doctors are experimenting with injecting this protein into cancer patients. The glowing protein points out cancerous tissue allowing the doctor to be more precise in his surgeries.

Gecko tape is a new idea in adhesives that attempts to mimic the way geckos move along the wall. This tape is designed with millions of microscopic fibers that are not sticky, but when the tape is pulled down the fibers slide and from a bond with the surface. When the pressure is released, the tape can be lifted off without leaving any residue behind. Other scientists are trying to develop an aerosol spray that operates similar to the way a bombardier beetle shoots out its defensive spray. The ideas for ways to mimic animals seems endless, and scientists are constantly looking to God's designs in nature for better ideas for solving human problems.

So what can we learn from biomimetics? First, we can see that even the "simplest" creatures are extremely complex. They have more to teach us than many people in the past have thought. Second, we see that God's design is better than man's design. Man can always learn from what God has created. Third, we see that God's creation declares His glory. So even though you are studying "simple" animals, remember that they are not really simple at all.

31

Worms

Creepy crawlers

Why are some worms important and others dangerous to humans?

Words to know:

flatworm   segmented worm

roundworm   compost

Challenge words:

hydrothermal vent   plume

tube worm   hemoglobin

chemosynthesis

If you are a fisherman, then you probably know where to find worms. To many people earthworms are nothing more than fish bait. However, worms are much more important than that. There are three main groups of worms: segmented worms, flatworms, and roundworms. All are long and narrow and have very simple bodies.

Segmented worms, worms with rings, are the most common. Nearly everyone is familiar with the earthworm. This creature loves moist earth. It eats dead plant material, turning it into fertilizer, or compost, for plants to use. This is why worms are so important. Segmented worms are great composters. Many people raise worms to use in compost bins. You feed your food scraps to the worms and they

Segmented worm

turn it into compost or fertilizer for your garden. Sea worms, leeches, and ragworms are also segmented worms.

The second type of worm is the **flatworm**. As the name suggests, these are flat creatures. Most flatworms live in water or are parasites living inside animal hosts. Planarians are flatworms that live in water. They have arrow-shaped heads and are usually less than one inch (2.5 cm) long. Planarians have a great ability to regenerate and, if cut into pieces, all but the tail will grow into a new worm. Flukes and tapeworms are both parasitic flatworms. They survive by infesting a host animal and absorbing nutrients from it. Parasitic worms are very dangerous, and often deadly, to their hosts.

The third group of worms is **roundworms**. These long, thin, smooth worms are almost all parasites. They often live in the intestines of a host and suck the host's blood or absorb digested food. They are almost always harmful to the host. So, depending on the type of worm, it can be very harmful or very beneficial to humans.

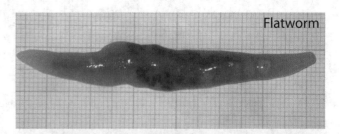
Flatworm

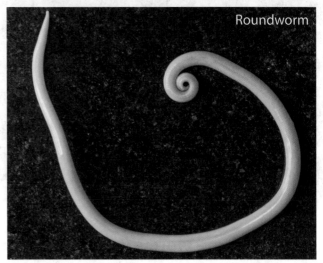
Roundworm

🧠 What did we learn?

- What kinds of worms are beneficial to man?
- How are they beneficial?
- What kinds of worms are harmful?

🚀 Taking it further

- How can you avoid parasitic worms?

Worm diorama

Make a scene in a shoebox showing an earthworm's habitat. Include dirt, rocks, dried leaves, and any other items you might find where earthworms live. Use gummy worms for the earthworms. Take a picture of your diorama for your animal notebook.

Wormy snack

Mix instant chocolate pudding according to package directions. Place about an inch of crushed chocolate cookie crumbs in the bottoms of four plastic cups. Put a gummy worm in each cup with one end hanging over the rim. Divide the pudding between the cups. Add another layer of cookie crumbs. Now you have four yummy mud pies with worms for dessert!

🎖️ Tube worms

Until the 1970s, it was believed that all ecosystems depended on sunlight and plants to perform photosynthesis for food; from all observations, every animal in an ecosystem either eats plants or eats other animals that eat plants. However, in the 1970s a very unusual ecosystem was discovered that changed this belief. On the bottom of the ocean floor, scientists discovered hydrothermal vents, areas where superheated water flows from under the ocean floor. This water contains large amounts of hydrogen sulfide and other minerals.

Living around these hydrothermal vents are very special kinds of worms called giant tube worms, which can grow up to 8 feet (2.4 m) long. These tube worms do not eat plants or animals, yet they are thriving. So how do they get their food? Living inside the tube worms are millions of tiny bacteria. The tube worms absorb oxygen, hydrogen sulfide, and carbon dioxide from the water. The bacteria convert these compounds into carbohydrates which provide energy for the tube worms. This process of converting chemicals into energy is call chemosynthesis.

Just as coral and algae have a symbiotic relationship, the tube worms and the bacteria also have a symbiotic relationship. The tube worms provide protection and shelter for the bacteria, and the bacteria convert chemicals into food for the worms.

Tube worms live inside tubes made of chitin, the same material that forms the exoskeletons of insects and crustaceans. These tough tubes protect the worms' soft bodies from potential predators. The bodies of the tube worms are soft and round like other worms. The end of a tube worm's body is called its plume. The plume on many tube worms is bright red, due to the hemoglobin that flows through the plume. Hemoglobin is a substance that turns bright red in the presence of oxygen. Some tube worms are missing their plumes because crabs or other animals living nearby are sometimes fast enough to get in a bite before the worm is able to pull into its tube.

It is a testimony to God's incredible design that anything can live in the deep dark waters near hydrothermal vents. The surrounding water is extremely cold, the water coming from the vents is extremely hot, there is no sunlight, and the pressure is unimaginable. Yet, there is a thriving ecosystem containing at least 500 different organisms that survive due to God's great design. Draw or paint a picture of this amazing ecosystem to include in your animal notebook.

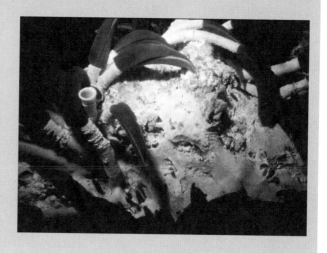

UNIT 6

Simple Organisms

32 Kingdom Protista

33 Kingdom Monera
    & Viruses

34 Animal Notebook—Final
    Project

35 Conclusion

◊ **Describe** the differences between monerans and protists.

◊ **Identify** the relationship between human health and protists, monerans, and viruses.

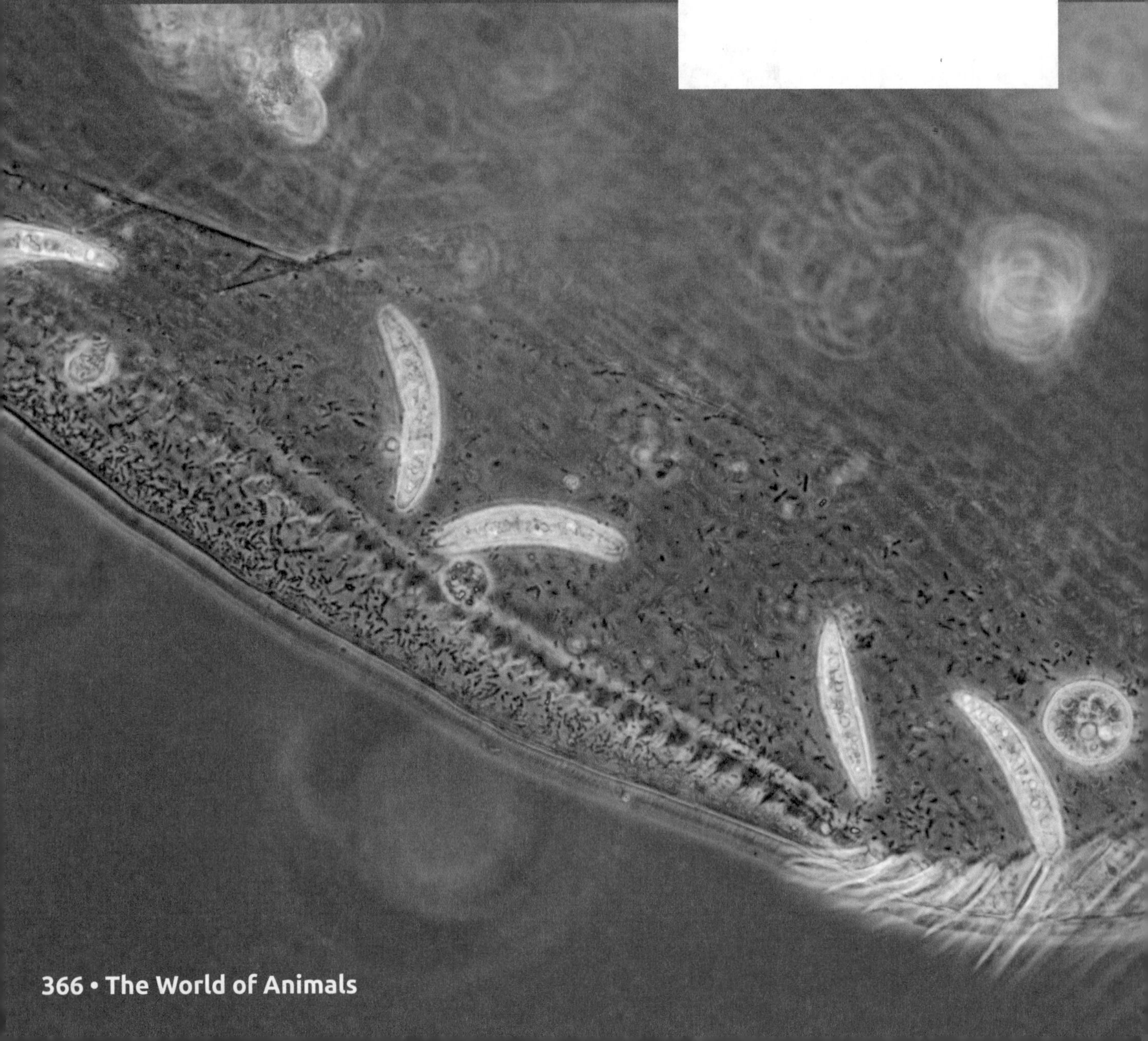

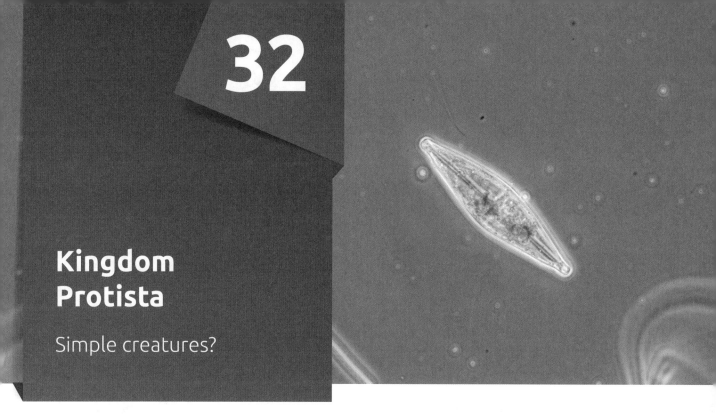

32

Kingdom Protista

Simple creatures?

Are protists simple?

Words to know:

protist	flagellum
cell membrane	sarcodine
nucleus	pseudopod
cytoplasm	ciliate
mitochondria	cilia
vacuole	gullet
flagellate	

Challenge words:

sporozoan	plasmodium

Some of the simplest life forms are protists. However, these microscopic creatures are more complex than you might think. Protists have all of the basic parts of an animal cell including cell membrane, nucleus, cytoplasm, mitochondria, and vacuoles. The **cell membrane** acts like skin—providing protection. The **nucleus** acts like the brain and controls the cell's functions. The **cytoplasm** provides a transportation network for the various parts of the cell. The **mitochondria** are the cell's power plants; they break down food and provide energy. And the **vacuoles** are the cell's warehouses, providing food storage.

In addition, most protists have specialized parts that allow them to perform many of the functions that larger creatures do. They eat and digest food, move, and protect themselves. There are thousands of protists. Scientists have grouped them by the way they move.

Flagellates are single-celled creatures that move by using a **flagellum**, or whip-like structure, at the front of the cell. A euglena is a common

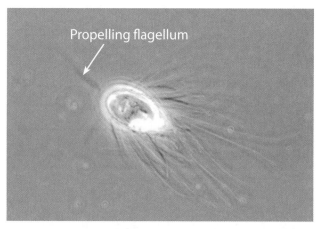

Propelling flagellum

The flagellate above is propelled by the single flagellum on the left. The other flagella are not used for movement.

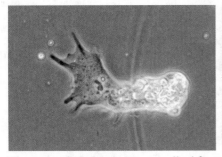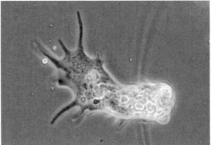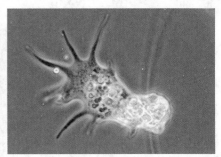

The amoeba above is propelled forward by several pseudopods.

flagellate found in freshwater lakes and ponds. It uses its flagellum like an outboard motor to propel itself through the water.

The euglena is a puzzling creature because, even though it has the characteristics of an animal and has the ability to catch food, it also has chlorophyll in its body and can produce its own food. Because of this and other anomalies, protists are put into a kingdom of their own (Protista) and are not part of the animal kingdom.

The second type of protist is the sarcodine. These are single-celled creatures with a pseudopod. Pseudopod means "false foot." A sarcodine moves by extending one part of its cell membrane in a finger- or foot-like projection and then moving the rest of the cell into that area. The amoeba is the most familiar creature with pseudopods. It is continually moving by changing its shape. An amoeba generally has several pseudopods sticking out at any one time. An amoeba ingests food by extending two or more pseudopods to surround the food and then take it into its cell.

The third type of protist is the ciliate. Ciliates are single-celled animals that are surrounded by cilia, or hair-like projections, that propel them through the water. A paramecium is a common ciliate. A paramecium is a submarine-shaped cell. The actual paramecium is covered all over with cilia. Its

Cilia

A ciliate uses its cilia to capture food while anchoring itself on a stalk.

cilia not only move it around, but also push food into its gullet, an opening that serves as its mouth.

Algae are plant-like organisms that are classified as protists. There are both single-celled algae and multicellular algae. Microscopic forms that live suspended in the water column of the ocean (called phytoplankton) provide food for many small marine animals.

Most protists live in water. Many are parasitic and cause some very serious diseases such as malaria, African sleeping sickness, and amoebic dysentery. Protists generally reproduce by some sort of division where one cell divides to form two new cells. Even though some people consider these to be simple life forms, they are actually very complex, and God's amazing design is obvious in their complex functions.

What did we learn?

- How are protists different from animals?
- How are they the same?

Taking it further

- Why is a euglena a puzzle to scientists?
- Why are protists not as simple as you might expect?

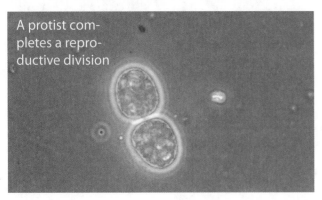

A protist completes a reproductive division

Paramecium model

Make a model of a paramecium. For the body outline, trace your shoe on a piece of construction paper and then cut it out. Glue short pieces of yarn around the edges to represent the cilia. You can cut different colors of paper to represent the nucleus, vacuoles, and mitochondria and glue them to the model. Note: this is a two dimensional or flat model. Actual paramecium are more submarine shaped and covered all over with cilia. Add this model to your animal notebook.

 # Observe microscopic creatures

If you have a microscope available, examine a drop of pond or stream water. Look for tiny creatures that live in the water. You may be able to observe some of the creatures discussed in this lesson as well as slightly larger creatures.

 # Sporozoans

One group of protists, called sporozoans, are very dangerous to people and animals. Sporozoans are single-celled creatures that produce spores that infect animals and humans with dangerous diseases. These protists generally have very complicated life cycles. They reproduce asexually, by dividing, and later on they reproduce sexually with sperm and eggs.

One of the most well known sporozoan is the plasmodium, which causes malaria. The plasmodium is injected into a human host when an infected mosquito bites a human. The spores of the plasmodium enter the blood stream where they are carried to the liver of the victim. Inside the liver, the spores begin reproducing. Eventually the new spores break out of the liver and enter the blood stream. Here the spores infect red blood cells.

Inside the red blood cells the sporozoans again reproduce asexually until the cell bursts open. This releases new sporozoans into the blood stream where they again infect more red blood cells. It also releases toxins into the blood. These toxins are what cause the symptoms of malaria including chills, fever, thirst, and fatigue.

Eventually, inside the red blood cells, female and male cells are produced. When these cells enter the blood stream they do not infect other cells. However, when a mosquito bites an infected person, some

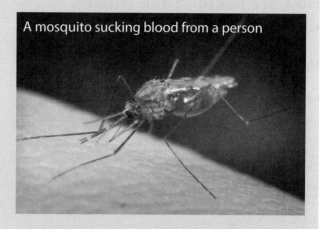
A mosquito sucking blood from a person

of these male and female cells are ingested by the mosquito. Inside the mosquito's digestive system, these cells combine to form new sporozoans. The new cells travel to the mosquito's salivary glands where they are then transmitted to a new victim.

This complicated life cycle has made it difficult for doctors to treat malaria. Many anti-malaria drugs kill the sporozoan cells in the blood stream, which relieves the malaria symptoms. However, the sporozoans in the liver can stay hidden for months and may cause a new outbreak of symptoms after the patient thinks he is cured. Some drugs treat both the spores in the blood and in the liver. Malaria infects approximately 500 million people each year and nearly 2.7 million people die annually from the disease.

Simple Organisms

33

Kingdom Monera & Viruses

Good and bad germs

How are bacteria and viruses different?

Words to know:

bacteria

moneran

virus

antibiotic

vaccine

Challenge words:

antibiotic resistant

The final kingdom we will look at is king-dom monera. Monerans are mostly single-celled organisms that have a cell wall but do not have a well-defined nucleus. The largest group of monerans is bacteria. Although bacteria are alive, they are not considered plants or animals and are classified in a separate kingdom.

Bacteria are single-celled creatures. Some bacteria can produce their own food while others feed off other cells or dead plants and animals. Some bacteria make humans sick. Bacteria can cause plague, pneumonia, and tuberculosis. But not all bacteria are harmful. Most bacteria are very helpful. Bacteria are vital in the breakdown of dead plants and animals. Also, bacteria are necessary in the human digestive system. Without bacteria, our bodies cannot properly digest the food we eat.

Viruses are some of the smallest "creatures," yet they present some of the biggest puzzles to scientists. Scientists do not consider viruses as living things. A virus has genetic information like a cell but it does not directly reproduce. Therefore they are not part of any kingdom. Instead, a virus invades a host cell and reprograms it to reproduce more viruses. Many of the diseases we are familiar with are caused by viruses, including flu, the common cold, chicken pox, and measles.

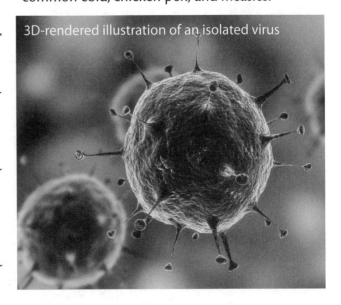

3D-rendered illustration of an isolated virus

Scientists have discovered antibiotics, which are substances that can be used in the treatment of bacteria-induced diseases. However, few treatments have been found to cure diseases caused by viruses. Many of the more serious diseases can be prevented by the use of vaccines, which are substances that encourage your body to build up defenses against certain viruses but cannot cure the diseases. Your own immune system is the best defense against viral diseases. But in the case of certain serious diseases, antiviral medications are sometimes used. Antivirals either stimulate the body's natural immunities so it can better fight off the disease, or they interfere with the virus's ability to reproduce. More work is being done to improve both antibiotics as well as antivirals.

 # What did we learn?

- How are bacteria similar to plants and animals?
- How are bacteria different from plant and animal cells?
- How are viruses similar to plants and animals?
- How are viruses different?

 # Taking it further

- Answer the following questions to test if a virus is alive:

  Does it have cells? Can it reproduce? Is it growing? Does it move or respond to its environment? Does it need food and water? Does it have respiration? Is it alive?

- How can use of antibiotics be bad?

 # Anti-bacterial hunt

Many of the items in our homes are anti-bacterial—that is, they kill bacteria. Search your house looking at things like hand soap, laundry soap, and cleaning supplies to see how many of them say "anti-bacterial" on them. Also, check medical supplies such as anti-bacterial creams or sprays, bandages, etc. People have become concerned about germs and want products that get rid of them in hopes of staying healthier.

Antibiotic resistance

Antibiotics are very important in treating bacteria-induced diseases. However, scientists have seen a rise in antibiotic resistant strains of bacteria—bacteria that are not killed by a certain antibiotic like they have been in the past. Some scientists claim that this is a form of evolution and that the bacteria are evolving to fit their environment. But is this really true? Let's look at what is really happening.

Many bacteria, such as the bacteria that cause strep throat, can be killed with a drug called penicillin. Some of the strep bacteria are able to produce an enzyme called beta-lactamase. This enzyme breaks down the penicillin, which makes it harmless to the bacteria.

When a person takes penicillin, the bacteria that do not produce the enzyme will be killed first and the ones that do produce it will survive and reproduce. The bacteria in the next generation are more likely to be able to produce the enzyme and thus are more likely to survive and reproduce again. Eventually, enough of the bacteria can produce the enzyme that the patient does not get well and a different antibiotic must be used. Thus the bacteria are now said to be resistant to penicillin. But is this evolution?

Molecules-to-man evolution requires that new information be added to the DNA of the next generation. The bacteria did not acquire a new ability. They already had the ability to form the enzyme. So there is no new genetic information added and no evolution has taken place. It is survival of the fittest, but not evolution. This is no different than the faster deer being able to survive longer than the slower deer that are more likely to be eaten by predators.

In fact, bacteria actually provide great evidence against evolution. Because bacteria reproduce very quickly we see many generations of bacteria in only a few days. In thousands of years bacteria go through millions of generations. There is a chance for changes to occur in the DNA of a creature each time it reproduces, so if changes in DNA cause evolution to occur, as the evolutionists claim, we should see the greatest changes in bacteria since they have gone through more generations than nearly any other living creature. However, when we compare fossilized bacteria to today's bacteria, there are very few differences, showing that even after millions of generations, no evolution has occurred. Even the smallest creatures support what the Bible says.

Louis Pasteur—Got Milk?

1822–1895

If you've got milk in your refrigerator, you might want to thank a French chemist named Louis Pasteur who was born two days after Christmas in 1822. His father had served in Napoleon's army and afterward worked as a tanner.

Louis Pasteur did a lot of work that we are still thankful for today, like what he did for milk. He came up with a way of processing the milk to kill off the bacteria so it will stay good for more than a couple of days. The process was named after him. We call it pasteurization. Look on your milk container to see if it says pasteurized on it.

He helped us in many other ways, too. Today, a woman can go to the hospital to deliver a baby and is able to enjoy the gift of a new life coming into the world without the fear of dying from infection. In Louis Pasteur's day, about one-third of the pregnant women in Paris died from childbirth fever or infection. Pasteur convinced the medical community that their sloppy practices were spreading germs and hurting their patients.

However, most of his ideas were not accepted easily. When he said doctors should wash their hands and sterilize their instruments, he really upset the medical community. He was called a menace to science. They said, "Who does Pasteur think that he is? He isn't even a medical doctor . . . just a lowly chemist."

The wife of the emperor asked Dr. Pasteur to come explain his radical views to the French Court. He told the emperor that the hospitals in Paris were death houses and that most of the doctors carried death on their hands (referring to germs). Even when he accurately predicted the death of the emperor's sister-in-law, he was condemned as a fraud and banned by the emperor from speaking out in public about medicine.

After this, Pasteur moved to the countryside where he spent the next ten years working to

discover the causes of anthrax, the black plague of sheep. Anthrax had been ravaging the sheep across France. Pasteur invented an anthrax vaccine, which he gave to the farmers to use on their sheep for free.

At this time, the French government needed more sheep to pay the 5 million francs they owed to Germany for their war indemnity. They came to the area where Pasteur had been working with the farmers to find out why their sheep were so healthy. When Pasteur told them of his vaccine, he was again mocked as a fool by the Academy of Medicine. He showed them the truth by taking 50 sheep and vaccinating 25 of them. Then all 50 were infected with blood carrying anthrax. To everyone's amazement, only the sheep that had been vaccinated survived. Because of Pasteur's work, we now have a reliable cure for anthrax for both livestock and humans.

Even with this wonderful success, the medical establishment was slow to accept Pasteur. However, after nearly 40 years of work, he was elected as a member of the Académie Française in 1882. There he undertook the task of finding a cure for rabies. Three years later he was able to save the life of a young boy named Joseph Meister who had been bitten by a rabid dog. The boy survived and later become the caretaker of Pasteur's tomb at the world-famous Pasteur Institute in Paris. Louis Pasteur headed work at the Pasteur Institute, which was inaugurated in Paris in 1888, until his death on September 28, 1895.

Dr. Pasteur's work has saved millions of lives, but his discoveries came too late to save three of his daughters, who died from typhoid fever. Pasteur selflessly taught that the benefits of science are for all of humanity, not for the benefit of the scientist, and today all of humanity is reaping the benefits of his work.

34

Animal Notebook: Final Project

Putting the animals together

What have you learned about animals?

After learning about many of the differ-ent creatures that God created, we can see that He created a wonderful world of life. From the most complex vertebrate to the single-celled protist, we can see the hand of the Master Designer. You have been making a notebook with all of your projects from this book. Now take what you have learned and finish up your book so you can share the world of animals with someone else.

What did we learn?

- What do all animals have in common?
- What is the difference between vertebrates and invertebrates?
- What sets protists apart from animals?

Taking it further

- What are some of the greatest or most interesting things you learned from your study of the world of animals?
- What would you like to learn more about?
- Read Genesis 1 and 2. Discuss what was created on each day and how each part completes the whole.

Simple Organisms

Animal notebook

As you have been studying the world of animals, you have been building a notebook. Below are some ideas for completing the notebook. You can make this as simple or complex as you desire.

It will be very beneficial to have library books available to provide additional information and ideas for the pages of your notebook.

It will probably take several days to complete this book. When you are done, you will have something that you can be proud of.

Some ideas for making pages in your notebook:

- Older children can write a report for each section of the book.

- Use your computer to find pictures of animals on the Internet. Print out pictures of your favorites and include them, along with a short description, in your notebook.

- Be creative; don't make every section look like every other section.

- Clip pictures from old magazines or coloring books to add to your book.

- If you are artistic, you can draw pictures of many animals.

- Take photographs of projects you have completed in previous lessons and include them in your notebook.

- Add photographs of field trips you have taken.

- Include the worksheets you completed in previous lessons.

- Make a colorful title page.

- Make a table of contents; this will allow readers to find information quickly.

Vertebrates Section:

This should include information for all five types of vertebrates.

1. Mammals
2. Birds
3. Fish
4. Amphibians
5. Reptiles

Invertebrates Section:

This should include information for all six types of invertebrates.

1. Arthropods
2. Mollusks
3. Cnidarians
4. Echinoderms
5. Sponges
6. Worms

Protists and Monerans Section:

Even though they do not belong in the animal kingdom, include information for these interesting creatures.

1. Flagellates
2. Sarcodines (pseudopods)
3. Ciliates
4. Algae
5. Bacteria
6. Viruses

 # Invertebrate collage

Demonstrate your knowledge of invertebrates by making a collage of pictures of various invertebrates to be included in your animal notebook. You can draw the pictures, cut them out of magazines, or print them from your computer. Try to include invertebrates from all six groups mentioned in the lesson. Use an animal encyclopedia or other source for ideas.

Simple Organisms

Conclusion

Reflecting on the world of animals

Thank God for animals.

We have studied the world of animals with its tremendous variety of creatures. As we think about the world of animals around us, we should be thankful to God for making such a wonderful world and giving us such variety. Take a few minutes and contemplate how glorious God's creation is. When God rested on the seventh day, it was indeed very good. And even though God's perfect creation has been corrupted by sin, He still wants us to study it, enjoy it, and take care of it.

Read Job 38:39–40:5 and discuss all the wonders mentioned in this passage. Discuss Job's response to God's questions. How should we respond to God's creation?

Use a Bible concordance or Bible encyclopedia and see how many different animals you can find mentioned in the Bible.

Now write a poem or prayer of thanksgiving to God for the amazing world of animals.

World of Animals — Glossary

Abdomen   Back segment of an insect or other arthropod body

Airfoil   Shape that causes air to flow faster over a surface than under it creating lift

Amphibian   Animal that begins life breathing water and changes to be able to breathe air

Anal fin   Fin on the underside near the back of the fish

Antibiotic   Substance used to treat bacterial diseases

Apes   Primates without tails including chimps and gorillas

Arachnid   Animal with two body parts and eight legs

Arthropod   Animal with segmented legs or feet

Bacteria   Single-celled creatures without a defined nucleus

Baleen   Comb-like structures in a whale's mouth for straining food

Binocular vision   Eyes on the front of the head—each eye produces a slightly different view which when combined provides depth perception

Bivalve   Mollusk with two-part shell

Blowhole   Hole on the top of the head through which an aquatic mammal breathes

Cartilage   Flexible material replacing bone in some fish

Caudal fin   Tail fin

Cell membrane   Outer covering of cell, acts like skin

Centipede   Animal with segmented body with one pair of feet per segment

Cephalopod   Mollusk with a merged head and foot and often no outer shell

Cephalothorax   Body part that is a combined head and thorax

Chitin   Starchy substance forming the exoskeleton

Chrysalis/Pupa   The stage in which the larva turns into an adult

Ciliate   Protist that moves using cilia

Cilia   Tiny hairs that cover a surface

Cloaca   Part of a bird's digestive system that releases waste

Cnidarians   Animals with hollow bodies and stinging tentacles

Cold-blooded   Animal that does not maintain a constant body temperature

Colubrid   Most common group of snakes

Complete metamorphosis   Change occurring in insects that look very different from their parents when they hatch

Compost   Decomposed material, fertilizer

Concertina movement   Moving by coiling and uncoiling

Constrictor   Snake that kills its prey by squeezing

Contour feathers   Feathers that cover a bird's body

Coral colony   A collection of thousands of coral connected together

Coral reef   A large collection of thousands of coral colonies connected together

Coral   Tiny cnidarians that grow a crusty shell around their bodies

Crop   Sac that releases food continuously into the bird's stomach

Crustacean   Animal that has two body parts and crusty exoskeleton

Cytoplasm   Liquid that fills a cell

Dorsal fins   Fins on the top of the fish

Down feathers   Fuzzy feathers providing insulation

Echinoderm   Sea creature with spiny skin, often has five legs

Endoskeleton   Internal skeleton

Esophagus   Tube between the mouth and stomach

Exoskeleton   Outer covering providing protection and support

Flagellate   Protist that moves using a flagellum

Flagellum   Whip-like structure that moves like a motor

Flatworm   Non-segmented worms with flat bodies

Flight feathers   Feathers that cover a bird's wings

Fluke   Tail fin on an aquatic mammal

Gastropod   Mollusk with one-part shell

Gills   Organs for removing oxygen from water

Gizzard   Rough organ to grind bird's food

Gullet   Opening that serves as a mouth

Head   Front segment of the insect body

Hibernation   A type of extended period of sleep

Incomplete metamorphosis   Change occurring in insects that look like their parents when they hatch

Insect   Animal with three body parts, six legs, wings, and antennae

Invertebrate   Animal without a backbone

Jacobson's organ   Special organ for smell found in snakes and some other reptiles

Joey   Immature marsupial

Keratin   Material that forms hair, fingernails, and baleen

Larva/Larval stage   Early stage of an animal that undergoes metamorphosis

Lateral undulation   Moving in sideways waves

Mammal   Warm-blooded animal with fur and mammary glands

Mammary glands   Glands that secrete milk for feeding young

Mantle   Organ that secretes a substance that forms a shell

Marsupial   Mammal with a pouch for carrying developing young

Medusa   Adult stage of a jellyfish's life cycle when it has a bell shaped body

Metamorphosis   A significant change in form

Millipede   Animal with segmented body with two pairs of feet per segment

Mitochondria   Cell's power plants

Mollusk   Soft bodied invertebrate with a muscular foot and usually a shell

Moneran   Micro-organisms without a nucleus, including different bacteria

Myriapod   Animal with many feet, specifically centipedes and millipedes

New World monkey   Monkeys that live in the western hemisphere, have a prehensile tail

Nictitating membrane   Clear eyelids that protect a reptile's eyes

Nocturnal   Active at night

Nucleus   Control center of the cell

Nymph   Immature insect that experiences incomplete metamorphosis

Old World monkey   Monkeys that live in the eastern hemisphere, do not have a prehensile tail

Parasite   Animals that take nutrients from a living host

Pectoral fins   Front fins used for angling up and down

Pelvic fins   Fins on bottom of fish in center of body

Planula   Worm-like stage in a jellyfish's life cycle before it becomes a polyp

Polyp   The stage in a cnidarians life when it has hollow body with tentacles

Pore   Small openings or holes

Preening   Running the feather through the beak to re-hook the barbs

Prehensile tail   One which has the ability to grasp

Primate   Mammal with five fingers, five toes, and binocular vision

Protist   A diverse group of simple creatures with a nucleus

Pseudopod   Foot or finger-like projection of a cell

Rectilinear movement   Moving by contracting and stretching to move in a straight line

Regenerate   To regrow a lost body part

Rostrum   Beak of a dolphin

Roundworm   Non-segmented worms with round bodies

Sarcodine   Protist that moves using pseudopods

Scavengers   Animals that eat dead plants or animals

Segmented body   Animal with distinct sections of its body

Segmented worm   Worm with rings or segments to its body

Side winding   Moving forward at an angle by moving sideways at the same time

Spinnerets   Organs which produce silky thread

Sponge   Simple animal with many pores

Swim bladder   Balloon-like sac used for buoyancy

Symbiotic relationship   Two or more creatures living in a mutually beneficial way

Tadpole/Pollywog   The larva or infant form of an amphibian

Talons   Claw-like feet

Thorax   Middle segment of the insect body

Vaccine   Substance that causes a body to build immunity to disease

Vacuole   Storage area in a cell

Venomous   Snakes that have a poisonous bite

Vertebrae   Small bones that protect the spinal cord

Vertebrate   Animal with a backbone

Virus   Sub-microscopic agent that causes disease

Warm-blooded   Animal that maintains a constant body temperature

World of Animals — Challenge Glossary

Abomasum   Fourth chamber of a ruminant's stomach

Antibiotic resistant bacteria   Bacteria that are not killed by certain antibiotics

Asymmetrical   Having no symmetry

Bilateral symmetry   Can be divided symmetrically by only one lateral line

Bioluminescence   Process producing light in an animal through chemical reactions

Biomimetics   Study of living creatures for human technology

Buoyant   Able to float

Carapace   Top part of a turtle shell

Casque   Large bony structure on the head of a cassowary bird

Ceratopsians   Horned dinosaurs

Chemosynthesis   Process of converting chemicals into food

Circular canal   Central canal pumping water to the ray canals

Compound eye   Eye with multiple lenses

Counter-current exchange   Air and blood flow in opposite directions through the lungs

Cud   The food that is regurgitated for more chewing

Digitigrade   Walking on the base or flats of the toes

Echolocation   Sonar used by animals for communication

Fiber optics   Use of tiny glass tubes to transmit light

Hemoglobin   Substance that turns bright red in the presence of oxygen

Hydrothermal vent   Area on ocean floor where super-heated water flows out

Lateral line   Series of nerves covering the head and sides of a fish

Leptoid scales   Scales on bony fish that grow as the fish grows

Madreporite   Openings through which water enters the water vascular system

Olfactory lobe   Part of the brain responsible for the sense of smell

Omasum   Third chamber of a ruminant's stomach

Open circulatory system   One with no blood vessels to carry the blood

Optic lobe   Part of the brain responsible for the sense of sight

Placoid scales   Scales on cartilaginous fish that do not grow

Plantigrade   Walking on the soles of the feet

Plasmodium   Sporozoan that causes malaria

Plastron   Bottom part of a turtle shell

Plated dinosaurs   Dinosaurs with large plates along their backs

Plume   End of a tubeworm's body

Radial symmetry   Can be divided symmetrically by any lateral line through the center of the circle

Ray canals   Tubes carrying water to the rays of the starfish

Reticulum   Second chamber of a ruminant's stomach

Rorqual   Whales with grooved expandable throats

Rumen   First chamber of a ruminant's four chambered stomach

Ruminant   Animal that regurgitates and rechews its food

Sauropods   Large dinosaurs with long necks and tails

Siphonophore   A colony of cnidarians living together to form one organism

Spherical symmetry   Can be divided symmetrically by any line through the center of the body

Spiracles   Openings in an insect's side for air flow

Sporozoan   Protist that produces spores

Stance   The way an animal walks on its feet

Theropods   Meat eating dinosaurs

Tube feet   Rows of tubes on the underside of each starfish ray

Tube worm   Worm that thrives near hydrothermal vents

Ungulates   Animals with an unguligrade stance

Unguligrade   Walking on the tips of the toes, usually with hooves

Urticating hairs   Barbed hairs on a spider that produce irritation in enemies

Water vascular system   Series of tubes that carry water throughout the starfish's body

Index

abdomen   336, 338, 341-345, 378

abiogenesis   14, 17, 135

adventitious   58-59, 133

aerial roots   58-60, 64, 110, 133

aggregate fruit   99-101, 133

airfoil   291, 293, 378

algae   23, 70, 105, 126-128, 133, 135, 325, 356, 359, 365, 368, 376

alveoli   226-227, 229-230, 254

amoeba   368

amplitude   191, 254

angiosperm   21, 23, 38-39, 88, 133

animal communication   173, 310

annuals   87, 102-103, 133

anther   95-96, 133

antibody   224, 243-245, 254

antigen   222, 224

appendicular skeleton   150, 152, 256

aqueous humor   188-190, 256

artery   214-216, 219-221, 225, 254-255

arthropod   333-335, 348, 378

association neuron   257

atrium   219-220, 254

axial skeleton   150, 152, 256

axolotl   313

bacteria   17-18, 44, 108, 127-128, 130, 204, 229, 233, 243-245, 252, 256, 272, 283, 365, 370-373, 376, 378-380

bark   38-41, 60-61, 66-68, 84-85, 110, 132-133, 270

berry   99, 101, 135

bicuspid   201-202, 254

biennial   87, 102-103, 133

bile   198, 200, 256

bioluminescence   339, 341, 380

biomimetics   361-362, 380

blood pressure   175, 215, 218, 256-257

blood type   222, 224, 242, 256, 258

botany   18, 24, 133

Braille   185, 187, 256

brain stem   174-175, 177, 254-255

bronchi   226, 229, 254

Bronchial tube   227

cambium   66-68, 119, 133

camouflage   324

canine teeth   201-202, 254

capillary   215, 217, 223, 226, 229, 254

carapace   326, 328, 380

carbohydrate   200, 206, 211-212, 254

carnivorous   105-108, 133, 349

cartilage   150-152, 158, 161, 193, 254, 298, 304, 333, 378

Carver, George Washington   52-53

catalyst   70-71, 133

caudal fin   301, 378

cell   26-29, 39, 55, 57, 63, 65-68, 71, 75, 119, 123, 126, 128, 133-136, 146-147, 164, 184, 196, 212, 215, 217, 220, 222-223, 228, 244, 246, 248, 254-257, 367-370, 378-379

cell membrane   26-29, 63, 133, 146, 254, 367-368, 378

cellular respiration   15, 47, 71, 226, 228, 256

cell wall   26-29, 133, 370

centipede   347-349, 378

cephalothorax   342-343, 345, 378

cerebellum   174-175, 254, 303

cerebral cortex   177, 254

cerebrum   174-175, 177, 179, 254, 303

chameleon   323-324

chemosynthesis   363, 365, 380

chemotropism   112, 114, 135

chitin   333, 335, 365, 378

chlorophyll   19, 23, 27-28, 59, 70-71, 74, 81-82, 106, 120, 126, 128-129, 133, 368

chloroplast   26-28, 71, 73, 128, 133

chrysalis   339-341, 378

chuckwalla   323

ciliate   367-368, 378

classification   13, 18, 21-23, 101, 133, 135, 205

cloaca   295-296, 378

cloning   117, 119, 135

cold–blooded   308-309

colubrid   319, 378

composite flower   88, 90, 97, 135-136

compound leaf   80, 135

coniferous   38, 85

constrictor   319-320, 378

coral   306, 320, 354-356, 361-362, 365, 378

Corpus callosum   174, 176, 254

cotyledon   45-47, 62, 133-134

cranium   153-156, 159, 254

crop   295-296, 338, 378

crustacean   345-346, 378

cuticle   66, 133

cytoplasm   26-29, 133, 135, 146, 254, 367, 378

Darwin, Charles   289-290

deciduous   31, 38-40, 65, 81, 85, 133

dermis   236-238, 254

diaphragm   30, 162, 165-166, 184, 226-227, 254

dichotomous key   18, 20, 135

dicot   23, 31, 45-47, 50, 68, 78-79, 113, 133

dinosaur   265, 314-318

dispersal   48-51, 100, 133, 135

DNA   16, 29, 119, 135, 242, 246-248, 252, 254, 256-257, 372

dolphin   279-280, 379

dominant   25, 246-247, 249, 254, 274, 289

dormant   42-44, 47, 65, 104, 133, 135-136

echidna   263, 266, 271

echolocation   278, 281, 380

eel   317

elastin   233, 237, 254

endocrine system   142-143, 257

endosperm   45-46, 133

ephemeral   102, 104, 135

epidermis   66-67, 133, 236-237, 254

epiphyte   58, 60, 135

esophagus   164, 166, 198-199, 229, 254, 295, 378

euglena   28, 367-368

eustachian tube   191-193, 257

evergreen   31, 38-40, 77, 81-82, 133

excretory system   142-143, 257

exoskeleton   107, 333, 335, 339-340, 346, 378

external respiration   226, 228, 257

fats   200, 211

femur   153-154, 156, 254

fern   23, 105, 120-122, 133, 135

fibrous roots   55-56, 58, 60, 133

filament   95-96, 126, 128, 133, 135

flagellate   367-368, 378

flower   21, 23, 32-33, 35-38, 40, 46, 48, 55, 61, 65, 75-76, 82, 84-85, 87-93, 95-97, 99-100, 102-104, 110, 120, 123, 126, 133-136

food group   199, 206-208, 212

forensic science   239-240, 242, 257

frequency   191, 254, 303, 310

friction skin   167-168, 239-240, 254

frond   120-122, 133, 135

fruit   16, 21, 23, 32, 38, 40, 42, 48-50, 71, 73, 82, 84-85, 87-88, 90-92, 99-101, 110, 117-119, 133-136, 207, 212, 273, 275

fungi   18, 21, 105, 129-130, 133, 245

genes   119, 135, 169, 246-250, 254, 290

geotropism   112-114, 133

germination   42-47, 133, 135-136

Gila monster   323

gizzard   295-296, 338, 378

GMO   117, 135

grafting   117, 119, 135-136

grain   35, 90-92, 99, 101, 102, 132-133, 135, 211, 282

gymnosperm   23, 38-39, 88, 133

hair follicle   186, 236-239, 254

haustoria   58-59, 109-110, 133

heartwood   66-67, 133

heliotropism   112-114, 133

hemoglobin   219, 221, 223, 255, 363, 365, 380

herbaceous   38-39, 61, 66-68, 133

hippocampus   174-175, 177, 255

Hooke, Robert   30

hormone   65, 75, 142-143, 257

hydrotropism   112-114, 133

incisor   201-202, 255

insect   106-108, 283, 329, 336-341, 378-380

Internal respiration   226, 228, 257

internode   64, 133

invertebrate   331, 352, 376, 379

involuntary muscle   165

jellyfish   263, 330, 332, 354-357, 362, 379

keratin   233, 236, 238, 255, 278-279, 318, 322, 328, 379

kidney   238

koala   284

Komodo dragon   325

lamprey   304-305

larva   339-341, 355, 359, 378-379

larynx   226-227, 255

lateral line   301, 303, 380

law of biogenesis   14, 16-17, 136

leaf   15, 19-21, 23, 28, 32, 35, 37-38, 40-41, 45-47, 55, 60-64, 68-89, 97, 103-104, 106-107, 110, 113-116, 118, 120-123, 126, 129, 133-136, 349

leaf margin   77, 80, 135-136

legume   99, 101, 136
Leonardo da Vinci   144-145,
ligament   159, 161, 201, 203, 257
Linnaeus, Carl   18, 22, 24-25, 133
Lucy   277
lungs   14, 146-148, 151-152, 155-156, 162, 172,
  212, 214-215, 219-221, 226-231, 252, 254-257,
  265-267, 271, 278, 281, 286, 291, 297, 299, 301,
  308, 311-312, 314, 338, 380
lymph nodes   243-244, 255
mammary gland   282
manatee   279-280
Man O' War   357
mantle   351-352, 379
marsupial   282-284, 379
meiosis   26, 29, 136
Mendel, Gregor   249-250
metamorphosis   307, 311-313, 329, 339-341, 348,
  378-379
metaphase   26, 29, 136
mildew   129
millipede   347-349, 379
mitochondria   26-28, 134, 146, 255, 367, 369, 379
mitosis   26, 29, 135-136
molar   201-202, 255
mold   129-130, 245
mollusk   351-352, 378-379
moneran   18, 21, 370, 379
monocot   23, 31, 45-47, 55-56, 68, 78-79, 133-134
moss   17, 105, 109-111, 120, 123-125, 136
Motor neuron   257
nautilus   353
nectar   91-93, 106, 108, 134, 136, 287
Nightingale, Florence   209-210
node   64-65, 74-75, 133-135
nucleus   26-29, 134, 146, 184, 248, 255, 367, 369-
  370, 378-379
Nymph   339, 379
orthodontics   204-205, 257
osmosis   61, 63, 136
ovary   21, 46, 88-92, 96-97, 99-100, 114, 133-134
ovule   29, 88-89, 91-92, 96-97, 99-100, 119, 134
palmate   77-79, 134
paramecium   368-369
parasite   105, 109-111, 133-134, 304-305, 379
passenger plant   109, 111, 134

Pasteur, Louis   373-374
patella   153-155, 255
peat   123, 125, 136
pectoral fin   301-302
pelvic fin   301-302
perennial   102-103, 134
petal   33, 75-76, 88-91, 93, 95-99, 134
phalange   153-156, 255
phloem   61-62, 66-68, 77-78, 133-134, 136
photosynthesis   15, 18-19, 32, 59, 69-75, 81, 100,
  106, 111, 113, 127-129, 132-135, 228, 365
phototropism   112-114, 133
pinnate   77-79, 134
pistil   88-92, 95-97, 99-100, 133-134
pistillate   88, 134
pituitary gland   174-176, 255
plaque   204, 255
plasma   222-223, 255
plastron   326, 328, 380
platelet   156, 222-223, 255
platypus   266-267, 271
pollen   29, 88-89, 91-93, 95-96, 114, 119, 133-134,
  136
pollination   87, 91-93, 95, 99-100, 114, 134
polyp   354-355, 379
positive tropism   112, 114, 136
preen   291-293, 379
prehensile   273, 275, 302, 379
prophase   26, 29, 136
protein   158, 165, 200, 207-208, 211-212, 244, 254-
  255, 318, 341, 362
protist   21, 367-368, 375, 378-380
pseudopod   367-368, 379
pupa   339-340, 378
receptacle   95-97, 100, 136
red blood cell   146-148, 151, 156, 213, 215, 217,
  222-224, 244, 255
Redoute, Pierre–Joseph   94, 98
reflex   175, 182-183, 255
regenerate   358, 361, 364, 379
reproductive system   142-143, 257
respiration   14-15, 43, 47, 71, 134, 226, 228,
rhizome   117-118, 121-122, 134
root hairs   55-58, 63, 136

roots 14-15, 23, 32, 35-37, 45-46, 54-65, 68, 71, 73, 76, 78, 98, 103, 109-110, 112-114, 118-123, 125-126, 129, 133-136, 203

rorqual 278, 281, 380

ruminant 272, 380

saliva 194-196, 198, 243

sarcodine 367-368, 379

seahorse 301-302

seed coat 42, 44-46, 134-136

self-pollination 91, 134

sensory neuron 182, 184, 257

sepal 88-89, 95-96, 134

shark 279, 300, 304-305

siphonophore 354, 357, 380

smooth muscle 165-166, 256-257

spider 330, 342-344, 380

spinal cord 147, 156, 171-173, 175, 182, 184, 254, 263-264, 303, 379

sponge 332, 361-362, 379

spontaneous generation 14, 16-17, 135-136

spore 23, 120-121, 123, 129, 131, 134

sporozoa 367, 369, 380

stamen 88-90, 95-97, 133-134

staminate 88, 134

starch 46-47, 70-71, 73, 136, 200, 257, 335

starfish 330, 332, 358-362, 380

stem 23, 32, 35, 37-40, 46-47, 54-55, 58-59, 61-68, 71, 73-75, 79-80, 89, 96-97, 109-110, 113, 115-116, 118-119, 121, 123, 131, 133-136, 174-175, 254-255

sternum 151-154, 256

stigma 89, 95-96, 134

stingray 305

stolon 61-62, 117, 134

stoma 70-71, 76, 134

style 23, 52, 89, 95-96, 134

subcutaneous 236-237, 256

succulent 74, 76, 99, 101, 115, 135-136

sucrose 70, 73, 136

symbiotic 354, 356-357, 365, 379

tadpole 311-313, 379

tarantula 344

taxonomy 18, 21, 24, 134

telophase 26, 29, 136

tendon 148, 150-151, 162-163, 256, 283

tendril 61-62, 76, 114, 134

thorax 336-338, 342, 378-379

tortoise 326, 328

trachea 226-227, 229, 256

transpiration 61, 63, 136

tropism 112, 114, 135-136

tube feet 358-360, 380

turtle 326-328, 380

ungulate 266, 268, 380

vacuole 26-28, 135, 146, 256, 367, 379

vascular tissue 21, 23, 55-57, 68, 120, 135-136

vegetative reproduction 117-119, 135

vein 78-79, 164, 215-217, 219-220, 225, 227, 255-256

venomous snakes 320, 379

ventricle 218-220, 256

Venus flytrap 106-107

vertebrae 152-154, 156, 159, 256, 264, 316, 328, 379

vine 32, 62, 89, 107, 109-111, 114, 135

virus 244-245, 370-371, 379

vitreous humor 188, 190, 258

warm–blooded 266, 308-309, 379

water vascular system 358, 360, 380

whale 41, 278-281, 346, 352, 378

white blood cell 146-148, 151, 156, 222-225, 244, 256

worm 354, 363-365, 379-380

xanthophyll 81-82, 136

xylem 61-63, 66-68, 77-78, 133-136

yeast 130, 133, 211

Photo Credits

165в Getty Images/iStockphoto
167т Getty Images/iStockphoto
167в ©2008 Jupiterimages Corporation
168 ©2008 Jupiterimages Corporation
169 Getty Images/liquidlibrary
170 Getty Images/Hemera
171т ©2008 Jupiterimages Corporation
171в ©Eraxion | Dreamstime.com
174 Getty Images/iStockphoto
175L Getty Images/iStockphoto
175R ©Cammeraydave | Dreamstime.com
177 ©2008 Jupiterimages Corporation
178т Getty Images/Stockbyte
178в Getty Images/Dorling Kindersley RF
180 ©2008 Jupiterimages Corporation
182т Getty Images/iStockphoto
182в ©2008 Jupiterimages Corporation
184 Getty Images/iStockphoto
185т ©2008 Jupiterimages Corporation
185в Shutterstock.com
187 ©2008 Jupiterimages Corporation
188т Getty Images/Hemera
188в Creative Commons | Kruusamägi
189в Getty Images/iStockphoto
191 Getty Images/iStockphoto
192 Getty Images/iStockphoto
194 Getty Images/Wavebreak Media
196 ©2008 Jupiterimages Corporation
197 ©2008 Jupiterimages Corporation
198 Getty Images/iStockphoto
199 Credit Mariana Ruiz Villarreal
201 Getty Images/iStockphoto
202 Getty Images/iStockphoto
203 Getty Images/iStockphoto
204 ©2008 Jupiterimages Corporation
205 ©2008 Jupiterimages Corporation
206 ©2008 Jupiterimages Corporation
207 Getty Images/iStockphoto
209 Public domain
211 Getty Images/Zoonar RF
214 ©2008 Jupiterimages Corporation
215 Getty Images/iStockphoto
216 Public domain
219 Getty Images/iStockphoto
220 Credit Mariana Ruiz Villarreal
222т Getty Images/iStockphoto
222в Courtesy National Cancer Institute/
Bruce Wetzel
225 ©2008 Jupiterimages Corporation
226 Getty Images/iStockphoto
227 Getty Images/iStockphoto
229т Getty Images/iStockphoto
229в ©Eraxion | Dreamstime.com
230 Getty Images/moodboard RF
232 ©2008 Jupiterimages Corporation
233 Getty Images/Stockbyte
234 ©2008 Jupiterimages Corporation
235 ©2008 Jupiterimages Corporation
236 Getty Images/iStockphoto
237 Getty Images/iStockphoto

239 Getty Images/iStockphoto
240 Public domain
243т Getty Images/Hemera
243в Credit CDC/Janice Carr
244 Credit CDC/Janice Carr
245 Shutterstock.com
246т ©2008 Jupiterimages Corporation
246т Shutterstock.com
248 Credit Genome Management
Information System, Oak Ridge National
Laboratory
249 Public domain
251 ©2008 Jupiterimages Corporation
253 ©2008 Jupiterimages Corporation
259 Getty Images/iStockphoto
261 Getty Images/ Digital Vision
262 ©2008 Jupiterimages Corporation
263 ©2008 Jupiterimages Corporation
264т ©2008 Jupiterimages Corporation
264в ©Glenjones | Dreamstime.com
265 ©Dannyphoto80 | Dreamstime.com
266т ©Apresident | Dreamstime.com
266в ©2008 Jupiterimages Corporation
267 Getty Images/iStockphoto
268т ©2008 Jupiterimages Corporation
268в Shutterstock.com
269т ©2008 Jupiterimages Corporation
269в Getty Images/Stockbyte
270т Getty Images/Fuse
270BL Getty Images/Photos.com
270BR Getty Images/iStockphoto
271 Getty Images/iStockphoto
272 Getty Images/Dorling Kindersley RF
273т ©2008 Jupiterimages Corporation
273в Shutterstock.com
274TL Getty Images/iStockphoto
274TR Getty Images/Purestock
274MR ©istockphoto.com/Nico Smit
274BR Getty Images/iStockphoto
275 ©Clivia | Dreamstime.com
276 ©Dejavues | Dreamstime.com
277 ©2008 Answers in Genesis
278 ©2008 Jupiterimages Corporation
279 ©2008 Jupiterimages Corporation
281 ©2008 Jupiterimages Corporation
282 ©2008 Jupiterimages Corporation
283L ©2008 Jupiterimages Corporation
283R Getty Images/iStockphoto
284 ©2008 Jupiterimages Corporation
285 Getty Images/iStockphoto
286 ©2008 Jupiterimages Corporation
287 ©2008 Jupiterimages Corporation
288TL Getty Images/iStockphoto
288TR Creative Commons | Rainer Jung
288BR Getty Images/Fuse
290 Public domain
291т ©2008 Jupiterimages Corporation
291в ©2008 Answers in Genesis
292т ©2008 Jupiterimages Corporation
292м ©2008 Answers in Genesis

292в Creative Commons |
Hoodedwarbler12
293т Getty Images/Fuse
293м Getty Images/iStockphoto
293в ©Otvalo | Dreamstime.com
294L Credit Maungatautari Ecological
Island Trust
294R ©2008 Jupiterimages Corporation
295т ©2008 Jupiterimages Corporation
295в Getty Images/Dorling Kindersley RF
297 Getty Images/Dorling Kindersley RF
298т ©2008 Jupiterimages Corporation
298в Shutterstock.com
300т Creative Commons | Isurus2
300T Creative Commons | Rajesh dangi at
English Wikipedia
301 ©2007 John McNeal
302т Getty Images/iStockphoto
302в Getty Images/Ingram Publishing
304т Getty Images/iStockphoto
304в Credit U.S. Fish and Wildlife Service
305т Credit U.S. Fish and Wildlife Service
305в NOAA/U.S. Department of
Commerce.
306 Getty Images/iStockphoto
307 ©2008 Jupiterimages Corporation
308 ©2008 Jupiterimages Corporation
309TL ©2008 Jupiterimages Corporation
309TR ©2008 Jupiterimages Corporation
309BR Creative Commons | Uajith
310 ©2008 Jupiterimages Corporation
311т ©istockphoto.com/Thomas Mounsey
311в ©2008 Jupiterimages Corporation
313 Getty Images/iStockphoto
314т ©2008 Jupiterimages Corporation
314в ©istockphoto.com/Norma Cornes
316 ©2008 Answers in Genesis
317 ©2008 Answers in Genesis/Dan
Rockafellow
319 ©2008 Jupiterimages Corporation
320т Shutterstock.com
320в ©2008 Jupiterimages Corporation
322 ©2008 Jupiterimages Corporation
323 ©2008 Jupiterimages Corporation
324 Getty Images/iStockphoto
325 Getty Images/iStockphoto
326 ©2008 Jupiterimages Corporation
327TL ©Prairierattler | Dreamstime.com
327TR ©2008 Jupiterimages Corporation
328 ©2008 Jupiterimages Corporation
329 ©2008 Jupiterimages Corporation
330т Getty Images/iStockphoto
330BL ©Photosaurus | Dreamstime.com
330BR Getty Images/amana images RF
331 Creative Commons | Matt Reinbold
332TL 76t Getty Images/iStockphoto
332TR Getty Images/iStockphoto
332BL CC BY-SA 4.0
333т ©2008 Jupiterimages Corporation
333в ©Tommyschultz | Dreamstime.com

GOD'S DESIGN
FOR SCIENCE SERIES

EXPLORE GOD'S WORLD OF SCIENCE WITH THESE FUN CREATION-BASED SCIENCE COURSES

GOD'S DESIGN FOR LIFE
GRADES 3-8

Learn all about biology as students study the intricacies of life science through human anatomy, botany, and zoology.

GOD'S DESIGN FOR HEAVEN & EARTH
GRADES 3-8

Explore God's creation of the land and skies with geology, astronomy and meteorology.

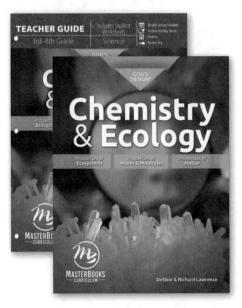

GOD'S DESIGN FOR CHEMISTRY & ECOLOGY
GRADES 3-8

Discover the exciting subjects of chemistry and ecology through studies of atoms, molecules, matter, and ecosystems.

GOD'S DESIGN FOR THE PHYSICAL WORLD
GRADES 3-8

Study introductory physics and the mechanisms of heat, machines, and technology with this accessible course.

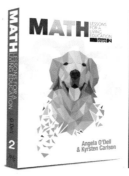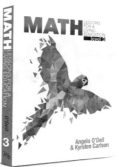
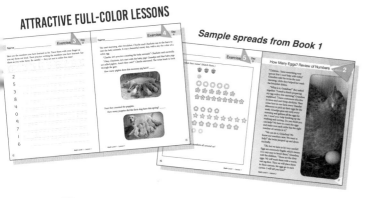

CHARLOTTE MASON INSPIRED
ELEMENTARY CURRICULUM THAT CONNECTS CHILDREN TO
AMERICA'S PAST... AND THEIR FUTURE!

Through this unique educational style, children develop comprehension through oral and written narration, and create memories through notebooking and hands-on crafts. This is not just facts and figures; this is living history for grades 3 through 6.

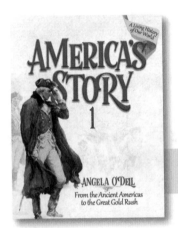

FROM THE ANCIENT AMERICAS TO THE GREAT GOLD RUSH

Part 1: Begins at the infancy of our country and travels through the founding of our great nation, catching glimpses of the men who would become known as the Founding Fathers.

America's Story Vol 1   *Teacher Guide*
978-0-89051-979-0   978-0-89051-980-6

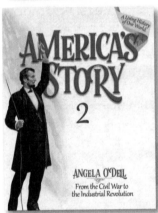

FROM THE CIVIL WAR TO THE INDUSTRIAL REVOLUTION

Part 2: Teaches students about the Civil War, the wild West, and the Industrial Revolution.

America's Story Vol 2   *Teacher Guide*
978-0-89051-981-3   978-0-89051-982-0

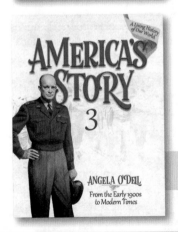

FROM THE EARLY 1900S TO OUR MODERN TIMES

Part 3: Carries the student from the turn of the 20th century through the early 2000s.

America's Story Vol 3   *Teacher Guide*
978-0-89051-983-7   978-0-89051-984-4

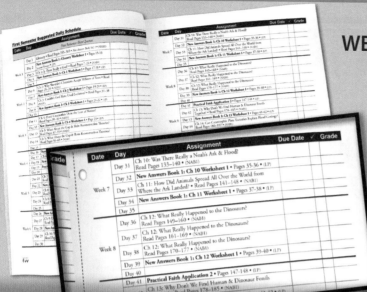